Linux® Toys II

Linux® Toys II

9 Cool New Projects for Home, Office, and Entertainment

Christopher Negus

Wiley Publishing, Inc.

Linux® Toys II: 9 Cool New Projects for Home, Office, and Entertainment

Published by
Wiley Publishing, Inc.
10475 Crosspoint Boulevard
Indianapolis, IN 46256
www.wiley.com

Copyright © 2006 by Wiley Publishing, Inc., Indianapolis, Indiana

Published simultaneously in Canada

ISBN-13: 978-0-7645-7995-0
ISBN-10: 0-7645-7995-9

005.432

Manufactured in the United States of America

10 9 8 7 6 5 4 3 2 1

1B/RY/RQ/QV/IN

For general information on our other products and services or to obtain technical support, please contact our Customer Care Department within the U.S. at (800) 762-2974, outside the U.S. at (317) 572-3993 or fax (317) 572-4002.

Wiley also publishes its books in a variety of electronic formats. Some content that appears in print may not be available in electronic books.

Library of Congress Cataloging-in-Publication Data
Negus, Chris, 1957–
    Linux toys II : 9 cool new projects for home, office, and entertainment / Christopher Negus.
        p. cm.
    Includes index.
    ISBN-13: 978-0-7645-7995-0 (paper/cd-rom+online)
    ISBN-10: 0-7645-7995-9 (paper/cd-rom+online)
    1. Linux. 2. Operating systems (Computers) 3. Multimedia systems. I. Title.
    QA76.76.O63N4233 2005
    005.4 32—dc22
                            2005025375

As always, I dedicate this book to my wife, Sheree.

About the Author

Christopher Negus landed a job in 1984 at AT&T Bell Laboratories in Summit, N.J., in the group that developed the UNIX operating system. Because he had used UNIX before (and had even written programs in BASIC), he was considered "technical" and started out writing about computer network protocols.

Over the next eight years, Chris helped write (and rewrite) the thousands of pages of documentation that accompanied the UNIX operating system. He stayed with the same organization, even after AT&T spun it off into UNIX System Laboratories and then to Univel, before the organization was sold (with the UNIX source code) to Novell in 1992. (Yes, this is the infamous SCO source code!)

Over the following decade, Chris wrote or contributed to about a dozen UNIX books. In 1999, he made the transition to Linux with a vengeance when he wrote *Red Hat Linux Bible*. Since that time, the book has become a computer book bestseller and in its various editions has sold well over 240,000 copies worldwide.

Between editions of *Red Hat Linux Bible*, Chris wrote *Linux Bible, 2005 Edition* and co-wrote *Linux Troubleshooting Bible* with Thomas Weeks. (Tom contributed two chapters to this book as well.)

The original *Linux Toys* and now *Linux Toys II* reflect Chris's attempts to put together open source software into fun and useful projects. The projects in this edition reflect Chris's collaboration with leaders and maintainers from a handful of excellent open source initiatives.

Credits

Executive Editor
Carol Long

Acquisitions Editor
Debra Williams Cauley

Development Editor
Sara Shlaer

Technical Editors
Bharat Mediratta (Gallery)
Brandon Beattie, François Caen (MythTV)
Roberto De Leo (eMoviX)
John Andrews, Robert Shingledecker
    (Damn Small Linux)
Charles Sullivan (Heyu X10)
Tim Riker (BZFlag)
Heiko Zuerker (Devil-Linux)
Michael Smith (Icecast)
Jim McQuillan (Linux Terminal
    Server Project)

Contributing Authors
Thomas Weeks
Jesse Keating

Copy Editor
Nancy Rapoport

Editorial Manager
Mary Beth Wakefield

Production Manager
Tim Tate

**Vice President and Executive Group
Publisher**
Richard Swadley

Vice President and Executive Publisher
Joseph B. Wikert

Project Coordinator
Ryan Steffen

Graphics and Production Specialists
Carrie Foster
Denny Hager
Stephanie D. Jumper
Barbara Moore
Heather Ryan

Quality Control Technicians
Amanda Briggs
Leeann Harney

Media Development Project Supervisor
Laura Moss

Media Development Specialists
Angela Denny
Steve Kudirka
Kit Malone
Travis Silvers

Media Development Coordinator
Laura Atkinson

Proofreading and Indexing
TECHBOOKS Production Services

Contents at a Glance

Contents

Part I: The Basics   1

Chapter 1: Introduction to Linux Toys II 3

Part IV: Small Business Projects   265

Chapter 10: Running an Internet Radio Station with Icecast 267

Chapter 11: Building a Thin Client Server with LTSP 289

Part V: Appendixes   319

Acknowledgments

Leaders of many of the open source projects covered in this book graciously agreed to provide technical reviews of the chapters that covered their work. There's nothing like having someone who eats, sleeps, and breathes a project suggesting corrections and enhancements to your writing. So my first special "thank you" goes to the following technical reviewers of this book (by project):

- Bharat Mediratta, creator of the Gallery Project

- Brandon Beattie, contributor to the MythTV project and creator of the Linux HTPC HOWTO

- Roberto De Leo, creator and maintainer of the MoviX and eMoviX projects

- John Andrews, creator and maintainer of Damn Small Linux

- Robert Shingledecker, developer responsible for most of the customizing DSL features described in this book

- Charles Sullivan, maintainer of Heyu version 2 X10 software

- Tim Riker, maintainer of the BZFlag tank battle game server and client software

- Heiko Zuerker, founder and developer of the Devil-Linux firewall project

- Michael Smith, contributor to Icecast and other projects sponsored by Xiph.Org

- Jim McQuillan, president of the Linux Terminal Server Project

As far as contributing writers go, Thomas "Tweeks" Weeks tops my list of important contributors to *Linux Toys II*. Tweeks wrote the chapters on MythTV and firewalls. He did a great job taking on the most complex of our *Linux Toys II* projects. Check out Tweeks's pictures of the beautiful personal video recorder PC he put together in Chapter 4. It just makes me want to cry. Thanks, Tweeks!

Because of the complexity of the MythTV project, we brought in a few other people to help as well. Jesse Keating did a wonderful job on the FireWire descriptions used in Chapter 4. We relied extensively on Jarod Wilson's work configuring MythTV in Fedora Core (http://wilsonet.com/mythtv). To do some last-minute, heavy testing of MythTV on Fedora Core 4, we were lucky enough to get François Caen (www.spidermaker.com) to offer invaluable feedback.

I would like to acknowledge Linus Torvalds and the Linux kernel developers (kernel.org), Richard Stallman and the GNU Project (gnu.org), and Red Hat, Inc. (redhat.com), as major contributors to the Linux distributions used as the foundation for projects in this book. Also, I'd like to thank contributors to the KNOPPIX project for creating some of the bootable CD technology used via Damn Small Linux, and Xiph.Org for its important work in creating free ways for us all to use audio (Ogg Vorbis) and video (Theora) without threat of lawsuits.

These and other projects attest to what can be achieved through the open source development process.

I'd like to thank Debra Williams Cauley at Wiley for her strong leadership in keeping us on track to meet our publication dates, Sara Shlaer for steering the book through the development and production stages, and Nancy Rapoport for putting the final polish on the book's content. Thanks to Margot Maley Hutchison at Waterside Productions for contracting the book with Wiley.

On the personal side, thanks to my wife, Sheree, for keeping our home a wonderful place to live. Thanks to Caleb and Seth for being great kids. (This book is almost done. I'll be down to play soon.)

Introduction

Supporting the Linux operating system are thousands of open source initiatives, building code for everything from word processors, to Web servers, to programming tools. While many of these initiatives help to make Linux the world's most powerful operating system, others produce software that is just flat-out fun.

Linux® Toys II is here to show you some of the fun stuff!

In *Linux Toys II*, I give you the software, the shopping list, and the steps to put together interesting projects using open source software and PC hardware. Some projects will run even on a 486 machine with 32MB of memory (for example, a client in the Linux Terminal Server project), while others encourage you to build a completely tricked-out entertainment system–style PC (for example, the MythTV project).

Most projects will run on any standard PC built in the past ten years . . . so you can decide how fancy a computer you want to use. Once you have built your *Linux Toys II* projects, you don't have to stop there. You can further enhance your projects because of the way open source works:

- **The building block nature of Linux**—You can continue to add software from the thousands of open source software components available for Linux. So you can add your favorite applications to your custom Linux pen drive, incorporate a database application to store images or music for a server, or include a graphical front end to control your home lighting.

- **Thriving open source communities**—Most of the *Linux Toys II* projects are built on open source initiatives that have active, thriving communities supporting them. You can learn more about each project by participating in forums or joining mailing lists. You can become a contributor to each effort by creating software or documentation . . . or buying a T-shirt.

If you are new to Linux, you can learn the basics of using Linux in Appendix B and procedures for installing a particular version of Linux (Fedora Core) in Appendix C. All the projects should run on most Linux systems (if you are willing to compile them yourself). However, if you are a first-time Linux user, following instructions for Fedora Core Linux and using the pre-built software packages (in RPM format) can save you some trouble.

So, welcome to *Linux Toys II!* To get started, all you need is this book and a PC for the most basic projects. In fact, in some cases, you can just boot the *Linux Toys II* CD itself (which contains a custom version of Damn Small Linux) to get started. For other projects, you need an installed Linux system and some extra hardware that I describe throughout the book.

How This Book Is Organized

There are five parts to this book. Part I has introductory material. Parts II, III, and IV contain the actual projects. The appendixes contain information on getting and installing software, as well as a few basics on using Linux (in particular, Fedora Core or Red Hat Enterprise Linux). Here's a larger description of those sections.

Part I: The Basics

Chapter 1 lays out the approach to the *Linux Toys II* projects. Chapter 2 goes into detail about finding hardware and software.

Part II: Multimedia Projects

Chapters in this part contain sound, video, and digital image projects. Chapter 3 describes how to set up a Gallery, a Web-based server for sharing digital images over a network. Chapter 4 shows you how to put together the hardware and software to make a MythTV personal video recorder that's suitable for your home entertainment unit. Chapter 5 shows you how to use eMoviX to turn your personal videos into bootable movies. It then covers how to play a variety of multimedia content using MoviX^2.

Part III: Home Projects

These chapters contain fun and useful personal and home projects. Chapter 6 describes how to create a customized Linux distribution from Damn Small Linux that runs on a pen drive. Chapter 7 shows you how to use Heyu and BottleRocket software to control lights and devices in your home using the X10 protocol. Chapter 8 describes how to set up a gaming server with the BZFlag tank battle game, which you can play in your home, small office, or even over the Internet. To protect your home or small office computer network, Chapter 9 describes how to build and configure a custom firewall device using Devil-Linux.

Part IV: Small Business Projects

While intended more as exercises than as real business opportunities, the projects in this section help you configure a couple of useful server types. Chapter 10 describes how to set up an Icecast server so you can create your own streaming radio station on the Internet or other network. Chapter 11 tells how to use the Linux Terminal Server project to fill a home, school, or small business with fully functional thin client computers for a fraction of the cost of complete computer workstations.

Appendixes

The appendixes contain supporting information for the rest of the book. Appendix A describes the *Linux Toys II* CD that is included with the book. Appendix B describes some of the basic Linux skills you need to use this book. Appendix C walks you through installing Linux (using Red Hat Fedora Core or Enterprise Linux as examples).

Conventions Used in This Book

On occasion, there will be code or commands I want to highlight during a procedure. Here are some examples of text that is marked differently along the way.

Sometimes in a procedure, I want to make a distinction between what you type and what is returned. In those cases, the entire input and output is marked as code, while the part that you type is marked in bold. For example:

```
# ssh toy
root@toy's password: *******
Last login: Tue Nov 22 12:58:49 2003 from music.linuxtoys.net
#
```

In this example, someone typed ~~ssh toy~~, and then typed a password (indicated by the asterisks in bold). The rest are the responses from the computer. This example shows a command typed to the shell. If you are new to Linux, remember that you typically open a Terminal window to get to the shell. When you see a prompt ending in a pound sign (#), it means you should be the root user when you run the command; when you see a dollar sign ($), you can be any user.

Special icons for Note, Caution, and Cross-Reference appear from time to time. Those paragraphs contain an extra bit of information or a special way of doing something, something to watch out for, or a pointer to another chapter, respectively. Here's an example:

A Note contains an extra bit of information.

What You Need for the Projects

For all the projects, you need a PC, the accompanying CD, and this book. Because the book includes a bootable Linux operating system on the CD, you can do a few of the projects without having Linux installed (most notably, the bootable pen drive project in Chapter 6). Most other projects require that you have a Linux operating system installed. I recommend Red Hat Enterprise Linux or Fedora Core. Other Linux systems will work as well, but you will need to either compile the software yourself (the CD includes the source code) or get pre-built binaries from somewhere else.

The projects in this book were all built and tested using Red Hat Fedora Core 4 (although they should work on Red Hat Enterprise Linux 4 as well). If you are unfamiliar with Linux, I recommend my book *Red Hat Fedora and Enterprise Linux 4 Bible* (Wiley, 2005). It includes the complete Fedora Core 4 Linux operating system as well as more than 1,000 pages of descriptions for using Fedora Core and Red Hat Enterprise Linux.

Check Chapter 2 for an overview of the hardware and software requirements for *Linux Toys II*. Then refer to each project chapter to determine the special requirements for each particular project.

The Linux Toys II CD

The CD that comes with this book contains the software you need to complete the *Linux Toys II* projects. Each chapter describes which packages from the CD you need for the project. Most of the *Linux Toys II* software is in RPM format (which is the format used to install software in Fedora Core and Red Hat Enterprise Linux).

Although binaries of *Linux Toys II* software were built and tested to run on Fedora Core, the source code is included on the *Linux Toys II* CD as well. If you are predisposed to do so, it should be possible to build most projects on other Linux distributions. (See Appendix A for descriptions of the software included on the *Linux Toys II* CD.)

The Linux Toys (and Linux Toys II) Web sites

There are two separate Web sites associated with *Linux Toys II*:

- **Linux Toys at Wiley** (www.wiley.com/go/negus)—Wiley Publishing, Inc., the publisher of *Linux Toys* and *Linux Toys II*, maintains a Web page that pertains to issues surrounding the purchase and features of the book.

- **Linux Toys Web Site** (www.linuxtoys.net)—Come to the LinuxToys.net site for further information about the *Linux Toys II* projects.

On with the Show

I hope that you are as excited to try out these projects as I am to bring them to you. If you are a Linux expert, feel free to jump right into the project of your choice. If you are new to Linux, be sure to go through the introductory materials and step through the appendixes to get a feel for how to use Linux. Okay, let's go!

The Basics

part

Introduction to Linux Toys II

The same building blocks used to create the world's most powerful computer system (Linux) can also be used as the foundation for creating fun, interesting, and useful projects. If you have a PC and this book (and are okay with adding a few extra pieces of hardware, which I describe later), you're ready to start.

Welcome to *Linux Toys II*.

Linux Toys II is my second attempt (the first being *Linux Toys*) to gather up a few cool projects based on open source software and create a book that steps through how to make them. In the few years since *Linux Toys* was published, the pool of open source software on which to base *Toys* projects has grown astronomically. As a result, you'll find *Linux Toys II* projects to be both more solid and more engaging than those in the first book. (See the description of the differences between the two books later in this chapter.)

Besides being fun, *Linux Toys II* projects offer you other opportunities:

> **Learn Linux** — While this book might be a bit challenging if you have never used Linux before, I've done what I can to simplify instructions and add some primers (see Appendixes B and C) for using and installing Linux. You might consider getting a more detailed book on installing, configuring, and using Linux (such as *Red Hat Fedora and Enterprise Linux 4 Bible*) to back you up if you are a first-time Linux user.

> For experienced Linux users, I've tried to remove a lot of the hunting and pecking you often have to do to get a project going and to expose you to some areas of Linux you may not have tried before.

> **Exercise your freedom** — By building these computer projects with open source software, you are generally free to add, take apart, recompile, or change out the software elements of these projects without breaking proprietary licensing agreements. (See the description of what you can and can't do with "free" software later in this chapter.)

- The spirit of open source software is sharing the pieces of software you add so that together everyone can benefit. Examples of this spirit include the ease with which you can share virtual worlds in the BZFlag tank game or download selected games, office applications, or network tools to your customized Damn Small Linux pen drive.

- **Reuse an old PC** — While the latest Windows operating system won't run on that eight-year-old PC sitting in your closet, many of the projects in this book will. If you can get an Ethernet card for it, even your old 486 machine can probably be used for the Linux Terminal Server Project.

  Most PCs that can boot from a CD will work for the bootable Linux projects (such as the *Linux Toys II* projects based on eMoviX and the Devil-Linux firewall CD). At the very least, you should be able to boot the *Linux Toys II* CD to try out Damn Small Linux (which includes a graphical interface with streamlined desktop applications).

- **Play with computer hardware** — While some of the projects are purely software-oriented (so they can run on most PCs), a few give you the chance to put together and play with the hardware as well. Follow the instructions in the MythTV project to build a personal video recorder with a wireless keyboard, a remote control, and a slick case that will fit in any entertainment center. Create a firewall box for Devil-Linux that includes the switch for attaching the computers in your home or small office LAN. Add X10 hardware modules around your house wherever you want to interact with lights and appliances using BottleRocket or Heyu software.

To make sure the projects are accurate and backed up by experts, most chapters have been reviewed by the creator or project lead for the featured software. Many of the projects closely follow open source initiatives that have active, on-going development efforts and vibrant community forums and mailing lists. Those facts will help you if you get stuck or want to continue to grow with the *Linux Toys II* projects you build.

Learning About Linux

The projects in *Linux Toys II* reflect the growing phenomenon of open source software and the Linux operating system. For the computer enthusiast or professional, Linux is now in so many places (PCs, enterprise computers, handheld and wireless devices, and so on) that you can hardly ignore it. And if you're going to need it anyway, why not learn about it while you build some toys?

 Note If this is your first exposure to Linux, see the "How Can This Software Be Free?" section later in this chapter. It describes how the licensing for open source software works.

Using Specialized Linux Systems

Freedom to use the software you choose in the way that you want to use it has always been at the heart of Linux and the open source software movement. Because you can take apart all the component parts of Linux and put them back together again as you like, you can end up with Linux systems that include everything you might ever want or only the exact components you need.

Here are some ways in which *Linux Toys II* projects let you use specialized versions of Linux:

- **Multimedia player** — The eMoviX and MoviX^2 projects include a specialized Linux system, geared toward playing multimedia content. Not only does the resulting Linux system not have to be installed on a hard disk, but it is small enough to run from RAM. So you can remove the CD containing Linux and insert a CD containing video, music, or digital images to play.

- **Efficient portable desktop system** — Damn Small Linux (DSL) fits on a bootable business card (about 50MB), but contains enough components to do basic Web browsing, email, word processing, and other desktop activities. (The project based on DSL describes how to install it to a rewriteable pen drive.)

- **Thin client** — While the other special Linux systems just described typically boot from CD or other removable medium, the Linux Terminal Server Project (LTSP) helps you get the Linux system that runs on a client computer from a server on the network. LTSP can be configured to boot from a DHCP server via a network card (using PXE or Etherboot) on a cheap PC or stripped-down workstation.

Each of the projects just described can help you learn about the most basic issues related to booting a Linux system. Once you get familiar with those concepts, you will probably want to begin customizing your own Linux systems to do just what you want.

Working with Servers

Several of the *Linux Toys II* projects describe how to set up and offer particular kinds of services on a network. Sharing services from your computer to the Internet is not something that should be done lightly (I'll give you about a billion warnings before the book is done). However, learning how to set up services from the safety of your home or small office LAN (provided you're behind a sturdy firewall, which I also describe) is a great thing.

Here are some of the server projects you can try out in *Linux Toys II*:

- **Sharing photos** — Web servers can do more than just serve HTML pages. The Gallery project includes a full-featured Web-based interface for controlling and sharing albums of digital images. In this project, you touch on features for setting up a Web server, managing access, and organizing digital content.

- **Multi-user gaming** — While many commercial PC games don't run in Linux, many servers that allow you to play those games against multiple opponents over a network do run in Linux. To play with the concept of hosting your own gaming server, the BZFlag project is a great choice. It includes server and client software for battling tanks in a virtual world.

- **Internet radio station** — You can serve up streaming audio content to make your own Internet radio station using Icecast software. The *Linux Toys II* project covering Icecast describes tools for both creating the content to feed to your Icecast server and the server itself for broadcasting the stream over the Internet.

Video and Audio Recording and Playback

The open source community now has its own ways to compress and store video and audio content. So once you have created your home movies, recorded your favorite TV shows, and saved your music, you can compress and store them using Ogg Vorbis (audio) and Theora (video) open source codecs and tools.

Several of the *Linux Toys II* projects focus on working with audio and video content:

- **Personal video recorder** — With MythTV, you can download a Web-based listing of television shows in your area. From that listing you can select to record those shows either immediately or queue them to record when they come on later. With MythTV you can manage and play back your recorded audio/video files as well.

- **Bootable movies** — With eMoviX, you combine a video/audio file with the movie player and Linux software to create a movie that can boot up and play on most PCs. You can record any type of content supported by the MPlayer multimedia player.

- **Streaming audio** — The Xiph.Org Foundation is a champion of open source multimedia-related projects. Using software sponsored by that project, in particular Ogg Vorbis (for compressing audio) content and Icecast (for streaming it to the Internet or other network), I describe a project for creating your own Internet radio station.

Hardware Tinkering

While most of the projects will run on most PCs, I selected a few projects to incorporate some hardware gathering and tinkering as well. If you want the box to look as sweet as the software, I suggest you check out these projects:

- **Entertainment center PC** — For the MythTV project, Tom Weeks combined a PC case that's slick enough to place in your entertainment center for recording, storing, and playing video content. The hardware Tom put together includes a SilverStone Technology LaScala case, two Hitachi hard drives, a Hauppauge TV capture card (with remote control), an NVidia video card, and a wireless keyboard.

- **Firewall/network switch PC** — A firewall for a small office/home office (SOHO) LAN won't require much of a PC. (Tom uses a P133 with 128MB of RAM that someone might be giving away these days.) However, you can add a few extra hardware components to outfit it like commercial dedicated firewall devices you might purchase. Besides a couple of inexpensive network cards (one facing your LAN and the other facing the Internet), Tom incorporates a cheap 100Mbit switch with at least eight ports. It makes a nice little box when you are done.

Aside from those two projects, most of the other *Linux Toys II* projects can be done with smaller bits of extra hardware. For the X10 projects, you need hardware to connect your PC to your location's power source to send X10 signals (usually from the PC's serial port). Then you can add as many X10 hardware modules around your place as you like. For the bootable pen drive project, you need to pick a pen drive (1GB pen drives are now available for just over $50).

The topics of interest covered in *Linux Toys II* projects that I've just described here are just the tip of the iceberg of what you can do with Linux and open source software. But the skills you learn in building these projects will scale down to handheld devices or up to enterprise computing clusters.

About the Linux Toys II Projects

Behind each *Linux Toys II* project are one or two primary open source initiatives. In most cases, these initiatives started because someone had an idea to create something with software. They pulled in existing open source software and created what they needed to fill in the holes.

Here are the *Linux Toys II* projects described in this book and the primary open source efforts the projects are built on.

Web Photo Gallery (Gallery)

A big reason Bharat Mediratta created Gallery was so his mom could easily display and print photos of her grandchildren on the Internet. Today, Gallery is probably the most popular open source software for sharing digital images. The Web Photo Gallery you build in Chapter 3 with Gallery software can be used to organize, manage, display, and print your images from a Web browser over private or public networks (such as the Internet).

Figure 1-1 shows a snippet containing two albums from a Gallery front page.

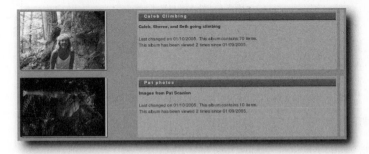

FIGURE 1-1: Share albums of digital images with Gallery.

Personal Video Recorder (MythTV)

Video recording and playback have long been a challenge in Linux and other open source systems. The MythTV project described in Chapter 4 has separated itself from the short list of open source Personal Video Recorders (PVRs) by combining an excellent graphical interface for searching out, selecting, and recording TV shows as well as by including good support for a range of useful recording hardware devices.

Of all the projects described in this book, MythTV is probably the most challenging from both the hardware and software perspective. But if you step through the *Linux Toys* procedure for configuring MythTV, you'll have a fully configurable PVR for recording and storing your television shows or other video input. And you'll end up with a neat new component to go into your entertainment center as well.

Figure 1-2 shows an example of the MythTV PC you build in Chapter 4.

FIGURE 1-2: Tricking out a SilverStone Lascala case for a MythTV PVR

Bootable Movie Player (eMoviX)

By adding a home movie, a movie player (MPlayer), and a Linux system needed to play the movie to one disk, you can be sure that anyone with a standard PC will be able to play your movies. The *Linux Toys II* project described in Chapter 5 steps you through creating video content in Linux and mastering that content (using eMoviX) to a bootable CD or DVD. The chapter also describes how to use the related MoviX[2] project, which can be run as a bootable player for many different types of multimedia content.

Custom Bootable Pen Drive (Damn Small Linux)

If you like projects that are compact, cool, and contain everything you need, you'll probably find the *Linux Toys II* project in Chapter 6 to be both fun and useful. Using Damn Small Linux (a bootable business card–size Linux that takes up less than 50MB space), the procedure steps you through how to install and configure a fully customized Linux system that you can boot from a pen drive.

Figure 1-3 shows a custom version of Damn Small Linux being booted from a 1GB pen drive, with a personal set of applications, desktop themes, and personal data files (music, documents, digital images, and so on) included on it.

Pen drive boots custom Damn Small Linux

FIGURE 1-3: Boot to your customized Linux desktop from a pen drive.

Personal Firewall (Devil-Linux)

Protecting your workstation or LAN from intruders has been the goal of many different Linux firewall distributions. Devil-Linux, described in Chapter 7, is a 200MB firewall distribution that provides a simple way to configure a secure firewall using a standard PC or by making a firewall PC with a built-in network switch. Figure 1-4 shows a PC that was modified to include a network switch so it could be used as a dedicated firewall.

FIGURE 1-4: Create a firewall PC with built-in network switch.

Multi-User Tank Game Server (BZFlag)

Linux is an extremely popular platform for professional and amateur gamers to set up the servers they need to do multi-user, networked gaming. Chris Schoeneman built the BZFlag multi-user, networked tank shoot-em-up game from a graphical demo program he created as a student at Cornell University. Chapter 8 steps you through how to set up a BZFlag server and play the game against multiple opponents on your LAN or the Internet. As shown in Figure 1-5, BZFlag lets you move your tank around a virtual world, picking up flags and destroying opponents.

X10 Home Controller (HeyU and BottleRocket)

Using inexpensive X10 devices, you can control a variety of lights and appliances in and around your home or office. With X10 hardware kits starting at under $50, projects such as BottleRocket and HeyU enable you to dim lights, react to motion detectors, or turn on a sprinkler system from your computer (in real time or using scripts). These X10 projects are described in Chapter 9.

FIGURE 1-5: Set up your own BZFlag multi-user, networked tank game.

Internet Radio Station (Icecast)

The people at Xiph.Org that brought you free audio (Ogg Vorbis) and video (Theora) codecs also bring you tools for streaming multimedia content over a network. The Icecast software featured in Chapter 10 can be used to set up streaming audio content so you can broadcast your own music or news radio station on the Internet or other network. Related software from that project called Ices can be used to feed content to your Icecast server, while streaming audio directories on the Internet can be used to advertise the availability of your radio station to the world.

Thin Client Server (Linux Terminal Server Project)

Using old throwaway PCs or stripped-down, diskless workstations, you can fill an entire classroom, small business, or non-profit organization with usable computers. The Linux Terminal Server Project procedure in Chapter 11 steps you through setting up and managing a group of inexpensive workstations from a single LTSP server. The project describes a variety of ways to boot up your clients (such as a CD or from your network card), as well as ways to manage your client computer from your LTSP server.

How Can This Software Be Free?

In recent years, the term "free software" has generally been replaced by the term "open source software" in hopes of clarifying what the movement is all about. Just as "freedom" in society doesn't mean you can do anything you want (such as restrict other people's freedom), freedom with open source software comes with some responsibility. The responsibilities are meant to encourage continued development of free software, when you use the code in certain ways. (See the "Open Source Software Definition" sidebar.)

A programmer who creates open source software typically attaches one of many available open source licenses to it, defining how it can be used. The intention of most open source licenses is to encourage people to make changes to the software and share those changes with others.

Understanding GPL and Other Licenses

The most popular of the open source licenses (and the one that covers most software in Linux distributions) is the GNU General Public License (GPL) from the Free Software Foundation (www.gnu.org). You can see that license at the end of this book or at www.gnu.org/licenses/gpl.html. As the GPL states, when software authors commit to making their software GPL, the license allows you to:

- Distribute copies of free software (and even charge for this service if you wish)
- Receive source code or get it easily if you want it
- Change the software or use pieces of it in new free programs
- Know you can do these things

There are lots of other licenses that can be used to cover open source–ish kinds of software. The Free Software Foundation maintains a list of some of these licenses (with their own comments about how well they conform to the GNU view of free software) at its Web site (www.gnu.org/licenses/license-list.html).

Building Projects with Open Source

As for using Linux and other open source software for building useful and expandable projects, there are several reasons why I think open source software is the best way to go:

- **No licensing fee for each toy** — You can build 1 or 1,000 of each toy. Other than the time you spend, it won't cost you any more than the nothing you paid in the first place (or just the one copy of Fedora Core, Red Hat Enterprise Linux, or other Linux system you bought).
- **No hiding the code** — You can see and change all the code in your *Linux Toys II*. If you don't like what it does, rewrite it yourself.

Open Source Software Definition

The Open Source Definition, written by Bruce Perens, sets down ten points defining open source software (see `www.opensource.org/docs/definition_plain.html` for the complete definition). Here are the points, with my interpretations of what they mean to you as someone creating or using open source software:

- **Free Redistribution**—The software creator can't keep you from selling or giving away the software as part of your software project and the creator can't make you pay a fee for it.

- **Source Code**—The software creator must give you source code or make it available.

- **Derived Works**—The software creator must let you redistribute the software, with your changes, under the same license.

- **Integrity of the Author's Source Code**—If you modify the software, the software creator can ask you to change the name or version, to protect the original code's integrity.

- **No Discrimination Against Persons or Groups**—The software creator can't say, "XYZ people can't use my software because I don't like them."

- **No Discrimination Against Fields of Endeavor**—The software creator can't say, "This software can't be used to study extraterrestrials or create recipes for moonshine."

- **Distribution of License**—Everyone who uses the software can use it under the same license, without needing to add a license.

- **License Must Not Be Specific to a Product**—The software creator can't restrict use of the code to a particular operating system or other software.

- **The License Must Not Restrict Other Software**—The software creator can't restrict you from distributing other software with the open source software. (The example given is that the license can't say that the software can be distributed only with other open source software.)

- **License Must Be Technology-Neutral**—The software creator can't restrict the software in such as way that it must be used with a specific interface style or technology.

- **Get enhancements going forward**—The open source projects that make up the projects described in this book will continue to go forward and offer enhancements to their projects.

- **You can learn Linux**—Every *Linux Toys* project can benefit from the fact that you are building it on a full-service operating system. Learn Linux features for configuring a network connection, a TV capture card, or a Web interface, and you have multiplied the power of your *Linux Toys* project. At the same time, you'll be learning a powerful, professional-quality operating system.

Remember that open source licenses are built on commitments to freedom and community. There are those who would equate people who create or use open source software with thieves and scoundrels. In my experience from Linux mailing lists and my local Linux User Group (LUG), I have found open source devotees as a group to be:

- **The first ones to help you** — Open source supporters always lend a hand if you have a problem with or a question about Linux.

- **Respectful of copyrighted material** — Most open source supporters believe that CDs, DVDs, books, and software should be obtained legally, with proper compensation given to the works' originators. However, they also believe that people should be able to play their legally obtained music and movies on the players they choose (including their PC-based Linux systems).

- **Interested in making things work** — There is a commitment in this community to getting your Linux box to work with any application or computer on your network. Compare that to a company that has a vested interest in selling you more of their products and fewer of the competitor's products. Sometimes they go out of their way to break software that tries to interoperate with their products.

The bottom line is that there are people around who will try to help you overcome obstacles you run into with Linux. Get on a Linux newsgroup or mailing list. Check out the resources at LinuxToys.net. If you can get on the Internet, there's help out there.

There are also other ways to support your own growth with Linux and open source software. For example, if you want to meet other Linux enthusiasts in your area, search out a local Linux User Group (LUG). Many of these groups offer monthly meetings, mailing lists, and Web sites to support their users. To search a list of LUGs for one that is near you, go to the Linux Online User Groups page (www.linux.org/groups/index.html).

Improvements from Linux Toys

If you read the first *Linux Toys*, by me and Chuck Wolber (Wiley, 2003), you will notice some improvements in this sequel. Doing that first book was a real learning experience for me and certainly increased my respect for people who run open source projects.

Here are some of the ways that I set out to improve on the approach we took in *Linux Toys*:

- **More depth to each project** — In *Linux Toys II* there is more depth to each project. While in *Linux Toys* we just got each project up and running, here I've taken more time to give you a deeper understanding of the technology behind each project and helped you get it working better.

- **Technical review by project leaders** — Nearly every project has been reviewed by the creator or project lead for the software featured in each project. And as I've asked each project to help us, I've also asked how I should encourage others to help them improve their projects.

- **Tarballs of each project** — *Linux Toys* offered RPMs and source RPMs for each project. *Linux Toys II* includes tarballs of each project as well, to make it easier for those who are installing the projects on Linux systems other than Fedora or Red Hat Enterprise Linux.

- **Bootable Linux Toys CD** — In *Linux Toys II*, the CD that accompanies the book is an actual bootable Linux CD, running Damn Small Linux. This offers several advantages. For one thing, you can use it as the basis for customizing a bootable pen drive project in Chapter 6. However, the CD can also be used to start trying out a reduced Linux system without having to install to hard disk. (Of course, the CD contains the packages needed to install the projects to hard disk as well.)

- **Reliance on other open source initiatives** — By keeping the *Linux Toys II* projects close to (or exactly the same) as the software that is delivered by open source projects, as I did with Gallery, BZFlag, Icecast, and others, readers can go directly to those projects for updates and help. Likewise, if you want to help contribute to these initiatives, there are better mechanisms in place than for the first *Linux Toys*.

In other words, *Linux Toys II* is more of a celebration of existing open source projects than attempts to piece together my own projects. What this book offers is detailed instructions for getting the most out of these very fine open source projects. If you enjoy the projects contained in this book, I strongly encourage you to pursue the people or organizations that created them and find ways to help those open source initiatives grow.

In each chapter, I tell about the major contributors to the software efforts behind each *Linux Toys II project* and what you can do to support or become more involved to help improve the software into the future. So if, in the course of using *Linux Toys II* you find that you have something to add or questions to ask, you will be able to find out just where to go.

Summary

Making useless, old PCs useful again, learning stuff about Linux, and just having fun playing with computer software and hardware are some of the benefits you'll get from the *Linux Toys II* projects contained in this book. The projects in this book cover a range of elements, including bootable Linux systems, open source audio and video playing and streaming, and Linux server configurations.

Projects in *Linux Toys II* have been reviewed directly by creators and maintainers of the open source software each project covers. Because *Linux Toys II* projects stick closely to these popular, well-supported open source initiatives, you have the advantage of having a place to continue to grow your *Linux Toys II* projects beyond the boundaries of this book.

Finding What You Need

Nearly every project in this book can be completed with an old PC (cheap), a Linux operating system (free), and a few pieces of extra hardware (reasonable). Some projects, such as the MythTV personal video recorder in Chapter 4, will work better with more expensive hardware, and others, like the Linux Terminal Server Project in Chapter 12, are designed specifically to take advantage of minimal hardware.

The cool thing is that if you are short on cash and long on time, you have few limitations on what you can accomplish with these projects. The software you need either comes with this book or is freely available. The hardware can range from an old 486 you found in a dumpster to the best multimedia PC you can find.

This chapter describes the general kinds of software and hardware you need to complete the *Linux Toys* projects. It also tells you where to go to find other projects that are available out in the world.

Getting Software

Linux Toys II software projects can be completed entirely with software covered under the GPL or similar open source licenses. The exact terms under which you can use and redistribute the software are included with each software project (typically in a file called COPYING or LICENSE). For the most part, however, the software described in *Linux Toys II* can be used without much restriction.

Because most of the projects illustrated in this book rely on software that is not included in core Linux distributions, building the *Linux Toys* projects requires a combination of software from at least two sources:

> ➤ **Linux distribution** — Every project in *Linux Toys II* either requires a Linux distribution be installed on your hard disk or includes a Linux distribution that is run live when you boot the project. When an installed Linux distribution is required, I recommend Fedora Core or Red Hat Enterprise Linux, although other distributions will work as well in most cases.

in this chapter

☑ Choosing a Linux distribution

☑ Getting Linux Toys software

☑ Connecting to open source projects

☑ Choosing hardware for different projects

■ **Open source initiatives** — Many of the projects described in *Linux Toys II* are based primarily (or entirely) on open source initiatives that offer software development, forums, and documentation that are ongoing and active. (Because these open source initiatives are also usually referred to as "projects" I'll try to be careful to distinguish between the *Linux Toys II* projects you create with and the projects/initiatives on which this *Linux Toys* book draws.)

The software for each *Linux Toys II* project is included on the CD that comes with this book (with a couple of exceptions where it is more appropriate to download the latest copy of software instead).

The following sections describe how to choose a Linux distribution to use with *Linux Toys II* and how to get involved with the open source projects that *Linux Toys II* and similar projects rely on.

Choosing a Linux Distribution

All of the projects in *Linux Toys II* have been tested and run on Fedora Core, the community-driven Linux system sponsored by Red Hat, Inc. In cases where you are constructing a self-contained project (such as eMoviX where the result includes an operating system on a disk), the procedure for putting together the software side of those projects is done on Fedora Core. However, if you have another Linux operating system installed, most of the projects can be adapted to run in those systems.

Note Because the *Linux Toys II* CD includes a version of Damn Small Linux, there are some aspects of the *Linux Toys II* projects you can do without having a Linux system installed at all. For example, the "Customizing a Live Linux Pen Drive" project (Chapter 6) can be done directly from a booted *Linux Toys II* CD, regardless of what operating system is installed on your hard disk.

Choosing which Linux distribution to install is, for some people, almost a religious matter. Most long-term Linux enthusiasts will try out many different Linux distributions. For example, a Linux person might use Red Hat Enterprise Linux or SUSE at work, Debian or Fedora Core for a small office server, and Gentoo or Slackware for their personal use.

Because most major open source software components are available for the major distributions, people will choose a Linux distribution for reasons other than what they can run with it. Different Linux distributions offer different approaches to software packaging, different quality levels of testing, and communities with very different personalities.

The following sections describe how to choose a Linux distribution to use with the *Linux Toys II* projects.

Using Fedora Core Linux

The Fedora Project is sponsored by Red Hat, Inc., and supported by the Fedora community. Twice a year it has produced a Linux distribution called Fedora Core. While Fedora Core is not a supported product of Red Hat, it is used as a proving ground for software that goes into

Red Hat Enterprise Linux products. It is freely distributed, has a great deal of community support, and (in my opinion) is an excellent platform on which to build *Linux Toys II* projects.

If you are a first-time Linux user, I recommend trying the projects in this book with Fedora Core. I chose to use Fedora Core for several reasons:

- **RPMs** — The *Linux Toys II* CD comes with software that was pre-built into binaries and put into packages in RPM format for most projects. RPMs save you the trouble of compiling and installing the components manually. Typically, one command can install the software package for the project you are building. After that, you can use the rich set of options to the rpm command for each package to list contents, display descriptions, or remove the package completely.

- **Stability** — When I say stability, I don't just mean that Fedora Core will work (although it should). I mean that you can depend on a certain set of well-tested core features in Fedora, and that there is a strong company (Red Hat, Inc.) and vibrant community (FedoraForum.org) backing it up.

- **Updates** — As bugs are found and security issues are uncovered, the Fedora Project offers updates to keep your Fedora system working and secure. Fedora includes tools for downloading and installing these updates, such as the up2date, yum, and apt utilities. Particularly if you are doing one of the *Linux Toys II* projects that can be used as an Internet server (such as Gallery or Icecast), you want to be sure that you have all the latest security enhancements.

Red Hat, Inc., uses Fedora Core as a test bed for features that go into Red Hat Enterprise Linux products. Although they make no guarantees that Fedora Core will work (or that they or anyone else will fix it if it doesn't), Red Hat relies on the testing and community support that goes on with Fedora to ensure the quality of their Enterprise products. I have found it to be quite reliable.

Every *Linux Toys II* project was tested on Fedora Core 4. (One exception is the MythTV project in Chapter 4, for which Fedora Core 3 is recommended.) However, it's quite likely that the projects will run on other versions of Fedora Core as well. Although the *Linux Toys II* projects have not all been tested in Red Hat Enterprise Linux (RHEL), most should simply install and work without modification in RHEL. You may find, however, that there are some differences in packaging and features between Fedora and RHEL.

Fedora Core features an easy-to-use installer, referred to as Anaconda. Using Anaconda takes a lot of the guesswork out of initially configuring your computer and installing Linux. Once Fedora Core is installed, you can use features such as yum and up2date to get critical software updates for your system.

Fedora Core includes hundreds of desktop, server, and workstation applications you can use. It makes an excellent and reliable platform as a desktop system, small office server, or programmer's workstation — as well as a good platform for *Linux Toys II*. Figure 2-1 shows an example of the Fedora Core desktop.

FIGURE 2-1: Fedora Core can be a desktop, server, or a platform for Linux Toys.

In addition to the packages included in Fedora Core, Fedora Extras is an initiative that allows community members to package software into RPM format so Fedora users can easily install it (see `http://download.fedora.redhat.com/pub/fedora/linux/extras`). Fedora Core 4 comes configured so that, if you know a package that exists in a Fedora Extras repository, you can install it from the Internet by typing `yum install` *package*.

There are already hundreds of software packages in Fedora Extras repositories that can be added to the basic Fedora Core. In particular, Fedora Extras offers choices. If you don't like the Web browser, mail client, or word processor supported by Fedora Core, you can choose from several other applications in those areas in Fedora Extras.

There are many ways to get Fedora Core because it is freely distributed. Here are a few:

- *Red Hat Fedora and Enterprise Linux 4 Bible* — Several books include the entire Fedora Core operating system with it. I like this one particularly because, well, I wrote it. Besides including both a full DVD and a reduced two-CD set of Fedora Core, the book contains about 1100 pages of information on user and system administrator topics.

- **Download** — If you have the bandwidth, you can download the entire Fedora Core distribution from the Internet and burn your own CDs or DVD. For instructions on how to do that, and links to sites that have Fedora Core, refer to the Fedora download site (`http://fedora.redhat.com/download/`).

If you decide to use Fedora Core to create your *Linux Toys II* projects, refer to Appendix C, which describes how to install Fedora Core on your computer.

Using Other Linux Distributions

Unlike the original *Linux Toys*, where the CD supplied only RPMs and source RPMs that were intended for Fedora and Red Hat Enterprise Linux, this book makes it a bit easier to install projects on other Linux distributions. If you are willing to create the projects from source code, you can try extracting and compiling the source code provided on the *Linux Toys II* CD on any Linux system.

There are some issues with using other Linux distributions, however. Because the projects have not been checked on every different type of Linux, there may be dependency issues that may cause the project not to work. In other words, you may need a particular utility or library that is not included with the Linux distribution you are using. While you can probably get whatever component is missing for your distribution, it may take some detective work.

The following is a quick rundown of a few popular Linux distributions:

- **Debian GNU/Linux** (www.debian.org) — Debian is known for being extraordinarily stable. The Debian project is committed to an open development process, in terms of sharing code, and providing public bug tracking facilities and support programs. There are more than 15,000 software packages associated with the Debian project. Because of its excellent software packaging tools and stability, many other Linux distributions are based on Debian. These include KNOPPIX, Ubuntu, Damn Small Linux, and others.

- **SUSE Linux** (www.novell.com/linux/suse) — Like Red Hat Enterprise Linux, SUSE is geared toward Enterprise computing. SUSE is owned by Novell, Inc., which was once the world's most successful computer networking company with its NetWare operating system. With SUSE, you can get professional support, training, documentation, and other commercial offerings that may be helpful to companies that need to deploy many Linux systems. SUSE includes the YaST interface, which offers graphical tools for administering your Linux system.

- **Slackware Linux** (www.slackware.com) — As one of the earliest Linux distributions still in existence today, Slackware offers a very streamlined approach to Linux. Many users consider Slackware to be among the best ways to learn Linux because it doesn't use a lot of graphical tools to support the basic operations of your Linux system. The distribution is compact, requiring only a two-CD set to get going. You can configure versions of Slackware that will run well on older computers with less power.

- **Gentoo Linux** (www.gentoo.org) — For people who like to fine-tune and tweak their Linux systems, Gentoo is an excellent choice. Every component of Gentoo can be built from scratch to specifically match your computer hardware and desired software configuration. Like Slackware, Gentoo is a good way to learn what goes on inside your Linux system because installation and setup instructions contain many manual features that are hidden from you with distributions such as SUSE and Red Hat Enterprise Linux. Gentoo features the portage tools for software installation, which are based on the BSD ports system.

Visit the Web sites for any of these Linux distributions to find out where you can download their software. There are also dozens (maybe hundreds) of other Linux distributions available today that you might want to try out. You can get an overview of what Linux distributions are available and links to where you can download and find out more about them at www .distrowatch.com and LinuxISO.org.

Tip   For more complete descriptions of different Linux distributions, refer to *Linux Bible, 2005 Edition* by Christopher Negus. Besides including a DVD and CD with ten different Linux distributions to try out, the book describes how Linux distributions differ, what each is best suited for, and how to find forums, mailing lists, and other resources to learn more.

Getting Linux Toys Software

After you have Fedora Core or another Linux operating system installed, you just have to add the software that is specific to each *Linux Toys II* project you want to build. All of the software needed to create the *Linux Toys II* projects is included on the CD that comes with this book (or is easily downloaded) in the following forms:

- **RPMs** — Pre-built binaries for each of the *Linux Toys II* projects are included on the CD in the form of RPM Package Management (RPM) files. These RPMs were created specifically to run on Fedora Core or Red Hat Enterprise Linux systems. However, it might be possible to use them on other systems that support RPM packages or by extracting the software from these packages and installing them on other Linux systems.

    RPM packages can be installed and managed using the rpm command. You can also use software packaging tools such as yum or apt to install and maintain software packages over the network.

- **Tarballs** — A tarball is a single file that contains a whole set of files. The name comes from the tar command, which is used to make the tarballs. Tar stands for *Tape ARchiver*, because when tar was created back in the old UNIX days, magnetic tape was the primary medium for archiving software. The tar command has many, many options for creating, comparing, listing, appending, and extracting tar files. For the projects in this book, you are most interested in extracting files from a project's tarball directory, and then possibly compiling and installing the software to use on a Linux system.

    If you are using a Linux distribution other than Fedora or RHEL, installing from the tarballs included with this book's CD is probably the best way to go. Tarballs are the most common way for a project to distribute the source code for open source projects for several reasons. For one thing, you can put all the files in an entire project into one file (making it easy to pass around). For another, every Linux and UNIX system includes the tar command, so you can be sure that you can extract all the files you need to your system.

    Usually the tar file will be compressed, often by the open source gzip utility. So instead of just ending in .tar, the tar archive file ends in .tar.gz. Because tar includes an option to uncompress gzipped archives, you can extract the entire project to your system in one step. After that, you usually need a C compiler and make utility to compile and install the software on your Linux system. Some projects these days, however, don't need to be compiled at all because they are built in languages such as perl that can be executed directly. (Gallery and Linux Terminal Server Project included with this book are examples of tarballs that include software that doesn't need to be compiled.)

- **Source RPMs** — Along with the RPMs you can install and use on Fedora and Red Hat Enterprise Linux systems, the CD provides source RPMs (SRPMs) for each project described in the book. Using SRPMs, you can change or tune the source code, and then rebuild the RPM packages.

- **ISO images** — Several of the *Linux Toys II* projects are available on what are referred to as ISO images. An ISO image is a single file that is intended to be burned to a CD or DVD (or other removable media) and accessed or run from either of those media. Linux Live CDs, installation CDs, or just a CD of backed-up data files come in ISO images. Several *Linux Toys II* projects rely on ISO images I have included on the *Linux Toys II* CD (e.g., the eMoviX, Devil-Linux, and Linux Terminal Server Project ISOs).

For Linux distributions that don't encourage a formal packaging format, such as Slackware, installing from source code is a good way to go. Source code for most open source projects is expected to run on many different operating systems. Not only will the source code for many of the projects in this book work with most Linux systems, but they may run in other UNIX-like systems (FreeBSD, NetBSD, OpenBSD, OS X, or Solaris, to name a few). For non-Linux systems, however, I recommend checking with the projects themselves to see if they have specific versions to run on other operating systems. Some will even offer Microsoft Windows versions of their projects.

By installing from tarballs that come directly from a software project (as are included with this book), you have a better chance of making sure your software will run exactly as the software creators intended.

If you have a Linux system other than Fedora or RHEL, you can look for software packages of projects that are stored in other formats. Although the CD that accompanies this book doesn't include packages in these formats, if you can find a package that is specifically built for the Linux distribution you are using, there is a good chance that it will have been tuned to run well on your system. Here are a few popular Linux software-packaging methods:

- **Deb packages** — Packages intended to run on Debian systems are packaged in .deb format. Therefore, other distributions that are based on Debian (such as Ubuntu, Damn Small Linux, and KNOPPIX) can use .deb packages as well.

- **Emerge for Gentoo Linux** — Applications built to run in Gentoo are made available through the portage installation system. For example, you can get Gallery Web photo software (described in Chapter 3) from the `www-apps/gallery` section of the portage database. You can install the Gentoo version of Gallery by typing **emerge gallery**.

- **RPMs for SUSE** — Like Fedora and RHEL, SUSE uses packages in RPM format. To use RPMs in SUSE for projects included with this book, however, you may need RPMs that were built particularly for SUSE.

Appendix A describes how the software is organized on the *Linux Toys II* CD and how you can use it to install the *Linux Toys II* projects.

Connecting to Open Source Projects

There are literally thousands of open source projects available to you. Many of these projects offer forums, mailing lists, documentation, and free downloads of their software. Larger projects offer formal support options and consulting service (if you want customized enhancements). Nearly every kind of software category you can think of has multiple open source offerings for you to choose from.

A goal of *Linux Toys II* is to help you connect to the projects you like, whether they are projects described in this book or ones that you find while you are exploring on your own. In the original *Linux Toys*, we pieced together much of software for the projects ourselves and offered our own forums. In *Linux Toys II*, I've encouraged a much closer connection to the open source initiatives I drew from in this book by:

- Sticking closely to existing open source projects, instead of piecing together software from several different open source initiatives

- Pointing you to existing forums, mailing lists, FAQs, and other resources from these open source initiatives to learn more about them

- Encouraging you to contribute to the open source software communities you like directly, by helping maintain code, write documentation, or give cash donations

Volunteers maintain most open source projects. Small contributions by many people can go a long way. If you make enhancements to the code or fix bugs, feed it back to the project so that others can gain from your work. In each chapter I describe how to connect to the open source initiatives that are included and described in this book so you can contact the projects directly if you want to find out more about them.

If the *Linux Toys II* projects in this book have sparked your interest, there are lots of ways that you can pursue other open source projects. There are gathering places on the Internet where you can find links to information and downloads for literally thousands of open source initiatives. Among the most popular places to start are SourceForge.net and Freshmeat.net.

Note   SourceForge.net and Freshmeat.net are both part of the Open Source Technology Group (www.ostg.com), which is a wholly owned subsidiary of VA Software (www.vasoftware.com). Other OSTG technology sites include Slashdot.org (where you get the latest open source news), NewsForge.com (another open source news site), and Linux.com (a resource for enterprise Linux products).

Finding Projects at SourceForge.net

SourceForge.net (http://sourceforge.net) touts itself as the world's largest open source software development site. It recently surpassed 100,000 registered open source projects and 1,000,000 registered users. If you want to find out what open source projects are available and the status of each one, SourceForge.net is a great place to start.

SourceForge.net offers free Web hosting to the thousands of projects that are registered to it. To each project, SourceForge.net provides its Collaborative Development System (CDS), which the project can use to support its development and connections to the open source community. SourceForge.net helps project administrators bring their projects to the public in the following ways:

- **Offering downloads** — SourceForge.net lets administrators package and store their projects for download by project users.

- **Providing project exposure** — Administrators can enter information about their projects that makes it easier for people to find the projects through the software map and keyword searches. Projects can be selected as the "SourceForge.net Project of the Month" to be particularly showcased at the SourceForge.net site. Special exposure is also given to projects that are being heavily developed or have very high download rates.

- **Posting news** — SourceForge.net offers tools administrators can use to post news items that can be exported using HTML export and RSS feeds. Several news items each day are placed on the SourceForge.net front page.

- **Posting screenshots** — Administrators can post screenshots of their projects so people can see what they look like before they download the projects.

- **Offering communications tools** — SourceForge.net offers tools to help developers communicate with each other, as well as with those who want to use each project. For managing bug reports, feature requests, and support requests, SourceForge.net offers the Trackers feature. To allow on-going discussions of each project, a project can take advantage of Web-based, searchable forums. Users and developers can also communicate using mailing lists.

Linux Toys II projects include many different open source projects that are hosted at SourceForge.net. By searching that site for software used in this book, you can also find related projects. For example, if you search for "gallery," you will find the Gallery project described in Chapter 3, as well as dozens more projects that can be used for managing images.

Finding Projects at Freshmeat.net

While SourceForge.net hosts open source projects, Freshmeat.net (http://freshmeat.net) provides a huge index of open source Linux and UNIX software, themes, and related stuff. Freshmeat.net also offers a huge selection of desktop themes, which it incorporated into its site in May 2002 from themes.org.

You can browse the Freshmeat.net site by software category, development status, intended audience, operating system, network environment and other variables. For each project, you can find links to its home page, downloads in available formats (tar, RPM, and so on), and communications tools (forums, mailing lists, and the like).

Freshmeat.net also includes articles related to open source software. If there are articles available related to a project, you will find links to those articles on that project's page at Freshmeat.net.

Choosing Hardware

An original concept of *Linux Toys* was to be able to reuse old, otherwise useless computer hardware to make fun stand-alone projects. While reusing old hardware is still a great goal for some of the projects in *Linux Toys II* (in fact, the LTSP project in Chapter 11 is a better project for reusing old PCs than anything in the first *Linux Toys*), some projects go to the other extreme. For example, Chapter 4 on the MythTV project describes a personal video recorder that doesn't skimp on hardware.

Each project chapter in this book describes any special hardware requirement for doing the project. You can view the information in this section as a bunch of tips and guidelines for reusing or purchasing the computer hardware you need to do these projects. That information is presented in the form of a Frequently Asked Questions list.

"Can I Use Any of These Projects on My Old 486?"

Yes! The Linux Terminal Server Project (described in Chapter 11) supports client machines as low as an Intel 486 processor with a minimum of 32MB of memory (text-only mode). That's because the client computer is running a minimal Linux system that is just enough to drive the graphical interface (or shell interface), mouse, and keyboard. The rest of the work is done on the server.

Because many of the projects in this book start with an assumption of Fedora Core 4 as the base operating system, the minimum requirements of that system set the minimum supported hardware. That minimum is a Pentium II, with different amounts of RAM required, depending on whether you want to use a GUI or just run from the command line. (See Appendix C for hardware requirements for installing Fedora Core 4.)

If you want to try a different Linux system, however, using a 486 on all but the most demanding projects (such as the MythTV project in Chapter 4) might be possible. I recommend trying Slackware, Debian, or Gentoo Linux distributions, and then installing the *Linux Toys II* software from the tarballs included.

With an old machine, a problem bigger than the processor in successfully running Linux could be the RAM and hard disk. If the old computer holds only 32MB of RAM, you won't be able to run GNOME or KDE desktops well (if at all). You're stuck in text mode or perhaps a very minimal window manager. Older computers may not have the disk space for a reasonable Linux install. Disks of 500MB were not uncommon only a few years ago and the minimal Fedora Core install is about 600MB.

Bottom line: I'd try the LTSP project for very old hardware. For any machine that has a CD drive, you can try any of the bootable images included with *Linux Toys II* (including booting the *Linux Toys II* CD itself). Start with a Pentium II or better processor for most of the other projects.

"Can I Get Linux Pre-Installed on a Computer?"

Yes. Everything from low-cost home desktop systems to high-end workstation and servers are being sold today with Linux preinstalled. The Linux.org site maintains a list of vendors who sell computers with Linux preinstalled. You can find that list at www.linux.org/vendor/system.

Companies such as Pogo Linux (www.pogolinux.com) and Penguin Computing (www.penguincomputing.com) offer workstations with Fedora or Red Hat Enterprise Linux preinstalled for under $1,000 or $1,800, respectively. With a PC from those companies, you can start right in installing and building *Linux Toys II* projects.

If you are looking for a laptop computer with Fedora preinstalled, check out Linux Certified (www.linuxcertified.com). Laptops with Fedora installed start at under $1,000.

There are also very low end PCs being mass-marketed with Linux preinstalled. A company called Linare offers desktop computers starting under $200 with Linux preinstalled and laptops for under $500 that are being sold through Wal-Mart and Amazon.com. They come with a Linare operating system installed. If you want to take a chance on one of those computers, you can try installing Fedora or RHEL on them if the projects don't work in Linare.

The trend is toward more and more inexpensive computers becoming available with Linux installed on them. Buying a computer with all hardware components certified to run Linux can save you some of the problems that put off many first-time Linux users. For example, to get Linux running on a computer that had Windows pre-installed often requires resizing the disk, dealing with winmodems and winprinters (software-driven hardware that is tricky to get working in Linux), and potentially messing up the boot loader when you install Linux.

"How Do I Pick Hardware for an Entertainment System?"

There are several qualities to look for in a PC that you plan to put in your entertainment system. Some specific issues for choosing an entertainment system PC are included in the MythTV PVR project (see Chapter 4). Here are a few of the highlights:

- **Quiet** — You don't want a fan that makes a lot of noise. Spend a few extra dollars and get one that is particularly quiet.

- **Elegant case** — You don't want to put a standard desktop case on your stereo system. The case used for the MythTV project was an LC11M from SilverStone Technology (www.silverstonetek.com). The dimensions are similar to a common stereo component (424 mm wide by 96 mm high by 430 mm deep). Using a Micro ATX motherboard allows the case to be smaller than you would need for a standard ATX motherboard, and still have room for the video cards, hard disks, and other components you need. Figure 2-2 shows a picture of this case.

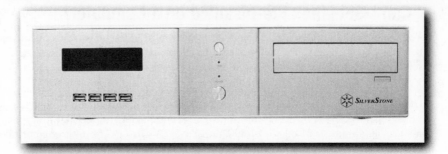

FIGURE 2-2: The SilverStone Tek LC11M case fits well in an entertainment center.

Another type of case that I used in the first *Linux Toys* book was the ShuttleXPC (www.shuttle.com). It is shaped like a large loaf of bread and is built to use a Micro ATX board.

■ **Ports** — You want to be able to plug headphones and other components into the front of the case. With the MythTV configuration, there are four USB 2.0 ports, one 1394 FireWire port, one earphone jack, and one microphone jack.

■ **Hard disks** — Music can take up a lot of disk space, but video can take up a lot more. The computer used for the MythTV project in Chapter 4 includes two Hitachi T7K250 drives. In standard mode, it can operate at 1.5 Gbit/second. However, it can also operate in SATA II mode and achieve speeds of 3 Gbit/second. Each disk holds up to 250GB of data.

■ **Wireless keyboard/mouse** — So you don't have to have wires strung all over your living room, a wireless keyboard with a built-in mouse is a good idea. A BTC 9019URF wireless multimedia keyboard is used for the MythTV project. It has a dual-mode joystick.

"How Do I Choose Hardware for Thin Clients?"

As I described with the "my old 486" question, the computers you use as thin clients can be almost throw-away computers these days. If you are using them in a professional setting, however, the key is that you can leave off almost everything you would expect in a PC (hard disk, CD/DVD, and floppy drive) and include just a motherboard and a network card. Check out www.disklessworkstations.com for new thin client workstations that are certified to work with the Linux Terminal Server Project.

The server you use with your thin client setup, however, must be up to the task of supporting as many thin clients as you expect to be using it simultaneously. That means:

■ **Lots of RAM** — Because all of the applications run by each client are actually running on the server (aside from the GUI, which runs on each client), you need to have enough RAM to support all those clients. You might figure on at least 128MB of RAM for each thin client simultaneously using the server.

- **Lots of disk space** — Depending on how you plan to use your thin clients, you may need a lot of hard disk space. If the thin clients are just being used to access the Web and play games, you may not need much space at all. If all users are going to have their own login accounts and home directories where they will want to store their work, you need to take into account the type and amount of content each person needs to store.

- **Peripherals** — You can save money by having only one of each type of component you need attached to the server, rather than having separate components attached to each client. So you should consider getting a good printer, backup medium, and other peripherals to be able to service the number of thin clients you use.

"How Do I Choose Hardware for a Server?"

Projects such as the Gallery project (Chapter 3) and Icecast Internet Radio Station project (Chapter 10) can be used as a public Internet server to share photos and audio broadcasts, respectively. While there are no special hardware demands, per se, for putting a server on the Internet (if you have an Ethernet card, an IP address, and a connection to the Internet, it will work), there are some issues you should consider.

If you are betting your business on the servers you use for these projects, it will be important that the hardware you choose is reliable. You can start by getting hardware that is certified to run Linux (as I described earlier in the question about getting pre-installed Linux computers).

There are hosting companies, such as RackSpace.com, that set up and maintain hardware that they know to work well in Linux. If something goes wrong, they have lots of spare parts on hand and can get your server back up and running again in a very short time. RackSpace.com is also good for *Linux Toys II* projects because it runs Red Hat Enterprise Linux servers, which will work for the projects described in this book.

"How Do I Know if My Computer Will Run Linux?"

There are ways of getting almost every computer hardware component known to humankind working in Linux (one way or another). Some hardware, however, may not work without some extra tweaking and some may not work for your particular version of Linux.

Here are some reasons why particular hardware components may not "just work" with the Linux system you are installing:

- **Only Windows drivers available** — Some hardware manufacturers do not publish the specifications of the drivers needed to access their computer hardware. This can make it very difficult for open source developers to create drivers needed to use the hardware in Linux. Drivers for certain software-driven modems (called winmodems), printers (called winprinters), and Webcams have been created by the open source community by sheer tenacity. In some cases, open source developers have created wrappers that can take advantage of existing Windows drivers. For example, the ndiswrapper project can be used with Windows drivers to support a variety of wireless networking cards that don't have native Linux Drivers.

■ **Not ported to the latest kernel** — When the Linux kernel goes through a major upgrade (as it did when it went from the 2.4 to the 2.6 kernel), not all drivers for all hardware supported by the earlier kernel will be upgraded. This can happen when the hardware is so old that it is not worth it for anyone to maintain support for it any more. In that case, an earlier kernel may be required to use the hardware. However, it's more likely that a few dollars will get you a more modern component to replace it with.

■ **Not yet supported by the latest kernel** — When new hardware that doesn't specifically meet known standards is introduced, a driver for that hardware that works in Linux can take a while to create. In particular, new TV cards, video cards, wireless cards, and other video and communications hardware can take a while to become supported in Linux. It's usually safest to check whether the specific item you want to purchase is already supported in Linux before you buy it.

Besides buying a computer that was certified to run Linux, with Linux already pre-installed (as I described earlier), you can check whether or not the hardware you have is supported in Linux before you start installing to your hard disk. Here are a few suggestions on how to do that:

■ **Google** — For each hardware component, use the Google.com search engine with the word "Linux" plus the name and model number of the hardware component in question. Chances are that someone else has already tried to install on a computer that includes that component. Googling will tell you if they have had success and if there is something special you need to do to get it working.

■ **Researching laptops** — Because they contain more non-standard components than you will find in the average desktop computer, laptops can be particularly tricky to get working in Linux. There's a Linux Laptop-HOWTO that can give you some insights (`http://en.tldp.org/HOWTO/Laptop-HOWTO.html`). The Linux on Laptops site (`www.linux-on-laptops.com`) shares experiences people have had getting different versions of Linux to run on their laptop computers.

■ **Hardware compatibility lists** — Fedora Core, which I recommend for the projects in this book, does not have an official hardware compatibility list. However, you can find information about specific known problems with hardware when you try to install Fedora Core in the release notes (`http://fedora.redhat.com/docs/release-notes`). Red Hat Enterprise Linux, however, does maintain a list of hardware that is certified to work with RHEL (`http://bugzilla.redhat.com/hwcert`). Searching the Red Hat bug database (`bugzilla.redhat.com`) is itself a good way to learn about troubles people might be having with a particular piece of hardware.

If you are using a different Linux distribution, few offer complete hardware compatibility lists. Your best bet is to search Web sites and forums for your Linux distribution for any particular hardware item that is in question.

As for places where you can read about general hardware support in Linux, you can start with the Hardware section of the LDP HOWTO-Index (`www.tldp.org/HOWTO/HOWTO-INDEX/hardware.html`). That will provide you with links to other HOWTOs about hardware for Linux.

- **Try a bootable Linux** — With bootable Linux distributions, such as KNOPPIX and Damn Small Linux, you can boot a working Linux distribution from CD or DVD without touching your computer's hard disk. The *Linux Toys II* CD includes, and can be booted directly to, Damn Small Linux. You can use that CD to try your hardware (configure a printer, dial out with a modem, hook up your TV card, and so on) to make sure it works. If it does, you can be pretty sure that is will work (or that you can get it to work) once you install your permanent Linux distribution.

Both *Linux Bible, 2005 Edition* and *Red Hat Fedora and Enterprise Linux 4 Bible* include bootable versions of KNOPPIX that you can use to test out your computer hardware before installing Fedora Core to your hard disk. KNOPPIX includes a larger set of software than is included in Damn Small Linux (although DSL is great for the basics!). You can also download your own version of KNOPPIX and burn your own CD from several locations on the Internet. (I suggest starting at `www.knoppix.net`.)

Summary

All you really need is a common PC, a Linux distribution (I suggest Fedora Core or Red Hat Enterprise Linux), and the software that comes with this book to build most of the *Linux Toys II* projects. However, this chapter describes some of the issues you may encounter for some of the projects that are more demanding (MythTV) or less demanding (Linux Terminal Server Project) of your computer hardware.

If you are interested in pursuing other open source projects or if you want to try *Linux Toys II* projects on Linux systems other than the ones I recommend, this chapter describes how to do that. Sites such as SourceForge.net and Freshmeat.net offer vast resources for researching and downloading software associated with thousands of open source projects.

Multimedia Projects

part

Creating a Web Photo Gallery

While taking tons of digital photographs is easy, sharing digital photos has turned out to be a lot more challenging. Email systems weren't designed to handle multi-megabyte attachments. Printing out every picture cousin Millie might like to see just isn't feasible. Creating your own Web photo gallery is a great alternative.

Gallery (`http://gallery.sourceforge.net`) is a high-quality, open source project for publishing and managing your digital photographs on the Web. Gallery gives you a lot of control over your content. You can authenticate users to manage what each person can see or even add to the gallery. With Gallery, you also have minute control over every aspect of the look-and-feel of your photo albums.

This chapter describes how to install, set up, configure, and maintain your own Gallery digital image server.

Overview of Gallery

Gallery is a Web-based software package that allows you to publish and maintain collections of photo albums. The package contains extraordinary flexibility in configuring how the main gallery, the albums in that gallery, and the photographs themselves are displayed and managed.

To set up and control Gallery, you need to have an administrative (admin) user assigned to your personal gallery. That user has total control over the functioning of your Gallery server. A Web-based configuration wizard lets the admin user check that all the components needed by Gallery from the operating system are available. It then lets you define specific settings that relate to your personal gallery and albums.

Gallery provides lots of ways for visitors to browse, search, and sort the images in your photo gallery. Hooks in Gallery let you or any visitors send images from your gallery to professional printing services to have prints made of the images you choose. (The admin needs to choose which printing service to make this feature available on a particular gallery.)

By creating user accounts, the admin also can allow selected users to create their own albums and then add, delete, and modify the images in those albums.

Bharat Mediratta created Gallery originally, but there is now a large community of developers, testers, and other contributors to the project. Along with Bharat, contributors to Gallery include Alan Harder, Andy Staudacher, Andrew Lindeman, Beckett Madden-Woods, Chad Kieffer, Chris Kelly, Chris Smith, Christian Mohn, Dariush Molavi, Dave Moore, Donald Webster, Douglas Cau, Ernesto Bachny, Felix Rabinovich, Jay Rossiter, Jens Tkotz, Jesse Mullan, Joan McGalliard, JoEllen Drazan, Michael Kleinert, Michael Schultheiss, Pierre-Luc Paour, Robert Balousek, Ross Reyman, and many, many more.

Note Gallery has too many contributors to list here. See the Gallery Development Team page at `http://gallery.sourceforge.net/wiki.php?page=Development%20Team` for a more complete list of contributors.

Gallery software is available for free. If you like the software, however, I encourage you to support the project in any of several ways. On the Gallery project home page (`http://gallery.sourceforge.net`), you can click the Donate to Gallery button to give a donation to help keep the project going. Or, select the Paid Support link to find out how you can pay to have the Gallery team install or fix your Gallery installation.

To get more information about Gallery or to become involved with the Gallery community, select the Wiki link from the Gallery home page. From there, you can find out about Gallery mailing lists, tutorials, documentation, development, and other ways of getting to know more about Gallery. The Gallery Development Team page listed earlier also tells how to join the team.

Linux Toys II includes and describes the well-tested Gallery 1.5. As of this writing, Gallery 2.0 is in development. So, by the time you read this, Gallery 2.0 will probably be available.

Gallery 2.0 features a complete rewrite of the Gallery interface, but includes all the features described in this chapter. You can check the Gallery Web site for information on upgrading from Gallery 1.5 to 2.0 or simply choose to download the later 2.0 version and use that instead of the software included with this book.

Installing Linux

To run Gallery in Linux, you need to at least have Apache Web server software and PHP4 scripting software installed with the Linux system on your server. There is also a variety of optional tools you will want for tasks such as photo manipulation (such as NetPBM or ImageMagick).

I tested this project using Fedora Core 4, installed as described in Appendix C, with the packages mentioned added. The only software package needed (aside from the Gallery tarball described in the next section) that doesn't come in Fedora Core 4 is the jhead package. The jhead utility is needed if you want to work with EXIF header information in your images. You can install that package from the *Linux Toys II* CD as follows:

1. Insert the *Linux Toys II* CD in your CD drive. If your CD mounts automatically, you can skip the first command. If it doesn't, run the following (possibly replacing /media/ cdrecorder with the location where your CD was mounted) as root user from a Terminal window:

```
# mount /media/cdrecorder
```

2. Next, change to the RPMS directory for Gallery and run the installme script as follows:

```
# cd /media/cdrecorder/RPMS/ch03-gallery
# ./installme
```

This installs all RPMs needed for this project (in this case, just the jhead package).

Installing Gallery

The following is a procedure for initially installing Gallery on your Linux server:

Note The copy of Gallery on the *Linux Toys II* CD comes directly from the Gallery project Web site. Before you install it, though, check the Gallery site at http://gallery.sourceforge.net to see if any critical patches are available. In fact, if Gallery 2.0 is available, you should consider downloading that instead (although much of the user interface will differ from what is shown here). At the very least, I strongly recommend subscribing to the gallery-announce mailing list (low-bandwidth) to get notices of any critical updates.

1. Unpack Gallery to a directory accessible to your Web server. Wherever you unpack the software, it will create a subdirectory called gallery/. If you are going to make your Gallery albums public (or at least available on your LAN), you need to install them in a location that can be accessed by the Web server. For example, a personal Gallery installation for a user named chris, might go in the directory /home/chris/public_html/gallery/. A system-wide installation might go into /var/www/html/gallery/.

   Here is what you type from a Terminal window to unpack Gallery from the *Linux Toys II* CD for a personal installation of Gallery (substitute your user name for *chris*):

```
$ mkdir /home/chris/public_html
$ cd /home/chris/public_html
$ tar xvfz /media/cdrecorder/Sources/ch03-gallery/gallery*gz
```

2. In your gallery/ directory, create .htaccess and config.php files and a directory called albums, and set ownership to your user name (for this example, I use the user name chris) and group to apache as follows:

```
$ touch gallery/.htaccess gallery/config.php
$ mkdir gallery/albums
$ chown chris:apache gallery/.htaccess gallery/config.php
$ chown chris:apache gallery/albums
$ chmod 664 gallery/.htaccess gallery/config.php
```

3. To make sure that your Apache server can access the Gallery files if they are installed in your home directory, you can change permissions as follows:

```
$ chmod 711 $HOME
$ chmod 775 $HOME/public_html
```

4. If you are installing Gallery to the /var/www/html/gallery directory, you don't need to configure Apache in any special way to access Gallery. However, to have Apache access Gallery from your home directory, you need to modify the file /etc/httpd/conf/httpd.conf to allow the public_html directory for the selected user to be able to publish Web content. First, you should comment out the UserDir disable line to appear as follows, so that feature is not disabled:

```
#   UserDir disable
```

Next, add the following Directory entry to allow content to be published from the chosen directory. For example, here is what you would put if Gallery were installed in the /home/chris/public_html directory:

```
<Directory /home/chris/public_html/gallery>
    AllowOverride Options FileInfo
</Directory>
```

At this point you should be ready to start checking and configuring the Gallery software you just installed.

 Note   There is a lot more you can do to configure an Apache Web server, if you like. Some more detailed Apache setup is covered in books such as *Red Hat Fedora and Enterprise Linux 4 Bible*. Also, Apache itself comes with an extensive online manual that is very useful once you understand the basics (http://localhost/manual).

Checking and Configuring Gallery

To check that your basic Gallery setup is working properly, you can run the Gallery Configuration Wizard. To run the wizard, start your Web server, and then open the index.php file in your Gallery's gallery/setup directory. Here's how to do that:

1. To start your Apache server, type the following as root user:

```
# /etc/init.d/httpd start
```

2. To start the configuration wizard, use any Web browser and open the index.php file from your Gallery setup directory. For example, if your setup meets these conditions

- Apache was set up to allow users to publish Web content from the public_html directory in their home directories.

- A user named chris installed Gallery to the gallery directory in /home/chris/public_html on the localhost.

you would type the following in your browser's location box to start the Gallery Configuration Wizard:

```
http://localhost/~chris/gallery/setup/index.php
```

Figure 3-1 shows an example of the first screen in the Gallery Configuration Wizard.

FIGURE 3-1: Starting the Gallery Configuration Wizard

The following steps describe how to use the wizard to check and set up Gallery.

Step 1: Check the System

In the first step (shown in Figure 3-1), the system check page displays the results of checking your Linux system for the components that Gallery needs to run properly. You should correct any problems that are noted on this page before proceeding.

For components that meet Gallery's needs, you will see a green "Success" box; components that fail show a red "Serious Warning!" or yellow "Warning" box. A "Serious Warning!" needs to be corrected, while a "Warning" might require a fix in certain situations or may not be a problem at all (I talk about specific cases later).

The system check page checks the following items:

- **Gallery version** — Checks the version of Gallery you are using. A link is provided to the Gallery project page, so you can check for a more recent version. If the site recommends a later version than you have, consider downloading that version instead and starting this procedure over again.

- **PHP version** — Checks if you have a version of PHP that will work with your version of Gallery. PHP, which recursively stands for PHP: Hypertext Preprocessor, is a scripting language often used with Web development that is incorporated into Gallery. If you need a different version of PHP, go to your Linux distribution's Web site and see if the version you need is available in binary form (such as an RPM or DEB package), or download the source code from the PHP Web site (www.php.net).

- **PHP predefined variables** — Checks whether or not your version of PHP handles predefined variables in a way that is required by Gallery. If this step fails, you probably need a later version of PHP.

- **PHP register_globals** — Checks whether or not the register_globals option is turned off. Gallery suggests that it be turned off for security reasons. If the option is turned on, you can turn off register_globals for the whole system or for your personal Gallery installation. To change it for your whole system, edit the /etc/php.ini file (as the root user) and change the register_globals = On line to read:

```
register_globals = Off
```

If you have a personal installation of Gallery (for example, in the directory /home/chris/public_html/gallery), you need to make two changes. First, add the following line to your .htaccess file in your gallery directory:

```
php_flag register_globals 0
```

Next, have the system administrator make the following addition to the Apache httpd.conf file (probably in /etc/httpd/conf/httpd.conf). Replace /home/chris with the name of your home directory (or other directory) where you have Gallery installed:

```
<Directory /home/chris/public_html/gallery>
    AllowOverride Options FileInfo
</Directory>
```

- **PHP safe_mode** — Checks whether PHP is running in Safe mode. Safe mode is too restrictive for Gallery to run, so the safe_mode option must be off. If it is not off, you can turn it off by changing the safe_mode line in the /etc/php.ini file to read as follows:

```
safe_mode = Off
```

- **Enabled exec function** — Checks that the exec function is enabled on your system. (Gallery uses exec to start image manipulation tools, such as ImageMagick and jhead.)

- **Access to .htaccess file** — Checks that Gallery has access to the .htaccess file from your gallery directory. Without having read access to that file, you won't be able to change settings.

- **PHP magic quotes** — Checks whether or not magic quotes are enabled. Off is recommended because magic quotes can result in unexpected behavior if you use single quotes, double quotes, or backslash characters in Gallery titles or captions. To turn off magic quotes, edit the /etc/php.ini file and make sure that magic_quotes_gpc, magic_quotes_runtime, and magic_quotes_sybase are all set to Off.

- **Short URLs enabled** — Checks whether the Apache Web server includes the mod_rewrite modules. This module lets you direct people to images in your gallery using shorter, easier-to-read URLs. If the module is being loaded, you should see a line similar to the following in your system's `/etc/httpd/conf/httpd.conf` file:

```
LoadModule rewrite_module modules/mod_rewrite.so
```

It is also possible to provide mod_rewrite support for your personal gallery, provided that your `.htaccess` file is accessible (which it should be at this point).

- **NetPBM image tools** — Checks that a set of NetPBM tools, used primarily for converting images into different formats, is available on your system. (For Fedora Core, these tools come in the netpbm-progs package.)

- **Image** — Checks that a set of ImageMagick tools for manipulating image files is available on your system. (For Fedora Core, these tools come in the ImageMagick package.)

- **Access JPEG EXIF headers** — Checks if the jhead utility is installed. Gallery uses jhead to examine and extract EXIF headers that are embedded in JPEG images created by many digital cameras. (To download or get further information about jhead, check the following site: www.sentex.net/~mwandel/jhead.)

- **Lossless rotation of JPEG images** — Checks if the jpegtran utility is installed. This utility is needed for Gallery to be able to do lossless rotations of JPEG images.

- **PHP support for fast translations** — Checks if your version of PHP includes support for GNU gettext. Support for gettext is needed to support fast translations into different languages.

- **Number of languages available** — Checks how many languages are supported by your version of Gallery. If the language you need is not there, go to the Gallery download page and look for gallery language packs. (The version I installed includes support for 35 different languages. There are about 70 languages available from the Gallery site.)

- **Multilanguage capabilities** — Checks if all supported Gallery locales are available on the system. Gallery needs these locales to enable multilanguage and appropriate date/time formats for supported languages.

- **Latest Gallery files** — Checks that the latest versions of Gallery files are being used. If you use a pre-release version of Gallery, you may see a warning that files are more recent than expected. You can probably continue without a problem.

Correct any problems that were encountered. Then reload the page to see if the change solves the issue raised by Gallery. When installation looks okay, click Next Step to continue.

Step 2: Do Initial Gallery Setup

The second Gallery configuration screen offers a ton of ways to configure and customize your Gallery albums. Gallery starts you off with a good set of defaults. So, despite the fact that you can change a lot of settings, you probably won't need to. Figure 3-2 shows the Gallery Configuration screen.

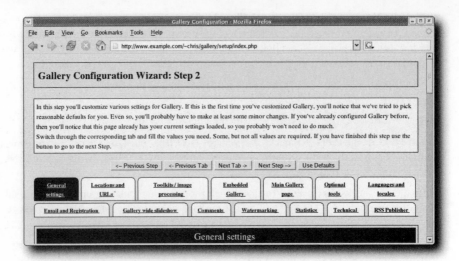

FIGURE 3-2: Customize your Gallery settings.

With Gallery, as with most software packages, it's not a bad idea to go through all the configuration setting just to see how Gallery is set up and where there are opportunities to tweak it. Each tab contains a different set of options. Some configuration settings are required (they appear with a red asterisk).

The following is a combination of required settings and options I recommend you consider changing to suit the way you want to use Gallery.

General Settings Tab

You will almost surely want to add your own title, password, and initial skin (which provides the look and feel of your gallery). Here are descriptions of those fields.

- **Gallery Title** — Choose a name to appear on your gallery.
- **Admin Password** — Enter a password for the administrative (admin) user account.
- **Skins** — Choose a skin (layout and color scheme) for your gallery. (See the "Changing Gallery Attributes" section for details on setting the look and feel of your gallery.)
- **Default upload method** — A form-based upload will be the default style of upload that Gallery users can use to upload images to your gallery. Other choices include Mini-Applet, Full-Applet, or URL.

Locations and URLs Tab

You need to tell Gallery where your albums, temporary directory, and gallery itself are located on your hard disk. You must also identify the Web addresses (URLs) of your gallery. From the Locations and URLs tab, you can make the following changes:

- **Album Directory**—Type in the location of the directory where you will store your digital photo albums. If you own the computer, you might set this directory to `/var/www/html/albums`. If you don't have root privilege on the computer, a common place to put your albums is in the gallery directory on your home directory. For example: `/home/chris/public_html/gallery/albums`. (The latter is how I had you create that directory earlier in the chapter.)

- **Temporary Directory**—Type the name of the temporary directory. Often the `/tmp` directory is used. However, if the `open_basedir` option is set in your `/etc/php.ini` file, limiting the area in which Gallery is able to write to the file system, you will have to assign the temporary directory to a point in the file system below the `open_basedir` directory. Also, whatever temporary directory you choose must be writeable by the apache user.

- **Gallery URL**—The Web address of the Gallery software. For example, with Gallery installed in the home directory for the user named chris, in the directory `/home/chris/public_html/gallery`, the Gallery URL would be `http://localhost/~chris/gallery`. If Gallery were in `/var/www/html/gallery`, the Gallery URL would be `http://localhost/gallery`.

- **Albums URL**—The Web address of your Gallery albums. For example, if the albums directory were `/home/chris/public_html/gallery/albums`, the Albums URL would be `http://localhost/~chris/gallery/albums`.

Email and Registration Tab

This set of options has to do with using email with your gallery. To use any of the options, you must first set the Enable email option to yes on the Email and Registration tab. Before turning this feature on, however, I recommend you refer to the "Managing Gallery Users" section. This will help you decide the level of user interaction you want to allow on your Gallery server.

If you do set the Enable email option to yes, you can then use the following options with Gallery:

- **Admin email address**—Enter an email address to which users can email questions and concerns. That email address can also be used to automatically alert you of activities from the users of your gallery.

- **Sender email address**—Enter an email address that Gallery will use as its return address when it sends out email. This can be the same as the Admin email address.

Again, the other settings on this tab let you do such things as allow users to register to create their own albums, have the administrator monitor changes users make to the albums, and identify how Gallery interacts with the mail server. You can also create a Welcome message that will be sent to new users (into which you can add placeholders that will read in information such as the Gallery name, admin email address, and the user's name and password.

Other Setup Sections

I've skipped over several sections from the Gallery Customize Settings screen that are less criti-cal for just getting your gallery up and running. Some of these settings are covered later in this chapter. Here is a brief overview, however, of the tabs I have skipped over, to help you decide if you want to change any of those settings before going forward:

- **Toolkits/image processing** — Gallery allows you to use several different tools for con-verting and otherwise manipulating images. The settings on this tab let you identify which tools to use (if you have a choice) and where those tools are located. By default, ImageMagick is used for manipulating images, although you can also use NetPBM if it is installed on your system. If both toolkits are missing, you can download NetPBM binaries from the Gallery Web site.

- **Embedded Gallery** — If Gallery is embedded in a content management system (CMS) environment, and you need to add some additional options to get the CMS to work with Gallery, you can add those options on this tab.

- **Main Gallery Page** — The settings on this tab let you define the appearance of the main Gallery page. Refer to the "Changing Gallery Attributes" section later in this chapter for information on tuning these settings as you would like.

- **Optional tools** — Settings that define the tools that Gallery can use to manage a bunch of image files at once that are grouped together in formats such as zip and rar, are set on this tab. The tab also lets you identify the locations of some tools that can be used for working with JPEG files.

- **Languages and locales** — Gallery is delivered with support for 35 different languages. This tab lets you set the language to use by default (English is set initially). You can set to displays of available languages. You can also set which date/time stamps to use.

- **Gallery wide slideshow** — Because the slideshow feature can be a big performance hit on your Gallery server, it is disabled by default. If you select either Ordered or Random for your Slideshow preferences (instead of Off), slideshows of the albums will be avail-able to visitors.

- **Comments** — You can choose to allow visitors to comment on the images in your gallery, based on settings on this tab. Comments can be allowed per photo, per album, or both. Many options are available to set who can make comments and who can view them. (See the section "Changing Gallery Attributes" later in this chapter for more information on settings related to comments.)

- **Watermarking** — If you want watermarks placed on your images, you can identify the directory that contains the watermark images (in PNG, TIFF, or GIF formats). The directory must be accessible by the apache user to have them applied to the images in your Gallery.

- **Statistics** — You may want to display information about each photo thumbnail, along with that thumbnail itself. Also, as you get a feel for the size and activity of your gallery, you might want to adjust settings related to caching. Those actions can all be done from the Statistics tab.

- **Technical** — The settings on the Technical tab are there mostly to deal with problems that might arise. See the section "Maintaining and Troubleshooting Gallery" later in this chapter for information on when you might uses these settings.

- **RSS Publisher** — You can add support for making your images available in RSS format. RSS can provide quick links to sets of images or information in a Web browser or news reader. Gallery supports RSS (Really Simple Syndication) 2.0.

If you are happy with your initial Gallery settings, click the Next Step button.

Step 3: Set Initial Album Options

The settings on the New Albums page define the layout and appearance of new albums you create. These settings do not affect any existing albums — only the new ones you create. Figure 3-3 shows the New Albums page of the Gallery Configuration Wizard.

FIGURE 3-3: Configure new album settings from the Gallery Configuration Wizard.

You don't need to change any of these settings. If you don't however, here is what you get by default:

- **Layout** — Each new album will have images appear in three columns and three rows per page.

- **Appearance** — Each image will have a black border 1 pixel wide and Arial font type.

- **Image processing and display** — Each image added to an album will have a thumbnail size of 150 pixels and an intermediate image size of 640 pixels. By default, JPEG and

PNG image sizes will not be limited. Original names of uploaded images will be retained. Images that are added will go to the end of the album. Images will not be automatically resized to fit the viewer's browser and visitors won't have the option of viewing full-size images instead of intermediate sizes.

- **Options** — Visitors will have the option of sending images from your albums to one of several different printing services to order prints of these images. There are other options on this tab as well, such as the ability to limit access to albums to registered users only (instead of the default permission of allowing Everybody access).

- **Data displayed** — Along with each image, Gallery displays the click counts within the album and a Description field. Available image dimensions for each image, however, will not be displayed under each thumbnail.

- **Item owner** — The owners of each photo can modify (edit, flip, and rotate) and delete their own photos. The photo owner will not be displayed, however.

- **Polling configuration** — The ability to vote on each photo is off (determined by the voter class being set to Nobody). If the feature is turned on, various options exist that set choices viewers have for voting on each image.

- **Album slideshow** — Slideshows are off by default with Gallery. If you turn them on (by setting the slideshow type to Ordered or Random), there are several settings that determine whether or not images are shown in a loop or shown recursively from subfolders.

- **Micro thumb photo navigation** — You can use micro thumbnail images for navigating photos. By turning this feature on (it's off by default), a tiny navigation panel appears containing tiny thumbnails of photos around the photos being viewed,

- **Frames** — Solid frames are set to appear around thumbnails and images. Sub-album frames are set to Original Style, which causes the frame style you set during Step 1 to be used on sub-album frames.

Select the Next Step button to continue.

Step 4: Save Configuration Settings

This step lets you see the settings you selected from the previous steps and save them to your .htaccess file. If you see a warning that the .htaccess file is not writeable by your Web server user (probably apache), you will need to open the permissions on that file. For example, if your .htaccess file is in /home/chris/public_html/gallery/.htaccess, you can open the permissions wide by typing the following from a Terminal window:

```
$ chmod 777 /home/chris/public_html/gallery/.htaccess
```

Refresh the page after you have changed the permissions. Then click Save Config to have you changes written to the config.php file. You should see a message that says:

```
Your configuration has been successfully saved!
```

As recommended on the screen, you should close the permissions on your Gallery configuration files by running the `secure.sh` script from the gallery directory as follows:

```
$ ./secure.sh
Your Gallery is now secure and cannot be configured. If
you wish to reconfigure it, run:
  % ./configure.sh
```

As noted, you won't be able to change the settings in the gallery without reopening permissions. You will be able to do that by running the `configure.sh` command, as shown above.

You are ready now to enter your gallery. Click the Enter the Gallery link. The main albums page for your Gallery site appears, as shown in Figure 3-4.

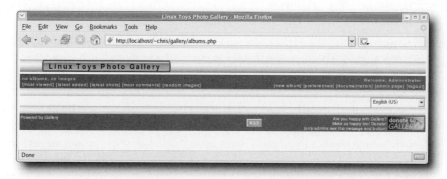

FIGURE 3-4: Begin adding photo albums to your main Gallery albums page.

Creating Photo Albums

If you just installed Gallery for the first time, you will see an empty main Gallery page. You are ready to begin creating albums and adding photos to them. To start this process, click login from the upper-right corner of the main Gallery page.

When the Gallery configuration login pop-up window appears, type in the admin user name and the password you assigned to it, in the appropriate boxes. The main Gallery page will now appear with several administration buttons added so you can begin creating your photo albums. Here's what you do next:

1. **Create an album.** Click the `new album` button. The new album appears, empty and untitled, in the current window. You are ready to start configuring the new album.

2. **Name the album.** Click the `album actions` box and select `rename album`. In the pop-up window that appears, type the name that you want to represent the album (this will actually be used as the album's file name) and click Rename.

3. **Add a title and summary.** Click the `album actions` box and select `properties`. From the Album Properties window that appears, you are able to set most of the attributes associated with this particular album. At first, this will contain the defaults you set when you first configured Gallery. I describe many of these attributes in the "Changing Gallery Attributes" section later in this chapter. However, for the moment, you will probably want to at least set the following:

   ■ **Album Summary** — Write a sentence or more describing the contents of the gallery. That summary appears near the top of the album's main page.

   ■ **Album Title** — Create a title for the album. This title appears at the top of the album's main page.

   After changing any other settings you choose from the Album Properties, select Apply. The changes will appear on the album's page. Click Close to close the Album Properties window.

4. **Add photos.** Click the `album options` box and select `add photos`. The Add Photos window appears. This pop-up window offers several ways of adding photos to your new album, which are described in the "Adding Photos to Albums" section. For now, you might just add a few photos that reside on your local hard disk as follows:

   ■ Select the Form tab.

   ■ Choose how many photos you want to copy from your hard disk to your album.

   ■ Type the file name (or browse for it) and caption for each photo.

   ■ Click the Upload Now button to load the images into the album. Status information appears as each photo is compressed and resized as needed.

   ■ Once the photos are added, click Dismiss.

5. **Edit photos.** The photos you just added should now appear in your photo album. Because you own the album, you can now make changes to it. Click the `Photo actions` drop-down box under any photo you want to change. Here are some things you can do to each photo:

   ■ **Edit Text** — Use this option to change the caption under a photo. From the pop-up window that appears you can also add descriptions and keywords that will help you search for the pictures later.

   ■ **Edit Thumbnail** — Use this option to select only part of the image to use as the thumbnail representing it (a thumbnail of the whole image is used by default).

Note

Using the Edit Thumbnail feature requires that the Java Runtime Environment (JRE) package be installed. Because that software is not open source, I don't include it on the *Linux Toys II* CD. You can get JRE from the Sun Web site (http://java.sun.com/j2se/1.5.0/download.html). The file I downloaded was jre-1_5_0_04-linux-i586-rpm.bin. You can execute that file as root (it's a self-installing RPM), but to get it working properly in Fedora Core 5, download and run the script java-post-install.sh (available from http://fedoranews.org/tchung/java).

- **Rotate/Flip** — Use this option to rotate or flip the image.

- **Set as Highlight** — Use this option to highlight the photo as the thumbnail for the album.

- **Move** — Use this option to move the photo to a different album. Entering numbers for First and Last lets you choose a range of photos to move. (Use the same number for First and Last to move just one photo.)

- **Reorder** — Use this option to move the selected photo to another location within the current album. Change the location number to move the photo to a different place in the album.

- **Hide** — Use this option to hide the image from everyone but the owner of the album.

- **Delete** — Use this option to remove the photo from the album completely.

- **Change Owner** — Use this option to change the ownership of the selected image to someone other than the current owner. Until you create other users, the admin user owns each album. However, ownership can be opened to everybody who visits the site, to an anonymous user that is logged in, or to the Nobody user account.

Figure 3-5 shows an example of a gallery I created called "Linux Toys Lost Weekend."

FIGURE 3-5: While logged in as admin, modify and load images into your album.

6. **Edit Gallery main page.** Once you have finished one or more albums, you should edit the main Gallery page. On the upper-right corner of your album page, click the name of the album you just created next to the word "Gallery" (or click the up arrow). Your main Gallery page appears displaying all your albums. Figure 3-6 shows an example.

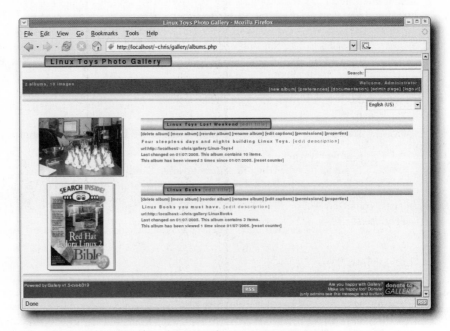

FIGURE 3-6: Main Gallery page, ready to be modified by the admin

If you are still logged in as admin, there are a lot of things you can do with the albums in your gallery at this point. You will probably at least want to edit the description of each album on the Gallery page. However, you can also change the album's name, title, order in the gallery, permissions, and other properties.

7. **Log out.** When you are done creating and modifying your gallery and its albums, click the logout button. You can now see the gallery as it will appear to your visitors.

You should have a working gallery at this point. The other sections in this chapter cover more ways of working with Gallery, such as adding users (so they can create their own albums), exploring other ways of adding photos, and finding more ways to change the look and feel of your gallery.

Caution

Although it is not that difficult to put Gallery on a public network, there are some security risks (as there are with any public server). If you plan to publish your gallery (on the Internet or other public network), check the "Maintaining and Troubleshooting Gallery" section later in this chapter.

Using Gallery

To visit your Gallery albums, your friends and family simply have to type the Web address of the location of your gallery directory on the server (assuming you have made your gallery accessible to the Internet). For example, if you had configured Gallery in the `/home/chris/public_html/gallery` directory (as described earlier) on a server named `www.example.com`, to visit that site, someone would simply type the following into the location box on their Web browser:

```
http://www.example.com/~chris/gallery
```

From your gallery site, people can access and display your gallery photos in a variety of ways. They can even have photographs they like sent to any of several vendors to purchase printed copies. The following sections describe how visitors can search, display, print, and bookmark your gallery images.

 Note As administrator, you can assign user accounts for people you choose. A person with a user account to your gallery can click on the login button to log in before going through the gallery. By assigning user accounts, you can give other people much greater control to add content (images, comments, and so on) and even create or control whole albums. See "Managing Gallery Users" later in this chapter for information on setting up gallery users.

Browsing the Albums

From the main Gallery page, visitors select albums they want to see. The first page of the album appears, containing thumbnails of images in that album. Clicking a thumbnail produces a full-size copy of the image. If the album contains an embedded album, clicking the image representing that album allows you to view its contents.

Left and right arrows in the header let you step through multiple pages of photos for each album. Also in the header, click the up arrow to go back to the main Gallery page (or, if you are in an embedded album, to the album above the current one).

Sorting the Photos

Visitors can sort the photos in Gallery in various ways. Because sorting can be a resource drain on the server, a visitor can use the Sort Album feature only if she is logged in. From the main Gallery page, a visitor can select the `album actions` drop-down box, and then choose `sort items`. The following options are then available from the Sort Album pop-up window:

- By Upload Date
- By Picture-Taken Date
- By Filename
- By Number of Clicks

- By Caption
- By Number of Comments
- Randomly

From a box at the bottom of the Sort Album pop-up window, a visitor can choose to display images in ascending or descending order, based on their selection above. Clicking Sort then sorts the images on the album page as requested.

Searching for Photos

Gallery will search captions, comments, keywords, and descriptions for any word you enter into the Search box at the top of the main Gallery page. Figure 3-7 shows an example of a Gallery search for the word "Kevin."

FIGURE 3-7: Search albums for words associated with Gallery images.

The search results show any albums containing the search word. After that, you can see thumbnails of each image that includes the search word. Notice that Gallery tells you if the search word is in the caption, keyword, comment, or description associated with an image.

Displaying Photo Properties

While displaying an image from an album, you can request to see a lot of different kinds of information about the photo. If you are not used to working with digital images, you might not even know that information is in there.

With an image displayed in Gallery, select Photo Properties from the header. A Photo Properties pop-up window appears, as shown in Figure 3-8.

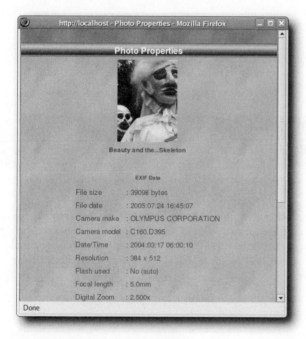

FIGURE 3-8: View the size, date/time, and other information about a photo.

The amount of data you see depends on how much the camera or image software stored in the EXIF area stored with the image. In this example, you can see the EXIF data contains information about when the image was created (date/time), its file size, and the resolution. In many cases, you can even see information about the make, model, and other attributes of the camera that took the image.

Printing Photos

While displaying an image from an album, the viewer can select to have that image sent to a photo service for printing (provided that the admin has enabled this feature). From the "Send photo to . . ." box in the header, with the photo selected, select a printing vendor. The ones currently offered include:

- **PhotoWorks** — A digital printing service from Seattle, WA (www.photoworks.com)
- **Shutterfly** — A digital printing service in Redwood City, CA (www.shutterfly.com)
- **Fotoserve** — A digital printing service in Great Britain (www.fotoserve.com)
- **Fotokasten** — A photo printing service out of Germany
- **mPUSH** — A service for pushing digital images to mobile devices (www.mpush.cc)

In most cases, the image selected is automatically transported to the site. At that point it is up to the user to determine if the available service is a good choice. Besides hard copy photos, some of the companies (such as Shutterfly) will also print images on mugs, note cards, mouse pads, and tote bags.

Bookmarking Albums with RSS

Gallery is enabled to support Really Simple Syndication (RSS), which essentially lets someone add a bookmark to an album or whole Gallery. Once bookmarked, however, when the person returns to the bookmark, it will contain a listing of the current items (photos or albums) in the Gallery or album you bookmarked.

Go to a gallery page from a browser that supports RSS (such as Mozilla Firefox), and select the RSS button (in Firefox, it's in the lower-right corner of the screen). When prompted, create a bookmark name. The next time you open your Bookmarks tab and select the Gallery book-mark, a "loading bookmarks" message will appear and load the names of the current albums and photographs in the selected gallery.

The gallery's admin can set the attributes of the gallery's RSS feed from the RSS Publisher tab on Step 2 of the Gallery Configuration Wizard.

Adding Comments to a Gallery

Unless you configured your gallery differently, by default a person visiting the gallery can add comments to images in your albums, but not otherwise modify the images or albums themselves.

Note To allow visitors to your gallery to do more than simply add comments to photos requires some additional configuration. See the following section for details on adding user accounts and allowing users to add, move, change, or delete photos from your gallery.

To add comments to a photo in an album, select the thumbnail for the photo you are interested in. Under the picture click the Add Comment button. From the pop-up window that appears, write your name into the Commenter box and your comment into the Message box and click Post.

To see all the comments entered for the album, select View Comments from the main page for the album. Thumbnails for all commented images are displayed.

Administering Gallery

Although initial configuration of your gallery can be pretty simple, there are a lot of ways you can change your gallery setup to modify the look of your gallery and configure what others can do to it. The following sections describe features that you can do as administrator (admin login) to further configure a running gallery.

Adding Photos to Albums

Using the default photo dialog box, you can type the file names and captions for up to five photos to be added to an album at a time. This section explains how to add *more* than five individual images at a time to an album.

After you have selected the album you want to add images to, click the login button and log in as admin. Then, from the album actions box, select add photos. From the Add Photos pop-up window, here are a few ways to add groups of photos to an album:

- **Increase Form** — You can increase the number of photos you can upload to Gallery on the Form tab of the Add Photos window from 5 to 10, so you can add up to 10 photos and captions at a time from your local hard disk.

- **Zip files** — Instead of entering an individual photo file into the Form tab, you can enter the name of a zip file on your local hard disk. Gallery will expand the contents of that zip file into individual image files. To create a zip file on most Linux systems, you could use the zip command. For example, to zip up all JPEG images (assuming they ended in .jpg) from the current directory to a zip file called myzip.zip, you could type the following:

```
$ zip myzip *.jpg
```

- **Web address** — Click the URL tab from the Add Photos pop-up window and type a Web address of an image file or zip file (containing images) to the location box.

- **Local directory** — Click the URL tab from the Add Photos pop-up window and type a local directory name on the server. A list of image files contained in that directory appears. You can check the images you want in that list and click Add Files to install the selected images in the current album.

- **Slurp Web page** — Slurp all images located on a selected Web page. Just add a URL to a Web page, and then select from the images on that page to load them on the server.

Besides identifying the image (or group of images) you want to load, you can also identify files of metadata to download along with your images. That metadata can contain such information as captions, keywords, and other relevant data for the images.

Changing Gallery Attributes

If you want to modify the look and feel of your gallery, the easiest way is to run the Gallery Configuration Wizard again (as described earlier in this chapter). From the wizard, you can set the overall appearance of your gallery (by assigning a skin), the arrangement of elements on the main Gallery page, the look and feel of each album, and attributes of individual photos.

If you want to look for more skins than are shown in the General Settings tab of the first page of the Gallery Configuration Wizard, there are several sites that offer more Gallery skins. Here are some places to look:

- **PowNuke** (www.pownuke.com/galleryskins) — Contains a handful of Gallery skins
- **Ithought Gallery** (http://gallery.ithought.org) — One-stop location for Gallery skins, borders, and other add-ons

Download the zip file for the new skin you want to install and unzip it in the gallery/skins directory of your Gallery configuration. To change to the new skin, you can edit the config.php file in your gallery/ directory. For example, to use the skin named border001, you could change the skinname line in the config.php file to read as follows:

```
$gallery->app->skinname = "border001"
```

Figure 3-9 shows my Gallery after I have changed the skin to border001.

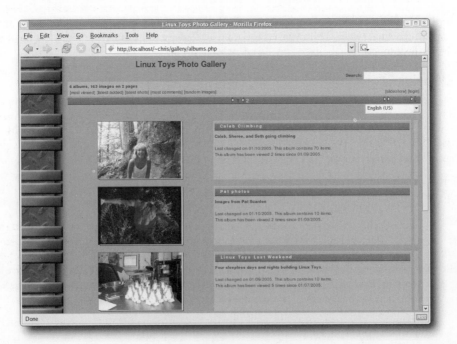

FIGURE 3-9: Adding a different skin can change the whole look of your gallery.

Changing the Main Gallery Page

In Step 2 of the Gallery Configuration Wizard, click the Main Gallery Page tab. From that tab, you can change the basic attributes of your main Gallery page. Here is what you can change:

- **Show the album tree** — Using the default, Complete Tree, you will be able to see every album (even embedded albums) in your gallery on the main Gallery page. If you have lots of embedded albums, you might want to restrict this feature, so as not to clutter up your main page too much. You can choose No Tree (to not show any albums below the main level) or select a specific level to go only one, two, three, four, five, or ten levels deep.

- **Highlight size** — Shows the number of pixels used to display the highlighted image (that is, the image representing the album on the main page).

- **Show owner** — The owner of the album is not identified on the main page, by default. You can change that by changing this value to yes.

- **Albums per page** — Up to five albums will appear on your first main Gallery page. You can change that to any number you like.

- **Accurate photo count** — With this value set to no (as it is by default), counts for the number of photos in your gallery can be inaccurate. By setting this to yes, the count will be exactly accurate, but will cause the display of your Gallery pages to be much slower.

- **Frame around albums** — You can choose the frame that appears around the thumbnail images on the main Gallery page.

Once you have set these general attributes the way you like, you can go to your main Gallery page and further tune the information on that page. For each album shown on that page, you can edit the title, modify the album (delete, move, reorder, or rename it), change captions, and set permissions.

Changing Each Album

Step 3 of the Gallery Configuration Wizard lets you set the layout and appearance of your albums. On the Layout tab, you can set the number of columns and rows for each album page; On the Appearance page you can set the border color and width, as well as the font used by default. You can also change ownership issues on the Options and Item Owner (which are discussed next in the "Managing Gallery Users" section).

Here are a few other things you can change for your albums from the Gallery Configuration Wizard:

- **Polling configuration** — Under this tab, you can turn on the polling feature (it's off by default) and set how it will work in your albums. You can change NOBODY to either EVERYBODY (to let any viewer vote on the images) or LOGGEDIN (to let only people who are actually logged in vote on the images). Poll types can be Critique (to give points to images without restriction) or Rank (to select from a set number of choices). You also have control over how the poll information is displayed.

- **Frames** — You can choose frames for thumbnails, images, and images in nested albums.

When you visit each album individually, most of the configuration is done from the `album actions` pull-down menu on the album's page. This is where you can do such things as add nested albums, set album permissions, and choose how poll results are displayed. You can also use this menu to manage all images in the album at once to do such things as edit captions, set permissions, rebuild thumbnails, resize all thumbnails, and sort the images.

Managing Gallery Users

As the Gallery admin, you can add user accounts to your gallery and (as you choose) decide who can access and possibly change each gallery. To create, modify and delete users, go to the Manage Users window from the main Gallery page by selecting admin page → manage users.

To create a new user for your Gallery, click the Create button. Then enter a user name, password for the user, a full name, email address, and the language in which the user will see the Gallery. Here is also where you select to allow the user to create albums, if you like (select yes).

To set default user permissions to your albums, go to Step 3 of the Gallery Configuration Wizard and select the Options tab. From that tab, you can set whether or not someone has to be logged in to even see the gallery (not required by default).

Also on Step 3 of the Gallery Configuration Wizard, you can select the Item Owner tab. From there, you can indicate whether the owner of an album can modify and delete photos, as well as whether or not to display the owner of the photo.

While the admin can change any album in your gallery, by default, a user will be able to change only an album that user owns. From each album itself, however, you can click album actions → permissions. The Album Permissions window that pops up can be used to assign user permissions associated with the album. Figure 3-10 shows the Album Permissions pop-up window.

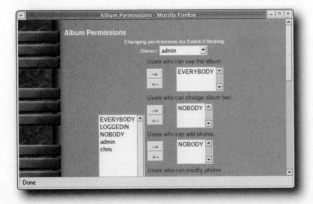

FIGURE 3-10: Define what different people can access and change in a gallery.

All user accounts created for your gallery will appear in the box on the left. You can use those names, or the names EVERYBODY, LOGGEDIN, or NOBODY, to assign who can see, change, add photos to, or delete photos from the album. You can also decide who can create sub-albums, view full images, add comments, and view comments. If you like, you can even change the owner of the current album.

Maintaining and Troubleshooting Gallery

Any server that is exposed to the Internet requires some watching and occasional maintenance. A Gallery photo server is no exception. The following section describes some administrative tasks for your Gallery server that might be helpful to you.

Forget Your Admin Password?

If you forget your admin password, you can add a blank file named `resetadmin` to your `gallery/setup` directory. Go to the login page, refresh it, and you should be able to get in again.

If you are not able to change your configuration, run the following command from your `gallery/` directory:

```
$ ./configure.sh
```

Now go to your Web browser and request setup under the gallery directory to run the configuration wizard again. For example, `http://localhost/chris/gallery/setup/index.php` will open the Gallery Configuration Wizard given the examples shown in this chapter.

Performance and Debugging

The Gallery Configuration Wizard screen (presented in Step 2 of the "Checking and Configuring Gallery" section) has a Technical tab with several settings that can help you debug and tune your Gallery server. If you are having problems with your Gallery server, set the Debug mode to "High (former Debug on)" instead of "No Debug" for a while. Be sure to turn it off when you have figured out the problem because debugging can be a strain on system performance if left on for a live system.

To tune the performance of your Gallery server, you can try many of the other options in Step 2 of the Gallery Configuration Wizard. You can set the time limit to something other than 30 seconds (the default) if operations are timing out without enough time to complete. You can turn on the Use Syslog option to report user login, logout, and errors using the Linux syslog facility. There are also options for caching data.

Patches and Updates

It is very important that you keep up with patches and updates for Gallery. Keep an eye on the Gallery Project page (`http://gallery.sourceforge.net`) to see when updates are available. If you are using Gallery as a public server, you must also keep up with patches from the Linux distribution you are using with Gallery. It's a good strategy to subscribe to the low-volume Gallery Announce mailing list `http://gallery.sourceforge.net/lists.php`) where you'll receive notifications about important updates.

Summary

Gallery is a powerful, open source application for publishing and managing all of your digital images so that you can publish them on your local LAN or on the public Internet. With Gallery, you can define who has access to view and change the contents of your Gallery server. You also have a lot of control over the look and arrangement of elements in your gallery and its albums.

Creating a Personal Video Recorder with MythTV

We're at a key point in history, where doing separate activities such as watching TV, surfing the Web, checking out local weather, and flipping through the family photo album is in the process of fundamentally changing. Convergence of several key multimedia and Internet technologies is making it possible for all things audible, visual, and informational to be consolidated into a single device in the home or office.

Personal Video Recorders (PVRs) such as TiVo lead the way in this media revolution. But similar technologies like MythTV and others are picking up the ball and running with it. No longer limited to just recording and playing back TV shows, these Media Centers are taking on every aspect of our multimedia lives.

MythTV is an open source, modular PVR project that is evolving faster and gaining more features than any other media convergence system. With its add-on modules, it has grown from just a PVR to a full-blown Media Center suite. In addition to performing all the normal PVR-type functions of recording and archiving your favorite shows to VCD (Video CD) or DVD, it also stores your music collections in countless formats.

MythTV can intelligently play back the songs it notices that you like more often than others, detect and skip commercials (which many PVRs no longer allow you to do), and serve as a family photo gallery. MythTV can provide local real-time weather information with animated satellite radar views, act as a real arcade game simulator console, and even keep track of your favorite recipes. It can even make the data available to non-Linux computers all over your home or across a network, all from one device. This is what the MythTV/Media Center buzz is all about.

This chapter takes you past all the jargon and tells you what to buy, how to put it together, and how to get it all working. When you're done, you'll have a MythTV Media Center that will make Bill Gates jealous.

in this chapter

☑ **Choosing your hardware**

☑ **Installing and preparing the OS**

☑ **Installing MythTV and drivers**

☑ **Configuring and testing MythTV**

☑ **Other tricks and tips**

Putting together the MythTV project (www.mythtv.org) as described in this chapter will result in an extraordinary multimedia center that can grow as MythTV continues to develop in coming years. However, if you are new to Linux, this should *not* be the first project you attempt. Some of the more advanced features described here for partitioning your disks and getting special hardware components working are challenging, even to an experienced Linux user.

If you are committed to trying the project, even without a lot of Linux experience, you can skip most of the partitioning and hardware configuration information. The project will work with little more than a supported video card, TV capture card, and a reliable Internet connection. Focus on the software configuration and be sure to have a PC with a reasonably powerful CPU, and plenty of RAM and hard disk space, and you can still have some fun with this project.

Choosing Your Hardware

This section explains the various configurations that MythTV can be set up in, and the ramifications this will have on your required hardware set. Your media playing and recording needs dictate what type of hardware you need to build the home-wide PVR system of your dreams.

Frontend Only or Backend Plus Frontend?

MythTV is not just a "single recorder/player" type device like TiVo. MythTV is actually an advanced client/server multimedia system that serves entertainment content much as a network Web server serves HTML content to a Web browser.

Put another way, the MythTV system is divided into a MythTV backend (server) component that schedules, captures, and stores most incoming content, and a MythTV frontend (player) that displays and interacts with you, the end user. The frontend component communicates with the MythTV backend system to pull the content and interact with the gallery, A/V archives, and other parts of the MythTV system, and display the requested media wherever you want to view it. This could be on a remote laptop somewhere on the home network, or on the same machine that is running the backend and which also happens to be connected to your TV.

Because MythTV is divided into client and server components, you can have one large beefy backend and storage system in a home, and then several frontend systems located in different parts of the house (over a LAN), all accessing the single myth backend media center for content. This is a very nice design feature that no other home media system at this price range can match.

The MythTV backend is usually centrally located wherever your TV inputs and connectivity are situated. That also happens to be where most people end up actually watching or interacting with their AV systems. So if you're building only one system for now, that system will need to run both the client (frontend) and the server (backend).

In a smaller MythTV frontend system (player only) you can get away with running MythTV on a fairly modest hardware set, such as a 1 to 2 GHz system with 256MB of RAM and a 10GB hard drive. If you need to run a single backend plus frontend (player + recording/re-encoding/storage) setup, as this chapter guides you through, the hardware requirements are much higher. I recommend a full 2.5 to 3 GHz processor, 256 to 512MB of RAM, and

120GB to 1TB+ (a terabyte = 1,024GB) of backend drive storage! It all depends on what you want to do with your PVR system, and how you want it configured.

Hardware Requirements for MythTV

Because this chapter guides you through setting up a combination MythTV backend plus frontend system with multiple input sources, the hardware requirements are going to be steep. The system I recommend includes:

- No less than a 2 to 3 GHz processor
- 512MB of RAM (I used 1GB)
- One (or two) 250GB SATA-II drives (two for running in a RAID-1 configuration for hardware redundancy/safety — see the sidebar "RAID Versus Data Backups" for more on RAID)
- A dual tuner cable card for tuning to or recording two different programs at the same time (or a FireWire port and FireWire digital cable receiver)
- An output video card with NVidia chipset
- Either S-Video output or a DVI connector to go out to the TV/monitor

Of course, you will also need the regular case, power supply, keyboard, mouse, audio, and so forth, but it needs to be in a layout that's quiet, aesthetically pleasing, and not overly geeky looking. It should look like it all belongs there next to your large screen TV and other AV equipment. Figure 4-1 shows the MythTV configuration I put together for this project.

RAID versus Data Backups

RAID-1 is a hardware redundancy/availability technology that allows you to take two drives (or partitions on different drives) and mirror the exact same data on each. When you write to drive 1, the same data goes to drive 2 at nearly the same moment.

Mirroring drives with RAID-1 is automated at the system or hardware level. So if one of the drives eventually dies, the other one will preserve your data integrity and the system will continue running. This system will also notify you that there is a problem so that you can replace the bad drive and "rebuild" the RAID-1 mirror.

The hardware redundancy I've just described, while not required for a project like MythTV, does protect you and your system data from failed hardware because the data is written to both disks simultaneously. While this is a nice feature, it does not protect you from user-deleted files, file system corruption, or getting hacked. To get protection from these, you need to also back up your important data at specific points in time to a place off the system.

Where RAID gets you hardware redundancy and availability, data backups give you data retention over time. Because of this, if you must choose only one type of redundancy because of cost limitations, choose backups over RAID.

FIGURE 4-1: My MythTV TV system put together for the living room

Note
If you are constructing a High Definition (HDTV)–based MythTV, a 3 GHz processor is the minimum I recommend. You will also want more RAM and storage resources, depending on how you are encoding your content when saving it to disk.

Table 4-1 presents the hardware set that I came up with to meet the specs of a higher-end MythTV backend plus frontend living room system, with around 200GB of RAID-1 (high availability) content. The major components are shown in Figure 4-2.

Table 4-1: Recommended Parts List for a High-End MythTV Setup

Part	Part Description	Price
Motherboard	MSI K7N2GM2-LSR, 3200+, 400FSB, nForce/NVidia+snd (use MSI K7N2GM2-IL if you need FireWire/IEEE1394)	$70.00
CPU	Athlon XP3000+/512M (AXDA2800DKV4D)	$140.00
CPU fan	Apache Copper K7 CPU Cooler, AP2CA-725(34dBA)	$28.00
Memory	Two 512MB PC2700/DDR333 Kensington	$100.00
Case	SilverStone Lascala SST-LC11M HTPC w/VFD and remote	$150.00

Part	Part Description	Price
Capture card	Video: Hauppauge PVR-500MCE Dual Tuner Card	$150.00
Hard drive(s)	Two Hitachi T7K250 250GB SATA-I/II, 7200, 8MB	$200.00
DVD-RW	NEC Dual Layer 16x DVD-RW Burner	$60.00
Keyboard/mouse	BTC Wireless 9019URF with Integrated Joystick/Mouse	$45.00
Total		**$943.00**

See www.linuxtoys.net for hardware URLs. Of course, all of the items you see here are likely to be offered at different prices from a variety of vendors.

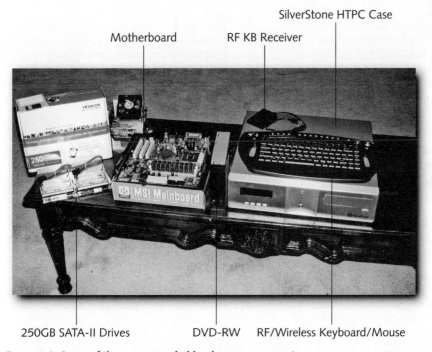

FIGURE 4-2: Some of the recommended hardware components

Note A big thanks goes out to Hitachi for supplying this project with the very large, very fast 250GB SATA-II drives, and the folks at SilverStone for the best overall HTPC case, the LC-11m.

Balancing Price and Performance

Now before you recoil at the $943 price tag when the street value for a TiVo is about $120 (plus a $250 lifetime subscription membership for a total of about $370), keep in mind, a MythTV media center is not just another TiVo-like PVR. The MythTV system is a full-blown media center that also has PVR capabilities (plus the capability to mark and delete commercials). It includes features and modules such as fully integrated Internet access, photo gallery/browsing, a DVD/movie archive, network jukebox, and audio jukebox. It also includes news and Web feed displays, real-time local weather center reports, a real arcade simulator gaming console, a DVD/VCD player and ripper, and modules for much more. If you're still not sure, check out the features page and screenshots at `http://mythtv.org/modules.php?name=MythFeatures`.

Note   While I used around $1,000 in hardware for my system, I have several friends who have put together fairly nice systems (with the nice case) for under $350 (one drive, 2 GHz, 256MB RAM, single tuner card instead of dual, and so on).

The motherboard I used, the MSI K7N2GM2-LSR, is one of many that could be used for this project, but I chose it because of its status as a proven MythTV performer as well as its nice well-rounded feature set and low price tag. It features the NVidia/nForce2 chipset to give you the accelerated direct S-Video output direct to your TV/monitor, surround sound and digital SPDIF sound outputs, and a built-in serial port (in case you need to control a cable box for changing channels). It includes both SATA and PATA drive controllers and a micro-ATX form factor that is compatible with the chosen case and its special PCI riser card.

Channel Changing Hardware

In this chapter, I step you through using either an analog cable signal (directly into your MythTV tuner card) or using FireWire from a digital cable box such as the DCT 6200. Channel changing is done differently for analog and digital channels:

- **Analog channel changing**—When changing analog cable channels directly on a tuner card (such as the PVR-500CE), you control the channel changing directly over the PCI bus via the i2c bus (via the i2c/tuner kernel modules).

- **Digital cable channel changing**—If you are running digital cable and have a FireWire output from your cable box, you can not only capture the video directly over FireWire (more on this later), but you can also control channel changing of your cable box over FireWire.

You may, however, have an older, external, analog cable box that you need to control channels via the MythTV. If this describes your home setup, you need to look into using a MythTV IR control interface to your older analog cable box. If so, check out `http://lircsetup.com/` for more information on the software side of IR to cable box remote control. You might also want to consider picking up an IR-Blaster from `http://irblaster.info/`.

Video I/O Hardware

Although this chapter focuses primarily on setting up an all-analog MythTV setup, there are several video input/output options you need to be aware of.

Video Input Options

For PVRs to play, pause, and rewind incoming content, content signal has to be brought in, or captured, from an external source to your PVR's system's hard drive. There are two ways to go about this: the old-fashioned coax cable analog way and the newer all-digital way.

- **Analog input** — For analog video inputs, the Hauppauge PVR series capture cards have fairly good TV capture quality, are easy to configure with MythTV, and have built-in MPEG2 compression hardware. Those features allow you to move multiple input streams to the hard drive without any resource hiccups (if you have a dual tuner card, or multiple cards).

  Use the PVR-150 if you need only one input (that is, you don't need to watch one show and record another, or watch different analog sources from two MythTV frontend stations). Because I think two tuners are the minimum for a cool MythTV setup, the PVR-500MCE is the dual tuner of choice in an analog setup. The software support is solid (tuner chip types vary, however), and setup is nice because the system just sees the card as two PVR-150s.

- **HDTV input** — For OTA (over the air) or broadcast HDTV, look at the hd3000 HDTV card for Linux (http://pchdtv.com/hd_3000.html). With this card, you can receive HDTV over antenna from your local broadcasters, something many people still have to do to get local HDTV signals (as some cable providers are restricted from retransmitting local HDTV programming over their lines). If you plan on doing HDTV out to your HDTV capable TV/monitor, you might want to look into this capture card to catch some of the incoming HDTV programming.

- **FireWire input** — For FireWire (digital) input into your PVR from popular digital cable boxes like the Motorola DCT 6200 (which serves both SD and HDTV), either your motherboard needs to have onboard FireWire ports or you need a FireWire PCI card. A FireWire port is needed to take in this type of digital signal (unencrypted mpeg 2 TS stream). This all-digital input configuration can greatly simplify your MythTV setup because you have no Capture Card to mess with.

  You can also usually control channel changing on the cable box directly through a FireWire interface; plus, you have direct digital-to-digital quality all the way to the hard drive. If you have digital outputs to your HDTV, then you're pure digital end-to-end. If you've been thinking about taking the digital plunge, this might be a good time to make the switch.

What Is FireWire?

FireWire is Apple Computer's trademark name for the IEEE (pronounced *eye triple e*) 1394. FireWire is a very fast external connection bus that can connect up to 63 devices and transmit data at up to 400 Mbps. It supports plug-and-play connectivity and is a very common interface on today's computer hardware. FireWire has become the de facto standard for high-performance digital video devices such as camcorders and now cable receivers, such as the Motorola DCT 6200.

The Motorola DCT 6200 cable receiver has become a very popular device for cable television providers to lease or sell to their customers. This unit is very nice and has an added bonus of a FireWire port. (The port is an optional feature, so you must request a unit with the FireWire port from your cable TV provider.) FireWire is not as recognizable a term in the television industry as in the PC industry, so be prepared to describe the port or show pictures of it, as some customer service people may not be familiar with FireWire.

Starting with version 0.17 of MythTV, functionality was added to support content capturing via FireWire. The Motorola DCT 6200 device was one of the first to be supported and continues to be the most tested/supported device. The DCT 6200 device decodes the cable stream and transcodes (or re-encodes it) to an unencrypted mpeg2 TS stream, which it then offers over the FireWire port. The unit will do this for both standard and high-definition channel streams. Capturing of both standard-definition and high-definition streams is supported. With MythTV version 0.18.1 (current release at the time of this writing), support was added to be able to change channels on the DCT 6200 device from within MythTV via the FireWire cable. Previously, an external program and/or external hardware was necessary to change the channel on the device. This was a major step forward for FireWire users of MythTV.

The use of FireWire with MythTV has a few advantages. One of the biggest advantages is that it eliminates the need for a TV capture card. In the case of HDTV, this could save a significant amount of money. The system requirements for capturing via FireWire are lower as well because the DCT 6200 provides a straight MPEG stream. There is no need for transcoding the video. This is yet another money-saving advantage. Finally, it is very easy to add multiple recording sources via FireWire. Just connect more cable receivers to the built-in FireWire ports that are built in, or the ports on an add-on PCI card.

Video Output Options

This is how the content (whether analog of digital) gets to your TV, monitor, or physically attached display device. While this chapter focuses on using the analog SVideo output option, there are several output options to choose from to best match your video display equipment and environment.

- **Analog television output** — Analog TV/RF output directly to a TV is probably the least desirable, but sometimes easiest to implement if you have an older TV without SVideo, RGB, or digital video inputs. For this type of setup, you need a TV tuner card that features the optional TV-output RF/F connector (like cable out on your VCR). This is not as desirable because you're taking the signal from baseband analog, back up to RF again, which picks up more signal noise (signal degradation and lack of fidelity) along the way. But if your display technology limits you to this option, you need to use a TV capture card that has this TV-out option, such as the Hauppauge PVR-350, probably the most popular card for this type of setup.

- **Analog SVideo output** — Analog SVideo output directly to a TV/monitor with SVideo cable inputs is the best way to get a very good display out of an all-analog setup, but your TV/monitor must have this SVideo input option. For this type of output, you must have a motherboard with an embedded GeForce/NVidia chipset, or a GeForce-based video card with the SVideo output connector. This is a nice configuration because some of MythTV's video signal conditioning features (such as deinterlacing and flicker smoothing) can be offloaded from your machine's main processor to the NVidia chipset to handle. This gives you both a better display at the maximum resolution your set can handle, plus additional signal enhancing effects handled by the special chips on the graphics card. If your TV/monitor does not have an SVideo input, you can also use the composite output of your GeForce card, although with noticeable signal quality loss compared to SVideo out.

- **Analog RGB/xVGA output** — Either 15-pin or discrete BNC output directly into a high-resolution TV/monitor or LCD/DLP projector is an even better all-analog option (technically, RBG is actually an analog signal). Although not many readers probably have a TV-sized RBG display, if you do and you have no digital display options (such as DVI or HDMI) this is probably your best option.

  Using RGB/xVGA output is as good as analog gets, as you are staying as close to the original signal as possible with analog; plus you can still get the all NVidia chipset special features, and the additional bandwidth capacity of the RGB signal format. This configuration is especially nice if you have a large-screen LCD or DLP projector. Some home theater–ready projectors can display HDTV via RBG connectors, although FireWire and DVI is becoming the predominant way to display HDTV on projectors and other HD devices.

  Be careful about running RGB cables more than 6 to 10 feet as signal loss, noise induction, and ghosting can occur. For required long-distance hookups (such as cable up to a ceiling-mounted projector), there are after-market RBG long haul amplifiers as well as wireless transmitters. Just be aware that these amplifiers add a stage into your content signal's path and as such will introduce some signal quality loss.

- **Digital DVI or HDMI** — Digital DVI or HDMI to your TV/monitor is probably the most common way to get digital to your HDTV/monitor. While some high-end HDTV plasma and projection sets have DVI, newer sets come with HDMI inputs (with the signal being backward-compatible with DVI if you use an adapter).

If you have FireWire out from your digital cable box to your MythTV and digital out to your TV/monitor, you can run pure digital all the way from your cable box to your set. This is a very desirable configuration and will yield the best results. A good output card for doing this on a MythTV PVR would be the NVidia eVGA GFX 5200 fan-less video card. Not only does it give you all the power of the NVidia chipset, but also features RBG/xVGA, SVideo, and DVI out — all without a cooling fan (which makes the room quieter during silent parts of the movie).

Putting It All Together

Assembling a system like this is like putting together Legos: Everything just snaps together. There are some things that are unique about a system like this, however. Be sure that you're mindful of them or you may damage your system.

Because a picture is worth a thousand words, Figure 4-3 shows an assembled view of the recommended system. This view shows the motherboard and components peering in from the underside of the beast. Yes, this means that the motherboard and all components are mounted upside down to the top inside surface of the case. Strange, I know, but this is part of SilverStone's new cooling system design.

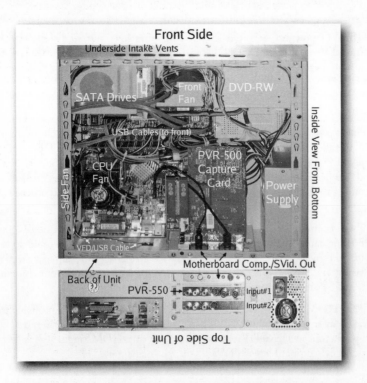

FIGURE 4-3: Inside bottom and back views of the assembled system

Assembly Tips

Here are a few details to watch for when assembling your system:

- **Cooling in this system is absolutely critical.** Be sure not to cover any vent holes on your drives with the case metal (your drive should have "do not cover" indicators if it is important). Also, on the recommended Silverstone case, all the air pulled into the system comes from the bottom and front bottom intake vents and center bottom parts of the case, and is ejected at the side (next to the CPU fan) and rear (power supply). Be sure that these areas are open and the case is not "boxed in" or your PVR can become a small oven that will slowly cook itself and any surrounding electronics.

Probably the most critical cooling component of your system is your CPU heat sink/fan assembly. In particular, the interface between your CPU and heat sink is the most critical, micro-fine adjustment that you can make.

Many stock CPU heat sinks (even some of the expensive/pretty ones) simply do not have a mirror-smooth finish. This is critical for an efficient CPU to heat sink heat conduction and cooling. This is even more critical in a PVR system because you're trying to do more with less (more cooling with less fan rotations and noise).

To get the absolute best performance out of your heat sink/CPU cooling system, clean and hone, or lap, your heat sink surface (where the CPU touches it) to a mirror finish using progressively finer and finer grits of abrasives until you can see your reflection in it. Make sure you definitely cannot see any patterned groves, scratches, or surface "lines." Then you can go back and apply a little heat sink compound, install the heat sink/fan assembly, and you'll now have the best CPU/sink interface possible; resulting in a CPU temperature that is 10–20° (F) cooler than before. For tips on CPU heat sink lapping, see this overclocker site: http://overclockers club.com/guides/heatsinklappingguide.php.

- **Don't crimp SATA cables.** If using SATA drives, be sure not to crimp the SATA cables. Doing so can cause major data I/O errors and endless headaches. If you need to bend them or tie wrap them, do as shown in Figure 4-3. Just loosely bend them no tighter than the diameter of a pencil. Going much farther will cause problems.

- **Adjust fan controls.** Take advantage of BIOS/motherboard auto fan control settings and use fairly low temperature activation thresholds (around 104° but no hotter than 120°). You will also have control over these if you enable the linux kernel i2c and lm_sensor kernel modules (as mentioned later in the chapter). Experiment with the 2.6 kernel's /sys/bus/i2c/devices/.../pwm settings to explore the best speed parameters for your i2c controlled fan speeds.

- **Separate cable runs.** When routing your external power, digital, and audio cables, be sure that you don't run them all together in parallel or zip tie them all together. Running highly dynamic, copper audio cables alongside power cables can induce humming and noise. Although this is less of a problem with digital SPDIF links (and moot with optical links), you should still keep your "big voltage," "analog little voltage," and "digital signals" (USB cables, VGA, mice, keyboards, Ethernet, and so on) physically separate as much as possible.

Installing and Preparing Fedora Core

You can drop MythTV on top of any of a dozen Linux distributions and then do weeks of battle trying to get it all working. There are even distros built around MythTV such as knoppMyth. But this chapter takes one of the easier paths to MythTV Nirvana and uses an established procedure based on the "Step-by-step guide to building a MythTV System on Fedora Core 3 w/Atrpms," by Jarod C. Wilson, available at http://wilsonet.com/mythtv/fcmyth.php.

Jarod's guide, as it is called, installs MythTV atop the quick moving and well-supported Fedora Core distro, and is an excellent choice for getting a well-rounded distro as well as PVR system. In addition, when combined with the apt for RPM system and ATrpms repository, installing MythTV becomes almost trivial.

Note Jarod's guide focuses mostly on the software side of MythTV. For a great resource on drilling into the hardware issues around Myth, see Brandon Beattie's HTPC/MythTV HOWTO at www. linuxis.us/linux/media/howto/linux-htpc/. Brandon kindly reviewed this chapter and offered his suggestions for improving it.

Note Apt is a port of Debian's apt tools that was adapted to work with RPM-based distributions. It provides the apt-get utility that provides a simpler, safer way to install and upgrade packages. Apt features complete installation ordering, multiple source capability, and several other unique features. This, combined with the ATrpms.net repository, allows you to install non–Red Hat–based packages (such as MythTV) that are built upon the original Red Hat–sourced OS packages.

Don't Stray Too Far from the Path

This chapter and the package versions seen are all based on the aforementioned hardware set, Fedora Core 3, and MythTV 0.18 running on MySQL 3.23 on the backend. At the time of this writing, Fedora Core 4 has just been released, and MythTV v0.18.1 is verified to work on it per these instructions. However, by the time you read this, later versions of Fedora Core may be available. Even so, the basic steps of installing both the OS and the MythTV suite atop Fedora should remain pretty much the same. I try to ensure that these directions will be future Fedora–compatible, but keep in mind that you may need to fill in some blanks with newer distributions. In such cases, you will find that following Jarod's guide may help.

If you decide to use a different distribution, or a radically different hardware set, you can still use this chapter as a guide; however, don't be surprised if you wander off into the dark wood and become devoured by wolves. Again, if you run into problems, look for help in the authoritative Jarod's guide, and the MythTV mail lists at http://mythtv.org/mailman/listinfo.

Before Installing the Operating System

You should not install MythTV atop any old system unless you know what you're doing, and that you meet all the hardware and software dependencies for MythTV and your hardware set.

This chapter provides an overview of the specialized Fedora install that you will need to perform for MythTV.

If you are not familiar with the Fedora Core installer or comfortable manually creating and tweaking partitions sizes and the like, please refer to Appendix C for details on general Fedora Core installs. After you're familiar with the Fedora install environment, the general partition, and packaging GUI look and feel, feel free to come back to this section for the quick but specialized OS install requirements for the upcoming MythTV packages and drivers.

About Your Disks and Partition Layout

I assume you want to store your TV shows, videos, and family photo albums locally on the same box that you're building. Given that, you want this system to be rock solid and the data secure, but also remain flexible and allow for future file system growth.

To meet both of these demands you should, if possible, use two hard drives run in a software RAID-1 mirror (for the redundancy and stability) and then on top of that run a growable Logical Volume (LVM2) file system. If this sounds daunting, don't sweat it. Fedora Core includes built-in support for both LVM2 and software RAID.

Note

Software RAID-1, or mirroring, between drives will ensure that if one drive dies you don't lose all of your home videos or family photos. In the event of a drive failure, it emails you that there are problems. A logical volume "device" positioned on top of your stable RAID mirror partition device adds the ability to grow your video content file system by simply adding more drives in the future and merging them with your existing video partition.

The following partition directions allow for either a single drive with logical volume setup or a dual drive with software RAID-1+LV configuration. If you are going to use only one drive plus LV, on that drive you will set up four primary partitions, the last of which will be an LV-type partition. If you chose the dual drive RAID-1 plus LV setup, you will need two identical (large) drives, each having a total of four partitions, mirroring each partition between them, and later setting up the logical volume manually after the first boot.

Caution

If you're not very comfortable with modifying partitions, setting partition types, and generally getting under the hood in Linux, this section may be a little advanced. Because you're starting with seemingly blank drives, there's no harm it playing around and getting the hang of this level of partition customization, but just be sure that you have it all right before continuing on past this section.

When you start your Fedora install (not yet!), the file systems of /boot and / will be manually partitioned for around 100MB and 12GB, respectively. You will also set a swap partition, which is typically between one-half to two times the amount of RAM on your computer (e.g., 512MB swap to 2GB RAM in my case). The last partition, named /video (where MythTV keeps its large file content), will take up the rest of the drive and be formatted as a ReiserFS file system, per the upcoming custom install directions.

Using One Drive with a Logical Volume

If you are going to use only one hard drive (no RAID mirror) with an LV file system, you can set all of this up on one drive only, all from within the installer (see Figure 4-4).

Using Two Drives with Software RAID-1 Plus a Logical Volume

If you are going to run the dual-drive RAID-1 mirror plus LV setup, things are a bit more complex than setting up a single drive with LV.

- First, you need to create four identical partitions on your two drives.

- Next, merge each partition with its twin on the other drive by using the RAID button on the partitioning screen to make your RAID devices. When you do this, give the first three RAID devices their formatted file system (ext3) and mount points (/boot, swap, and /), but do not format or provide the last RAID device (/dev/md3) a file system or mount point. The last RAID partition will get set up with LVM and formatted later.

Tip

See the Red Hat Enterprise Linux 4 System Administration Guide documentation, located at `http://redhat.com/docs/manuals/enterprise/RHEL-4-Manual/sysadmin-guide/ch-software-raid.html`, if you need help on visualizing this in the GUI.

Specifically, in the installer you need to set up the same four raw partitions on each of your two disks (100MB /boot, 512MB swap, 12GB /, and the rest of the drive), as type "software RAID" partitions with no file system or mount point yet (Step A in Figure 4-4). You then mirror each partition pair across the disks (still in the installer) under the RAID tab (Step B), setting up ext3 file systems (or swap) and mount points for the first three partitions on top of their software RAID-1 device names. (See Step B: "boot" to /dev/md0, "swap" to /dev/md1 and "/" to /dev/md2.)

The last partition on each drive (/dev/md3 using the remaining drive space) will also be manually made into a RAID mirror, but you will not format it or mount it during the install (Step C). Later, *after the install*, you will build your Logical Volume atop of it (Step D), format the LV, and then permanently mount it as /video. That's where all of your content will be safely stored and what will allow for future file system expansion.

Figure 4-4 shows what the manual partitioning arrangement and optional RAID-1 creation steps look like (note the device names).

During the OS install (don't start yet!), you need to manually partition from within the Fedora Installer, as shown in Figure 4-4.

If you are doing this on a standard IDE/ATA drive(s), you will be using the device name /dev/hda (and /dev/hdc for a dual drive config). If you are using a SCSI or SATA drive(s), it will appear as /dev/sda (and /dev/sdb for your second drive).

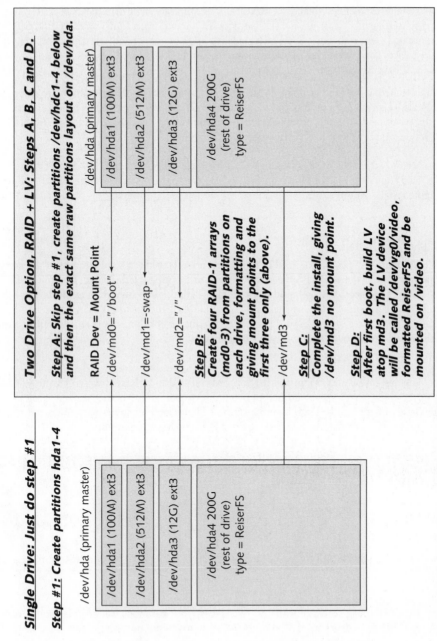

Single Drive: Just do step #1

Step #1: Create partitions hda1-4

/dev/hda (primary master)

| /dev/hda1 (100M) ext3 |
| /dev/hda2 (512M) ext3 |
| /dev/hda3 (12G) ext3 |
| /dev/hda4 200G (rest of drive) type = ReiserFS |

Two Drive Option, RAID + LV: Steps A, B, C and D.

Step A: Skip step #1, create partitions /dev/hdc1-4 below and then the exact same raw partitions layout on /dev/hda.

/dev/hda (primary master)

RAID Dev = Mount Point

/dev/hda1 (100M) ext3	/dev/md0="/boot"
/dev/hda2 (512M) ext3	/dev/md1=-swap-
/dev/hda3 (12G) ext3	/dev/md2="/"
/dev/hda4 200G (rest of drive) type = ReiserFS	/dev/md3

Step B:
Create four RAID-1 arrays (md0-3) from partitions on each drive, formatting and giving mount points to the first three only (above).

Step C:
Complete the install, giving /dev/md3 no mount point.

Step D:
After first boot, build LV atop md3. The LV device will be called /dev/vg0/video, formatted ReiserFS and be mounted on /video.

FIGURE 4-4: Installing OS on RAID-1, and /video on LVM-RAID-1

If using the recommended dual drive RAID+LV configuration, be sure to set all of the "partition type" settings to "Software RAID" (or type "fd" viewed from fdisk) on each disk, combining them into their respective RAID device (such as /dev/mdX) and only then assigning the RAID devices their respective file systems and mount points. Otherwise, you'll mess up your install and have to start over.

Again, if you're doing the two-drive RAID plus LV setup, during the install you are setting up four RAID-1 arrays /dev/md0-3, but configuring only the first three at this time to house /boot, swap, and /. Later in the chapter, I step you through making the last /dev/md3 into a growable logical volume and mounting it as /video.

Note If you need to access hard disk partitions from a bootable Linux, such as Damn Small Linux, you should know that many of them (including DSL) cannot access hard disk partitions that are configured for LV and/or RAID.

Starting Your Install

When you start the install, you need to type **linux reiserfs** at the boot: prompt of the installer so that it will offer the ReiserFS file system as one of the supported file systems. You need ReiserFS support because it, or another large-file–friendly file system such as xfs, is best suited for handling large files and many files as you have on a PVR. But to get install time and RPM package support for ResiderFS, you need to tell the install boot prompt that you want it as an install option. At the boot prompt, type **linux reiserfs**:

```
boot: linux reiserfs
```

Select Custom install and "Manually partition with disk druid." Refer back to Figure 4-4 and create all of your partitions as outlined previously (depending on whether you're setting up a single drive or a dual-drive RAID configuration). The accompanying table shows what my partition layout looks like, running a dual-drive RAID+LV configuration.

Device	Mount Point	File System	Size
/dev/md0	/boot	ext3	100MB
/dev/md1	swap	swap	512MB
/dev/md2	/	ext3	12GB
/dev/md3	not used yet	(eventually, Reiserfs)	rest of drive(s)

Note If you are not running software RAID on two drives, your partitions will be /dev/hda1-/dev/hda4 (or /dev/sda1-/dev/sda3 if SCSI or SATA). Also, if you are not using a two-drive RAID-1 setup, you may set up your last partition at install time (probably either /dev/hda3 or /dev/sda3) as a ReiserFS-formatted volume and mount it to /video.

Tip

Although ReiserFS is considered superior to the ext3 file system, on any Red Hat–based system, if you ever find yourself in an emergency boot/recovery situation, the Red Hat environment (including the boot CD's rescue mode) is more ext3 friendly. So with ext3, you will have a better chance of getting your data back. Additionally, if an ext3 file system is ever corrupted beyond the point of being able to mount it, ext3 allows for the fallback mount options of ext2 r/w or ext2 r/o modes to assist you in recovering your operating system data. This is why we still use ext3 on the /boot and / partitions.

Network/Firewall Settings

For these install settings, set the following:

- Use DHCP (if on a DHCP network, but use static IP if possible)
- Firewall on (allow SSH, HTTP, and HTTPS)
- SELinux = warn

Installing Packages

According to the recommendations in Jarod's guide, along with a few of my own additions, install the following package groups and subpackages:

- X Window System
- KDE Desktop Environment
- Web Server (if you want to use MythWeb Web frontend interface for MythTV)
- MySQL Database (be sure mysql-server is selected under the "Details" section)

Other packages that you might want to consider installing include:

- Xfce-desktop (in case the KDE is too resource-hungry)
- Editors
    - +vim-X11
- Graphical Internet
    - Gaim
    - Firefox (handy for copying and pasting from Jarod's guide)
    - +Thunderbird (checking email with a friendly interface)
- Text-Internet
- Sound and Video
    - +dvgrab (for grabbing ieee1394/firewire input)
- Windows File Server

- Network Servers
  - vnc-server (nice for remote access options)
- Development-tools (you will need to compile a couple things)
- Admin-tools
- System-tools
  - +tsclient
- Printing Support (nice for hooking up a photo printer)

Now complete the install (this will take 30–40 minutes), and then reboot the system.

The system should boot up into graphical mode and run the First Boot GUI, asking you to enter some setup settings. Do the following:

- Enable NTP and point the pointer to `pool.ntp.org`.
- Set `resolution` to 800 × 600 (if running normal analog inputs).
- Create the user `mythtv` and set the password.

After this, the system should present you with a login screen. Log in to the GUI login screen as your mythtv user and let the desktop come up.

Some Final Fedora RPM Tweaks

After the KDE system and desktop appear to be done loading, go to the Red Hat icon menu and select System Tools → Terminal. This will pull up a bash shell in a kterminal. Now become root with `su -` and then enter the root password you set at install time.

Note To add any menu item from the Red Hat menu to your toolbar, just place it where you want by dragging and dropping it.

Now you will need to import all the default Fedora GPG keys, and then the ATrpms GPG key with the following commands:

```
# updatedb
# rpm --import $(locate GPG-KEY|grep rhn | tr \\n " ")
```

The first command may take a few minutes to run the first time. The second command will find all the GPG keys on your system and import them into the RPM system in case you decide to pull down any stock Fedora RPMs later. Next, fully patch your new Fedora install with this command:

```
# up2date-nox -uf --nosig
```

This command will take a while to run, and you will need a good, fast Internet connection as it updates all of your installed packages. If it fails before it completes, you may have to run it a couple of times. It will pick up each time where it failed in the previous attempt.

Next, try installing a new package, usbutils, like this:

```
# up2date-nox -i usbutils
```

If this works, you will be able to probe USB devices hooked to your system (as root) with the lsusb command. You will make use of this later when you hook up your USB/VFD (if you're using the recommended Silverstone case).

Tip

If you want a convenient way of looking for RPMs in Fedora Core's stock RPM repository, run the command up2date-nox --show-all > RPM-showall.txt once in a while. This will allow you to browse through all the Red Hat–sourced RPMs instantly, whether online or not.

Installing and Setting up the ATrpms System

The MythTV suite, as installed by Jarod's guide, relies not on the stock Red Hat–sourced RPM/yum repository, but instead uses the atrpms.net source of apt-based RPMs. It's a pretty nice system, but on the frontend it works a bit differently than the stock up2date/yum method of downloading RPMs. To get this new package repository and download engine working on your system, you first need to prep your system to trust the signed RPMs that it provides. You can do this with this one-line command:

```
# rpm --import http://atrpms.net/RPM-GPG-KEY.atrpms
```

Next, the quickest way to get apt for RPM installed on your system is to use ATrpm's own atrpms-kickstart package to get you up and running:

```
# rpm -Uvh  http://dl.atrpms.net/all/atrpms-kickstart-28-
1.rhfc3.at.i386.rpm
```

Note

If you are running a different version of Fedora, go to the main ATrpms.net Web page, click your version of Fedora, and locate and download the appropriate atrpms-kickstart package. For example, at the time of this writing, the Fedora Core 4 version of the package is located under http://atrpms.net/dist/fc4/atrpms-kickstart/. Click the first atrpms-kickstart file link and Firefox downloads and installs the package for you after you provide your root password.

If you have problems getting it going, check the manual install directions on the atrpms.net site at http://atrpms.net/install.html, or look for updates on Jarod's guide at http://wilsonet.com/mythtv/fcmyth.php#apt.

After you get the apt-get system installed, test your ability to talk to the repository by updating your local apt package data files:

```
# apt-get update
```

This should update your local package list and dependency tree.

Note If you run into any package conflicts in this section (between Fedora and AtRPMs packages, you need to either remove the offending Fedora package with `rpm -e packagename`, or use the possibly safer option of adding it to the apt-get "Allow-Duplicated" list. See the command `apt-config` for more information.

Now you're ready to install apt-get–based atrpm packages. Try using apt to update your entire system against the apt RPM repository:

```
# apt-get dist-upgrade
```

This last command will take a while as it updates your system against the atrpms.net reposi-tory. If you would like a GUI tool for apt in the future, install the package synaptic like this:

```
# apt-get install synaptic
```

All of these new package management systems, such as Apt, that ride atop RPM now resolve dependencies and install all dependent packages along with the ones you request. Just be sure that after you get your system set up and running, you don't install or upgrade packages that could take your system down, such as kernel, ivtv, or other packages that your system is finely tuned against.

Last, before you move on to the hardware driver section, you need to set up an environment variable that makes things much easier with the apt for RPM system. I'm talking about setting up the $KVER environment to hold the contents of your kernel version information. Here's how to set it up to work every time you boot the system.

```
# echo "export KVER=\`uname -r\`" >> /etc/profile.d/kver.sh
# chmod 755 /etc/profile.d/kver.sh
# reboot
```

Be sure to use backticks and not single quotes around the `uname -r` command. Now after rebooting, from anywhere in the system you should be able to type `echo $KVER` and see your kernel version.

Tip A font-based bug in Fedora Core 3's urw-fonts package makes mythfrontend display fonts onscreen that are too large for the user GUI display. You can determine if you have this problem by going to MythTV's Weather service and viewing your local weather. If your local temperature for today looks chopped off on the bottom, or you cannot read all of the text, you are suffering from this font bug. To fix this, you can forcefully downgrade to an older (or newer fixed) version of the package as per the directions at www.users.on.net/~jani/dvico-mythtv-10.html#ss10.1.

Setting up a Logical Volume for /video

If you are using a single drive configuration and you set up your logical volume during the install, you can skip the bulk of this section and move on to the section "Installing MythTV and Drivers." However, if you are running the recommended dual-drive RAID+LV configura-tion, this section will step you through setting up your LVM2 logical volume on top of the RAID-1 mirror /dev/md3. You might want to at least check out the LVM Terminology 101 sidebar for getting started with LVM.

Now that most of the OS is set up and running, you need to finish that wild partition layout of a logical volume on top of software RAID (/dev/md3). This section is not required, but if you want the ability to add more drive space to your system in the future, this is the way to prepare for it now without some day having to move GBs of data around between drives. With LVM, you simply add more drives to the system (let's hope in the form of more RAID arrays), and add those resources to the logical volume. No reformatting, copying files, or even so much as a reboot (if you're using USB or ieee1394 drives!). LVM or no LVM? It's your call.

On my system I run SATA drives, which appear as SCSI devices (/dev/sda instead of /dev/hda), but no matter. Setting up a logical volume atop your software RAID-1 mirror /dev/md3 device (if you're using RAID) will look pretty much the same regardless (except when you poke around with fdisk at the raw partition level).

Caution

If you're planning on really using LVM and adding more and more drives to your logical volume in the future, then you probably want to do it in the form of RAID (either hardware RAID-5 or 1, or software RAID-1). That's because adding multiple drives together under one file system (like LVM) decreases the overall reliability of that file system. So you can balance this stats game by adding not single drives, but RAID-1 arrays. This will reduce your chances of losing all of your data some day!

Step 1: Verify Your Drives and Partitions

Before you mark, allocate, create, and format your logical volume for use, you really, really want to make sure that you're working on the correct drive(s) and partition(s)! I can't stress how careful you need to be here. Read through this whole section a couple of times, take comparative notes for your system device names, and get a feel for how this works *before* doing anything to your running system.

First, take a look at what you have physically, partition-wise. Running fdisk -l as root will list all the partitions that it can see on all the disks that it can see:

```
# fdisk -l
Disk /dev/sda: 250.0 GB, 250059350016 bytes
255 heads, 63 sectors/track, 30401 cylinders
Units = cylinders of 16065 * 512 = 8225280 bytes

   Device Boot    Start     End    Blocks   Id System
/dev/sda1   *       1      13    104391   fd Linux raid autodetect
/dev/sda2          14    1580  12586927+  fd Linux raid autodetect
/dev/sda3        1581    1711   1052257+  fd Linux raid autodetect
/dev/sda4        1712   30401 230452425   5 Extended
/dev/sda5        1712   30401 230452393+ fd Linux raid autodetect

Disk /dev/sdb: 250.0 GB, 250059350016 bytes
255 heads, 63 sectors/track, 30401 cylinders
Units = cylinders of 16065 * 512 = 8225280 bytes

   Device Boot    Start     End    Blocks   Id System
/dev/sdb1   *       1      13    104391   fd Linux raid autodetect
```

```
/dev/sdb2       14      1580    12586927+ fd Linux raid autodetect
/dev/sdb3       1581    1711    1052257+ fd Linux raid autodetect
/dev/sdb4       1712    30401   230452425  5 Extended
/dev/sdb5       1712    30401   230452393+ fd Linux raid autodetect
```

This shows that I have a number of identical partitions on two drives, /dev/sda and /dev/sdb (if running older IDE/PATA, you should see /dev/hda and /dev/hdc).

Because I'm running software RAID, and my big 200GB partition is actually running in a RAID-1 mirror set on /dev/sda5 and /dev/sdb5, I should see them somewhere under the software RAID status file of /proc/mdstat here:

```
# cat /proc/mdstat
Personalities : [raid1]
md1 : active raid1 sdb2[1] sda2[0]
    12586816 blocks [2/2] [UU]

md2 : active raid1 sdb3[1] sda3[0]
    1052160 blocks [2/2] [UU]

md3 : active raid1 sdb5[1] sda5[0]
    230452288 blocks [2/2] [UU]

md0 : active raid1 sdb1[1] sda1[0]
    104320 blocks [2/2] [UU]

unused devices: <none>
```

The output showed all of my RAID arrays, and md3 looks like the largest one. But how can you tell which array is not really being used? Try this:

```
# df -h
Filesystem      Size Used Avail Use% Mounted on
/dev/md1        12G 6.4G 4.9G 57% /
/dev/md0        99M 12M 83M 12% /boot
none            490M  0 490M  0% /dev/shm
# cat /etc/fstab
# This file is edited by fstab-sync - see 'man fstab-sync' for details
/dev/md1        /                    ext3    defaults        1 1
/dev/md0        /boot                ext3    defaults        1 2
none            /dev/pts             devpts  gid=5,mode=620 0 0
none            /dev/shm             tmpfs   defaults        0 0
none            /proc                proc    defaults        0 0
none            /sys                 sysfs   defaults        0 0
/dev/md2        swap                 swap    defaults        0 0
/dev/hda        /media/cdrecorder    auto
pamconsole,exec,noauto,fscontext=system_u:object_r:removable_t,managed 0 0
```

The output shows that md0 is /boot, md1 is /, and md2 is swap. That verifies that /dev/md3 is the big unused RAID device that I need to put a LVM logical volume onto.

Tip

If you would like to see more information about your RAID arrays, check out the new software RAID admin tool called mdadm. That tool will allow you to make, break, and fail partitions in a software RAID array, but you can also use it to check out all the settings on a specific RAID array. Try running it on one or all of your arrays like this: mdadm --detail /dev/md3.

Step 2: Mark Your Partition/Device as a Physical Volume

Before you can use a partition or device (or RAID array) as a part of a *Logical Volume*, you first need to mark your device as a *physical volume* for the system to see and use, using the command pvcreate:

```
# pvcreate /dev/md3
Physical volume "/dev/md3" successfully created
```

(or /dev/hda3 if you're not using a two-drive RAID mirror).

Here is how you can see that you have successfully marked your device as a physical volume:

```
# pvdisplay
--- NEW Physical volume ---
PV Name               /dev/md3
VG Name
PV Size               219.78 GB
Allocatable           NO
PE Size (KByte)       0
Total PE              0
Free PE               0
Allocated PE          0
PV UUID               E3kyqV-ki6t-ijH5-SpIg-3dw0-zjwt-Bf24vG
```

This shows that you have a 219GB physical volume available to assign to any Volume Group, which you eventually allocate to a logical volume that can be formatted.

Now that you have your physical volume (or PV) set up, create a volume group to tell your system to chop up and assign your PV using 32MB PE chunks, and give this pool of storage resources a volume group name, vg0, as follows:

```
# vgcreate -s 32M vg0 /dev/md3
Volume group "vg0" successfully created
# vgdisplay
--- Volume group ---
VG Name               vg0
System ID
Format                lvm2
Metadata Areas        1
Metadata Sequence No  1
VG Access             read/write
VG Status             resizable
MAX LV                0
Cur LV                0
Open LV               0
```

```
Max PV              0
Cur PV              1
Act PV              1
VG Size             219.75 GB
PE Size             32.00 MB
Total PE            7032
Alloc PE / Size     0 / 0
Free PE / Size      7032 / 219.75 GB
VG UUID             jERnx7-SN5Z-sfsG-29zu-Vq7V-ZELL-TuIZRa
```

The output shows that you have created a *volume group* named vg0, and that it is using a PE size of 32MB from the PV previously marked for use (/dev/md0 in my case). It also verifies that it has allocated all of your PEs and has made available all the space on the PV that you expect to see (in my case, 7032 PEs, which equals the full 219GB). The output from the command vgdisplay shows that your allocated PEs are equal to 0 at this point, and that all PEs are free for use in your volume group, which you now create like this:

```
# lvcreate -l 7032 vg0 -n videoLVM
/dev/cdrom: open failed: Read-only file system
  Logical volume "videoLVM" created
# lvdisplay
  --- Logical volume ---
  LV Name                /dev/vg0/videoLVM
  VG Name                vg0
  LV UUID                MkkHtO-QgJD-9HNH-sYb3-SQ7t-MsUm-2rid57
  LV Write Access        read/write
  LV Status              available
  # open                 0
  LV Size                219.75 GB
  Current LE             7032
  Segments               1
  Allocation             inherit
  Read ahead sectors     0
  Block device           253:0
```

That created your Logical Volume called /dev/vg0/videoLVM. Take a closer look:

```
# ls -la /dev/vg0/videoLVM
lrwxrwxrwx 1 root root 24 Jul 1 01:03 /dev/vg0/videoLVM ->
/dev/mapper/vg0-videoLVM
```

It seems that /dev/vg0/videoLVM is actually a symlink to this real physical device:

```
# ls -la /dev/mapper/vg0-videoLVM
brw------- 1 root root 253, 0 Jul 1 01:03 /dev/mapper/vg0-videoLVM
```

That's the actual drive file that you want to format and mount now, as follows:

```
# mkreiserfs /dev/mapper/vg0-videoLVM
mkreiserfs 3.6.18 (2003 www.namesys.com)
[...]
Guessing about desired format.. Kernel 2.6.11-1.27_FC3 is running.
Format 3.6 with standard journal
```

LVM Terminology 101

A *physical volume* is just that: a single physical partition or disk (i.e., hardware) that you have marked as usable by the LVM system. A *physical volume*, or *PV*, gets cut up into small chunks (called *Physical Extents* or *PEs*) at the time that it is assigned to a new or existing *volume group* (such as /dev/vg0).

A volume group is just a logical abstraction of one or more physical volumes, so that you can refer to this grouping of PV/PE resources by a name for management purposes. For example, you could have one volume group dedicated to low-cost IDE drives, one for faster SCSI drives, and one for higher-cost RAID arrays. The name that I've given my volume group in this section is vg0, and this is the name that allows me to reference the association of my eventual logical volume to a specific set of volume group resources (/dev/md3 in my case).

The volume group is also the level at which you control the size of the chunks that you chop your physical volume into. The default small chunk, or PE size, is 4MB (from the command line), but I will be using 32MB chunks because I want to be able to grow file systems very large.

Some or all of these PV/PE chunks get associated with a volume group, and then glued together, or *allocated*, from your volume group to form your *logical volume* or *LV* (for instance, /dev/vg0/videoLVM), which is now like a raw partition that you can then format and mount. The difference between just using a single drive versus your new logical volume is that this logical volume "device" can now have more PE chunks added to its parent volume group (from other drives in the system). PE chunks can then allocated to your logical volume, which can now become larger than any single drive in the system!

To grow your logical volume, you simply add a new drive to the system (even hot swap USB or FireWire based), mark it as a physical volume, pull PV/PE chunks to the volume group, and finally allocate more (or all) of them to the mounted logical volume. That's like making a partition larger without even rebooting! You just don't have this type of storage flexibility on old-fashioned single drives and partitions.

After growing the LV, the only thing that remains to be done is growing the file system that resides on top of the LV to get access to the additional space. Both ext3 (using `ex2tonline`) and ReiserFS (using `resize_reiserfs`) support this feature now on the fly without so much as a reboot or a file system remount. Very powerful indeed!

```
Count of blocks on the device: 57606144
Number of blocks consumed by mkreiserfs formatting process: 9969
Blocksize: 4096
Hash function used to sort names: "r5"
Journal Size 8193 blocks (first block 18)
Journal Max transaction length 1024
inode generation number: 0
```

```
UUID: 0ac470f3-d9f1-4f17-8ced-fa2f802c2e82
ATTENTION: YOU SHOULD REBOOT AFTER FDISK!
    ALL DATA WILL BE LOST ON '/dev/mapper/vg0-videoLVM'!
Continue (y/n):y
Initializing journal - 0%....20%....40%....60%....80%....100%
Syncing..ok
[...]
ReiserFS is successfully created on /dev/mapper/vg0-videoLVM.
```

Done! Very quickly, too, for a 200GB+ format job.

Note   If your system does not have the `mkreiserfs` command, you somehow did not get the reiserfs-utils package. You can install it via the command `up2date-nox -i reiserfs-utils`.

The next step is to create the mount point, set up `/etc/fstab`, and mount it!

```
# mkdir /video ; chmod 777 /video
# vi /etc/fstab
    ...
    /dev/mapper/vg0-videoLVM /video reiserfs defaults,noatime 1 2
    ...
# mount /video
# df -h
Filesystem         Size Used Avail Use%    Mounted on
/dev/md1           12G 7.4G  3.9G  66%     /
/dev/md0           99M  12M   83M  12%     /boot
none              490M    0  490M   0%     /dev/shm
/dev/mapper/vg0-videoLVM   220G  33M 220G  1% /video
```

There you go. You're probably the only one on the block running LVM on top of software RAID. Notice also in the `/etc/fstab` file that I added the mount setting addition `noatime`. This will speed up drive access a bit.

For much more information on LVM2 and what you can do with it, see this valuable resource: `http://tldp.org/HOWTO/LVM-HOWTO/`.

Installing MythTV and Drivers

Now that you have the base OS and special file systems all set up and running, you can install the base myth-suite and then get some of the specialized hardware drivers that you need installed and configured on this system.

First, you'll use apt and the atrpms.net repository to make quick work of installing the bulk of the MythTV system.

Second, and the hardest part of the MythTV project, is getting all the related drivers for your specific hardware installed and configured. You need kernel modules set up and configured before the system will be usable. This includes:

- The NVidia GeForce 4 video card, for S-Video rendered output (if using)
- The lm_sensors, for controlling fan PCM/speed
- The ivtv audio codecs and video kernel modules for Hauppauge capture cards
- The lirc infrared receiver/interpreter system for your IR remote
- The kernel source (if you're recompiling any kernel modules)
- Optional drivers for the USB-based VF display on your case (if using the SilverStone)

Installing mythtv-suite from ATrpms.net

This is probably the easiest step of the whole process. It takes only these two commands:

```
# apt-get update
# apt-get install mythtv-suite
```

This will install approximately 70 to 80 different RPMs on your system, paving the road for the rest of this section.

If any errors are thrown, be sure to follow up and fix the problem before continuing. Most errors can be tracked down and fixed by referencing the ever-useful Jarod's guide online.

Setting Up NVidia Graphic Card Drivers

These drivers are the graphics card drivers for the recommended motherboard with embedded GeForce 4 NVidia graphics card with integrated S-Video output, which yields a superior quality output, especially for a PVR. You will probably want to use these drivers if you're using a regular GeForce card also.

These graphics card drivers are dependent upon your kernel version, and as such, need the output information from the command uname -r on your specific install. If you have not upgraded your kernel yet (done in the previous up2date and apt-get dist-upgrade steps), take care of that before continuing.

Because you previously set up the $KVER variable in your startup scripts, you should now be able to get and install the NVidia-graphics packages for your system. To make sure, verify your $KVER variable like this:

```
# echo $KVER
2.6.11-1.27_FC3
```

That's the output for my system. Yours will probably be different. This is the same output you should get from the command uname -r.

Now install the proper kernel modules:

```
# apt-get install nvidia-graphics7174-kmdl-$KVER
# apt-get install nvidia-graphics7174
```

Note This package version varies based on Fedora version. For example, FC3 is version 7174 and FC4 is version 7667. Go to `http://atrpms.net/`, click on your version of Fedora, then the `nvidia-graphics-4kstacks` link, and the first at-rpm RPM package is the version you want.

To enable the modules, you need to drop out of X Windows using the command `init 3`, and then set up the X driver for the NVidia graphics card, as follows:

```
# init 3
# nvidia-graphics-switch 7174
# cd /etc/X11
```

Note If after typing init 3, you get some locked-up looking screen, try pressing Ctrl+Alt+F2 or Ctrl+Alt+F1 to get to the correct virtual terminal screen.

Now edit your `xorg.conf.nvidia` file:

```
# vi xorg.conf.nvidia
```

In the `"Module"` section of the new, but inactive backup, `xorg.conf.nvidia` configuration file, add the following load line for the v4l (video 4 linux) system:

```
...
Section "Module"
    Load "v4l"
    Load "dbe"
    Load "extmod"
    Load  "glx"
...
```

Note If you are missing the "glx" module, you may need to add it to get the full advantage of the NVidia card.

You may also want to add one or more of these options in the `"Device"` area of your `xorg.conf.nvidia` file, depending on whether you're using an S-Video or RGB monitor:

```
Section "Device"
## GF4 Options
    #Option    "RenderAccel" "1"
    Identifier "Videocard0"
    Driver     "nvidia"
```

```
        VendorName "Chaintech"
        BoardName  "nVidia GeForce 4 MX 440"
        #Option    "ConnectedMonitor" "SGVA"
        Option     "ConnectedMonitor" "SVIDEO"
        Option     "TVStandard" "NTSC-M"
        Option     "TVOutFormat" "SVIDEO"
    EndSection
```

Next, back up your current (active) `xorg.conf` file, and then overwrite the original with the `xorg.conf.nvidia` configuration file you just created:

```
# cp -a xorg.conf xorg.conf-BAK
# cp -af xorg.conf.nvidia xorg.conf
```

Next, set up the NVidia drivers to reload their settings each time you start X. Do this by creating an init file in the `/etc/X11/xinit/xinitrc.d/` directory and making the file executable:

```
# vi /etc/X11/xinit/xinitrc.d.nvideo-settings.sh
```

Put the following in the file

```
#!/bin/bash
nvidia-settings --load-config-only &
```

and make the file executable:

```
# chmod 755 /etc/X11/xinit/xinitrc.d.nvideo-settings.sh
```

Reboot and make sure that when X comes up, you see the NVidia logo flash on the screen before your X sessions begins.

Tip

This chapter is setting up an NTSC standard PVR, outputting to the embedded GeForce video card's S-Video output. If you're using the TV/RF output from (for example) a PVR-350, or any capture card other than the recommended PVR-500MCE, refer to Jarod's guide on how to configure both your xorg file (shown previously) and your ivtv driver options (shown later in the chapter). Find this info at `http://wilsonet.com/mythtv/fcmyth.php#capture`. As for creating a PAL- or SECAM-based system, you need to look on the ivtv site and/or mail lists. But start out at the ivtv FAQ here: `http://ivtv.sourceforge.net/FAQ.html`.

Setting up i2c and lm_sensors (and Fan Control)

Think of your machine's internal i2c bus system as the way in which all the little components of your system can "talk" to each other. The i2c bus system is what tells your lm_sensors system how hot your processor is, how fast your fans are spinning (or if they've stopped), or if someone's opened the case. The i2c bus system also listens on some IR ports (in some cases) and allows you to control your capture card tuner(s).

Additionally, in a small hot system like a PVR, you definitely want to make sure that lm_sensors and i2c modules are set up correctly. If you run the following `lsmod` command and see your i2s_core and sensors lines, it may already be set up. Check it like this:

```
# lsmod |grep sensor
i2c_sensor          3521 2 w83627hf,eeprom
i2c_core            21953 11 msp3400,wm8775,cx25840,tuner,
tveeprom,i2c_algo_bit,w83627hf,eeprom,i2c_sensor,i2c_isa,i2c_nforce2
```

If you don't see at least i2c_core and i2c_sensor, here's how to set it up. In my case, w83627hf is my motherboard's i2c/lm_sensor chip. On your system, run the command `sensors-detect` and follow the directions for setting up lm_sensors. If you don't have that command on your system, you need to install the usbutils package and then run `sensors-detect`:

```
# up2date-nox -i usbutils
...
# sensors-detect
```

Follow the directions in the interface for setting up your `/etc/modprobe.conf` and `/etc/rc.d/rc.local` startup file. Later, I show you how to test the fan control PWM (speed control) circuits and what your `modules.conf` and `rc.local` files should look like. Be sure to reboot and verify that everything comes up.

Fixing Your CPU/MB Temperature Labels

Depending on your motherboard's lm_sensor chipset, you will probably need to fix your temperature read-out labels. To start this, run `sensors -f` to get a full read out. To get just the temperature labels, run `sensors -f | grep [0-9]..F` and you'll get the various temperature measurements that your system provides.

Play around with a cool blow dryer and figure out which temperature is which (being careful not to allow your system to overheat). After you know which is which, write them down, in order 1, 2, 3 as output from `sensors -f`, and note what you would like 1, 2, and 3 to be called. Hold that information, and find out whether your lm_sensor module "chip" is like this:

```
# sensors -f|grep -B1 "Adapter: ISA"|head -1
w83627thf-isa-0290
```

This shows you your motherboard lm_sensor's ISA adapter chip (usually used for the temperature and voltage measurements). Next, look for the "chip" line in your `/etc/sensors.conf` file, and for the area that looks like this:

```
    label temp1 "Case Temp"
    label temp2 "CPU Temp"
    label temp3 "Under CPU"
```

Modify these to whatever you want to call them, and reparse this configuration file via the command `sensors -s` to reload the config changes, and you're done!

Installing lirc_xx or lirc_imon IR Drivers

Lirc is the suite that takes IR input from an IR receiver that is hooked up to your system and translates it from remote control buttons into named functions (such as volume+, channel-, power, and so on). These functions get mapped to application-specific keyboard key combos through a user file, `~/.lircrc`. Ultimately, this allows you to control said apps via the remote and lirc.

If you are running a Hauppauge PVR-x50 card, you have an easy way out and can use the IR dongle that comes with your capture card. In that case, you will need nothing other than install the appropriate lirc packages from the ATrpms.net repository. However, if you're using the SilverStone LC-11m case with integrated USB/VFD and IR receiver, things are a bit more complex and you will need to do all the steps in this section.

Installing the Stock lirc-kmdl and lirc atrpms.net Packages

You will need the lirc-kmdl and lirc atrpms.net packages no matter what hardware you're running. They will give your kernel the required modules for setting up the lirc daemon, which watches for IR input and translates the input into key presses.

Grab both of the packages required for your kernel version like this:

```
# apt-get install lirc-kmdl-$KVER
# apt-get install lirc
```

If you are running some form of IR receiver other than the one that comes in the SilverStone case, you can try to use one of the kernel modules that comes in the stock package. You can locate these stock kernel modules with this command:

```
# locate lirc_|grep ^/lib/modules
```

If you're using one of the Hauppauge PVR-x50 cards with IR, you will probably be using the included lirc_i2c kernel module. If you're using a serial IR adapter, the lirc_ser is probably for you. These (and other lirc modules) are covered in both Jarod's guide and the LIRC Web site (`http://lirc.org/`).

If you're using some other strange piece of IR receiver hardware, you can try using one of the lirc_xx modules listed on your system from that `locate` command, and try to match your IR receiver to the proper kernel module. After you get it working, skip the upcoming "Custom lirc_imon" sections and continue at the "Configuring Your lirc_xx/lirc_imon IR Driver" section.

Tip

If you have an IR receiver other than the one that comes in the SilverStone case (motherboard IR interface, capture card IR, serial IR receiver, and so forth), load the appropriate module (with `modprobe lirc_XXX`) and test it by using `irrecord /tmp/test-output-lirc.conf`. If you don't see dots along the bottom of the screen while testing, that specific module is not working. Unload it with `rmmod lirc_XXX` and try another module. For more lirc troubleshooting help, see the lirc Web site and mail lists at `http://lirc.org/`.

Note

If you didn't use the SilverStone case, and you need to buy an IR receiver, see the lirc Web site under the "Supported Hardware" links, or just buy a general purpose IR/RS-232 unit from `http://zapway.de/e_index1.htm`.

If you are using the recommended SilverStone case with special VFD front display unit, you need to use the lirc_imon driver and do the work described in the next two custom lirc_imon sections.

Checking for the Custom lirc_imon Kernel Module

If you're using the really nice HTPC case, the SilverStone LC-11m with integrated USB-based Vacuum Fluorescent Display with included IR receiver, you need to jump through a few hoops here to get this specialized device working with MythTV. The apt-get install lirc commands you previously ran got you the base lirc kernel modules for most of the common IR hardware, but at the time of this writing, the ATrpms.net RPMs don't have the specific kernel module that this device needs, the lirc_imon module, as shown following. You can try to find it on your system by doing this:

```
# locate lirc_imon|grep modules
/lib/modules/2.6.11-1.27_FC3/misc/lirc_imon.ko
```

This file, which I manually compiled and put in place, shows what you're looking for. It contains the code that controls both the IR functions and the USB/VFD control features that I need. If you do have a lirc_imon.ko file driver somewhere under /lib/modules/*kernelversion*/ on your system, then try it out by loading it up with the command modprobe lirc_imon, and then run these commands:

```
# lsmod|grep lirc
lirc_imon       15748 0
lirc_dev        13636 1 lirc_imon
# ls -la /dev/lirc*
crw------- 1 root root 61, 0 Jul 3 14:59 /dev/lirc
crw------- 1 root root 61, 0 Jul 3 14:59 /dev/lirc0
srw-rw-rw- 1 root root   0 Jul 3 14:58 /dev/lircd
# ls -la /dev/lcd0
crw------- 1 root root 180, 144 Jun 8 22:48 /dev/lcd0
```

If lsmod shows you that the drivers are loaded, and you see the /dev/lirc* files as shown, and also see the /dev/lcd0 device file for USB output to the VFD, you're all set! Just configure your modprobe.conf and/or rc.local file, as you'll see shortly, and you're ready to start recording your remote control's IR output. If you didn't see at least part of the output shown, you need to jump through the following hoops.

Note The way the device files magically appear when a kernel module is loaded is a part of the udev (or devfs style) of dynamic device naming system. This is something that you do not see in all distributions, but which comes standard in Fedora Core. If you are using a distribution other than Fedora Core, or one that does not use the udev or devfs, see man mknod and man MAKEDEV for help.

Compiling and Installing the Custom lirc_imon k-mod

The custom compile of lirc_imon is a bit of a pain because you have to have the kernel source in place first. Red Hat has removed the kernel source RPM from FC3 and newer, so now you need to download the kernel-2.6.*xxx*.*yy*.src.rpm, kind of prebuild it into usable source, and then move the buried source code directories into the appropriate place. After that kernel-source prerequisite is met, download the lirc source code, set up and configure, it, and then just compile and install the single lirc_imon driver that you want.

Note Again, if you're not using the SilverStone LC-11m case with the Soundgraph USB IR/VFD, you need not continue with this section. Skip to the section "Configuring Your lirc_xx/lirc_imon IR Driver."

I've broken it down for you into seven easy-to-follow, discrete steps.

1. **Get your kernel's src RPM.** First, download the kernel src package for your specific kernel from wherever you got your currently running kernel (probably Red Hat via up2date):

   ```
   # up2date -d --get-source $(rpm -qa|grep kernel-2.6.*FC3|sort|tail -1)
   ```

   Note the name of the src.rpm that it downloads, and ensure that it is indeed the same version that you are running (or the kernel version that you intend to be running).

   If that reg-ex trickery doesn't seem to work for you, just download the kernel src.rpm from Red Hat:

   - FC3:

   ```
   http://download.fedora.redhat.com/pub/fedora/linux/core/updates/3/SRPMS/
   ```

   - FC4:

   ```
   http://download.fedora.redhat.com/pub/fedora/linux/core/updates/4/SRPMS/
   ```

   - FC5:

   ```
   http://download.fedora.redhat.com/pub/fedora/linux/core/updates/5/SRPMS/
   ```

   For example, for my FC3 Myth setup, I'm running the updated kernel:

   ```
   # uname -r
   2.6.11-1.27_FC3
   ```

   So if the up2date method didn't work for me, I could manually download this kernel src.rpm:

   ```
   http://download.fedora.redhat.com/pub/fedora/linux/core/
   updates/3/SRPMS/kernel-2.6.11-1.27_FC3.src.rpm
   ```

2. **Install and rebuild the source tree.** When using up2date, all RPMs download to the /var/spool/up2date/ directory. After you're sure that you have the right version, go ahead and install it (it will put the source files in place in /usr/src/redhat, but not touch your real kernel):

   ```
   # rpm -ivh /var/spool/up2date/kernel-*src.rpm # or wherever
   you downloaded it to
   # cd /usr/src/redhat/SPECS
   ```

```
# rpmbuild -bp -target=noarch kernel-2.6.spec # or whatever
your spec file name is
```

That will set up all the source files into a usable state for you.

3. **Move the linux-2.6.XX source directory.** For the system and other kernel module compiles to recognize the source, you must set up the source code in the correct directory (`/usr/src/`) with a compatibility symlink set up also, like so:

```
# mv /usr/src/redhat/BUILD/kernel-2.6.XX/linux-2.6.XX
/usr/src
# ln -s /usr/src/linux-2.6.XX /usr/src/linux
```

Replace *XX* with your kernel's subversion. For example, my kernel is 2.6.11, so I would replace *XX* with 11.

4. **Download and decompress the latest lirc tarball.** You can try to use the lirc version that I have listed here if you want, but I recommend just going to the LIRC Web site at `http://lirc.org/` and downloading the latest:

```
# wget http://prdownloads.sourceforge.net/lirc/lirc-0.7.1.tar.bz2
# tar xjvf lirc-0.7.1.tar.bz2
```

The latest version of lirc may not be what apt-get gave you. I highly recommend downloading only the exact same source tarball version as the RPM that apt-get previously installed. If you're not sure what version this is, run `rpm -qa|grep lirc-[0-9]` to see the RPM version that your apt-get installed. Be sure to get that exact version of the tarball.

5. **Configure the package to compile.** Use the following commands:

```
# cd lirc
# ./setup.sh
```

Next, a text configuration GUI pops up. Use it to configure the following settings for the SilverStone/Soundgraph VFD unit. Make the following selections, by pressing the indicated numbers:

1) Driver

8) USB

0) Soundgraph iMON . . . IR/VFD

3) Save configuration and run configure

6. **Compile and install only the lirc_imon module.** Now change to the `driver/lirc_imon` directory and run `make` and `make install`:

```
# cd driver/lirc_imon
# make && make install
```

This installs only the single `lirc_imon` binary, and pops it into place here:

```
# ls -la /lib/modules/2.6.11-1.27_FC3/misc/lirc_imon.ko
-rw-r--r-- 1 root root 124114 Jun 21:53 /lib/modules/2.6.11-
1.27_FC3/misc/lirc_imon.ko
```

That's it. Now you can pick up where those not using the `lirc_imon` version left off.

Configuring Your lirc_xx/imon IR Driver

In the previous lirc sections, you should have been able to download and install your specific lirc_XX driver (whether the imon or other hardware module). Now you need to test it, set up the system to permanently use it, program in your specific remote control codes for your remote, and then configure the daemon to run.

1. **Test load your lirc_xx kernel module.** You should have installed your specific lirc_xx module. Now you need to test load it. The first step (if not already done) is to load the module with modprobe like this

   ```
   # modprobe lirc_imon
   # lsmod |grep imon
   lirc_imon        15748 0
   lirc_dev         13636 1 lirc_imon
   ```

   substituting whatever your specific module name is (lirc_ser, for example). Don't proceed if you encounter an error at this stage.

2. **See if lirc dev files are in place and are working.** Next, check to see that the loading of your kernel modules properly created your device files (assuming a udev- or devfs-based distribution such as Fedora):

   ```
   # ls -la /dev/lirc*
   crw------- 1 root root 61, 0 Jul 3 14:59 /dev/lirc
   crw------- 1 root root 61, 0 Jul 3 20:47 /dev/lirc0
   srw-rw-rw- 1 root root  0 Jul 3 14:58 /dev/lircd
   ```

3. **Test the receiving of IR input using irrecord.** This step uses a program called irrecord to do some testing of your IR input. Make sure that your IR receiver is in clear sight, and that you have your remote ready to use (the SilverStone LC-11m also comes with an included remote that I used in my examples). Set `irrecord` to dump its output out to a junk test file, and follow the directions, watching for the "..........." dot output to show you that the lirc system is at least working:

   ```
   # irrecord /tmp/xxx
   irrecord - application for recording IR-codes for usage with lirc
   Copyright (C) 1998,1999 Christoph Bartelmus (lirc@bartelmus.de)
   This program will record the signals from your remote control
   and create a config file for lircd.
   [...deleted...]
   Press RETURN to continue.
   ```

```
Hold down an arbitrary button.
. . . . . . . . . . . . . . . . . . . . . . . . . . . . . . . . . . . . . . . . . . . . . . . . . . . . . . . . . . . . . . . . .
Found gap length: 235985
Now enter the names for the buttons.
Please enter the name for the next button (press <ENTER> to finish recording)
```

That means that it worked. Press Ctrl+C to break the process.

Note

For more information and useful tips on everything from universal remotes, to thumb mouse remotes, and "punch through" issues, see the Linux HTPC hardware setup guide at www.linuxis.us/linux/media/howto/linux-htpc/.

4. **Program your /etc/lircd.conf for your remote.** To map your remote's buttons and IR codes to desired functions, you need to create your remote control's own unique `/etc/lircd.conf` file by starting up the irrecord program as shown, and following the directions for setting up the required conf file for your remote:

irrecord /etc/lircd.conf

Just follow the directions for reading your remote's codes into your new `lircd.conf` file. Be sure to give the buttons meaningful names (such as "vol+," "vol-," "Power," and "Eject"). Do this for every button (and Shift/function key presses if you have Shift/function keys) before finishing.

Note

If you are using the SilverStone case with its Soundgraph USB/VFR IR module, you can find the `/etc/lircd.conf` and other resources online for this hardware. Check out the MythTV page at LinuxToys.net for more information.

Tip

If you're running the SilverStone/Soundgraph VFD module, at this point (if your module is plugged into one of your USB ports) you should be able to echo messages out to it like this: `echo -n "Hello World" > /dev/lcd0` and get output to the VFD display. Cool, eh?

5. **Map lircd.conf functions to application keys.** When mythfrontend starts, it is going to look for a file called `~/.mythtv/lircrc` that will map specific LIRC/Remote functions to application-specific keys. I recommend downloading Jarod's template file from either `http://wilsonet.com/mythtv/lircrc-RS.txt` (`lircrc` file for his Radio Shack remote) or from his page on the subject: `http://wilsonet.com/mythtv/remotes.php`. Also check the LinuxToys.net Web site for the latest updates on recommended hardware and SilverStone-included remote.

Tip

Remember, the `lircd.conf` file (in `/etc/`) is required first to define what incoming IR maps to what remote buttons (function names) for your specific remote. You should probably generate your own because the same make/model remotes can sometimes change little things. Second, you need the `~/.lircrc` file and/or the `~/.mythtv/lircrc` file (in the mythtv user's home directory). This is the file that maps the lircd button functions that you have in your `/etc/lircd.conf` file to application-specific key hits. You can probably download a template file for your `.lircrc` file (from Jarod's site) and modify it yourself. I recommend having one file called `/home/mythtv/.lircrc` and making a symlink to it called `/home/mythtv/.mythtv/lircrc`.

6. **Load module via /etc/rc.d/rc.local.** I do not normally recommend using `rc.local` to load kernel modules, but in this case, it gives you much finer-grained control over the module and application timing than doing so anywhere else.

Order-wise in your `/etc/rc.d/rc.local` file, before starting MythTV or doing anything to the LCD in your `rc.local` file, put something like this:

```
echo "-Installing LIRC/iMON Drivers"
modprobe lirc_imon
echo -n " " >/dev/lcd0                    # Only if you have the VFD module
echo -n "MythTV 0.18   Hello World ;\)" >/dev/lcd0
sleep 3
```

This loads the lirc_XX driver (as well as lirc_dev) in the order that you want relative to the other actions you will be taking in the `rc.local` file. If you're using some other lirc_XX driver (lirc_serial, lirc_i2c, or the like), you can just ignore the `echo/lcd0` lines. That's for outputting text to the VFD.

7. **Configure the lirc daemon for startup and examination.** Turn on the lirc daemon, and check for all its related files, as well as your LCD interface:

```
# chkconfig --list lircd
lircd        0:off  1:off  2:off  3:off  4:off  5:off  6:off
# chkconfig lircd on
# chkconfig --list lircd
lircd        0:off  1:off  2:on   3:on   4:on   5:on   6:off
# /etc/init.d/lircd start
Starting infrared remote control daemon:              [ OK ]
# ls -la /dev/lirc*
crw------- 1 root root 61, 0 Jun 27 21:01 /dev/lirc
crw------- 1 root root 61, 0 Jun 27 21:01 /dev/lirc0
srw-rw-rw- 1 root root    0 Jun 27 23:43 /dev/lircd
```

Lirc Troubleshooting Tips

Here are a few troubleshooting tips that you may find useful.

- If issuing a `/etc/init.d/lircd start` gives you no `Starting... [OK]` output, immediately type **echo $?** afterward. If it returns a 1, then the daemon had a problem starting. You're either missing the lircd binary `/usr/sbin/lircd` or `lircmd`, or, most probably, a `/etc/lircd.conf` config file.

- Test lircd and your remote by running `irw` and pressing keys on your remote. If you get no output, you have a problem with either your specific lirc module, the auto-loaded lirc_dev kernel module is not getting loaded, or there is no good `/etc/lirc.conf` file in place. Again, you have to build an `/etc/lirc.conf` file yourself by using the command `irrecord /etc/lircd.conf` or nothing IR-related will work.

- After getting lircd working and verifying this by seeing output from testing with `irw`, you next need to grab someone's `mythtv/mplayer/xine ~/.lircrc` file and modify it to map your remote/lircd.conf button functions to application-specific keyboard hits, and then place your `.lircrc` file in the mythtv user's home directory. This is what mythfrontend looks for to be able to take IR input in place of user keyboard input. You can download a template file for `.lircrc` from Jarod's site. However, another nice GUI-based shortcut you may want to explore is the lircrc_config package. It gives you a GUI for setting up your `lircrc` file.

Configure the LCD Daemon (Optional)

If you're not using the front LCD or VFD for your own purposes (temperature, load, time, and so forth) and want MythTV to use the front VFD for channel, volume, status, and so on, you can download, install, and set up the LCDd (daemon) so that your MythTV can talk to your display (using `localhost:13666`).

Note If using the USB/VFD module, this section is not required to output raw messages to the VFD. When you compiled the lirc_imon kernel module, and did a `modprobe` install of it, that should have given you the character device file `/dev/lcdproc0` that you can echo messages to. The rest of this step is just setting up the LCDd (daemon) that MythTV looks for to output PVR data to.

And again, this command

```
# ls -la /dev/lcd0
crw------- 1 root root 180, 144 Jun 8 22:48 /dev/lcd0
```

shows that the lirc_imon driver you set up also includes support for the VFD (front display) on your SilverStone case (although note that only root can write to it at this point). If you have this VFD, as shown set up here, root will now be able to echo commands and raw information out via that device file. For example:

```
# echo -n " "> /dev/lcd0                              #clears the display
# echo -n "12345678901234567890123456789012"> /dev/lcd0   #fills all 32 chars
# echo -n "MythTV 0.018\n  Hello World..."> /dev/lcd0      #says hello
```

The LCDd service that mythfrontend (as the mythtv user) is expecting to see is used to output its PVR-related data to. Setting up the LCDd service is fairly straightforward. Just follow these steps.

1. **Get and install the LCDd package.** Download the VFD-ready version of the package like this:

```
# wget http://venky.ws/projects/imon/files/lcdproc-0.4.5-imon.tgz
```

or just see the LCDproc section of this page: http://venky.ws/projects/imon/ for the latest lcdproc tarball.

2. **Expand the LCDd package.** Untar the package:

```
# tar xzvf lcdproc-0.4.5-imon.tgz
```

3. **Configure and compile the LCDd package.** To do this, change to the specific lcdproc directory and configure and compile the package:

```
# cd lcdproc-0.4.5-imon
# ./configure
# make && make install
```

4. **Set up the configuration file.** First, copy the generic LCDd.conf file into place:

```
# cp LCDd.conf /etc
```

Note that LCD remains uppercase. Now edit the configuration file to use the proper imon driver (if using the SilverStone/Soundgraph VFD):

```
# vi /etc/LCDd.conf              #set the Driver line like this
    ...
    [server]
    # Server section with all kinds of settings for the LCDd server
    Driver=imon
    ...
```

5. **Set up the configuration init script.** Copy and set up the init script as follows:

```
# cp scripts/init-LCDd.rpm /etc/init.d/LCDd
# chmod 755 /etc/init.d/LCDd
```

Next, fix the etc variable in the /etc/init.d/LCDd init script to what you see here:

```
    ...
    prefix=/usr/local
    exec_prefix=${prefix}
    bindir=${exec_prefix}/bin
    sbindir=${exec_prefix}/sbin
    etc=/etc

    LCDd=${sbindir}/LCDd
    configfile=${etc}/LCDd.conf
    ...
```

If you want the LCDd service to come up after reboots, configure it to automatically turn on at boot time:

```
# chkconfig --add LCDd
# chkconfig --level 345 LCDd on
# chkconfig --list LCDd
LCDd       0:off  1:off  2:off  3:on  4:on  5:on  6:off
```

Note

Unless you are loading your LCD driver in modprobe.conf, you may not want to use chkconfig to auto-start your LCDd. Instead, you can simply issue a service LCDd start or /etc/init.d/LCDd start command in your rc.local file right after you load your display's kernel module. You can do this right after you run modprobe lirc_imon (which includes the driver for /dev/lcd0). (I show you this in the example /etc/rc.d/rc/local file later in the chapter.)

6. **Configure MythTV to use the LCD/VFD.** Mark this step to come back to later, after you have MythTV up and running and operational.

After MythTV is working and TV playback works, enter the MythTV GUI menu under the Setup area. In the Appearance/LCD device display section, enable the LCD/VFD display (they work the same whether using the VFD or an aftermarket LCD display) so that MythTV will send all of the user interaction feedback to the VFD/LCD display. This really adds a nice professional touch to your MythTV setup.

Installing and Setting up the ivtv Package and Drivers

This is the package that allows you to watch TV using your Hauppauge TV/capture card. The various components include the main kernel module as well as the packages for the mpeg-2 encoder, decoders, and audio drivers as well. Installing them is as easy as pie:

```
# apt-get update && apt-get ivtv-firmware-audio
# apt-get install ivtv-kmdl-$KVER
# apt-get install ivtv
```

After completing the preceding step, add the following lines to the bottom of your /etc/modprobe.conf file for your capture card and ivtv:

```
# Setup ivtv (PVR-500MCE)
alias char-major-81 videodev
alias char-major-81-0 ivtv      # First video device
alias char-major-81-1 ivtv      # Second video device
alias tveeprom tveeprom-ivtv

alias tuner tuner-ivtv
alias msp3400 msp3400-ivtv      # Audio codec for TV sound

## Added this to fix my specific tuner a/v probs
options ivtv tuner=57,57    # Only add this if static/wrong channels
```

```
options msp3400 once=1 simple=1  # Sound options
options cx25840 no_black_magic=1

# Not loading here...
#install ivtv /sbin/modprobe --ignore-install ivtv
     # To get ivtv working.. I prefer to have
     # modprobe load it from my rc.localfile.
```

The options ivtv tuner=*XX* line is what forces the kernel module to use a specific tuner chipset type for your specific capture card. Because my PVR-500MCE has two tuners of type 57, that's why you see =57,57 in my settings. Using this line overrides the autodetected settings, so do this only if you're getting all static on your output or your channels don't match what's on the screen. To find out what your specific type is, check through your /var/log/messages file like this:

```
# cat /var/log/messages|grep tuner: |grep "set to"|tail -1
Jul 2 14:30:22 myth kernel: tuner: type set to 57 (Philips FQ1236A MK4) by
insmod option
```

That's where I found my tuner type so I could set the options tuner type=*XX* line. Yours may be different.

Tip

If you need to research a capture card problem, I recommend searching the myth-user mail list for relevant information. You can do this quickly via the site-specific search keyphrase site: mythtv.org/pipermail/mythtv-users plus whatever keywords you're trying to look for. For example, to find tuner information for your tuner (a PVR-500 for example), you might type +site:mythtv.org/pipermail/mythtv-users +tuner +type +"PVR-500" into the search tool. Also, check out the searchable MythTV mail list archive at http://gossamer-threads.com/lists/mythtv/.

After setting up your modprobe.conf file, reboot and do an lsmod to see if everything loaded:

```
# lsmod |grep ivtv
ivtv           1331812 0
i2c_algo_bit      9033 1 ivtv
videodev          9665 1 ivtv
# ls -la /dev/video  lrwxrwxrwx 1 root root 6 Jun 27 21:01 /dev/video -> video0
```

As a quick test, you should be able to grab video from the /dev/video0 device to a file for a few seconds, and then watch the file with mplayer. Try this:

```
# cat /dev/video0 > /tmp/video-file      # hit CTRL-C to stop
# mplayer /tmp/video-file
```

Setting up FireWire

The following sections provide the details for setting up MythTV without a capture card, instead using FireWire coming in from a digital cable receiver to your MythTV.

Hardware Requirements

The hardware needed to capture TV with MythTV via FireWire is a FireWire port on your machine and a MythTV-supported cable receiver. At the time of this writing, the following cable receivers are supported by MythTV:

- Motorola DC6200
- Motorola DC6400
- Scientific Atlanta 3250

Only the Motorola DC6200 supports changing the channel via the FireWire cable on MythTV.

FireWire ports can be provided in different ways. They can be included on the PC's motherboard, on a sound card such as the Creative SoundBlaster Live series, or provided by a stand-alone FireWire PCI card. FireWire included on the motherboard is the most convenient method, as it requires no additional hardware.

Unfortunately, not all on-board FireWire devices are well supported in Linux or by the FireWire video capturing software for Linux. If your PC does not have on-board FireWire, or the on-board FireWire is not supported by Linux or by the capturing software, you should look to a PCI device to provide a FireWire port. Obviously, you don't want to purchase a sound card just to get a FireWire port if the PC already has a functional sound card. The majority of PCI FireWire cards work well with Linux and capturing software. Be sure when purchasing such a card that the vendor has a good return policy should the card not be supported.

Software Packages Needed

MythTV packages now include most of the needed software packages to use FireWire capturing as dependencies. However, one extra package, libiec61883-utils, must be installed by hand. This package provides some utilities to work with the FireWire video subsystem. This package can be installed with the following command:

```
# apt-get install libiec61883-utils
```

Loading Kernel Modules

First load the two base modules to work with the FireWire ports. These modules are named ieee1394 and ohci1394. Use the lsmod command as root to ensure that these are loaded:

```
# lsmod |grep 1394
ohci1394              39177  0
ieee1394             302873  1 ohci1394
```

In order to capture video through FireWire, the raw1394 kernel module must be loaded. However, before this module can be loaded you must first create two device entries. These are necessary to interact with the udev subsystem. To create the necessary device entries, issue these commands as root on the MythTV system:

```
# mknod /dev/raw1394 c 171 0
# mknod /etc/udev/devices/raw1394 c 171 0
```

After these device entries have been created, the raw1394 kernel module can be loaded as follows:

```
# modprobe raw1394
```

To ensure that this module loads properly after the system reboots, you must edit the /etc/ modprobe.conf file. Open this file in a text editor and add the following as one continuous line to the bottom of the file:

```
install ohci1394 /sbin/modprobe --ignore-install ohci1394;
/sbin/modprobe raw1394
```

Attaching the Cable Receiver

At this point, the cable receiver can be attached to the PC's FireWire port. Should there be multiple FireWire ports on either the PC or the cable receiver, it does not matter which of these ports is used. Ensure that the cable receiver is powered off and then connect both ends of the FireWire cable. Now the cable receiver can be powered up. The log file /var/log/ messages can be checked for contents similar to the following:

```
ieee1394: Host added: ID:BUS[0-00:1023]  GUID[0090a94000003380]
ieee1394: Node added: ID:BUS[0-01:1023]  GUID[000f9ffffea323c6]
ieee1394: raw1394: /dev/raw1394 device initialized
```

This means that the cable receiver was detected via the FireWire port and the raw capture device associated with it was initialized for use. If all has gone well, the next step is to scan for the device and test a capture.

Scanning for the Device and Testing a Capture

In order to capture content from the cable receiver, the system must know which FireWire port and node the receiver device is connected to. You can scan for this by using the plugreport utility. The following is output from plugreport on a system with a cable receiver attached to port 0, node 1:

```
# plugreport
Host Adapter 0
==============

Node 0 GUID 0x0090a94000003380
--------------------------------
libiec61883 error: error reading oMPR
libiec61883 error: error reading iMPR

Node 1 GUID 0x000f9ffffea323c6
--------------------------------
oMPR n_plugs=1, data_rate=2, bcast_channel=63
oPCR[0] online=1, bcast_connection=0, n_p2p_connections=1
     channel=0, data_rate=2, overhead_id=0, payload=376
iMPR n_plugs=0, data_rate=2
```

Seeing values for oMPR, oPCR, and iMPR under Node 1 tells you that the device is attached there. The port and node information will be needed for testing captures and configuring MythTV.

Testing captures can be done with the use of `test-mpeg2`. This utility can capture content directly from the FireWire node and redirect it to a file, which can then be played with MPlayer. First, tune the cable receiver to a known working station. Use the remote or the buttons on the receiver itself to change the channel. Next, using the node information from the `plugreport` output, use the following line to capture content:

```
$ test-mpeg2 -r 1 > testcap.ts
libiec61883 warning: Overlayed connection on channel 0.
You may need to manually set the channel on the receiving node.
Starting to receive
(hit ctrl-C)
done.
```

Press Ctrl+C to stop the capture.

Now the file can be viewed with `mplayer` to ensure proper capturing:

```
$ mplayer -vo xv testcap.ts
```

If the capture plays back correctly, the next step is configuring MythTV to use this device. If the capture does not play back correctly, review the preceding steps and ensure that the correct node is being used and that the cable receiver is receiving the cable signal correctly. This can be tested with a normal TV.

Fine-Grain Control of Drivers via /etc/rc.d/rc.local

Many people have problems getting all of their drivers and modules to load in the correct order. For example, this is a rough idea of the order in which you want things to load on a MythTV setup:

1. OS boot

2. MySQL server

3. i2c/lm_sensors modules and fan control

4. ivtv hardware drivers and related modules and settings

5. LCD/VFD kernel module/driver (lirc_imon in my case)

6. LCDd

7. mythbackend service

8. mythfrontend application (can start in KDE user space as the mythtv user)

Up to the point where the MySQL server starts, I allow my OS to load via the standard boot runlevel (`chkconfig` settings). But for the remaining items, I found it easier to get the precise timing control that I needed via the `/etc/rc.d./rc.local` file. Admittedly, this is a dirty way to handle the startup of any package; however, it works in a pinch if you can't quite get your `/etc/init.d/` files all working smoothly and playing nice with the other required daemons (lirc, LCDd, backend, and so on). My startup `rc.local` file looks like this:

```
#!/bin/sh
#
# This script will be executed *after* all the other init scripts.
# You can put your own initialization stuff in here if you don't
# want to do the full Sys V style init type control dance.

touch /var/lock/subsys/local

echo "--------Running rc.local--------"
## TWW: First, set up motherboard specific i2c drivers and lm_sensors & fans
echo "-Setting up i2c drivers and fan control"
modprobe i2c-nforce2
modprobe i2c-isa
# I2C chip drivers
modprobe eeprom
modprobe w83627hf        # from sensors-detect, just for my motherboard..
# sleep 2 # optional
/usr/bin/sensors -s        # recommended
echo 40 > /sys/bus/i2c/devices/2-0290/pwm2 # Playing with fan speeds
sleep 2 # optional
echo 240 > /sys/bus/i2c/devices/2-0290/pwm2
sleep 1
echo 200 > /sys/bus/i2c/devices/2-0290/pwm2 # The final speed I want
echo
## TWW: Putting ivtv here and restarting mythbackend further down
echo "-Installing IVTV Vid.Card Drivers..."
/sbin/modprobe ivtv tuner=57,57
echo
## TWW: My VFD/LIRC Driver, and LCDd service startup
echo "-Installing my VFD & LIRC/iMON Drivers"
modprobe lirc_imon
echo -n " " >/dev/lcd0
echo -n "MythTV 0.18   Hello World ;\)" >/dev/lcd0
sleep 3
/etc/init.d/LCDd restart
## TWW: Here's where I restart the mythbackend to properly bind to ivtv
echo "-Restarting Mythbackend"
/etc/init.d/mythbackend restart
echo "-Done"
```

A Final Look at /etc/modules.conf

As I've indicated throughout this chapter, the `/etc/modprobe.conf` file is as centrally important to your setup as is the `rc.local` file, as it contains all the kernel module configuration information that mythbackend and the other parts of the system need to be able to talk to your hardware. Here's the `/etc/modprobe.conf` that I built:

```
## TWW: Everything in this section is from my stock OS install
alias eth0 forcedeth
alias scsi_hostadapter sata_nv
alias snd-card-0 snd-intel8x0
options snd-card-0 index=0
```

```
install snd-intel8x0 /sbin/modprobe --ignore-install snd-intel8x0
&&
/usr/sbin/alsactl restore >/dev/null 2>&1 || :
remove snd-intel8x0 { /usr/sbin/alsactl store >/dev/null 2>&1 || :
; };
/sbin/modprobe -r --ignore-remove snd-intel8x0
alias usb-controller ehci-hcd
alias usb-controller1 ohci-hcd

## TWW: Here is what I've added for my specific system thus far
# I2C module options
alias char-major-89 i2c-dev

# nvidia kernel module
alias char-major-195 nvidia-1_0-7174
alias nvidia nvidia-1_0-7174

# Setup ivtv (PVR-500MCE)
alias char-major-81 videodev
alias char-major-81-0 ivtv
alias char-major-81-1 ivtv
alias tveeprom tveeprom-ivtv
alias tuner tuner-ivtv
alias msp3400 msp3400-ivtv
## Added this to fix tuner a/v probs
options ivtv tuner=57,57         # New usage
install ivtv /sbin/modprobe --ignore-install ivtv
options msp3400 once=1 simple=1
# Setup if using FireWire
#install ohci1394 /sbin/modprobe --ignore-install
ohci1394;/sbin/modprobe
raw1394
```

Now that you have all the hardware driver issues taken care of, you're ready to follow through with the last of the MythTV configuration settings, the actual configuring of MythTV and various other related services.

Configuring and Testing MythTV

Now that you have MythTV installed and the drivers in place, you need to do the following before you can use MythTV:

- Configure the MySQL database for MythTV use
- Register your MythTV's channel data service with zap2it.com (aka "DataDirect")
- Configure MythTV backend and startup
- Configure MythTV frontend and startup
- Make KDE-specific adjustments

Configuring MySQL Server for MythTV

Follow these steps to prepare and configure MySQL Server for MythTV:

1. Check that you have MySQL server installed and ready to go:

```
# rpm -qa|grep ^mysql
mysql-3.23.58-16.FC3.1
mysql-devel-3.23.58-16.FC3.1
mysql-server-3.23.58-16.FC3.1
```

   Although your versions may differ, make sure that your packages appear to be installed. Also verify that the mysqld service is set to be on at reboot time, and start it:

```
# chkconfig mysqld on
# chkconfig --list mysqld
mysqld     0:off  1:off  2:on  3:on  4:on  5:on  6:off
# /etc/init.d/mysqld start
Starting MySQL:                       [ OK ]
```

2. Next, set MySQL's database root password to something that you will not forget (I recommend making it the same as the system's root password):

```
# mysql -u root mysql
mysql> UPDATE user SET Password=PASSWORD('ROOT_PWD') WHERE user='root';
mysql> FLUSH PRIVILEGES;
mysql> quit
```

   Change *ROOT_PWD* to what you want your MySQL database password to be.

3. Next, import the starter MythTV database into MySQL:

```
# mysql -u root -p < /usr/share/doc/mythtv-0.18.1/database/mc.sql
ERROR 1064 at line 4: You have an error in your SQL syntax near 'TEMPORARY
TABLES ON
mythconverg.* TO mythtv@localhost IDENTIFIED BY "mythtv"' at line 1
```

   Enter the MySQL root password that you just set. The error 1064 at line 4 is fine. You can ignore this if you see it. (Fedora Core4/MySQL4 and newer should not show this error.)

4. Now you need to make some slight changes in the mysql server settings as well as to the client side. The main server configuration file is /etc/my.cnf. Edit this file and change the contents under the [mysqld] section to roughly match the following for MySQL 3.23 (stock in Fedora Core 3):

```
[mysqld]
datadir=/var/lib/mysql
socket=/var/lib/mysql/mysql.sock
### Mythtv Adjustmests for MySQL 3.23 ###
set-variable = key_buffer = 16M
set-variable = table_cache = 128
set-variable = sort_buffer = 2M
set-variable = myisam_sort_buffer_size = 8M
```

If you're running Fedora Core 4 or newer, you're probably running MySQL 4.*x*, and will want to use the following additions instead:

```
[mysqld]
datadir=/var/lib/mysql
socket=/var/lib/mysql/mysql.sock
###Mythtv Adjustmests for MySQL 4.x ###
key_buffer = 16M
table_cache = 128
sort_buffer_size = 2M
myisam_sort_buffer_size = 8M
query_cache_size = 16M
```

5. Next, restart the MySQL server like this:

```
# /etc/init.d/mysqld restart
Stopping MySQL:                          [ OK ]
Starting MySQL:                          [ OK ]
```

Now you're ready to set up the online channel data service so that you can get all of your local channel listings.

Setting up the DataDirect Channel Listing Service

DataDirect is a free Internet-based channel listing service hosted by zap2it.com. It's a mostly free service that you get in three-month chunks for occasionally filling out their electronic surveys. This is the new way in which MythTV gets its channel listings. The old way, a setup that went down every time they changed the look and feel of their Web interface, hinged on libcurl and screen scraping. So this new DataDirect-based service is a real godsend.

Subscribing to DataDirect

To join the free (as in money) service, you just need your postal zip code and a few minutes free (and an Internet connection, of course). If the following instructions don't work, then something at MythTV has probably changed. If the service stops working as described here, refer to either the MythTV guide at `http://mythtv.org/docs/mythtv-HOWTO-5.html#ss5.3` or `http://labs.zap2it.com/` for updated information.

1. First, point a Web browser at `http://labs.zap2it.com/` and click New User? Sign-Up. Read the license agreement and click Accept.

2. On the Subscription Registrations screen, enter the Certificate Code from the MythTV.org HOWTO at

`www.mythtv.org/docs/mythtv-HOWTO-5.html#ss5.30`

3. Fill out the survey and click Submit.

4. Move on to the Lineup Wizard and plug in your zip code and cable provider, and start selecting the channels that you receive with whatever cable/provider package that you have (see Figure 4-5). (Remember to write down your user name/password for this zap2it.com service, as you will be poking this into your MythTV configuration so that it can pull down the channel listings every night over the Internet.)

Note Shows listed with a dash (-) are HD. If you're not doing an HD Myth box, don't select the HD channels.

FIGURE 4-5: Selecting your channel data on Zap2it's Lineup Wizard

Note If you do not have an always-on Internet connection, or can't at least start a modem PPP dial-up connection at night from your MythTV box, you may still be able to get things to work. But the system won't be as fully functioning as an always-on connected MythTV box would be.

Creating Needed Directories under /video/

Before you run the actual `mythtvsetup` program, you need to create some directories that the mythbackend service needs to store the large files that will be put on the drive as you start watching TV and recording content.

1. As the root user, create the following directories under your mounted `/video/` file system directory with the file/directory permissions of 777 on each directory like this

```
# mkdir /video/buffer ; chmod 777 /video/buffer
# mkdir /video/mythmusic ; chmod 777 /video/mythmusic
# mkdir /video/.mythtv ; chmod 777 /video/.mythtv
...
```

until you have the following directories under the `/video/` directory:

```
drwxrwxrwx  2 root    root     48 Jul 5  17:24 buffer
drwxrwxrwx  2 root    root     48 Jun 13 21:48 mythmusic
drwxrwxrwx  7 mythtv  mythtv  416 Jul 4  05:09 .mythtv
drwxrwxrwx  3 root    root     80 Jun 14 00:20 pictures
drwxrwxrwx  2 root    root    672 Jul 5  17:00 recordings
drwxrwxrwx  2 root    root     48 Jun 13 23:54 .tmp
drwxrwxrwx  2 root    root     48 Jul 1  00:16 videos
```

This will create the directories that myth needs, and allow the mythtv user full access into them.

2. Before continuing, log in as mythtv user (you don't need X yet), and set up the following symlink from `/home/mythtv/.mythtv` to `/video/.mythtv`:

```
$ ln -s /video/.mythtv/ /home/mythtv/.mythtv
$ ls -la /home/mythtv/.mythtv
lrwxrwxrwx 1 mythtv mythtv 15 Jun 13 21:35
/home/mythtv/.mythtv -> /video/.mythtv/
```

This is where mythfrontend will store all of its settings. And because it's actually located on your data array (`/video`), you have to back up only that one file system to get most of your content (if you decide to implement data backups).

Mythbackend Setup and Startup

For this stage of the configuration, you need to have X up and running. Open the MythTV setup GUI by running the command `mythtvsetup`. That will drop you into the main MythTV setup GUI, with the setup menu options:

- General
- Capture Cards
- Video Sources
- Input
- Channel Editor

General

Under the general settings for the mythtv backend, adjust the settings as follows:

- Host Address Backend Setup:
  - IP address: **127.0.0.1**
  - Port server runs on: **6543**
  - Port server shows status on: **6544**

- Master Server IP address: **127.0.0.1**
- Port master server runs on: **6543**

- Host-specific Backend Setup
  - Directory to hold recordings: **/video/recordings**
  - Directory to hold the Live-TV buffers: **/video/buffer**
  - *Leave remaining default settings*

- Global Backend Setup
  - TV Format: **NTSC** *(or your country's standard)*
  - Channel frequency label: **us-cable** *(or your country/provider's standard)*
  - *Leave remaining default settings*

- Shutdown/Wakeup Options
  - *Leave default settings*

- Wake On LAN settings
  - *Leave default settings*

- Job Queue (host, global, and Job Commands)
  - *Leave default settings*

Capture Cards

Under the Capture Cards menu, click (New capture card) and set the options as follows:

- Capture Card Setup
  - Card Type: **MPEG-2 Encoder card (PVR-250/350)** *or enter your card type*
  - Video device: /dev/video0
  - Default Input: **Tuner 0**

If you are using a second capture card, or are using the recommended PVR-500MCE dual-tuner card, continue and enter another set of capture card settings by clicking the (New capture card) option for the second tuner and setting the options as follows:

- Capture Card Setup
  - Card Type: **MPEG-2 Encoder card (PVR-250/350)** *or enter your card type*
  - Video device: **/dev/video1**
  - Default Input: **Tuner 1**

Note If you create a capture card that you want to get rid of, you can delete the entry by pressing **d**.

FireWire for Input

If you don't have a capture card and are using FireWire for your input, you need to use the following capture device settings:

- Capture Card Setup
    - Card Type: **FireWire Input**
    - FireWire Model: **DCT-6200**
    - FireWire Connection Type: **Point to Point**
    - FireWire Port: **0**
    - FireWire Node: **2**
    - FireWire Speed: **200Mbps**
    - Default Input: **MPEG2TS**

Note FireWire Model references the type of cable receiver you have attached to your FireWire port. At the time of this writing, the only two options are DCT-6200 and Other. If you select DCT-6200, the internal channel changing system will be used to change channels through FireWire.

Video Sources

Next, define the names and variables of your video provider sources, and map their XML TV listings to the MythTV interfaces. You need an Internet connection for this process. Click (New video source) and enter the following:

- Video source setup:
    - Video source name: **Cable-1** *(for example)*
    - XMLTV listing grabber: **North America (DataDirect)** *(or your country's service)*
    - User ID: *service user name*
    - User Password: *service password*

For *service user name* and *service password*, enter the user name and password you created when you signed up for the Zap2it service. Select Retrieve Lineups to auto-populate the rest of the form with your Linux details and your channel frequency setting.

Inputs

This section defines what MythTV should take as input from which physical sources. For example, the video device /dev/video0, paired with Tuner0, has its content associated with the provider stream channels of Cable-1 listings, or /dev/video1 paired with S-Video 1 and a DSS video source with its own external channel changing commands, and so on. This step may vary quite a bit depending on your specific video source setup (e.g., analog cable versus DSS dish).

With my MythTV setup, and for cheap basic cable, the configured setup is:

```
[MPEG : /dev/video0 ] (Tuner 0) -> Cable-1
[MPEG : /dev/video1 ] (Tuner 1) -> Cable-1
```

In other words, both of my usable video inputs are dedicated to the RF tuners on my single PVR-500MCE, whose signal (and channel data) is paired with the Cable-1 source.

Channel Editor

The channel editor allows you to associate specific channel names with different video sources. For example, I could have cable channels 2–66 associated with my Cable-1 video source and another range of channels with a different video source called DSS-1 for my dish. I could then have yet another single channel VCR that takes input from the video source called VCR-1 (for dubbing VHS tapes to VCDs or DVDs).

I recommend leaving this area alone until you get a feel for how your setup works, and what you might like the channels and various inputs to be dedicated to in your given system.

That's it for the various mythtvsetup settings. Press Esc to get out of the GUI.

Downloading Program Guide Data for the Backend

Now that you have all the settings plugged in, you need to store these settings in the mythbackend database (actually, the database name is mythconverg). To accomplish this, you need a live Internet connection. You start the mythbackend service, and then use the mythfilldatabase command sequence to populate the mythbackend system with its initial channel data and settings, like this:

```
# /etc/init.d/mythbackend start
Starting mythbackend:                   [ OK ]
# mythfilldatabase
```

It may run for several minutes as it pulls down your channel listings and populates the database.

Next, you can automate a nightly program listing download using mythfilldatabase so that your channel listing data is updated regularly from the online listing provider. This is most easily done by setting up a cron job for the mythtv user. To do this, log in as the mythtv user, type **crontab -e,** and it will throw you into a vi editor. Type **i** to go into insert mode, and then type the following (all on one line):

```
01 3 * * * sleep $(expr $RANDOM \% 14400) && mythfilldatabase >
   /var/log/mythtv/mythfilldatabase.log 2>&1
```

Note MythTV now has this nightly download feature built in so you can set it up from within the user interface's setup GUI and not worry about typos.

If you get lost, hit a wrong key, or the keyboard stops responding, press ESC a few times, press the i key to begin inserting text again. When you get it typed in, press ESC a couple of times, and then hold down Shift and press Z twice. This will save the file, and every night at around 3 a.m. it will auto-update the listings database.

Note Zap2it is providing the community this free service, and requests that people try to not schedule downloads at or around midnight. Please honor their wishes. Thank you, Zap2it folks! Also, if for some reason you stop using the MythTV project from this computer, be sure to remove the cron job so the updates don't continue.

Mythbackend Startup Automation

Now that you have the basic backend setup taken care of, start the mythbackend service either with chkconfig or via the /etc/rc.d/rc.local file. If you have been following the directions in the chapter, you probably have your mythbackend service starting toward the end of your rc.local file already, so you should be set. Or you could type the following:

```
# chkconfig mythbackend on
```

Mythfrontend Setup and Startup

The mythfrontend system can be a little picky with a stock KDE configuration. For example, KDE likes to take over control of the Open Sound System–based audio system, and not let anything it doesn't know about use the sound I/O system. In addition, getting MythTV to come up automatically and correctly can be a problem. So here are some solutions.

KDE Settings for mythfrontend

This section covers three main steps: First, make sure that KDE is the default display manager, as well as the default desktop. Next, enable auto-login (without password) for the mythtv user. Finally, you need to disable KDE's hijacking of the audio subsystem.

1. To make KDE the default desktop is easy. Simply log in as root; edit the file /etc/sysconfig/desktops, changing the desktop variable to "KDE"; and enter the variable for DISPLAYMANAGER like this:

   ```
   DESKTOP="KDE"
   DISPLAYMANAGER="KDE"
   ```

   With this in place, type **init 3** to back out of X and into runlevel 3, and then type **init 5** to kick back into X with the KDE display manager (login GUI).

   Log in to X as the mythtv user, as you will be making the other KDE changes through the KDE desktop and Control Center.

2. To make KDE auto-login the mythtv user, open the KDE Control Center by opening the Red Hat menu and clicking Control Center. Once there, expand the System Administration group. Click on the Login Manager, and then on the Administrator Mode button at the bottom. The system will immediately ask you for the system's root password. Type it in. Next, click the Shutdown tab and verify that the Allow Shutdown Local: field reads Everybody. Click Apply.

Click the Convenience tab and make selections to match those shown in Figure 4-6:

- Select the Enable password-less logins and Enable auto-login check boxes.

- Under "No password required for:" select mythtv.

- From the Preselect User choices, choose the mythtv user from the list.

- Farther down in this window (not shown) select the "Miscellaneous: Automatically log in again after X server crash" option.

Click Apply.

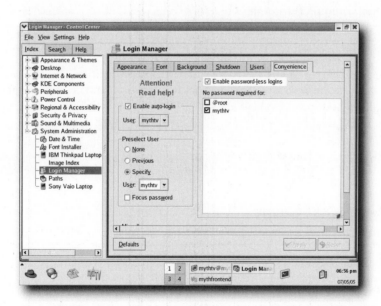

FIGURE 4-6: Set up auto-login for the mythtv user within KDE Control Center

3. To stop KDE from taking over the sound I/O system, go to the Control Center's Sound & Multimedia group and click the Sound System tool. On the General tab, clear the Enable the sound system check box, and then click Apply.

4. To ensure that the mouse will always work correctly as the MythTV frontend system pulls up and closes down multimedia child apps, open the Desktop group in the KDE Control Center. Then click the Window Behavior tool, and within the Focus tab, in the pull-down list, ensure that Focus Follows Mouse is selected. Don't forget to click Apply.

5. To ensure that the proper apps pop up every time, click the KDE Components group, and then click the Session Manager tool. Within that window, click the radio button for "Restore manually saves session," and then click Apply.

6. To ensure that the screensaver doesn't pop up in the middle of your favorite movie, click the Appearance & Themes group, and from there the Screen Saver tool. Clear the Start Automatically check box, click Apply, and close down the KDE Control Center. You should now be set.

7. Log out of KDE, and when the login GUI appears, press Ctrl+Alt+Backspace (not Delete). This will kill and restart X, as well as the login display manager. When X restarts, it should auto-log you into KDE. Make sure that this is working before continuing.

KDE Autostarting mythfrontend

To ensure that mythfrontend (the GUI) always pops up correctly (in front of all other windows), press Alt+F2 to get a Run Command pop-up window. When it pops up, in the command field, type **mythfrontend** and verify that the mythfrontend interface pops up. Don't get distracted by all the cool MythTV GUI stuff. Instead, immediately press the Windows key (or Alt+F1) to pull up the Red Hat desktop menu. Click Save Session. This saves all applications currently running, and their positions on the desktop (with myth on top).

To test everything that you've just done, still logged in and with mythtvfrontend running, press Ctrl+Alt+Backspace. As a result, mythfrontend, KDE, and X should all be killed. X should respawn, KDE should auto-log you in, and mythfrontend should start. Smooth as silk. If it does not, go back and step through each of the mythfrontend set and startup steps again, checking your work.

Mythfrontend Audio Settings

To ensure that MythTV now controls the OSS audio and mixer controls on the system, run mythfrontend, and navigate down into Utilities/Setup ➜ Setup. Press Enter three times to get to the Audio setup screen. Be sure that you have the correct audio output device selected (usually /dev/dsp), and if you're using a digital audio/SPDIF output from your PVR to your amp, check that you have "Enable AC3 to SPDIF passthrough" enabled. For the rest of the audio settings, ensure that you have "Use internal volume controls" selected, that you have the correct mixed device (usually /dev/mixer), and that the Mixer Controls are set to PCM.

MythTV Testing

You're probably eager to check things out by now. If you can reboot and everything comes up and the mythfrontend GUI is on the front screen and you can move the menu selections around with the arrow keys, you're halfway there.

Select Watch TV and check whether you get your channels. If you get a black screen, an error message about your /dev/video0 device, or snow or the like, and everything is hooked up correctly, you probably have some type of tuner/capture card problem.

Tip

Having problems? Look in `/var/log/`messages as you start MythTV frontend. You can often resolve problems by looking for key error messages there, and then using an Internet search engine to search for the text of the error message.

FireWire Testing

Testing MythTV for FireWire is just like testing it for any other input method. Go to Watch TV and tune to a channel to test the connection; you should see live TV content. Change channels to test the internal channel changing via FireWire if a supported device is being used. If things are not working as expected, you may need to do some troubleshooting.

Problems using FireWire with MythTV will either be with the cable receiver, the MythTV system, or with the FireWire cable itself. Here are a couple of suggestions for handling possible problems with FireWire.

- **Cable receiver** — Because replacing the cable is easy, that troubleshooting step is fairly obvious. On the cable receiver, check that the receiver is actually receiving video content and is able to display this content by other means than FireWire. It is also possible that the FireWire ports on the cable receiver are not functional. If this is the case, replacing the cable receiver with one with active FireWire port(s) would be the appropriate action. Ask your cable provider for a unit with operational FireWire ports.

- **MythTV system** — Problems not related to the cable receiver or FireWire cable can be attributed to the MythTV system. These problems could be anything from the FireWire ports on the PC itself to a misconfiguration within MythTV. Start with the easiest-to-fix possibility and work backward to avoid time-intensive steps. Triple-check all configuration information. Re-verifying the port and node information using the `plugreport` and testing captures with `test-mpeg2` can help you verify connectivity to the cable receiver. Checking `/var/log/messages` and `lsmod` output can help you determine whether the FireWire ports in the PC are detected and functional. Finally, stepping through all the setup instructions one more time may lend a clue to where the failure may be.

Tricks and Tips

MythTV is great, but it still has a few little quirks that evolve, appear, and disappear over time. Here are a few tricks and tips to help you get the most out of your new setup. If you need to get to a shell or menu outside of MythTV, press Ctrl+Tab. Select a different desktop (four are available by default), do the steps you need, then return to MythTV by selecting Ctrl+Tab again and selecting Desktop 1.

Problems with DVD Menus

The default media player for MythTV (MPlayer) does not support DVD menus. After searching various forums, and finally landing back on Jarod's page, I found that while MPlayer could not yet support DVD menus, xine does. To fix this problem, go into the mythfrontend setup, down into the DVD settings, and change the player line

```
mplayer dvd:// -dvd-device %d -fs -zoom -vo xv
```

to this:

```
xine -pfhq --no-splash dvd://
```

That will not only give you DVD menus, but allow you to control every aspect of DVD playback, plus an amazing set of frame advance, zoom, and slow motion controls . . . all of which work even in the DVD menus themselves! You can't do *that* with a store-bought DVD player!

Problems with Removable CD/DVDs

KDE is nice, but it can be annoying too. Sometimes you'll pop a CD in and KDE will see that it has content and mount it, and not allow the MythTV app to eject it. Once again, Jarod's guide to the rescue. Logged into KDE as the mythtv user, just nuke KDE's autorun feature for the desktop media, like this:

```
$ rm ~/.kde/Autostart/Autorun.desktop
```

And all your problems should go away.

Email Notification of Problems

Just like any other Linux system, when a RAID device fails, or there are file system or hardware errors, your MythTV will try to email the administrator of the server. As with any Linux system, email for all parts of the system goes to the root user. You can set the local root user's email address to be aliased somewhere else, either on or off the box, by editing the /etc/aliases file and changing the root user's email address like this:

```
# vim /etc/aliases
...
# Person who should get root's mail
root:           tweeks@example.com

...
```

Then just recreate the aliases db (the binary file that's built from the file that you just edited) as follows:

```
# newaliases
```

Now when there's a system RAID problem (such as a failed drive), you start running out of space, or the system has some other problem, you'll get an email about it. I wonder if Microsoft Media Center does that!?

Tastes Great and Less Filling!

Using the built-in MP2 encoder hardware in your PVR-xx0 card is a double-edged sword. It's nice in that it really frees up some serious bus bandwidth and CPU power as all the raw video to file compression is done on the capture card itself. However, the MP2 format is lower quality and takes up more space.

One trick to keep the quality high (tastes great) and space to a minimum (less filling) is to record in higher-resolution/quality settings for all of your programs to get the higher-quality master copy to disk. Then turn around and use the MythTV transcoder, which (after marking/stripping commercials) will re-encode for MP4 file format, discarding the old MP2 file after it's done. Details on setting this can be found at `http://mythtv.org/docs/mythtv-HOWTO-22.html#ss22.14`.

Wireless MythTV?

Yes, you can run a MythTV backend in a house over wireless to multiple Myth frontend player units. However, doing so over 802.11b (11 Mbps) is simply not feasible. You should run at least 802.11g or 54 Mbps if you actually expect to watch programs.

Verify that you have good signal strength and connection speeds and that appliances such as microwave ovens and 2.4 GHz wireless phones are not killing your connectivity. However, some people have problems getting smooth MythTV playback even over 54 Mbps. If this is true for you, make sure that other household appliances such as microwaves, cordless phones, or even a neighbor's wireless LAN isn't interfering with your wireless system. In some environments, the speed will get auto-negotiated down below usable levels. This is just the nature of high-speed WiFi.

Watching System Load and CPU Temperature

When you're first trying to get all the kinks worked out of your new PVR system, the last thing that you want to do is fry your new motherboard/CPU and components! I strongly recommend setting up a monitoring script on one of your virtual terminals that will let you keep an eye on the system when it's under full load to be sure that you're not slowly frying it. Additionally, you really don't want to walk away from the system and leave it simmering if you have not stress tested it to see how hot the system gets.

Normally you don't have to worry about frying your average desktop the first time you leave *it* alone, right? Well the point here is that if you want to truly create a home theater system, you need one that's quiet. And quiet means running CPU and system fans as slow as you can get away with — running them at a fraction of their normal speed. To do this safely, you must monitor your system (I recommend a week of watching) before trusting it enough to leave it on and toasting all the time.

To aid you in this temperature-testing quest, here's a short and simple script.

```
#!/bin/bash
## watchsys.sh
```

```
## Thomas Weeks
## Wiley Publishing 2005 (C)

watch --no-title 'echo "                       o----------Temp & Fan-----------o" ; \
sensors -f|grep -A1 "CPU T" ; echo;echo "                  o---------Load, \
CPU/RAM & PIDs--------------o" ; top -bn 1 |head -15'
```

Create the directory /home/mythtv/bin/ and poke this script in. Then set it up to run in one of your virtual terminals. Here's what the output looks like:

```
            o----------Temp & Fan-----------o
CPU Temp: +113.9F (high = +127F, hyst = +122F)  sensor = diode
Under CPU:+123.8F (high = +176F, hyst = +167F)  sensor = thermistor


            o---------Load, CPU/RAM & PIDs--------------o
top - 01:35:09 up 11:15, 5 users, load average: 0.89, 0.78, 0.69
Tasks: 105 total,  1 running, 104 sleeping,  0 stopped,  0 zombie
Cpu(s): 4.2% us, 1.0% sy, 1.7% ni, 91.2% id, 1.4% wa, 0.5% hi, 0.0% si
Mem:  1003060k total,  989068k used,  13992k free,  20220k buffers
Swap: 1052152k total,   304k used, 1051848k free,  785576k cached

 PID USER    PR NI VIRT RES SHR S %CPU %MEM  TIME+ COMMAND
11017 mythtv  15  0 208m 66m 30m S 9.9 6.8  6:51.20 mythfrontend
 9238 root    15  0 68620 29m 14m S 2.0 3.0  1:14.72 X
    1 root    16  0 1688 548 476 S 0.0 0.1  0:01.06 init
    2 root    34 19   0   0   0 S 0.0 0.0  0:00.03 ksoftirqd/0
    3 root    10 -5   0   0   0 S 0.0 0.0  0:00.24 events/0
    4 root    10 -5   0   0   0 S 0.0 0.0  0:00.01 khelper
    9 root    10 -5   0   0   0 S 0.0 0.0  0:00.00 kthread
   18 root    20 -5   0   0   0 S 0.0 0.0  0:00.00 kacpid
```

This is a great way to get a feel for your system.

Watching Temperature, Load, Time, and Capacity on Your LCD/VFD

This is a nice little trick that I used while monitoring system load and temperature levels, while being able to continue to watch my programs on the tube. To do this yourself, just take the last script idea and trim its output down a bit. You can format it to fit your 16×2 ASCII display, shut off the LCDd daemon (so that you can get write access to /dev/lcd0), and now you, too, can watch your system in real time via the front VFD display. Here's the script that I threw together to temporarily run in the background from the rc.local file:

```
#!/bin/bash
## lcd-show.sh
## Thomas Weeks
## for Wiley Publishing 2005 (c)

while true;  do
        TEMP=$(sensors -f|grep 'CPU T'|tr -s [:blank:]|tr \
```

```
                 [:blank:] ' '|cut -f3 -d ' '|grep -o [0-9\.]|tr \\n \\000)F
        LOAD=$(uptime |tr -s [:blank:] |cut -f3 -d','|grep -o [0-9\.]|\
           tr \\n \\000)
        VIDEO=$(df -h|grep video|tr -s [:blank:]|tail -1|cut -f5 -d' ')
        TIME=$(uptime |tr -s [:blank:] |cut -f2 -d" "|cut -f1,2 -d':')
        LCDOUT="T=$TEMP LD=$LOAD VID=$VIDEO $TIME"
        #FOR TESTING
        #echo $LCDOUT
        #echo 123456789012345612345678901234 56
        echo -n "  " >/dev/lcd0
        echo -n $LCDOUT > /dev/lcd0
        sleep 30
```

This little script simply dumps the following variables out to the case from the VFD or LCD display unit:

```
        T=115.7F,L=1.17,
        VID=5% 02:16:31
```

Simple, nice, and useful. For more LCD/VFD display fun, check out the `mythtvosd` command.

> **Tip**
>
> Don't have a nice front VF display or LCD? Want an aftermarket display? Check out some of the LCDs and VFDs that can be had at Matrix Orbital (`www.matrixorbital.com`). Most of these serial and USB displays now have support in Linux!

Using MythTV Frontend from Anywhere

Want to be able to watch your MythTV from anywhere in the house? Check out the Live CD distro called KnoppMyth! It's a live Linux CD distribution that you boot a machine from, and it can function as a MythTV frontend. This means that you simply point it to your MythTV backend (server) and *voilà*! You have all of your backend content, anywhere in the house that you can get a wired (or wireless) connection! For more info, see `http://mysettopbox.tv/knoppmyth.html`.

Other Troubleshooting Resources

Jarod's guide has a great set of Tricks and Tips at `http://wilsonet.com/mythtv/tips.php`.

Try Brandon Beattie's HTPC/MythTV HOWTO at `www.linuxis.us/linux/media/howto/linux-htpc/`.

Other useful troubleshooting tips can be found on the MythTV site at `http://mythtv.org/docs/mythtv-HOWTO-21.html#ss21.4`.

And while you're at it, you should at least browse through the documentation at `http://mythtv.org/docs/`.

Summary

Building your own MythTV media center can be a daunting task, but one that will give you a much more powerful and useful media center than anything that is currently on the market.

Step by step, I showed you how to take off the shell components and build your own Linux-based PVR media center system. With your MythTV project up and running, you can begin watching television, recording video, playing music, and managing digital images.

MythTV is much more than just another PVR. It really does change the way you watch TV and interact with streaming information sources such as news and weather. And it even gives you a video game console and digital photo album. MythTV gets you all this audio/video resource convergence, but still allows you remote access to those resources from anywhere on the network. Because a MythTV system is a full-blown (and powerful) computer system, you can hook up devices such as photo printers, scanners, faxes, answering systems, home automation hardware and software, motion detection cameras, and more.

By building your own MythTV media center, not only do you get some of the coolest, most cutting-edge multimedia convergence technology all in one box, you also learn a lot about multimedia and real-time technologies on Linux. Not to mention that you'll also bowl over all your friends by showing them the sleek, cool side of what Linux can do.

Making Bootable Movies with eMoviX

If you are like me and do all your video recording in Linux, you may wonder how you can share the TV shows, personal videos, and other multimedia content with friends and family who don't use Linux. How can you get the video from your hard disk to the people you care about in a way that you know they can play it?

Well, instead of just hoping they have a way to play your favorite video format, why not give them your home movie with a player that you know can play it? In fact, why not give them the whole operating system with it so you know that your player will run?

What I'm talking about here are bootable movies. Using eMoviX (a special version of the MoviX[2] multimedia Linux distribution), you can create a CD or DVD image that contains:

> **Video files** — You can put as much video content as will fit on the bootable CD or DVD. You can also add music files (MP3 and Ogg Vorbis are supported) or other types of content that can be played by the MPlayer media player included with eMoviX.

> **eMoviX** — This micro Linux distribution is geared specifically for playing movies. It doesn't contain much more than a mini Linux distribution (created using User-Mode Linux and Debian packages) and MPlayer (to play the movies). All the software adds only about 10MB to the disk space you need.

From almost any PC, your friends and family will be able to boot up and immediately begin playing your video from the CD or DVD you give them. It's also a great way to introduce them to the idea of using Linux as a multimedia system.

This chapter describes how to capture video in Linux, combine that video to make a bootable isolinux ISO image, burn that image to CD or DVD, and play back the content. If you enjoy eMoviX, you'll probably want to try out the full MoviX[2] distribution (also included with this book). Later in the chapter, I describe how to use MoviX[2] to play more kinds of multimedia content that you can grab from a local hard disk, network, or other CD or DVD media.

Overview of MoviX² and eMoviX

The MoviX project (`http://movix.sourceforge.net`) is a collection of several projects (eMoviX, MoviX², and MoviX) designed to create a small Linux distribution that can be used primarily to play movies. MoviX² contains the most complete set of multimedia playing components. MoviX is a stripped-down version of MoxiX², which you can use if you have less than 128MB of RAM on your computer. The eMoviX project was actually the first of the three projects and includes software for mastering ISO images of the player to include your own video content.

Because MoviX² is an actual, bootable Linux distribution, and not just a media player, you can play content on nearly any PC — essentially ignoring whatever operating system is on the computer's hard disk. The focus of this project is eMoviX, which is a micro version of MoviX² that was created to co-exist on a CD or DVD along with video content.

Understanding eMoviX

The eMoviX project lets you create your own customized, micro MoviX² version that can boot up and play your personal video content. The fact that eMoviX software is so small (under 10MB) allows most of the software to be contained on the initial RAM disk (`initrd.gz`). Once the RAM disk is loaded into memory and the kernel is booted, eMoviX has only to access the CD or DVD to get the video content.

The eMoviX software incorporates a RAM disk that was built inside a User-Mode Linux session (`http://usermodelinux.org`) using Debian GNU/Linux packages. Roberto De Leo created eMoviX to contain only those components that were needed for the dedicated media player itself, as well as some components needed to support the player (such as extra drivers for audio and remote controls). eMoviX includes BusyBox (`www.busybox.net`), a single utility that includes many common Linux commands. The parts needed to make the CD bootable come from the SYSLINUX Project (`http://syslinux.zytor.com`). As for the Linux kernel, the 2.4.22 kernel is included with the version of eMoviX that comes with this book.

MPlayer (`http://mplayerhq.hu`) is the multimedia player used with eMoviX, and Advanced Linux Sound Architecture, ALSA, (`www.alsa-project.org`) is the sound system. When you or your friends want to play back your bootable movies, MPlayer plays in fullscreen mode. You can use your keyboard to control the playback (later in this chapter, Table 5-1 provides an MPlayer cheat sheet to detail how to use the keys).

Limitations on what you can play with your eMoviX bootable movies are based on the codecs and video file formats that MPlayer supports and the size constraints of the medium (CD or DVD) you choose to use. In other words, the hardest part of this project can be getting the video you want to include onto your computer.

Understanding MoviX²

Instead of booting directly to a custom video, the basic MoviX² distribution boots to a set of menus that gives you more flexibility in the type of content you can play and how you play it.

MoviX² can fit on a mini CD (about 50MB). Once MoviX is loaded, you can eject the CD and insert your own content to play. That content can include:

- **Video** — As with eMoviX, with MoviX² you can play any video file that is supported by the MPlayer media player.

- **Music** — Along with supporting audio with your movies, MoviX² includes support for a variety of audio codecs that are popular for playing music. In particular, you can use commercial music CDs, WAV, Ogg Vorbis, and MP3 audio formats to play music.

- **Images** — You can display image files using the slideshow software included with MoviX². The images will change at set intervals. You can select music to play in the background music during the slide show.

- **Streaming audio** — With your PC connected to the Internet or other network, you can play streaming audio from SHOUTcast or Icecast Internet radio sites.

Note

In Chapter 10, I describe how to set up an Icecast server to create your own Internet radio station. Once you set up that project, you can use MoviX² to play your streaming music or other audio content from your own radio station.

The fact that MoviX² runs in such a small amount of memory, and doesn't require that your CD be mounted when you play content, gives you a lot of flexibility in where you get the content that you play. Here are some of the types of media from which you can play content in MoviX:

- **Music CD** — You can load the table of contents from a music CD and play selected songs. As the music plays, the current artist, album, and song names are displayed, provided that information has been embedded in the audio file.

- **Movie DVD** — Because it is not legal in many countries to distribute the libdvdcss library required to play most commercial movie DVDs in MPlayer, it is not included with the MoviX package. With that library added to MoviX² (where legal), you can play DVD movies.

- **Other CD and DVD content** — You can play any supported audio, video, or image files that you have on CD or DVD. (You don't even need more than one CD or DVD drive on your computer because you can remove the MoviX² CD once you boot MoviX².)

- **VCD and XCD video** — A VideoCD (VCD) can hold up to 74 minutes of video and audio, stored in a VCD-specific format of MPEG1. XCD is a data storage method that stores CD content in Mode 2 instead of Mode 1 format, to hold more data than you typically could on a regular CD.

- **Hard disk** — MoviX² automatically mounts (in read-only mode) any hard disk partitions it finds on the PC under the `/discs` directory. You can play any supported content from those mounted directories. This is a great way to play your multimedia content from a Windows system, while still using the Linux tools you have become comfortable with.

- **Network** — If you have an Ethernet card and a DHCP server on your network, you can play content in MoviX² that you get from the Internet or your private LAN. You can mount an NFS directory or access Internet radio stations. You can also launch an FTP server and upload content to your MoviX² system from another computer on the network.

Although the focus of the chapter is on creating bootable movies with eMoviX, if you find that you like eMoviX you might well want to use MoviX² as your own personal media player. After the section on creating your own bootable movies, check out the section "More Ways to Use MoviX²" later in this chapter.

Hardware Requirements

You can use nearly any PC running Linux to make eMoviX images and burn them to CD or DVD. You can play them back on almost any PC, regardless of what operating system is installed on it. Because eMoviX includes a minimal Linux operating system, it can run on machines with as little as 32MB of RAM (according to MoviX creator Roberto De Leo). I run it quite often on a 600 MHz Pentium with 64MB RAM, although I do some tweaking at the boot prompt (which I talk about later) to get best performance.

On the capturing side, there are a lot of ways you can get the video you want to share. In particular, you can use the hardware described for the MythTV project (see Chapter 4). Essentially, you need hardware for capturing video input (such as a TV capture card) and enough processing power and RAM to be up to the task of handling the recording and possibly encoding.

Note Refer to Chapter 4 for information on selecting a TV capture card. In most cases, the more money you spend on a supported TV capture card, the more processing you can offload to the card. In other words, you might be able to encode the video on a lower-end PC with a capture card that does a lot of the work.

Making a Bootable Movie

Getting a home video or recorded television show into a form where it can play on almost any PC is the point of this project. The basic steps for doing that include getting the recorded video, joining that recorded video together with eMoviX software to form a bootable ISO image, and burning that image to CD or DVD.

Although your bootable eMoviX movie will work on most PCs, there are a few limited cases where some boot options are needed to get the video to play (or at least to play well). So the last steps of this procedure are dedicated to describing boot options (for getting eMoviX to boot in special situations) and MPlayer keys (to control the movie from the keyboard once it's playing).

Figure 5-1 illustrates the general steps in making and playing an eMoviX bootable movie.

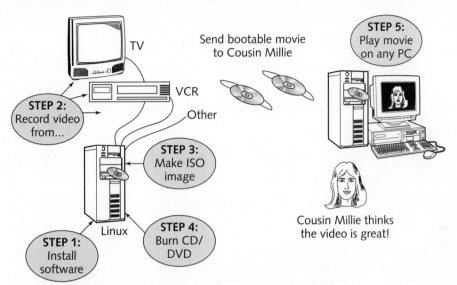

FIGURE 5-1: Making bootable movies . . . from Linux to cousin Millie

Step 1: Installing Linux and eMoviX Software

To build bootable movies from the descriptions in this chapter, you need to have a basic Linux system and the eMoviX software included on the *Linux Toys II* CD. The following bullet items describe what software to install to complete this procedure.

- **Install Linux** — To create bootable movies, I used Fedora Core 4 as my operating system. If you have Fedora Core 4 installed (as described in Appendix C), you can install the RPM packages made for this project. If you are trying the project from another Linux system, you should install the software for this project from tarballs. Both sets of software are included on the *Linux Toys II* CD.

- **Install eMoviX** — You can install the software needed to record video and create your bootable images by installing the software either from RPMs (for Fedora Core or Red Hat Enterprise Linux) or tarballs (for other Linux systems). To install from RPMs, insert the *Linux Toys II* CD on your CD drive. If your CD mounts automatically, you can skip the first command. If it doesn't, run the following (replacing /media/ cdrecorder with the location of where your CD was mounted if needed) as root user from a Terminal window.

Note

If you already have recorded video, you can skip the packages used for video recording by typing `rpm -Uhv emovix*` to install the eMoviX software, instead of running `./installme`.

```
# mount /media/cdrecorder
# cd /media/cdrecorder/RPMS/ch05-emovix
# ./installme
```

This will install all RPMs needed for this project. To install the software from tarballs, refer to the packages in the Sources/ch05-emovix directory and install them using the generic instructions in Appendix C.

Step 2: Recording Content

Any content that can be played with MPlayer (and associated audio/video codecs included with eMoviX) should be able to run in eMoviX. Many of the following audio and video formats are supported by the MPlayer that comes in eMoviX, but not all codecs are included with the version that comes with MoviX[2] because of patent issues (so you may need to get them yourself):

- **MPEG files** — Files in MPEG-1, MPEG-2 and MPEG-4 formats typically end in .mpg, .mpeg, and .m1v extensions.

- **AVI files** — The Audio Video Interleaf (AVI) format is a container format. So a file ending in .avi can actually contain video that has been compressed by any of a variety of different video formats, such as DivX or WMA, or audio formats, such as PCM. It can also contain uncompressed video. Most AVI files today contain content that was compressed in DivX format.

- **DivX files** — DivX is a popular codec for compressing video in Linux. The DivX 3 codec was based on the MPEG-4 V3 codec and made to fit in an AVI format file. The DivX 4 format was developed from scratch.

- **QuickTime files** — Common video format used with Macs and Apple in general. Many commercial movie clips are in QuickTime format, with .mov or .qt file extensions. Many new QuickTime files use Sorenson video and QDesign Music audio. Because these are proprietary formats, only players from Apple can play back these files.

- **Advanced Systems Format (ASF) files** — Another video format from Microsoft using a .asf file extension. This format is not as popular as AVI format for open source applications.

- **VIVO files** — These files follow the h.263 video standard and g723 or Vivo Siren codec for audio. Files of this type often end in the .viv file extension.

- **RealVideo files** — Developed by RealNetworks (www.real.com), these file formats follow RV10, RV20, RV30, or RV40 video standards. Audio formats are either COOK, SIPR, ATRAC3, or DNET. These files typically end in the .rm extension.

- **Windows Media Video (WMV) format** — This is a Microsoft Windows media format, with files that typically end in a .wmv file extension.

- **OGG Media files** — OGM (.ogm file extension) is a container format that is similar to AVI. It consists of OGG video and OGG audio streams (such as the OGG Vorbis open source audio codec). The OGG video stream can be DivX, XviD, or other video codecs.

- **Autodesk animations** — These are Autodesk automation files (.fli or .flc file extensions). This format is often used with scientific illustrations, morphing, and other animated applications.

- **NuppelVideo files** — This is a popular format for capturing video from TV cards on slower computers with MMX capability. It uses the RTjpeg2.0 codec. (Files of this type often have .nuv file extensions.)

- **MP3 files** — Compressed audio files are often stored in MP3 or MP2 formats (with .mp3 or .mp2 file extensions).

If there are codecs you are missing, you can check the MoviX project site to see what codecs are available (the package is named Codecs). Before building your bootable movie images, you can add any additional codecs to the /usr/local/share/emovix directory to have them included in your build.

You can go about getting video files on your computer to put into your bootable eMoviX CD or DVD in a few ways:

- **Get recorded video** — If you have downloaded or copied a video file to your hard disk of a supported video/audio type, you can just go to the next step. I recommend you try out the video first, to make sure that it will run in MPlayer, before you build the bootable movie. This can include such things as movie clips downloaded from the Internet or video files uploaded from a digital camera.

- **MythTV** — If you have installed and are using the MythTV project described in Chapter 4, you can include television and other video content you recorded from that project on your bootable eMoviX CD or DVD.

- **Command line capture tools** — In the rest of this step, I describe how to use several different command line tools for capturing video and audio input from a TV capture card to a file on your hard disk. In particular, I cover ffmpeg (and related nvrec tools) and mencoder (which is part of the MPlayer software project).

Note Although this chapter focuses on how to simply grab and compress an audio/video stream from a TV capture card to a file, there are a variety of tools available for manipulating video that can be used in Linux. The mencoder command described here to grab video can also be used to filter and transform existing video files. For simple open source video editing tools, I suggest looking into Linux Video Editor (http://lvempeg.sourceforge.net) and Cinelerra (http://heroinewarrior.com/cinelerra.php3).

Here are some steps you can follow for capturing video from a Linux system to use with eMoviX:

1. Get a supported TV capture card for getting video input from your television, VCR, or other video equipment. (See Chapter 4 for information on how to choose and set up a TV capture card.)

2. Make sure that your audio system is set up to record from the correct device. For my inexpensive analog TV capture card, I have Audio out patched to the Line in on my sound card. So I ran the aumix program, clicked on the left side of the Line indicator so a red "R" appeared next to it, and turned up the volume. I also turned up IGain. Then I clicked Save and Quit. An example of aumix configured as I just described it appears in Figure 5-2.

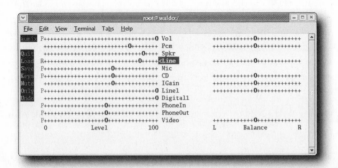

FIGURE 5-2: Use aumix to identify which audio device to use for recording.

Note

The aumix package is not included with Fedora Core 4. However, the tools for selecting an audio capture device that are included with Fedora Core 4 (alsamixer and the GNOME Volume Applet) appear to be broken in that feature. I installed the aumix package from FC3 and it seems to work fine.

3. Use xawtv or tvtime television viewers to set the channel you want to record from and modify any video settings (such as hue and contrast). Once the TV input (video4linux driver) is set as you want, turn off the TV viewer.

4. For recording video, the MPlayer project includes the mencoder utility. Assuming you have a TV capture card on your computer, here's an example of an mencoder command line for recording television input (the backslashes indicate that all three lines should actually be typed on one line):

```
# mencoder -ovc lavc -lavcopts vbitrate=312 tv:// -tv \
driver=v4l:norm=NTSC:device=/dev/video0:width=640:height=480\
-oac mp3lame -lameopts cbr:br=64 -o /tmp/test.avi
```

In this mencoder example, the lavc video codec is used at a bitrate of 312 (using raw instead of lavc gives you better video quality, but much larger output). Video capture is from television (tv://), and options related to video input indicate the video for the Linux (v4l) driver is used and set to the television standard typically used in the United States (NTSC). The video device is /dev/video0 with the image size set to 640 × 480 pixels. Audio compression is done with mp3lame with a constant bitrate (cbr) set to 64 bits. The output of the recording is sent to the /tmp/test.avi file.

If you want to try out some different recordings, I show some commands from the nvrec package (`http://nvrec.sourceforge.net`): `ffmpegrec` and `divx4rec`. They use many of the same options, but allow you to try different audio and video codecs. Before you run commands to capture video, you need to make some decisions:

Note

While the nvrec RPM package that came with the first `Linux Toys` book worked well through Fedora Core 3, a working RPM is not yet available for Fedora Core 4. I recommend you try the MythTV project in Chapter 4 for recording television content. I leave the descriptions of `ffmpegrec` and `divx4rec` in case RPMs for nvrec become available for Fedora Core 4 in the near future.

- **How long** — You need to tell each command how many frames to capture to determine how long to record. For example, to record a 30-minute show at 30 frames/second, multiply 30 frames × 60 seconds × 30 minutes to get 54,000 frames (`-F 54000` option).

- **Video codecs** — With the nvrec commands you have a choice of which codecs to use to record video. To check which codecs are available with ffmpegrec, type **ffmpegrec -vc help**. It lists mpeg1video, h263, h263p, rv10, mjpeg, mpeg4, msmpeg4v1, msmpeg4v2, msmpeg4, wmv1, huffyuv, and rawvideo. You can feed any of those values to `ffmpegrec` with the `-vc` option. (I give examples of a few I've found to work well.) You can also record video in DivX format, using the `divx4rec` command.

- **Audio codecs** — To see what audio codecs are available with ffmpegrec, type **ffmpegrec -ac help**. You will see ac3, mp2, vorbis, and a variety of pcm formats. With divx4rec you can use mp3 (`-ab` or `-aq`) or raw PCM (`-wav`) to record the audio portions of your videos.

- **Video size** — You can set the width and height (in pixels) to record your video. For example, to record video at 512 pixels wide × 384 high, use the `-w 512 -h 384` options.

- **Input** — You can set where to get input for your recording. For example, to get television input, use the `-input Television` option.

- **Video device** — You can identify the device from which to grab video to record. For example, `-v /dev/video0`.

- **Audio device** — You can identify the audio device from which to get the audio portion of your video. For example, `-d /dev/dsp`.

There are other options you can use with the `ffmpegrec` and `divx4rec` commands that you can see from the man pages for each of those commands (type **man ffmpegrec or man divx4rec**). Here are some examples (the backslashes indicate that the command line continues without pressing Enter):

```
# ffmpegrec -d /dev/dsp -s -v /dev/video0 \
   -w 640 -h 480 -vc mjpeg -input Television \
   -norm NTSC -vq 0 -sc mp2 -F 1800 -o test.avi
```

In the previous example, recording is taken from /dev/dsp and video from /dev/video0. Video is captured at 640 × 480 pixels. The video codec used is mjpeg. The audio codec is mp2. The recording is taken from Television input in NTSC format (common in the United States; PAL is used in Europe). A fixed quality scale of 0 is used. For the example, 1,800 frames are grabbed (one minute of video).

You can cut the size of the video file by more than half (with some loss of quality) by changing mjpeg to mpeg4. You can reduce the video size further by reducing the video height and width by half (320 × 240). Here's an example of the command line:

```
# ffmpegrec -d /dev/dsp -s -v /dev/video0 \
    -w 320 -h 240 -vc mpeg4 -input Television \
    -norm NTSC -vq 0 -sc mp2 -F 1800 -o test.avi
```

When I ran this second command, the size of the test.avi file went from 18MB to 6.8MB. You should run MPlayer on each output file to make sure that the video quality is acceptable before using those settings to capture the video you want to keep.

To create DivX encoding, you can use the divx4rec command. Here is an example:

```
# divx4rec -d /dev/dsp -s -v /dev/video0 \
    -w 320 -h 240 -input Television \
    -norm NTSC -F 1800 -o test.avi
```

I went with the lower frame size (320 × 240) because I was getting a lot of frames dropped at the higher size. In general, I got better quality video using mjpeg. A lot of factors are associated with your hardware and video input that can cause you to get different results. The key here is to try different codecs and frame sizes to find a level of quality and file size that you can live with.

Now you're ready to take the video files you created and make them into bootable movies.

Step 3: Creating Bootable Movie Images

After you have the video content you want to make into a bootable movie, you need to create an ISO image to later burn to a CD or DVD. You do that with the mkmovixiso command. Here's an example:

```
# mkmovixiso -t "2005 Vacation" -o movix_vacation.iso movie.avi
Your iso image is now in "/home/user/movix/movix_vacation.iso
You can safely delete temporary directory /tmp/movix-1106024960
```

In this example, the video content is named movie.avi in the current directory. You can add as many AVI files as will fit on the medium (they will play one after the other, by default). The title (2005 Vacation in this case) is entered after the -t option and is used as the Volume ID tag on the image. The title must be less than 32 characters. The name of the ISO image file follows the -o option (in this case, movix_vacation.iso).

The ISO image is created here using many default options. You can see a complete list of options by typing **mkmovixiso -h**. Here are a few options that might interest you:

- `--boot-label=label` — Instead of using the default boot label (which is MoviX), you can choose to have a different boot label used by default. The label that is entered from the boot prompt determines the kernel that is booted and the options passed to it. (See the section "Starting Play with Different Boot Labels" later in this chapter for information on other labels you can choose.)

The main reason for choosing a different label is to select one that boots eMoviX with a video driver and display options appropriate to the machine you are booting from. MPlayer uses this information to choose which video driver to use when it plays back video. Replace label with one of the boot labels listed in the boot/isolinux.cfg file on the ISO image you create.

- `--subtitleFonts=language` — Replace language with the name of the font set you want to use with MPlayer. Font sets available with MPlayer include centralEU-cp1250, centralEU-iso-8859-2, cyrillic, czech, greek, hebrew, polish, russian, and turkish.

- `--language=language` — Replace language with the name of the language you want used on the displays and menus that appear with eMoviX. The default is US English (us). However, you can also use de (German), es (Spanish), fr (French), hu (Hungarian), it (Italian), nl (Dutch), pt (Portuguese, or be (Belgian).

- `--bgVideo=file.avi` — Indicates what video file to use as the background when you are playing music files in eMoviX. By default, file.avi is replaced by movix .music.avi. Other choices include coresis.avi and black.avi. You can add your own AVI file to the /usr/local/share/emovix/backgrounds directory and indicate it with this option.

- `--loop=n` — Replace n with a number indicating how many times you want the video to play before quitting. Use 0 to have the video repeat forever.

- `--random` — Have the video files included on the CD/DVD play in random order.

- `--eject, --reboot, or --shut` — When the video finishes playing, have the CD/DVD eject, reboot the computer, or shutdown the computer, respectively.

You can add any codecs you like to your bootable eMoviX distribution to play any other content that is supported by MPlayer (but doesn't happen to be included with eMoviX). Options that add support for different video codecs to your bootable eMoviX movie include --hasQT (include DLLs for QuickTime content), --hasASF (include DLLs for .asf files), --hasWMV (include DLLs for .wmv files), --hasRP (include DLLs for RealPlayer files), and --hasXANIM (include DLLs for files from the xanim project). Codecs for the following media types are available for download by selecting Codecs from the MoviX SourceForge Web site (http://sourceforge.net/projects/movix).

- Win32 codecs (asf,wmv)

- QuickTime6 DLLs

- RealPlayer9 codecs

- RealPlayer Win32 codecs
- XAnim DLLs

Note The custom DLLs available from the MPlayer Web site (`http://mplayerhq.hu`) will not work with eMoviX. The DLLs packed into five different `tar.bz2` files at the MoviX SourceForge Web site will work with eMoviX.

After you download a codec, you can make it ready to be included in your bootable movie with the `mkmovixiso` command by creating a codecs directory and copying it there. For example:

```
# mkdir /usr/local/share/emovix/codecs
# cp whatevercodecs /usr/local/share/emovix/codecs/
```

You need to do research to determine whether the libdvdcss library is legal for you to use in the country you are in. You cannot play most commercial DVD movies in MPlayer without libdvdcss. If it is legal to use libdvdcss in your country, the `--css` option will add that library to your bootable movie with the `mkmovixiso` command, provided you add the `libdvdcss-1.2.6-1.i386.rpm` file to your `/usr/local/share/emovix/movix` directory. (Again, check for legality in your area.)

After you have created the eMoviX ISO image, you can burn it to CD or DVD as described in the next step.

Note If you prefer a graphical interface for creating your bootable movies, try the MoviXMaker-2 project (`http://savannah.nongnu.org/projects/movixmaker`).

Step 4: Burning Bootable Movie Images

Any application that can burn ISO images to CD or DVD can be used to burn your eMoviX movie to disk. If you are using a desktop Linux system, I recommend you use "K3b - The CD/DVD Kreator." If you prefer the command line, you can use the `cdrecord` command. Here is an example of how to use K3b to burn your ISO image.

Note To use K3b you must install the k3b package. You can install the k3b package from your Fedora installation medium or by typing **yum install k3b** as root user from a Terminal window. To use k3b also requires that you install the kdelibs package.

1. From the Fedora Applications menu (or most main KDE menus), select Sound & Video ➜ K3b. The K3b window appears.

2. From the K3b window, select Tools and then one of the following (depending on what you are burning to):

   - CD ➜ Burn CD Image: To burn an image to CD
   - DVD ➜ Burn DVD Image: To burn an image to DVD

Figure 5-3 shows an example of these menus from the K3b window.

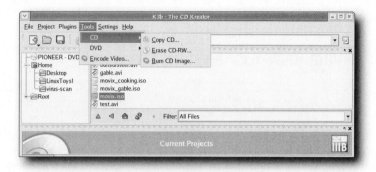

FIGURE 5-3: Burning CD or DVD images using K3b

3. In the Burn CD (or DVD) Image window that appears, enter the location of the ISO image you want to burn in the Image to Burn box (click the folder to browse there). Information about the ISO image will appear in the box (including the image type detected, size of the file, System ID, Volume ID, and other information).

4. Insert the blank CD or DVD you want to burn to. (You may need to close a CD Creator window if one pops up.)

5. Click the reload icon (two green arrows) next to the Speed box. The Speed box will then tell you write speeds that are supported for the medium you inserted. Select a speed.

Note

Be sure that the medium you are burning will support the speed you selected. Sometimes, simply reducing the burning speed can prevent getting a bad burn (that is, medium that won't boot).

6. Click Start. You will see the progress as the ISO image is burned to the disk. When the burn finishes, the CD or DVD will automatically eject.

Mark the disk appropriately or print a label for it. It's now ready to boot.

Instead of using K3b, you can use `cdrecord` from the command line to burn the image to disk. Here is an example of a `cdrecord` command line for burning an eMoviX image:

```
# cdrecord -data dev=/dev/hdb -eject movix_vacation.iso
```

In this example, the writeable CD or DVD device is located at /dev/hdb. For a SCSI device, you might enter something like dev=0,0,0 (for the first SCSI device). You can type `cdrecord --scanbus` to see the SCSI CD drives that are available on your computer. The image (`movix_vacation.iso`) is burned to the CD or DVD in CD-ROM mode 1 format (also called Yellow Book), based on the `-data` option. The CD will eject (`-eject` option) when the burn is done.

It's ready to play.

Note Because `cdrecord` is included with Damn Small Linux, you can boot the *Linux Toys II* CD and run the `cdrecord` command without having Linux installed at all. Open a Terminal window from the Damn Small Linux desktop and add `sudo` in front of the `cdrecord` command line shown previously.

Step 5: Playing Back Your eMoviX Video

An exact minimum PC you can use to play the bootable movie you just created is difficult to determine exactly. Important factors are the amount of RAM, processor speed, and the video card. Also, smaller size videos will play better than those run in full screen.

Feedback received by Roberto De Leo indicates that people are able to run eMoviX movies on a computer with as little power as a 600 MHz Pentium with 64MB of RAM. If you have an older PC, consider getting a higher-quality, if somewhat older, video card (such as an ATI mach64 or Matrox g200 video card).

To play your bootable movie, insert the CD or DVD into the appropriate drive on your computer. Then reboot the computer. You will see the MoviX splash screen and a boot prompt. At that point, you can:

- **Start playing the movie** — Press Enter or simply wait a few seconds and the movie will start. Press 0 and 9 keys to adjust the volume. Press m to display the Play menu. Press p to pause (or unpause) the playback. Press q to quit playback. See Table 5-1 for other playing options.

- **Run a different boot label** — When eMoviX boots automatically, it runs the MoviX label by default. The MoviX label causes eMoviX to choose the best driver to use for your video card. You can type **MoviX** manually and add additional boot options to it.

Figure 5-4 shows the eMoviX boot screen.

If the movie doesn't play properly, try some of the boot options described in the next section.

Starting Play with Different Boot Labels

The following boot labels are available, if the default doesn't work the way you would like. Simply type any of these labels at the eMoviX boot prompt to get them to work.

- `vesa` — Use the generic vesa driver, which should work on most video cards.

- `vesaFB` — Use the generic vesa frame buffer driver. There are also other labels that will use the vesa frame buffer drivers at specific resolutions. These include `vesaFB640` (640 × 480 resolution), `vesaFB800` (800 × 600), `vesaFB1024` (1024 × 768), or `vesaFB1400` (1400 × 1050).

- `aa` — Use the ASCII art driver to display the image. You can also use the aa1024 (1204 × 768 resolution) and aa1280 (1280 × 1024 resolution) labels.

- `TV` — Initialize any applications needed to activate the TV-out jack on your card.

FIGURE **5-4: Press Enter to play the movie or add more boot options.**

You can see these and other labels by pressing the F2 function key from the eMoviX boot screen. Press the F5 or F6 function key to see other boot-related options. F3 lets you see MPlayer playback keys.

Controlling Playback

After booting, eMoviX starts immediately playing the video you put on the disk. To control the video, use the keyboard shortcuts in the MPlayer cheat sheet in Table 5-1. Because no MPlayer control panel is displayed with eMoviX, you can refer to the cheat sheet to see what keystrokes you can use to go forward and back in the video, change the volume, and adjust the picture quality.

Figure 5-5 shows an example of a full-screen movie playing in eMoviX.

Table 5-1 shows the keyboard keys that can be used to control playback when you are playing a video with MPlayer. You should consider giving this quick reference to the people who get your bootable movies.

Space pauses and "q" stops the playback.

FIGURE 5-5: As movies play in eMoviX, text describes how to control playback.

Table 5-1: MPlayer Keyboard Shortcuts

Key	Action
Right arrow	Seek forward 10 seconds
Left arrow	Seek backward 10 seconds
Up arrow	Seek forward 1 minute
Down arrow	Seek backward 1 minute
Page up	Seek forward 10 minutes
Page down	Seek backward 10 minutes
p or space bar	Toggle pause/unpause movie (any will unpause)
q or Esc	Stop playing
m	Display MPlayer menu (Esc to remove menu)

Key	Action
j	Cycle on subtitles
+	Adjust audio delay by +0.1 seconds
-	Adjust audio delay by -0.1 seconds
/	Decrease volume
*	Increase volume
1	Decrease contrast
2	Increase contrast
3	Decrease brightness
4	Increase brightness
5	Increase hue (not supported with all -vo)
6	Decrease hue (not supported with all -vo)
7	Decrease saturation
8	Increase saturation
9	Decrease volume
0	Increase volume
o	Toggle OSD mode
f	Toggle full-screen mode
z	Increase subtitle delay by +0.1 seconds
x	Decrease subtitle delay by -0.1 seconds
r	Adjust subtitle position up
t	Adjust subtitle position down
>	Go to the next item in playlist
<	Go to the previous item in playlist
[	Reduce playback speed 10 percent
]	Increase playback speed 10 percent
{	Cut current playback speed in half
}	Double current playback speed
Backspace	Reset playback speed to normal
.	Pause, and then step forward one frame at a time
T	Toggle "stay on top"

Switching Consoles

You can stop the movie and switch to different virtual consoles. Press q or Esc to quit the movie, and then select Exit from the MPlayer eMoviX menu. Select Console Prompt. With the movie stopped from the console, you can press the following Alt key and function key combinations:

- **ALSA Mixer (Alt+F2)** — Displays the ALSA Mixer to change audio levels of your movie.

- **Shell prompt (Alt+F3)** — Displays a shell prompt, allowing you to run shell commands. As you might guess, you will have fewer commands than there would be on a larger Linux system. The shell prompt is most useful in eMoviX if you want to figure out why your sound card isn't working or otherwise debug your player. (Available commands are described in the next section.)

- **Movie (Alt+F1)** — Goes to a console prompt when done. Type **help** to see your options. Type **movix** to play the bootable movie again.

After the Movie Is Done

After the movie has finished playing, eMoviX displays the MPlayer eMoviX menu. Figure 5-6 shows the MPlayer eMoviX menu.

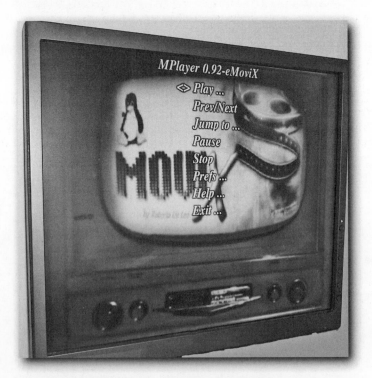

FIGURE 5-6: Start playing again from the MPlayer eMoviX menu.

The following selections are available from the MPlayer eMoviX menu:

- **Play** — Displays a menu of content you can select to play. You can play a CD, file, playlist, DVD, VCD, or audio CD. Because eMoviX is running in RAM, you can remove the CD or DVD and insert a CD or DVD containing the media you want to play. For files or playlists, you can select from any of the local removable media (CD, floppy, DVD, and so on) or from a local directory.

- **Prev/Next** — If there are multiple audio and/or video files on your medium, use the right arrow here to select the next track/file or right arrow to select the previous one.

- **Jump to** — Select Jump to see a list of available tracks on the selected medium. Move the arrow key to highlight the track you want and press Enter.

- **Pause** — Select pause to pause the playback of the current video or audio content.

- **Stop** — Select Stop to stop playing of content. When you select Play again, you will start at the beginning of the first file or track.

- **Prefs** — Select to set preferences related to your audio channel or subtitles.

- **Help** — Select to choose to see the Help Menu, MPlayer man page, or eMoviX credits.

- **Exit** — Select Exit, and then choose Console Prompt (to exit to a shell), reboot (to restart your computer), or Poweroff (to turn off your computer).

Because eMoviX contains a basic set of Linux commands (provided primarily by BusyBox utilities), you can get around in eMoviX as you would any Linux system (pwd, ls, cd, and other commands are available).

Because eMoviX is intended to be used to boot a single movie (or set of movies) on the local CD or DVD, it is not a full-featured media player. For playing different content from different locations (hard disk, network, and so on), I recommend you try out MoviX as described later in this chapter. However, a few features have been added to continue playing multimedia content.

To try some other features, after your movie is done playing, select Exit ➜ Console Prompt. You can use a handful of common Linux commands (type ls followed by /bin, /usr/bin, /sbin, or /usr/sbin to see what commands are available). Here are some specific MoviX commands you can try:

- help — Displays information about these commands.

- movix — Plays the video again or, if you inserted a different CD, plays that video.

- vcd *N* — Plays a video CD; replace *N* with the track number 1, 2, or other.

- dvd *N* — Plays from DVD; replace *N* with the track number (encrypted DVDs unsupported).

- dvd — Plays longest DVD track. (You can play only unencrypted DVDs.)

- acd — Plays audio CD.

- mcd — Plays CD containing MP3, Ogg, and Wav content.
- lim — Loads ISA modules (if ISA audio card is not detected automatically).
- reboot — Reboots the computer.
- poweroff — Shuts down the computer.

Note Whether the media described here will actually play depends on whether or not the codecs are included in eMoviX. Because eMoviX contains a reduced set of codecs, it's probably better to try to play other content in MoviX, as described later in this chapter.

To go beyond the bounds of what you can do with eMoviX, I recommend you try out the MoviX² distribution that comes on the *Linux Toys II* CD. The following section describes how to use MoviX².

Note To find out more information on eMoviX and how to use it, refer to the eMoviX Web site (http://movix.sourceforge.net/Docs/eMoviX).

Playing with MoviX²

With the MoviX² multimedia Linux distribution, you aren't expected to have the content on your CD. MoviX is small enough that you can boot it from your computer and have it load everything it needs into memory. You can then remove the MoviX CD and use that drive to insert other CDs or DVDs that contain the content you want to play.

I've used the term MoviX to generically describe this distribution. However, different versions of MoviX are available. The basic MoviX distribution runs without an X Window System interface, so you are running the non-X version of MPlayer. MoviX² includes a simple X interface, so you can run gmplayer (with graphical controls) to display your movies or other multimedia content.

Unless you expect to run on a machine with less than 128MB of RAM, you should use MoviX² instead of the MoviX distribution. In the rest of this chapter, I describe MoviX², which is included with the *Linux Toys II* software distribution.

Getting MoviX²

There is an ISO image of MoviX² on the *Linux Toys II* CD that you can burn to a separate CD to boot MoviX² directly. If you like, you can look for a later version of MoviX² from the MoviX site at SourceForge.net (http://sourceforge.net/projects/movix).

Here's a description of how to create your own MoviX² CD from the one on the CD:

1. With Fedora or other Linux system running on your computer, insert the *Linux Toys II* CD into your CD drive. It should mount automatically. (If it doesn't, type **mount /media/cdrecorder** to mount the drive. You may need to replace cdrecorder with cdrom or other another string, depending on the name of your CD drive mount point.)

2. Copy the MoviX^2 ISO image to your hard drive (you can skip this step if you have a recordable CD drive available on your computer other than the one holding the *Linux Toys II* CD).

   ```
   # cp /media/cdrecorder/isos/ch05-emovix/movix2*iso/movix2*iso /tmp
   ```

3. Eject the CD (either type **eject** or right-click the CD and select Eject).

4. Remove the CD and insert a blank CD.

5. Burn the CD image (`/tmp/movix2*iso`) to CD using any CD burning tools (such as cdrecord or k3b, described earlier in this chapter).

The CD you just created contains a bootable image of MoviX^2.

Selecting MoviX^2 Boot Options

As with eMoviX, MoviX^2 is created to boot quickly to a multimedia player (gmplayer in this case) and run from RAM. The ISO image of MoviX^2 is about 52MB, so it is still small enough to run in the memory of most systems that have enough RAM. (I had the best results with 128MB or more of RAM.)

To use MoviX^2, insert the MoxiX^2 CD you created in the previous section and reboot your computer. When the MoviX boot screen appears, to see what boot options are available, you can press the following function keys from the boot prompt:

- **F2** — Shows the boot labels available with MoviX^2. (These labels are described in the eMoviX section on using boot labels.)

- **F4** — Shows a description of the MoviX distributions.

- **F5** — Shows boot parameters available to run from the boot prompt. The parameters shown here will help you if you need to specify the driver to use with MPlayer or information about the monitor you are using (such as the horizontal and vertical frequency). These options also tell you how to identify X Window System–specific parameters, such as where your mouse is connected or the color depth of your display.

- **F6** — Shows many more boot-related options for identifying your TV card hardware (card type, tuner, remote, and so on) and other hardware features (such as whether or not to use DMA). If there is no DHCP server on your network, options shown here let you indicate your own IP address (provided you want to use a network connection with MoviX).

Here's an example of boot command lines. The first example boots MoviX^2 to display text in German (de) with a German keyboard (de). The mouse is set to a USB mouse.

```
boot: MoviX2 LANGUAGE=de KB=de MOUSE=usb
```

In the following example, there is no DHCP server on your network so you have to set IP addresses manually to get a network connection. Here, the computer's IP address is set to 10.0.0.99, the gateway machine (providing the route to the Internet) is 10.0.0.1, and the DNS server is located at 10.0.0.2:

```
boot: MoviX2 IP=10.0.0.99 GW=10.0.0.1 DNS=10.0.0.2
```

Having MoviX[2] start a connection to your local network can be useful because it allows you then to potentially play content that exists anywhere on your LAN. I talk more about using that network connectivity later.

Getting Around in MoviX[2]

When you first boot MoviX[2], you see an X screen ready to play video from the graphical MPlayer application (called gmplayer). Besides that mode of operation, you can switch between different virtual consoles to operate MoviX[2] in different ways. For example:

- **MoviX screen (Alt+F1)** — Displays the MoviX screen, where you can select from a variety of ways to play video, audio, digital images, and streaming content.

- **AlsaMixer (Alt+F2)** — Displays an audio mixer.

- **Shell (Alt+F3)** — Displays a shell command line prompt for operating the system from the shell.

- **Graphical MPlayer (Alt+F4)** — Return to the graphical, X-based MPlayer screen.

In most cases, if you just want to play video content, you can start from the graphical MPlayer screen, as described in the next section.

Choosing Video Content with MoviX[2]

Once MoviX[2] finishes loading, you'll see an X screen with the MoviX[2] logo in the background. Now you can select any of the following options:

- **Eject the CD** — MoviX[2] should be loaded and running entirely from RAM at this point so you can press the button on your CD drive to eject the CD.

- **MPlayer display** — Left-click the mouse to see a graphical representation of a DVD player, with buttons, time and volume read-outs, and the like.

- **MPlayer menu** — Right-click the mouse to see a menu of actions to take with MPlayer.

- **MoviX main page** — Right-click the desktop and select Switch to MoviX. From the MoviX main page that appears, you can select where to get your video content from, or choose to play other types of content (described later). Press F9 to return to the MPlayer GUI.

Figure 5-7 shows the MPlayer display and the MPlayer menu. You can use either of those ways to select the content you want to play.

FIGURE 5-7: Select multimedia content to play from the MPlayer display or menu.

Getting Content with MoviX²

Because there is nothing in your CD/DVD drive now, you can insert a CD, VCD, or DVD to play from MPlayer. Instead of just playing a video included on the CD or DVD you created with eMoviX, with MoviX², you can play content from different locations.

While the MoviX main menu is a text-based (ncurses) display, you can use your mouse to select from the menu at the top of the page. Unless you need to adjust some settings, however, you can select and play video, audio, and image content without leaving the MPlayer display. Here are some other ways to get content to play with MoviX².

From CDs or DVDs

From the MPlayer menu, you can select to play from a VCD or DVD, with options to display Titles, Chapters, and different languages, if they are available. (As already mentioned, you cannot play commercial, encrypted DVDs without the libdvdcss library's being installed in the /lib directory of MoviX².)

Another way to use MPlayer to open a video or audio file that is located on any removable medium (or even fixed media) is by selecting Open → Play file from the MPlayer menu. You can view the contents of the CD and DVD drives from /cdrom0, /cdrom1, and similar directories, depending on how many CD/DVD drives you have. Remember that you can remove and reinsert CDs and DVDs into your drive to change to different content while MoviX² is running in memory.

From Your Hard Disk

MoviX^2 looks for partitions on your hard disk and automatically mounts them (read-only) so you can play video, audio, or digital images from there. To select a file to play from your local hard disk, open the MPlayer menu (left-click the mouse) and select Open → Play file. Select the /discs directory.

In the /discs directory you should see your hard disk partitions mounted. In my case, there were three partitions on the first hard disk: disc0.part1, disc0.part3, and disc0.part5. Click to move to subdirectories of any of the mounted partitions and select video or audio files to play.

From the Network (FTP)

By starting up a network connection automatically (if a DHCP server is available) or by entering your own IP addresses (as described earlier in this chapter), you open the possibility of being able to grab content to play from other places on the network. One way to open your system to upload content is by turning on FTP service to your MoviX^2 system.

Follow these steps to start the FTP service so you can upload video to your MoviX^2 system:

1. Select Alt+F1 to go to the MoviX2 menu screen.

2. Select Play → Net → FTP Server → On. This should start the bftpd server.

3. Select Alt+F3 to go to the shell prompt.

4. Open a directory for writing on your MoviX^2 system so you can copy content there. To do that, unmount the directory you want to write to and remount it with read/write access. For example:

```
# umount /discs/disc0.part3
# mount -rw /dev/discs/disc0/part3 /discs/disc0.part3
```

The partition you want to open may be a different one (such as part1 or part2).

5. Type **ifconfig eth0** and look for your IP address (listed after inet addr:).

6. From another computer on your network (with the current directory containing the content you want to transfer to your MoviX^2 computer), use an ftp command to connect to your MoviX^2 player. For example:

```
# ftp 10.0.0.98
220 Welcome to the MoviX FTP Server.
Name (10.0.0.98:root):
```

Press Enter to log in to the MoviX^2 FTP server. It should drop you into the /discs directory on your MoviX^2 computer.

7. Next, change to the directory where you want to put the content and put the content there. For example:

```
ftp> cd /discs/disc0.part3
ftp> put myvideo.mov
```

You can now go to the MoviX² machine again and open the video you just copied to that computer using the MPlayer menu or controller.

From the Network (NFS)

You can mount a directory from another computer on your LAN that is shared using Network File System (NFS) and play content from there on your MoviX² player. NFS is a popular method of sharing directories of files among Linux and UNIX systems.

Before you can mount a remote NFS directory in MoviX², your MoviX² system must be connected to the network and the computer containing the directory you want to share must make it available on the network. While there's no room for a complete description of NFS here (you might check out *Red Hat Fedora and Enterprise Linux 4 Bible* for that), here is a quick procedure for sharing a directory using NFS from a Red Hat Linux (Fedora or RHEL) system:

1. From the computer sharing the directory (server), make sure you have an active network connection and that your firewall doesn't prevent access to the NFS service to your MoviX² system (open port 2049).

2. Add an entry (as root user) to your `/etc/exports` file that contains the directory you want to share. For example, if you put a copy of a video in the `/tmp/movie` directory on the server, you might share it with everyone on your LAN (read-only) by adding the following to your `/etc/exports` file on the server:

   `/tmp/movie *(ro)`

3. Start the NFS service on the server (as root user) by typing the following:

   # /etc/init.d/nfs start

4. Back on your MoviX² system, you can mount the remote directory from the MoviX² menu. First go to that menu (Alt+F1). Then select Play → Net → Mount Remote Volume to see the Mount Remote Volume form.

5. With the server name or IP address, you can identify the remote directory you want to mount and the location on the local system where you want to mount it. For example, if the IP address of the server is 10.0.0.2, you can fill in the following information to have the `/tmp/movie` directory mounted locally:

   ```
   Volume to mount:        10.0.0.2:/tmp/movie
   Mount point:            /discs/server1
   File system:            nfs
   Extra mount options:
   ```

   By default, you may not need any extra mount options. MoviX² should automatically mount it read-only. You can, however, view the mount man page (type **man mount** and search for NFS) to see options you may want to add to the NFS mount command.

6. Select Save. The directory `/discs/server1` should now be created, with the remote NFS directory mounted on it.

7. From either the MoviX² menu or the MPlayer menu, you can select to open a file, go to the `/discs/server1` directory, and open any content you want to play.

From the Network (Internet Radio Station)

MoviX^2 is configured to immediately connect to SHOUTcast or Icecast radio stations if you are connected to the Internet. To open a SHOUTcast or Icecast streaming audio radio station, do one of the following, respectively, from the MoviX^2 menu (Alt+F1):

■ **SHOUTcast** — Select Play ➔ SHOUTcast Radios. From that menu, select the type of content and then the exact station to connect to. For example, if you selected Jazz ➔ Swing, you would see the MoviX^2 audio display screen with the words "SHOUTCAST Swing radio: KCEA-FM Big Band Swing" displayed.

■ **Icecast** — Select Play ➔ Icecast Radios. From that menu, select the type of content and then the exact station to connect to. For example, to play classical music you could select Classical ➔ Symphonic. As with SHOUTCAST, you will see the audio screen with the name of the Icecast radio station displayed.

In both cases, press the Esc key to quit the radio station and go back to the MoviX^2 menu.

More Ways to Use MoviX^2

Although MoviX and MoviX^2 are meant primarily to play video content, they can play other content as well. You can play music directly from an audio CD or display a slideshow of images, as described in the following sections.

Playing Music CDs

To play a music CD, insert that CD into your MoviX player's CD drive. From the MoviX menu, select Play ➔ Audio CD ➔ Reload TOC (to load a table of contents of the CD). You can then select individual tracks to play (Play ➔ Audio CD ➔ PlayTrack) or play the whole CD (Play ➔ Audio CD ➔ Play). If the information is available, you will see the artist, album, and song information displayed for the music as it plays.

Playing Slideshows

From the MoviX menu, you can select a directory of images to play as a slideshow and choose music to play along with it. From the MoviX main page, do the following:

1. Select Play ➔ SlideShow ➔ Select Background Music.

2. From the menu that appears, select Set/change music.

3. Use your mouse or keyboard keys to choose the song you want to play from your local file system (hard disk, CD, DVD, remote-mounted directory, and so on).

4. Back at the main menu, select Play ➔ SlideShow. Then choose the disk you want to choose your directory of images from.

5. On that same screen, choose to randomize (or play in order), get images from subdirectories of the selected directory as well, and whether or not to loop through the images continuously (or just quit after going through them once).

The images will begin playing continuously, changing every few seconds, with the music you selected playing in the background. To control the slide show, you can: pause (p), scroll large images (arrow keys), zoom in (+), zoom out (-), go to the previous image (Page Up), go to the next image (Page Down or space bar), or go to a particular image number (type *N*g, replacing the *N* with the image number you want).

Getting More Information on MoviX² and eMoviX

The center for information on MoviX² and related projects is the MoviX Web site (`http://movix.sourceforge.net`). From there you can find articles, FAQs, tutorials, screenshots, slideshows, and links related to MoviX, MoviX², and eMoviX.

The MoviX projects were created by Roberto De Leo (`peggish@users.sf.net`). Like many open source projects, donations help make it possible for developers to spend more time developing the project. There is a "Support this Project" button on the MoviX home page you can click on if you would like to make a contribution.

If you have questions about or problems with MoviX or related projects, I recommend you go to the MoviX forums page (`http://sourceforge.net/forum/?group_id=61561`). There are help and open discussion forums. There is also a forum if you are interested in building a multimedia box, where MoviX can be permanently installed on a low-end PC.

Contributors to MoviX

Since it started in 2002, there have been a lot of contributors to the MoviX projects. The following is a list of major contributors, according to Roberto De Leo:

- **Balazs Barany** — Created most of the new eMoviX features, including the builder that allows anyone to build the eMoviX distribution from scratch. In the past year and a half Balazs has built all eMoviX binaries.

- **Pascal Giard** — Authored the Debian GNU/Linux eMoviX packages.

- **Jochen Puchalla** — Responsible for much of the testing of the MoviX distributions.

- **Clovis Sena and Kangur** — Co-authored the win32 MoviX packages.

- **Rémi Turboult** — Created a builder set of scripts for MoviX/MoviX², still unpublished but available on the CVS tree.

- **Vladimir Popov** — Created software for installing on USB pen drives and handled the Russian translations.

In addition, many others contributed to translations of the MoviX projects into different languages.

Future Directions for MoviX

Roberto De Leo has many plans for future development of MoviX projects. Here are some of the future plans he passed on to me. If you are interested in helping with any of these development efforts, please contact Roberto through the MoviX Web site.

- **Builder** — A set of scripts for compiling MoviX/MoviX^2 binaries from scratch is already in the works. The scripts were written by Rémi Turboult and will be released very soon. They could help users add and test new drivers or build their own dedicated distributions. The dedicated distributions could focus on other applications. Roberto suggested distros such as Musix, Doomix, or Whateverix could grow from this effort.

- **Encoding** — Currently, the process of grabbing and encoding video is not part of the MoviX projects. MPlayer comes with the mencoder utility, which Roberto hopes to add to a MoviX menu so a user could encode videos from an acquisition card from a MoviX distribution.

- **GUI** — Instead of the current interface, which lets users choose from three different selection screens, Roberto would like to have one high-quality GUI to operate the project (as MythTV does). In the best case, the GUI would be customizable to different dedicated distributions. (If any MythTV developers, or anyone else for that matter, would like to help port the MythTV frontend to MoviX or develop a new frontend, please contact Roberto.)

Once the current MoviX distributions are fairly stable, Roberto would like to branch out into other dedicated distributions. Here are some examples he mentioned:

- **ePictix** — A distribution that can autoboot and play a CD or DVD full of photos. If a similar feature isn't added to MPlayer, it could be done directly by eMoviX

- **eGamix** — A distribution containing your favorite game that you'll be able to play on every PC without wasting time installing anything. With eGamix including a network game (such as Doom and related games), eGamix could make setting up a LAN party quick and easy. You won't have to spend half your LAN party installing the games and fighting with Windows or other client operating systems trying to make everything work.

- **ePartix** — A distribution containing only QtParted that people could use to partition their hard drives before installing an operating system.

Using tools that the MoviX project will make available, Roberto encourages people to create distributions like these and others that would center around a single application that could benefit from being bundled with a simple, dedicated distribution.

Summary

Video is one of the more entertaining things to do with a computer. By combining several open source projects (MPlayer, a kernel, isolinux, BusyBox, and other components), the MoviX project has created a fun and useful way to manage multimedia content with a completely self-contained, bootable operating system.

The eMoviX project lets you combine a micro MoviX distribution with your own video content to create bootable movies. For this chapter, I've put together a step-by-step procedure for gathering video content, creating the bootable ISO image, burning it to CD or DVD, and playing back the content.

If you like making and using eMoviX bootable movies, you almost certainly will want to try out the full MoviX^2 multimedia distribution. Descriptions in this chapter tell you how to run various players (primarily MPlayer) to play your audio, video, and digital image content in MoviX^2. With features built into MoviX^2, you can gather multimedia content to play from a local hard disk, CD, DVD, VCD, remote directory (NFS), FTP upload service, or Internet streaming audio (SHOUTcast and Icecast).

Home Projects

part

Customizing a Live Linux Pen Drive

Ever wonder why you lug a computer around with you wherever you go? After all, there are PCs everywhere. What if you could carry something that fit in your hand and included your:

➤ Music, documents, and graphics

➤ Applications for playing, displaying, or manipulating your stuff

➤ Themes, backgrounds, and other desktop preferences

➤ Settings for connecting to your mail server, instant messaging buddy list, and Web browser bookmarks

➤ Favorite operating system (Linux, of course)

What I'm talking about here is a customized, bootable operating system that includes your own bootable Linux, settings, and data files. To use it, you just need access to a PC that can boot from a USB pen drive (the medium of choice for this project) or other removable medium (as I describe later). Then, within a few minutes you are working away from most any PC as though you were at your desk.

With bootable Linux systems such as Damn Small Linux (which is based on the KNOPPIX LiveCD), much of the work of creating a live Linux distribution you can carry around with you has already been done. Choose settings that make the distribution your own, add the applications you want, add your personal music and document files, and then put it all on a pen drive.

This chapter steps you through the process of:

➤ Understanding what a live Linux distribution is

➤ Choosing a pen drive

➤ Getting and installing a bootable Linux system (Damn Small Linux is included on the *Linux Toys II* CD)

➤ Customizing that system to include the stuff you want in your bootable Linux

Understanding Live Linux Distributions

The concept behind a live Linux distribution (often referred to as a LiveCD or LiveDVD) is to be able to separate the computer operating system from the fixed hard disk on a computer. By storing an entire operating system on a removable medium (CD, DVD, pen drive, or zip drive), you can:

- Bypass any operating systems stored on the computer's hard disk
- Carry around all your favorite applications and data, without carrying a computer
- Use an operating system and applications you are comfortable with to access data stored on the computer's hard disk

Beginning with KNOPPIX

KNOPPIX is the best known of the live Linux distributions. It was first created to fit on a CD, and was therefore referred to as a LiveCD distribution. Because KNOPPIX was made to run from a read-only medium, some tricks had to be performed to get it to work:

- A running operating system expects to be able to write to the file system, so RAM and swap area were used to act as the file system.
- Applications were linked from the CD to their proper locations in the file system and uncompressed and run on the fly when they were requested.

At first, everyone thought that live Linux distributions were so cool, no one cared much about their minor inconveniences. For example, because the file system was set up in memory, any applications you added, data you created, or settings you made disappeared when you rebooted. Also, because the CD was acting as a hard disk would, you couldn't just remove it if you wanted to use the same drive to write data to, play a music CD, or install software from.

As live Linux distributions became more popular, features were added to overcome some of the challenges of running Linux on a computer without requiring a hard disk:

- Options to save system settings and set up persistent desktops where data could be stored on hard disk or removable read/write media were added.
- Smaller distributions were created (such as Damn Small Linux) that could be run entirely in RAM even on low-RAM machines, so you could pop out your CD and use the drive while the live Linux was still running. This also makes the operating system run really fast! (I describe how to run DSL from RAM near the end of the chapter.)

Some people liked these live Linux systems so much, they came up with ways of installing KNOPPIX, Damn Small Linux, and others on hard disk.

Using Damn Small Linux

The live Linux included on the *Linux Toys II* CD is called Damn Small Linux (http://
damnsmalllinux.org). It is derived from KNOPPIX, but instead of fitting on a 700MB
CD, DSL can fit in only 50MB on the boot medium. This makes DSL an excellent choice for
running from bootable business cards, small pen drives, or specialized handheld devices with
limited memory.

Besides not taking up much disk space, applications selected for DSL were chosen to get
the maximum functionality while running as efficiently as possible. The small demands on the
system also make DSL a good live Linux project if you have less powerful hardware. The minimum computer you need to run DSL is a 486DX CPU and 16MB of RAM.

Because DSL is so small, the entire operating system can be run from RAM, with as little as
128MB of total RAM available. That, combined with efficient applications, can make DSL
run faster than operating systems installed on hard disk.

Another good feature of DSL that makes is appropriate to demonstrate how to set up a customized live Linux distribution is its capability for installing applications tailored specifically
for DSL and its ability to carry those applications across reboots. Likewise, any configuration
or other files you create during a DSL session can be saved and carried across reboots.

John Andrews created Damn Small Linux "as an experiment to see how many usable desktop
applications can fit inside a 50MB Live CD." Robert Shingledecker joined John in DSL version 0.5 and is the developer responsible for almost all the custom features (including those
described in this chapter). Both have been extremely generous in providing feedback to me on
this chapter.

There is a very active user forum and many user-contributed extension applications. Ken Porter
manages and interacts with the user community to support the library of user-contributed
extensions.

Damn Small Linux also has a very active user forum in which you can participate (http://
damnsmalllinux.org/cri-bin/forums/ikonboard.cgi). If you want to support the
project, DSL has an online store (http://damnsmalllinux.org/store) where you can
purchase DSL on a CD or pen drive, as well as purchase Mini ITX systems.

Choosing a USB Pen Drive

To create a customized live Linux installation from Damn Small Linux, I chose to use a pen
drive as the medium for several reasons. The first is that the medium is rewriteable, so that both
the operating system and data can be carried on the same medium. Also, the size is very appeal-
ing (they can be smaller than a cigarette lighter) and prices have come down drastically in recent
months. (I bought a 1GB USB pen drive for about $50 and it seems to be working fine.)

In choosing a pen drive to use for a customized DSL live pen drive, there are a few things you should know:

- Pen drive is just one name for solid-state USB storage devices that are typically shaped like a pack of gum. You might also hear people refer to them as flash drives, key drives, USB sticks, memory keys, thumb drives, or similar names. They also come in different shapes.

- All power for the pen drive comes from the USB port it connects to.

- Because pen drives are typically encased in plastic, they can't be harmed by scratches or dirt, the way that CDs, DVDs, and floppy disks can.

- Available versions of USB pen drives are USB 1.0, 1.1, and 2.0. The 1.0 and 1.1 versions run at speeds of either 1.5 Mbit/s or 12 Mbit/s. The 2.0 versions can do speeds of up to 480 Mbit/s (although the highest reading speed is probably around 100Mbit/s).

- Linux views USB pen drives as USB mass storage devices. Often, Linux desktop systems are configured to mount and display an icon for a pen drive automatically after it is inserted, without needing any additional drivers.

- Computers with recent BIOSes can be configured to boot directly from the USB pen drive (recognizing it as a USB-ZIP or USB-HDD device). Other computers may need to start the boot process from another medium before accessing the USB pen drive.

The combination of cost, convenience, durability, and support by most modern computers makes a USB pen drive a good medium for creating a customized, bootable live Linux.

Making a Custom Damn Small Linux

Starting with the Damn Small Linux on the *Linux Toys II* CD that comes with this book, this chapter takes you through the process of customizing your own Damn Small Linux to run on a USB pen drive. I recommend you start with the following:

- *Linux Toys II* CD

- A USB pen drive that holds at least 64MB, although at least 128MB will give you much more flexibility for configuring Damn Small Linux and adding your own data and applications. (I used a 1GB pen drive.)

- A PC with a USB port. If possible, the PC should be set up to connect to the Internet because you'll need a connection to download applications you want to add later. DSL can automatically connect to the Internet from a wired Ethernet connection that has a DHCP server on the line (as do most connections from an ISP). (If the PC can't boot from a USB port, you can use a floppy disk or CD to boot DSL and access the pen drive, as described later.)

The basic procedure for customizing your own DSL pen drive is to boot DSL from the *Linux Toys II* CD, install DSL to the pen drive, reboot DSL from the pen drive, and then add custom applications, settings, and data to the drive. Figure 6-1 illustrates these steps.

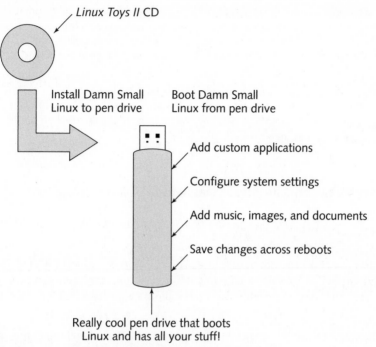

Linux Toys II CD

Install Damn Small
Linux to pen drive

Boot Damn Small
Linux from pen drive

Add custom applications

Configure system settings

Add music, images, and documents

Save changes across reboots

Really cool pen drive that boots
Linux and has all your stuff!

FIGURE 6-1: Customize your own live Linux on a pen drive.

Note

Because the *Linux Toys II* CD contains a customized Damn Small Linux, it is larger than the original 50MB DSL. If you are installing on a small pen drive, or don't want the *Linux Toys II* custom features, you can burn the original ISO image of DSL to CD and use that for this project instead. The image is located on the *Linux Toys II* CD as `dsl-1.3.1.iso` in the `isos/ch06-damnsmall` directory. See Chapter 5 for burning an ISO image to CD. Also, by the time you read this, a later version of DSL will be available. So you can download and burn a newer ISO image directly from `www.damnsmalllinux.org` to do this procedure if you prefer.

Step 1: Booting Damn Small Linux from a CD

In addition to including the software for creating the *Linux Toys II* projects, the CD that comes with this book includes a bootable Damn Small Linux distribution. The procedure for creating a custom Damn Small Linux on a pen drive begins by booting Damn Small Linux as follows:

1. Insert the *Linux Toys II* CD into the CD drive on your PC. As I noted earlier, you can also use an official copy of Damn Small Linux instead (`dsl-1.3.1.iso` is available on the CD as well).

2. Reboot your PC. The DSL boot screen appears.

3. Press Enter to start Damn Small Linux. If your PC is configured to boot from CD (as most are), DSL will boot from CD, try to detect your hardware, start up a desktop system, and connect to the network. (If you have a wired or wireless card on the PC and an available DHCP server on your network, DSL should be online automatically.)

If either you don't see the DSL boot screen or you see the boot screen, but the boot fails, refer to the "'What If I Can't Boot Damn Small Linux?'" sidebar.

DSL is configured to boot to a graphical desktop (init state 5). If you see the DSL desktop, you are now ready to start configuring your DSL pen drive.

"What If I Can't Boot Damn Small Linux?"

While Damn Small Linux will boot just fine on most PCs, in some cases you will need to give it a bit of help. Here are some things you can try:

- **Check BIOS** — If the boot process totally bypasses your CD, check that your PC's BIOS is capable of booting from CD. Do this by entering Setup when the computer first boots, checking boot order, and making sure that CD comes before your hard disk.

- **Try boot options** — If you see the DSL boot prompt, but the boot fails, try pressing F2 or F3 from the boot prompt. You will see available boot options. If video is scrambled, try `dsl vga=normal` (minimal VGA) or `dsl fb800x600` (or other fb options on a laptop). If DSL is not able to detect certain devices, try disabling those devices by entering `dsl` followed by one of the following: `noscsi`, `nopcmcia`, `nousb`, `noagp`, `noswap`, `noapm`, `noapic`, `nomce`, or `noddc`. Using `dsl failsafe` causes DSL to boot with almost no hardware detection.

- **Boot from floppy** — If your computer can't boot from CD at all, you can start the boot process from a floppy disk. The DSL project includes the `bootfloppy.img` and `bootfloppy-usb.img` files that you can use to start DSL from a floppy, and then continue the startup process from a CD or USB drive, respectively. I've included those images on the *Linux Toys II* CD (`isos/ch06-damnsmall` directory) or you can download them yourself from `damnsmalllinux.org`. So, from any Linux system, with bootfloppy.img in the current directory and a blank floppy in the first floppy drive, type the following to copy the DSL floppy boot image to floppy:

```
#dd if=bootfloppy.img of=/dev/fd0
```

The same concept can be used if you are unable to boot DSL from a pen drive. To use a boot floppy to boot DSL from a USB pen drive, change `bootfloppy.img` to `bootfloppy-usb.img` to create a floppy disk.

If your computer is not capable of booting Damn Small Linux to a graphical display, you should consider trying the project on another computer. Although DSL can run in text mode, most of the procedures in this chapter assume you have a working GUI.

Step 2: Preparing to Install DSL on Your Pen Drive

Before you begin installing DSL on your pen drive, check to make sure that:

- You are ready to completely erase your pen drive. (If there is anything on the pen drive that you want to keep, make a copy of it now.)

- Your PC has a USB port that matches your pen drive (USB 1.1 or USB 2.0).

- The pen drive is not mounted. (You can either not insert the pen drive until later in the process or unmount it, probably by typing `sudo umount /dev/sda1` or by unmounting it from the mount.app tool in the DSL panel.)

Note

To perform many of the steps in this chapter you need root access. Like KNOPPIX, DSL doesn't make you give a password to gain root access. However, it does have you ask for root access. Here are a few ways you can gain root access: right-click the desktop, select XShells → Root Access (to open a shell with root access); use the `sudo` command to run a command as the root user (as in the `sudo umount /dev/sda1` command shown previously). Or you could run emelFM (the default file manager) as root by selecting Apps → Tools → emelFM → emelFM as super-user to work with the file system as root. I'm told by Robert Shingledecker that future DSL releases will allow the regular `dsl` user to automatically have root permission (so, with a later DSL, you may not have to gain root access to proceed with this chapter).

Consider the type of computer you will boot from before you choose how to install DSL on your pen drive. Here are your choices:

- **USB-ZIP** — Most PCs that are capable of booting from a USB device will be able to boot a USB-ZIP device. Because USB-ZIP is an older standard, however, it has limitations. The boot partition on the USB drive must meet limited zip drive size specifications. To deal with this problem, a USB-ZIP pen drive install for DSL creates a small boot partition and then assigns the rest of the space on the pen drive to a separate partition. In cases where you want to boot directly from a lot of different computers, USB-ZIP is your best choice.

- **USB-HDD** — Newer computers will be able to boot the USB pen drive using the USB-HDD boot style. However, the USB-HDD boot option in not available in many older computers. Because the USB-HDD configured pen drive can be accessed once the computer boots, you can start the boot process for a USB-HDD drive from a floppy disk or CD boot and then continue it from the USB-HDD pen drive.

Note

See the "Starting up Your DSL Pen Drive" section later in this chapter for information on starting your DSL pen drive installation from a boot floppy or boot CD.

- **Embedded boot (within Windows or Linux)** — There is an embedded version of DSL available that you can use to boot DSL on a computer that is actively running Windows. DSL will appear in a window on your Windows desktop! When you do an install of that type of image on your pen drive, DSL includes the QEMU emulator. That combination allows you to launch DSL in its own window on your Windows or Linux desktop.

- **Five-way**—A recent addition to the DSL install family is the DSL 5-way install. The result of this install on your pen drive is that you will be able to boot DSL directly from a USB port, from floppy, from CD, or from within Windows or Linux.

  This install type requires a bit more manual setup and is therefore not included in this procedure. However, if you would like to try it, I've included the 5-way.tgz file on the *Linux Toys II* CD (`isos/ch06-damnsmall`). You can unpack that file, read the `README.txt` file for information on preparing your pen drive, and then run the `5way_install.sh` script to download and create your custom 5-way DSL.

Note

A good way to support the DSL initiative is to purchase a DSL pen drive from the www. damnsmalllinux.org Web site. It comes with the 5-way DSL preinstalled. I purchased one and I've been able to run DSL from it on computers from a Pentium II with 64MB of RAM (floppy boot) to a brand new IBM laptop from within Windows XP.

Step 3: Installing DSL on Your Pen Drive

With DSL running on your computer from the *Linux Toys II* CD, the following procedure describes how to format your pen drive, and then install DSL to it. To install DSL on your pen drive, follow these steps:

1. Insert the pen drive into a USB port on your computer (but don't mount it yet).

2. Determine the name of the device associated with your pen drive. In many cases, the drive device is `/dev/sda` and will include a single partition: `/dev/sda1` (for the first device on the first SCSI drive). If you don't know what the device name is, open a Terminal window (right-click the desktop, select XShells ➔ Root Access), and then type the following:

```
# /sbin/fdisk -l
Disk /dev/sda: 1024 MB, 1024966656 Bytes
32 heads, 63 sectors/track, 933 cylinders
Units = cylinders of 2016 * 512 = 1032192 bytes

   Device Boot    Start    End    Blocks    Id System
/dev/sda1          1        922    999813+   6  FAT16
```

In my case, the pen drive has 1GB of storage and is formatted for a single FAT16 (DOS) file system. The device name I would enter for the pen drive (that might be your device as well) is `sda`.

Caution

It's important that you get the right device name for your pen drive here. If you have more than one storage device appearing as a SCSI drive, your pen drive may be `sdb`, `sdc`, and so on. Be sure you have the right device name because in the next few steps you are going to erase everything on that drive! Also, don't enter the existing partition number (for example, `sda1`); enter the name that designates the entire drive to be erased (for example, `sda`).

3. The next step depends on whether you are doing a USB-ZIP, USB-HDD, or embedded install. Follow the instructions in the appropriate section.

USB-ZIP or USB-HDD Install

To create a DSL install that can be booted from your pen drive as USB-ZIP or USB-HDD, do one of the following:

- **USB-ZIP** — Right-click the desktop and select Apps → Tools → Install to USB Pendrive → For USB-ZIP Pendrive. A DSL USB Pendrive Installation screen appears. This install type will result in a pen drive with a small boot partition and a second partition that contains all your remaining disk space. Most computers will be able to boot the resulting pen drive.

- **USB-HDD** — Right-click the desktop and select Apps → Tools → Install to USB Pendrive → For USB-HDD Pendrive. A DSL USB Pendrive Installation screen appears. All data is placed on one partition on the pen drive for this install type. Only recent model PCs can be counted on to be able to boot USB-HDD formatted pen drives.

With either USB-ZIP or USB-HDD selected, when prompted select **y** to proceed. The following are the questions you are asked in the course of reformatting your pen drive and installing DSL for these two install types:

- **Installation or upgrade?** — If this is a new install (type **i**), your entire pen drive will be erased. For an upgrade (type **u**), new DSL files will overwrite the old ones.

- **Target device** — Enter the device name representing the pen drive (such as `sda`, as you determined earlier).

- **DSL ISO location** — Identify the location of your DSL ISO file. You can simply use the one included on the *Linux Toys II* or DSL CD (type the letter **l**), a file from your hard disk or other device (type **f**), or from the Web (type **w**). For this example, I chose the letter **l** (lowercase L), although you might be able to get a later version by choosing **w**.

- **Boot options** — You can type boot options to run every time your DSL pen drive boots. For example, if you know you will always run on a minimal video display, you might add `vga=normal`. If you know it will always run on a computer with lots of RAM, add the `toram` option (see the booting DSL section near the information for further information on running from RAM). Other boot options can let you automatically start services for allowing remote login (`ssh`), file sharing (`nfs`), system logging (`syslog`), printing (`lpd`), Web service (`monkey`), and file transfer (`ftp`).

- **Language** — If you are using a language/keyboard other than English, you can type a code for it here (`cs`, `da`, `de`, `es`, `fr`, `nl`, `it`, `pl`, `ru`, and `sk` are supported). Or just press Enter to continue in English with a U.S. keyboard.

This is your last chance to quit the DSL pen drive install. After the next step, DSL begins reformatting your pen drive.

■ **Continue?** — If you are ready, press **y** to continue. If necessary, the install will partition your pen drive (two partitions for USB-ZIP or one for USB-HDD), effectively erasing its contents, and then write the DSL system files to that pen drive. When you see the message USB installation has completed, press Enter as instructed.

After you press Enter, the window exits and your pen drive will contain the same Damn Small Linux you booted from your CD or downloaded from the Web. Next you need to boot DSL from the pen drive.

Embedded (Run Within Windows) Install

If you want to create a DSL pen drive that can start up in a window of a running desktop operating system (either Windows or Linux), use the following procedure (instead of the USB-ZIP or USB-HDD procedure just shown). Basically, all you need to do the install is unzip the dsl-embedded.zip file (included on the *Linux Toys II* CD) to the pen drive.

Here's how you would do that from a running Linux system:

1. **Insert the *Linux Toys II* CD.** Insert the CD containing the dsl-embedded.zip image into your computer's CD drive.

2. **Insert and mount pen drive.** Insert the pen drive into an available USB port and mount that drive.

3. **Mount CD and pen drive.** On most recent Linux desktop systems a formatted USB pen drive or CD will cause an icon of that drive to appear on the desktop. Simply double-click the icon to mount that drive. On the DSL desktop, a tool on the panel on the right side of the screen (mount.app) lets you cycle through the storage devices on your computer and click a button to mount the one you want (probably sda1 and cdrom for those devices). The pen drive must be mounted in a way that you can write to it.

4. **Unzip to the pen drive.** The last step is to unzip the dsl-embedded.zip file contents to the pen drive. The easiest way (and one that will work on any Linux system) is to open a Terminal window and gain root access. On a Fedora system, the CD might appear as /media/cdrecorder or /media/cdrom and the pen drive could be /media/usbdisk/. If those are true in your case, you could type the following:

```
# cd /media/usbdisk
# unzip /media/cdrom/isos/ch06-damnsmall/dsl-1.3.1-embedded.zip
```

Different Linux systems will have different mount points for your USB devices and CD drives, so be aware of that. The embedded DSL files are now installed on the pen drive and ready for you to proceed to the next step.

Step 4: Booting DSL from Your Pen Drive

To boot DSL directly from your pen drive, you need a computer that is capable of booting from a USB storage device (USB-ZIP or USB-HDD). This step describes how to determine if your PC can boot from your pen drive, and then tells how to configure your BIOS settings (from the CMOS setup screen) to boot from that pen drive.

Note If you find that your computer is not able to boot from a USB drive, refer to the "Starting Up Your DSL Pen Drive" section later in this chapter for information on starting the pen drive boot from a floppy or CD. Alternatively, if you created an embedded DSL, you can skip this step by simply booting your installed Windows or Linux system, and then starting your embedded DSL as described in the "Starting up Your DSL Pen Drive" section.

If possible, you should boot the pen drive from your normal desktop PC or other computer that contains all the information you want to add to your DSL pen drive. In later steps, I describe how to access your hard drive so you can copy over your documents, music, images, bookmarks, or other items from your hard drive to your pen drive.

1. Insert your pen drive (with Damn Small Linux installed on it) into a USB port on your PC.

2. Reboot your computer.

3. Before your computer can boot from hard disk, quickly enter Setup mode as noted on the screen (often by pressing the DEL key or F2 function key).

4. When the CMOS setup screen appears, look for entries that define which devices are booted and in which order. For example, you might see boot order as Floppy disk, then CD-ROM, then hard disk. You want to change the first boot option to be USB-ZIP (which will be the most common choice on older machines) or USB-HDD as is shown in Figure 6-2, so that your system will try to boot from your pen drive.

FIGURE 6-2: Change boot order for the BIOS in the CMOS setup screen.

5. Save your settings and continue with the boot process (again, look for indications on the screen for how to save and continue). DSL should boot after a few moments and appear on your screen as shown in Figure 6-3.

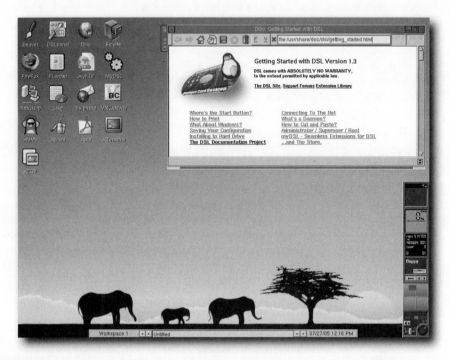

FIGURE 6-3: The Damn Small Linux desktop can boot up directly from a pen drive.

Step 5: Getting Access to Disks and Networks

While there is some configuration you can do without access to any outside resources (such as set up desktop preferences), to get other stuff you need on your pen drive you will probably want to have access to:

- **Hard disk**—Assuming you have booted your pen drive on your own personal computer (or other computer that contains the data you want), you can copy over many of the files and settings right from your own hard disk to your DSL pen drive. Damn Small Linux should detect all the partitions on your local hard disk so they can be easily mounted and accessed from DSL. You can then copy files across from your hard disk to incorporate them into your pen drive Linux system. (You can also use any content from the hard drive temporarily.)

- **Network**—If you have an Ethernet interface and an accessible DHCP server (which you typically do if you are plugged directly into your ISP's network equipment), DSL will boot directly up to the network. With access to the Internet, you can download lots of stuff you might want to add to your DSL pen drive. In particular, you can grab the applications you want to add to DSL, but you can also get themes, backgrounds, or more data files to add to your pen drive.

This step describes how to gain access to your hard disk partitions and network so you can get the stuff you need to add to your DSL pen drive.

Accessing Your Hard Disks

You don't need to access your hard disks to run DSL or other KNOPPIX-based LiveCD technology. You can simply run from your computer's RAM and removable media (CD, DVD, or pen drive). However, if you want to get stuff off of your hard disk to use with DSL, it's usually pretty easy to do so.

Mount a disk partition

A tool on the panel on the right side of your DSL screen (see the box marked *floppy* in Figure 6-3) lets you step through the available storage partitions on your computer and mount those that can be mounted. Click the right or left arrow keys to display partition names such as floppy, cdrom, sda1 (probably your pen drive), hda1 (probably the first partition on your IDE hard drive), and so on. To mount a device, simply click the icon to the left of those arrows (it turns green when it's mounted).

If you are interested in a more old-school, manual way to work with your disk partitions, refer to the "Understanding Partitions in Damn Small Linux" sidebar.

Note   Fedora Core uses the Logical Volume Management (LVM) file system type for the root file system (/) by default. Damn Small Linux cannot mount LVM file systems. You can get around this problem during Fedora Core installation by assigning your partitions as ext3 instead of LVM. If Fedora is already installed with LVM used, however, you will have to boot Fedora from hard disk to get the files you want. With Fedora booted, you can copy files directly to the pen drive or to another medium (such as CD) to get the files to DSL later.

Go ahead and mount any other partitions that you want to get files from during the DSL configuration process. Here are a few tips about working with these partitions:

- NTFS file systems can be mounted only read-only in DSL. While read/write support is available for NTFS partitions from Linux, it is not considered stable and is not included with DSL. So, you can get stuff from your NTFS partitions, but not write to them.

- Supported Linux partitions can be read from or written to from DSL. However, to protect you from yourself, DSL requires that you have root permission to write to a hard disk partition (for example, sudo cp file /mnt/hda3). Also, standard Linux file permissions apply, so a file that is readable only by root cannot even be copied without root permission.

Understanding Partitions in Damn Small Linux

When DSL boots up, it looks to see what storage media drives (hard disks, CD, floppy, DVD, pen drive, and so on) are connected to your computer. It then looks to see what file systems are available on separate areas of the disk (called partitions). An entry for each partition is added to the `/etc/fstab` file. Here's an example of an `/etc/fstab` file:

```
# Added by KNOPPIX

/dev/sda1 /mnt/sda1 ext2 noauto,users,exec 0 0

# Added by KNOPPIX

/dev/hda1 /mnt/hda1 ntfs noauto,users,exec,ro,uid=1001,gid=50 0 0

# Added by KNOPPIX

/dev/hda2 /mnt/hda2 vfat noauto,users,exec,umask=000,uid=1001,gid=50 0
0

# Added by KNOPPIX

/dev/hda3 /mnt/hda3 ext3 noauto,users,exec 0 0
```

This `/etc/fstab` file came from a system running Damn Small Linux where the hard drive was configured to boot both Windows and Linux. For clarity, I'm not showing lines from this file that don't apply to this discussion.

The lines in this example all were added after being detected by DSL (noted by the `Added by KNOPPIX` comments). The first entry (`/dev/sda1`) represents the pen drive from which DSL is running. The next two entries (`/dev/hda1` and `/dev/hda2`) are NTFS and VFAT partitions, respectively, that were created by the Windows system. The last partition (`/dev/hda3`) is a Linux ext3 file system where I have Fedora Core Linux installed. For each entry, the device name (`/dev/sda1`) is followed by the point in the file system where the partition will be mounted (`/mnt/sda1`).

To make any of the partitions just described accessible, you can use the `mount` command (as root user). Because most of the information needed to mount each partition is already in the `/etc/fstab` file, the `mount` command can be quite simple. For example, to mount the Linux partition, I use the `mount` command followed by either the device name or mount point, as follows:

```
$ sudo mount /mnt/hda3
```

■ For the purposes of being able to read and write from Windows or Linux partitions from DSL, use VFAT and ext3 file system types, respectively, when you first install those systems. Some people create a large, separate VFAT partition on computers that can be booted to different operating systems, to get the greatest flexibility in sharing data.

Browse your files

At this point, the mounted partition is part of your Damn Small Linux file system. You can use the shell, a file manager, or any application to access files from your mounted partitions.

DSL comes with the Emelfm file manager. Open it from an icon on your desktop. In DSL, storage devices are mounted under the /mnt file system. So, to browse to files on your hard disk, simply enter **/mnt** into the location box, and then click to enter the directory containing your mounted disk partition (hda1, hda2, and so on). Open a directory on the other side of the Emelfm file manager to copy files across from one directory to the other.

Accessing the Network

If you have an Ethernet card that is plugged into a high-speed Internet connection or a LAN switch that has a DHCP server on the line, you might have immediate access to the Internet when you boot DSL. DSL looks for a DHCP server when it boots and configures its network interface if it finds one.

DSL starts with the Dillo Web browser up on the screen. To check if your network is working, just type a Web address into the location box or click a link to the DSL site to make sure you can access the Internet. If you can, you're good to go.

However, if you don't have network access, there are a few ways to set up an Internet connection from DSL. Start by right-clicking the desktop to display the DSL menu. Then select System → Net Setup and choose from the following:

- **Wired Ethernet card (netcardconfig)** — If DHCP didn't get your network interface up when you started DSL, you can manually configure your wired Ethernet card. You will need to choose an IP address, netmask, broadcast address, default gateway, and DNS server. If you don't know this information, you should be able to get it from your Internet service provider (ISP) or network administrator.

- **Dial-up PPP** — Use this selection to create a Point-to-Point Protocol connection to your ISP over phone lines. To do this, you must have a supported modem, the telephone number of your ISP, DNS servers used, the type of authentication (PAP, CHAP, and so on), and the user name and password needed to complete your dial-up connection to the ISP. To dial the ISP, type the provider name you just created into the PPP Dial box and select Dial.

- **DSL/PPPoE** — If you have an Internet connection that goes through a DSL modem (that's Digital Subscriber Line, not Damn Small Linux), that service may require that you use PPP over Ethernet (PPPoE) to configure your connection. This selection lets you create a PPPoE connection using information provided from your ISP.

- **Wireless card (iwconfig, wlcardconfig, ndiswrapper, or prism2)** — Because wireless networking card drivers that are native to Linux are not as easily available as they are for wired cards, DSL offers several ways to configure your wireless networking cards. For wireless cards that were detected and had a Linux driver available, iwconfig lets you simply identify that interface and add information needed to use that card (such as its device name, channel number, as well as SID and WEP identifiers).

If a driver for your card wasn't found, selecting wlcardconfig gives you the opportunity to configure that card. When no Linux driver is available for your wireless card, you may be able to select ndiswrapper and configure your card to incorporate a Windows driver. The prism2 selection lets you configure wireless cards that use the Prism2 chipset.

Note Configuration files created when you set up your network connections in DSL are stored in the /opt directory. However, not every configuration file in /opt is saved automatically when you use the backup feature of DSL. Check the descriptions of the `.filetool.lst` file and `boot-local.sh` script later in this chapter for information on how to save configuration files and commands you want to rerun, respectively.

After you have the Internet and your hard disk accessible to DSL, you are ready to get all the stuff you need to build up your bootable Damn Small Linux pen drive.

Step 6: Adding Fun Stuff to Your DSL Pen Drive

Now the fun begins. It's time to fix up your DSL configuration so that it includes everything you want on your portable Linux system. The best place to start adding applications and preferences to your DSL pen drive is with the DSL Download Extension Panel. Open that panel by double-clicking MyDSL on the desktop or by right-clicking the desktop and selecting Apps → Tools → MyDSL Browser. Figure 6-4 shows the DSL Download Extension Panel.

FIGURE 6-4: Add multimedia players, office
programs, or themes to your pen drive.

Downloading extensions (even information on which ones are available) requires that you have a connection to the Internet. Once you do, you can begin by selecting applications, themes, and other components to download and install.

Getting Applications

When you download an application to DSL to use on your pen drive, you want to do it in such a way that it doesn't disappear the next time you reboot. The following procedure describes how to select, download, and install an application so it is available on your DSL pen drive across reboots.

To try out applications, it's best to download them to a temporary directory (such as /tmp) and install them from there. Later, you can copy over the applications to your pen drive all at once to keep them permanently.

1. Open the DSL Download Extension Panel by selecting MyDSL from the desktop.

2. From the DSL Download Extension Panel, select a category. For my example, I select Multimedia. The multimedia panel appears.

3. Scroll the application list and select one that interests you. I chose grip (CD player and ripper). In Figure 6-5 you can see the information that is displayed for grip from the multimedia list.

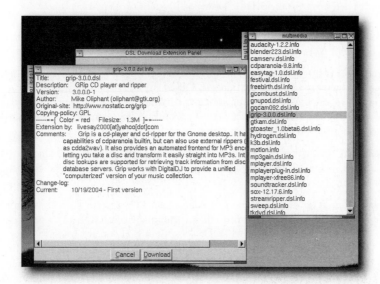

FIGURE 6-5: See descriptions of an application before you download and install.

4. If you want to install the application, click the Download button. A pop-up window asks what directory you want to put the application in.

5. Type the location of the root of your pen drive directory (in this example, I use /tmp as recommended by DSL) and select Download. The application is downloaded and installed on your DSL pen drive. For most applications, an icon will appear on the desktop immediately to indicate that the application is installed.

You can repeat this process for every application you want to install. Before you install any application, be sure to read the description. Some applications are quite large and will quickly fill up your pen drive and use up system resources. Also, because /tmp is assigned to your RAM disk, you can quickly run out of temporary space there as well. For example, the OpenOffice.org productivity suite requires about 66MB of disk space and 384MB of RAM to run.

Here are a few things you should know about any applications you install:

- The next time you boot your pen drive, DSL will look for available applications in the root of the pen drive directory and install those applications again.

- To start any of the applications you installed, look for an icon on the desktop or right-click on the desktop to display the DSL menu. On the DSL menu, select myDSL to see a list of your applications, and then click the one you want to run.

The following is a list of applications that, if you have the disk space, you might consider adding to your pen drive from the DSL Download Extension Panel:

- **Gaim** — If you just love to instant message with your friends, Gaim is a clone of the AOL Instant Messenger client that runs in Linux. To add it, select Net ➔ gaim.

- **OpenOffice.org** — This suite of word processing, spreadsheet, presentation, and related office productivity tools gives Microsoft Office a run for its money. If you have the space for it, it's a great way to take professional quality writing and presentation tools on the road with you. To install it, select apps ➔ openoffice. For a smaller, but capable word processor, you could try Abiword (apps ➔ abiword).

- **The GIMP** — If you have the space for it (about 26MB), the GIMP is the premiere photo retouching, image composition, and authoring tool available with Linux. To add it, select apps ➔ gimp.

- **Grip** — This application lets you play your music CDs and rip them to your pen drive or hard disk. Because DSL in our procedure is running from RAM and a pen drive, you can play CDs from your CD drive while DSL is running. If you are going to rip and encode music to add to your pen drive, however, I recommend you rip to hard drive first. Then copy the music files to your pen drive (perhaps /mnt/sda1/music), to avoid too much writing to your pen drive. To add Grip to your DSL pen drive, select Multimedia ➔ grip.

- **Gtkam** — If you want to download images from your digital camera to your pen drive, you can add the gtkam application. To add gtkam, select Multimedia ➔ gtkam.

- **Xine** — To play video, xine and mplayer both work well in DSL, provided you have enough processing power and a properly configured video card to handle it. You can install xine or mplayer by selecting Multimedia, and then either xine or mplayer.

The applications just described consume much more computing resources than do the ones that come with DSL. So if you are using a small pen drive (128MB or less) and have low system RAM (under 256MB), you'll probably do best using the applications that come with DSL and adding only a few special applications.

After you have chosen the applications you like, copy them from your /tmp directory to the root of your pen drive. At this point your pen drive (/dev/sda1) is probably mounted on the /cdrom directory. Gain root access to your file system (from Emelfm or from a shell) and copy the `*.dsl` files representing the applications you want to keep from your `/tmp` directory to the pen drive. For example, to copy the grip application, you could type:

```
$ sudo cp /tmp/grip-3.0.0.dsl /cdrom
```

Tables 6-1, 6-2, and 6-3 contain lists of general, multimedia, and game applications that are available for you to download. The applications are listed by the name of the button on the DSL Download Extension Panel.

Table 6-1: General Applications for Your DSL Pen Drive

Application	Description
abiword	Word processor
antiword	Converts Microsoft Word documents into text or PostScript
bc	Simple calculator program
chameleon	Adds pictures or colors to the desktop (X) background
cinepaint	Image retouching program for high-resolution images
dia	Diagram and blueprint creation program
dosbox	Runs old DOS applications and games
dsl-aterm	Terminal (aterm) extension for transparent background
endeavor	File manager suite to browse files, view images, and archive
figurine	Xfig vector graphics editor for X
gimp	For photo retouching, image authoring, and composition
gmoo	Graphical multi-user dungeon (MUD) client
gnuplot	Creates 2D and 3D plots.
gpsk31	Ham radio Phase Shift Keying, 31 Baud (PSK31) interface
gtkfind	Graphical file finding program
gtksee	Image viewer and browser, with slide show capability
gv	PostScript and PDF file viewer
ImageMagick	Image creation and editing tool collection
inkscape	SVG editor, similar to Illustrator and CorelDraw
kjvbible	HTML version of King James Version of the Bible
lifelines	Genealogical database software
nedit	Graphical text-editing software
octave	Math and numeric processing software

Continued

Table 6-1 (continued)

Application	Description
openoffice	Office productivity suite (works with many office formats)
parted	Disk partitioning and resizing tool
predict-gsat	Multi-user satellite tracking and orbital prediction program
pspp	Does statistical analysis of data using SPSS language
qcad	Two-dimensional computer aided drafting application
qsstv	Slow scan Ham radio program
R	Statistical and graphical R language testing tools
rkhunter	Scans for rootkits, backdoors, and other exploits
rox	Graphical file manager and viewer
sc	Spreadsheet that runs in a text-based (curses) environment
scite	Graphical programming editor
sketch	Interactive vector drawing program
soundmodem	Makes a sound card into a packet radio modem
ted	Rich text format (RTF) text editor
tux_commander	File manager with side-by-side panels
tuxpaint	Drawing program for children
tuxtype	Typing tutor for children
twisted	Framework for writing network applications
vim_full	Entire vim text editor, including help files, scripts, and more
wv	Converts and displays Microsoft Word documents
wvdial	Modem dialer program
xdesktopwaves	Makes your X desktop background appear to be under water
xephem	Ephemeris for charting planets, stars, and constellations
xfireworks	Plays fireworks on your screen
xfishtank	Displays moving fish on your desktop
xplanet	Displays an earth image on your desktop's X background
xscreensaverGTK	Reduced set of mpie xscreensavers
xv	Picture file viewer
xvkbd	Virtual keyboard for X Window System
zile	Text editor similar to Emacs

Table 6-2: Multimedia Applications for Your DSL Pen Drive

Application	Description
audacity	Editor for MP3, Ogg Vorbis, and other digital audio files
blender	3D modeling and animation program
camserv	Webcam server that works with video4linux
cdparanoia	CD music ripper
easytag	Views/edits tags in MP3, Ogg Vorbis, and other audio files
festival	Framework for speech synthesis systems
freebirth	Music sequencer and synthesizer
gcombust	CD burning frontend
gnupod	Collection of scripts for working with iPods
gqcam	Similar to QuickPict software for QuickCam
grip	CD player and ripper
gtkam	Graphical tool for downloading images from digital cameras
gtoaster	CD recording frontend
hydrogen	Drum machine software
k3b	KDE CD burning application
motion	Video camera software with motion detection features
mp3gain	Command line tool for analyzing mp3 gain fields
mplayer	Multimedia video and audio player for many content types
mplayerplug-in	Plays video/audio content in Mozilla and Firefox browsers
soundtracker	Sound editor and player
sox	Sound processing and conversion tools
streamripper	Rips streaming Shoutcast and Icecast content
sweep	Audio file editor/player for WAV, Ogg Vorbis, and others
tkdvd	DVD burning frontend
trommler	Drum machine application
xdrum	Drum machine application for small systems
xine	Multimedia video/audio player, supporting many formats
xmms	Set of applications for playing audio in a variety of formats
xwave	Wave recorder for small systems (runs on X)

Table 6-3: Games for Your DSL Pen Drive

Application	Description
abuse	First person shooter game
ace	Penguins card games collection
acm	Flying simulation game
a_steroid	XFree asteroids game
barrage	Barrage war game for destroying targets in a limited time
billard	Play billiards against the computer
blast	Shoot holes in your applications
briquolo	3D breakout game
buzz	Buzz Aldrin's race into space game
cgoban	Strategy board game
chromium	2D space shooting game
circuslinux	Circus Linux balloon-popping game
doom	Game engine for DOOM first-person shooter
dossizola	Strategy game to block your opponents
dsl-cube	3D shooter game
dsl-xjig	Jigsaw puzzle game
eboard	Chess board that can use different chess engines
enrapture	Role playing space game
falling_tower	Game where you try to jump up a tower
freeciv	Civilization clone
freecraft	WarCraft II fantasy strategy game clone
frozen-bubble	Colorful game for removing bubbles of like colors
gcompris	Educational software for kids from 2 to 10
gtetrinet	Multiplayer tetrinet game
hexxagon	Strategy board game
intellivision_gamepak	Clones of Intellivision games
invaders	Classic space invaders game for DosBox
koth	Two-player tank strategy game

Application	Description
koules	Competitive pushing game
lgames	Classic Linux game clones of Breakout, Tetris, LPairs, and the like
lincity	Strategy game
liquidwar	World domination game
mathwar	Math card game
nethack	NetHack role playing game
penguin-command	Missile command game clone
pente	Strategy game to get five-in-a-row
pipenightdreams	Game for redirecting sewage (a connect-the-pipes game)
quake2	3D Quake II gaming engine for X
sdlroids	Asteroids game
snake	Snake game
spearofdestiny	Spear of Destiny first-person 3D shooter
stella	Game emulator for Atari 2600 consoles
supertux	SuperMario clone
toppler	Tower Toppler strategy game
torcs	Car simulator 3D racing game
tuxracer	Race Tux the penguin down a mountain
Ultima-AOD	Classic Ultima role-playing games for DosBox from the 1980s
vba	Emulator for Visual Boy Advance
wesnoth	Turn-based Battle for Wesnoth strategy game
wof	Wings of Fury aircraft game for DosBox
xasteroids	Asteroids game
xbill	Splat Bill game
xboing	Breakout style game
xbubble	Frozen bubble clone
xgalaga	Space shooting game
xgammon	Backgammon game for X
xmahjongg	Mahjongg tile matching game for X
xmame	Classic game console emulator

Continued

Table 6-3 *(continued)*

Application	Description
xpat2	Card game collection
xpen	Penguins walking on your desktop
xpuyopuyo	Tetris-like game
xskat	Skat card game
zsnes	Game emulator for Super-Nintendo

Any of these games that you add to the root directory of your pen drive will be available the next time you boot your pen drive.

Getting Network and Administrative Tools

So far, the applications I've described that you can add to DSL are desktop oriented. There are also a variety of other tools you can download and install on DSL from the DSL Download Extension Panel. Here are some examples:

- **Net** — Applications for accessing resources on the Internet or other networks are available by selecting the Net button. Applications you might consider adding include Thunderbird Email client (mozilla-thunderbird), Samba file and print services for Windows (samba), and Bittorrent peer-to-peer download client (bittorrent-cli). You can also find a selection of Web browsers, ICQ clients, news readers, and other Web applications.

- **System** — Tools for administering and tuning your DSL system are available from the System button. Tools include iptables firewalls (iptables), dpkg to enable apt to get Debian applications for DSL, and GRUB bootloader (grub). If you have an NVidia video card, consider adding the NVidia driver (especially if you plan to play video or do gaming or other graphic-intensive applications).

Step 7: Changing Your DSL Desktop Features

While the DSL desktop is very attractive, it's likely that you'll want to change the look and feel of the desktop to some extent to suit your tastes and match how you use the computer. Here are some ways you can change your DSL desktop and save those changes so they are there when you reboot.

- **Change desktop themes.** DSL comes with several themes already installed. From the DSL Download Extension Panel, you can click the Themes button to download other themes that will work with the fluxbox window manager (which is the default with DSL). To change your current theme, right-click the desktop and from the DSL menu select Desktop ➜ Styles, and then choose the theme you want. Figure 6-6 shows the Liquidglass theme.

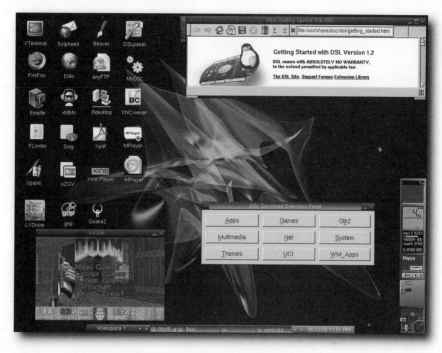

FIGURE 6-6: Select Liquidglass or other fluxbox themes (or download more).

- **Add window manager applications.** There are a bunch of little window manager tools you can add to spruce up your desktop. From the WM_Apps button on the DSL Download Extension Panel, you can add applets to dock in your panels such as clocks, calculators, and puzzles. You can even change your entire window manager from fluxbox to icewm, twm, or others.

- **Change desktop behavior.** You can change how desktop features such as focus, window placement, tabs, and icons are all used on the desktop. Right-click on the desktop to see the DSL menu. Then select Desktop ➔ Configuration and choose from a variety of desktop options.

Step 8: Configuring and Saving System Settings

Preferences for individuals are stored in the user's home directory (often in files beginning with a dot, so they don't appear normally in file listings). Because the /etc directory, where system-wide configuration is normally stored, is not all writeable from DSL, configuration information you want to persist across reboots in DSL is mostly stored in the /opt directory. For example, DSL tools for configuring a printer or PPP connection store resulting configuration files in /opt.

Although you may not know what hardware will always be attached to the computer you use with your DSL pen drive, you will probably want the settings associated with the applications you use to stay across reboots. Here are some applications you should consider setting up:

- **Email client** — You can identify your incoming and outgoing mail servers, account information, and various preferences for your email client. You can select Sylpheed to configure it, or you can download Mozilla Thunderbird or other email client.

- **Web browser** — While the default Dillo Web browser is fairly simple, you may want to add and save bookmarks you gather with it. If you use Firefox, you can import bookmarks or set different preferences for browsing. You can also configure the Links browser.

- **Chats and instant messaging** — You can store your buddy lists, favorite IRC channels, and other preferences related to only chat and instant messaging. DSL includes nAIM, nIRC, and nICQ clients in that category.

- **Music player** — You can set up playlists of music stored on your pen drive in applications such as xMMs.

Many of the system services you configure for DSL can also be saved across reboots, although you have to choose to do so explicitly in some cases. Right-click the desktop to see the DSL panel. Then choose System → Control Panel. From the DSL Control Panel, you can configure several different services for your computer, including login/ remote shell (`sshd` server), printing, file sharing (NFS), and FTP (BetaFTP) services. You can also configure networking hardware and interfaces, assuming that similar configurations work for other computers where you use your pen drive.

For the settings you just made to persist across reboots, you need to save the configuration files that were just created or modified. DSL has made that easy for you: Simply indicate a location for your settings to be backed up to, and it automatically backs up all settings from your home directory (personal settings) and some from your `/opt` directory (system settings).

Here's how to identify your backup files, set the location of your backed up settings, and backup the files:

1. Open the file `.filetool.lst` from your home directory (`/home/dsl`). Note that the file begins with a dot, so you need to type **ls -a** to see it from the shell. The file contains a list of files and directories to be backed up. Here's an example of what that file might contain:

   ```
   opt/ppp
   opt/bootlocal.sh
   opt/powerdown.sh
   opt/.dslrc
   opt/.mydsl_dir
   home/dsl/
   ```

2. Add any additional files or directories to that file that you want backed up and save the file. For example, there may be other files in the `opt` directory you want backed up.

3. Open the DSL Control Panel (select DSLpanel from the desktop).

4. From the Control Panel, choose Backup/Restore. It will ask you where you want to back up your saved files.

5. Type the name of the first partition on your pen drive (in most cases, it is `sda1`) and click Backup. A compressed archive of the saved files will be written to the `backup.tar.gz` file in the root of your pen drive, to be restored on the next reboot.

The `bootlocal.sh` file is where you can put any commands that you want run each time DSL boots up. Note that there is also a `.xfiletool.lst` file in the `/home/dsl` directory that *excludes* files that you don't want backed up (such as cache files).

An example of configuration information that is not saved is the basic network configuration setup you might enter if there were no DHCP server on your network (using the Netcardconfig tool). Let's assume you want to configure a network connection with an IP address of 10.0.0.2, a gateway address of 10.0.0.1, and a DNS name server with address 11.22.33.44 (use an address provided by your ISP). You could add these lines to your `/opt/bootlocal.sh` file:

```
ifconfig eth0 ip 10.0.0.2
route add default gw 10.0.0.1
echo nameserver 11.22.33.44 > /etc/resolv.conf
```

When you boot DSL, you should also add `dsl nodhcp` to the boot prompt so you don't have to wait for DSL to try and fail to get a DHCP server.

Step 9: Adding Documents, Music, and Images

With your pen drive inserted into a USB port, you can add the data files you want to the directory where your pen drive is mounted (probably `/cdrom`). You might want to create subdirectories to store your data (such as `/cdrom/music` or `/cdrom/documents`). You can copy files to those directories and use them with any applications that are available with DSL. (Remember that you need root access to copy files to your pen drive.)

Because space on the pen drive is a concern, consider compressing your music with Ogg Vorbis tools and zipping document and image files.

Step 10: Starting up Your DSL Pen Drive

Your live Linux pen drive should now be ready to roll. For the normal way to boot your USB-ZIP or USB-HDD pen drives, refer to "Step 4: Booting DSL from Your Pen Drive." However, there are cases where booting directly from one of those formats doesn't work or you might want to do something special when you boot. The following subsections include some different ways to boot your DSL pen drive.

Floppy Boot to Pen Drive

Some older computers can't boot from USB drives at all, even if they have USB ports. In those cases, you can create the pen drive as you would normally (USB-ZIP or USB-HDD), but also create a boot floppy using the file `bootfloppy-usb.img` as described in the "'What If I Can't Boot Damn Small Linux?'" sidebar.

CD Boot to Pen Drive

Same deal as with the floppy USB boot, but you can start the boot process from a DSL CD (such as the *Linux Toys II* CD). You tell the CD to continue from the USB pen drive by typing **dsl fromhd=/dev/sda1** from the boot prompt (assuming the pen drive to be on your first SCSI device). (You may be able to skip the boot prompt lines because the DSL CD seems to look for and find other DSL distributions on a pen drive that's inserted.)

Embedded Pen Drive Boot within Windows or Linux

If you did an embedded install of DSL to your pen drive, you can boot DSL directly from either Windows or Linux while those systems are still running. While you will take a performance hit running DSL inside of Windows or Linux, it's a good way to get your email or get on the Web from a computer without rebooting.

To try it out, start up any desktop Windows or Linux system. Then do the following:

1. Insert your DSL pen drive with the embedded DSL install into a USB port. In many Windows and Linux desktops, an icon will appear on the desktop or in the My Computer folder.

2. Open the icon representing your pen drive. You should see a folder displaying the top-level directory of that drive.

3. To start DSL so that it appears in a window on the desktop, launch one of the following two commands, depending on whether you are currently in Windows or Linux. For Windows, launch the following:

   ```
   dsl-windows.bat
   ```

   If you are in Linux, launch the following:

   ```
   dsl-linux.sh
   ```

As if by magic, a QEMU window will open on the desktop and a DSL desktop will boot up in that window. Click in that window to use it as you would any DSL desktop system. Press the Ctrl+Alt keys together to return mouse control outside of that window. You can shut down DSL as you would normally when you are done. Then close the QEMU window.

Although the embedded DSL pen drive install I described cannot boot up directly, using a DSL boot CD, you can boot your configured embedded DSL pen drive. With the pen drive inserted, you could type the following from the DSL boot prompt:

```
boot: dsl fromhd=/dev/sda1 qemu frugal
```

Booting DSL from RAM

When DSL normally boots, you must keep your CD or pen drive inserted during its entire operation. That's because much of the DSL system is mounted and accessed directly from the original medium. This allows DSL to run on computers with very little RAM (as little as 32MB).

If you have lots of RAM available, however, you can have all of DSL loaded into RAM and run from there. Not only will this give you a big performance boost, but you can also remove the boot medium if you like after DSL is running. This is especially nice, for example, if you are booting from CD and you want to use the CD drive to play music or backup files.

To run DSL from RAM you need at least 128MB of RAM on your computer. If you do, you can start booting DSL from RAM by typing the following from the DSL boot prompt when you first boot DSL:

```
boot: dsl toram
```

The initial boot will take longer than a normal DSL boot as the DSL image is copied to ramdisk. After that, however, you should see much faster performance out of DSL. Any of the supported boot formats can use the `toram` feature.

Summary

The features and usefulness of live Linux distributions have grown dramatically in the past few years. Not only can distributions such as KNOPPIX and Damn Small Linux have a Linux system up and running on your computer within a few minutes, they can also be customized and extended in many different ways.

The project covered in this chapter is a customized version of Damn Small Linux that runs on a pen drive and includes the applications, settings, and data that you want to carry around with you. Using the *Linux Toys II* CD, which contains a version of Damn Small Linux, I describe how to install DSL to the pen drive, add applications, customize settings, and then take the pen drive on the road so you can show everyone how smart you are.

Automating Home Lights and Gadgets with X10

By automating your home using X10 devices and software (provided with this book), you can control the lights, alarms, garage doors, sprinklers, or most any other appliance you can plug in or wire in. That control can come from a handheld remote, centralized switches, or (you guessed it) . . . Linux.

While there are lots of ways to turn your lights and appliances off and on with X10, managing X10 from your computer adds the ability to automate those activities. Using Linux as your operating system and open source software, you have the further advantage of being able to tailor those tools to your needs.

This chapter starts you off using two different X10 hardware starter packages and two X10 open source software projects:

➤ **Firecracker and the BottleRocket project** — Using an inexpensive Firecracker X10 starter kit and BottleRocket (mlug.missouri. edu/~tymm) you request simple on/off and dimming functions from X10 lights and appliances. Several Web-based and GUI tools are available that rely on BottleRocket.

➤ **ActiveHome and the Heyu project** — The Heyu version 2 project (www.heyu.org) includes a broad range of X10 features, including the ability to work with X10 hardware that communicates in two directions and offload X10 schedules to an ActiveHome device (so schedules continue, even with your computer off). With Heyu, X10 software can detect the status of devices and react to X10 events from those devices (such as turning on a light when motion is detected).

To do this project, all you need is a PC that has an RS232 serial port (and Linux installed) and a few dollars worth of X10 equipment. You can grow these projects to incorporate a large number of X10 devices and create scripts for automating X10 activities. For newer PCs supplied with USB ports but no RS232 serial ports, both BottleRocket and Heyu will work with a USB-to-Serial adapter. (Before purchasing such an adapter, make sure it is compatible with your version of Linux.)

Understanding X10

If you have electrical power running through your home or business, you can probably use X10 to control your lights and various devices. X10 is a simple protocol that allows X10 devices to communicate across power lines in your building. It is a protocol that broadcasts codes that each X10 device connected on the same power system can see. Each device responds to the codes based on its own settings.

X10 devices are identified by an address that is represented by a single-letter house code (from A to P) and a unit number (from 1 to 16). That lets you have up to 256 separately controllable devices in your location. Because all devices see every command, however, you can have multiple units associated with a particular house code/unit (for example, one house code/unit number might turn on several outside lights).

Although the X10 signals for turning devices on and off (or dimming them) are sent over your power lines, those signals can originate from radio frequency (RF) transmitters that talk to X10 devices (called transceivers). Those transmitters can be such things as handheld remotes or devices connected to your computer (which is what interests us most with this project).

Figure 7-1 shows an example of an X10 configuration that includes a variety of X10 devices controlled from both handheld remotes and computers running Linux X10 applications.

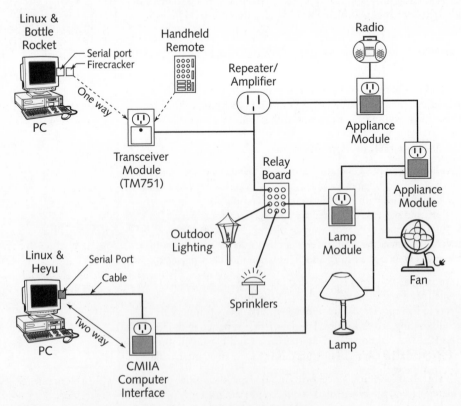

FIGURE 7-1: Control X10 devices from computers running Linux.

In Figure 7-1, two different Linux applications are illustrated for controlling X10 devices. BottleRocket software can communicate with an X10 Firecracker device — a little dongle that connects to your computer's serial port and uses RF to send X10 signals to a transceiver. Heyu software talks to ActiveHome hardware that connects to a serial port, but plugs directly into an electrical outlet to send X10 signals.

Once X10 signals are sent to your house's power lines, they can control a variety of modules. You can plug lamps or appliances directly into external modules that are plugged into your outlets. Or you can get modules that are wired directly into your lights or appliances, so they are hidden behind the walls.

To improve signal strength, you can get X10 signal amplifiers and receivers. Often, these devices are connected to 220-volt power outlets, to connect signals across multiple 110-volt power sources in a house. However, there are also signal boosters that can be hard-wired into your house wiring.

X10 protocol supports one-way and two-way communication. However, not all hardware for transmitting X10 signals can also receive feedback from X10 modules (and not all X10 modules are two-way). But regardless of whether you are using one-way or two-way transmitters, you can use lamp and appliance modules simply to turn devices on and off.

Getting X10 Hardware

A wide variety of X10 hardware is available from online sites and electronics stores. Although quality of X10 hardware can vary, most X10 hardware complies with X10 standards and should therefore work together.

Many online sites selling X10 hardware have pop-up windows, flashing text, and hot specials. I suggest you shop around a bit, however, because the noisiest sites don't always have the best deals. Here are a few sites you can check out that offer a nice range of X10 products:

- **Smarthome** (www.smarthome.com)
- **X10** (www.x10.com/home2.html or www.x10pro.com)
- **Home Controls** (www.homecontrols.com)
- **Outpost** (www.outpost.com)

While I haven't used all of these sites (and therefore can't personally recommend them) I have ordered from Smarthome and Outpost without any problems. Charles Sullivan suggests that the X10.com Web site offers some of the best deals on X10 hardware. If you check regularly and sign up for its mailing list, you can sometimes get 2-for-1, 3-for-1, or even 6-for-1 deals on "module mania" sales. If you prefer going to brick-and-mortar stores, you can try electronics retailers such as Radio Shack and Fry's Electronics.

Choosing X10 Starter Kits

If you don't have any X10 hardware, you should consider purchasing an X10 starter kit. As noted earlier, the two projects featured in this chapter (BottleRocket and Heyu), can be used with the Firecracker and ActiveHome starter kits, respectively.

I was able to purchase a basic four-piece Firecracker kit (one-way computer interface, remote control, transceiver, and one lamp module) for $39.99. The basic ActiveHome CK11A kit (two-way computer interface, remote control, credit card control, two-way transceiver, lamp module, and ActiveHome software for Windows) was available for $49.99. On occasion, you can find better deals, so be sure to shop around.

Beyond the basic X10 starter kits, you can purchase as many X10 lamp modules, appliance modules, switches, remotes, or other devices that you like. So, depending on which computer interface you are starting with, choose the other X10 hardware items that interest you, and then proceed to either the BottleRocket or Heyu sections that follow.

Choosing Transceivers

Although X10 works through the power lines in the house, often X10 requests are transmitted from wireless devices (such as key pads and computer modules) that send signals through the air to X10 transceivers. Those transceivers in turn transmit the X10 commands to the house wiring, where they can be picked up by other X10 devices.

Here are a few issues to consider when you are choosing an X10 transceiver:

- **Number of house codes** — Inexpensive X10 transceivers will operate only on a single house code (represented by a letter from A to P that you choose). So, if you have only one of those transceivers, all devices must be on that house code (and you can have only 16 of them). To talk to devices on multiple house codes (to communicate with more than 16 units), you need multiple inexpensive transceivers. You can, however, purchase a transceiver that can receive all 16 house codes.

- **Antenna** — Many X10 transceivers have a single antennae attached directly to the transceiver. To improve reception, some transceivers come with external antennas that can be placed several feet away from where the transceiver is plugged into a power outlet.

Instead of using an RF transmitter, you can use a device that sends signals directly into your power lines. An example of this type of device is the CM11A computer interface that plugs directly into a power outlet and receives signals from your computer's serial port.

Choosing Plug-in Modules

Plug-in modules are about the size of a large bar of soap and plug directly into a power outlet. There are plug-in lamp modules and appliance modules:

- **Lamp modules** — These modules typically allow you to plug in a lamp or other light source that is up to 300 watts.

- **Appliance modules** — These modules typically support lights up to 500 watts, but can also be used to turn on and off appliances. For example, the appliance might be a television up to 400 or 500 watts or a motor with up to one-third horsepower.

- **Heavy-duty appliance modules** — For high-wattage, 220V appliances (including water heaters, air conditioners, stoves, or pool pumps) you can purchase 20-amp appliance modules. For example, Leviton makes an appliance module that can turn your 220V devices on or off using X10 or a local switch (see www.smarthome.com/2210i.html).

On the whole, these plug-in modules are fairly inexpensive. You usually get at least one with an X10 starter kit. More expensive modules will support two-way communications and include the capability to save settings, even if the unit is unplugged.

Choosing Hardwired Modules

If you don't like those plug-in modules sticking out of the power outlets all over your house, there are some other options available. Many X10 devices are designed to be hardwired directly to your house wiring. Here are a few examples:

- **Inline modules** — You can get inline receiver modules that can go inside a lighting fixture or inside an electrical box.

- **Wall switch modules** — By installing an X10 wall switch, a light can be turned on and off either from an X10 signal or directly from the wall switch itself.

- **Screw-in lamp modules** — There are modules that screw directly into lamp sockets and receive X10 codes to turn the light bulb screwed into them on or off.

- **Motion detectors** — Most motion detectors will simply turn on a light that is connected to them. X10 motion detectors can be set to send a house code, so that they can turn on or off any X10 device in your house.

- **Wired X10 cameras** — These cameras can be configured to any house code and number, so that they can be turned on and off from your computer, a handheld device, or even a motion detector.

Choosing Other Interesting X10 Hardware

Besides lights, motion detectors, and cameras, there are interesting X10 hardware devices available that you might not have thought of. To control a whole set of low-voltage X10 devices from a single source, you can get a relay controller.

Relay controllers are very good for things like sprinkler systems, where you have multiple zones that you want to control from a single location. Relay controllers come in sets of four (www.smarthome.com/2310.html) and eight (www.smarthome.com/2315m.html) relay units. Instead of plugging lamps or appliances into these controllers, you simply connect the wires for the devices you want to the contact closures.

Caution

While it is possible to attach X10 modules to turn such things as fireplaces, heaters, HVAC dampers, and air conditioning units on and off, it is dangerous to do so. X10 is insecure by its nature. In fact, it's possible for noise on the power lines to turn a device on or off. Therefore, X10 devices should never be used to control devices that could injure people or property if they were to go off or on unexpectedly.

When you are using X10 devices that can send as well as receive, changes of temperature, movements, and other events can trigger X10 signals to be sent from these devices. You can set off alarm systems, turn on pool pumps and heaters, or simply report events to your X10 software to gather data. For example, there is a barking dog alarm that can go off when motion is detected (www.smarthome.com/7250.html), and then send an X10 signal to turn on lights or a radio.

Controlling X10 from Linux

While I've run into more than a dozen open source X10 projects for Linux, I've focused on two projects for this chapter: Heyu and BottleRocket. I've chosen Heyu (version 2) and BottleRocket because they offer support for two sets of inexpensive X10 computer interfaces: ActiveHome CK11A (two-way) and Firecracker (one-way), respectively.

Installing Linux and X10 Software

Software required to run the X10 procedures in this chapter include a Linux operating system and a set of X10 software packages contained on the *Linux Toys II* CD. The following sections describe what you need to do:

- **Install Linux** — Refer to Appendix C for information on selecting and installing a Linux operating system. If Fedora Core is your Linux system, you can install the RPM packages made for this project. If you are trying the project from another Linux system, you should install the software for this project from tarballs. Both sets of software are included on the *Linux Toys II* CD.

- **Install X10 software** — You can install the X10 software described in this chapter either from RPMs (for Fedora Core or Red Hat Enterprise Linux) or tarballs (for other Linux systems). To install from RPMs, insert the *Linux Toys II* CD on your CD drive. If your CD mounts automatically, you can skip the first command. If it doesn't, run the following (possibly replacing /media/cdrecorder with the location where your CD was mounted) as root user from a Terminal window:

```
# mount /media/cdrecorder
# cd /media/cdrecorder/RPMS/ch07-x10
# ./installme
```

This will install all RPMs needed for this project. To install the software from tarballs, refer to the packages in the Sources/ch07-x10 directory and install them using the generic instructions in Appendix C.

Using BottleRocket (One-way, Cheap X10)

Setting up and using a basic Firecracker configuration to use with BottleRocket can be pretty simple. The following steps take you through both hardware and software configuration.

Step 1: Setting up X10 Hardware

Follow these steps to make sure your hardware is working before you start using the
BottleRocket software.

1. **Connect the Firecracker hardware.** The X10 Firecracker interface is a little dongle
   about the size of a Fig Newton. Plug it into a serial port on your computer (by default,
   BottleRocket will look for it in the COM1 port, represented by /dev/ttyS0 in Linux,
   but you can identify a different one later). Plug the transceiver into any electrical outlet.
   Figure 7-2 shows the Firecracker and transceiver ready to go.

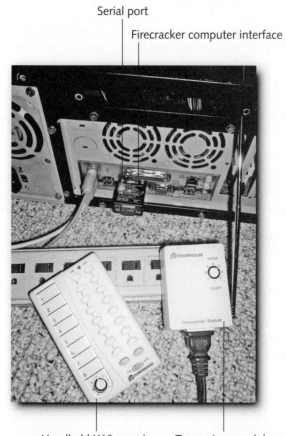

Serial port

Firecracker computer interface

Handheld X10 remote   Transceiver module

FIGURE 7-2: Firecracker requires a serial port and an electrical
outlet to start.

You can plug in one or more lamp or appliance modules that you want to control from your
computer or X10 remote control. Here, the module is shown plugged into a power strip.

Note The X10 model TM751 Transceiver supplied with the Firecracker kit has an outlet on it that allows it to be used as an appliance module. It will respond to number 1 for the house code you set on the unit. So, if you set the house code to C, you can control an appliance plugged into it by C1.

2. **Set house codes.** A basic transceiver can be set to only a single house code (from A to P). So using a screwdriver, turn the transceiver's code wheel to select the house code you want. Then, also using a screwdriver, set the code wheels on each lamp or appliance module to that same house code and to a particular unit code (number from 1 to 16), to set the value that will turn that unit off or on. So, for example, if you set your transceiver to house code C, you could set your lamp and appliance modules to C1, C2, C3, and so on up to C16.

Note Some transceivers (the more expensive ones) can receive signals for all house codes. This allows them to control up to 256 units without having to set anything on the transceiver.

3. **Attach lamps/appliances and test.** Plug lamps and/or appliances into your X10 modules, as appropriate. Then, if you received a handheld remote with your X10 kit, you should try it now to turn the attached devices off and on.

4. **Make the Firecracker device accessible.** By default, the port connected to your Firecracker device (/dev/ttyS0) is accessible only to the root user and uucp group (traditionally used for modem communications). To make your serial ports accessible to a different user, you can add that use to the uucp group. (It's a good security practice not to use the root user when it isn't necessary.) So, for example, to make your serial ports accessible to a user named chris, edit the /etc/group file as root user and change the uucp line to read as follows:

```
uucp:x:14:uucp,chris
```

At this point, you can use a regular user account (in this case, chris) to run the br command.

Step 2: Using BottleRocket Commands

BottleRocket (http://mlug.missouri.edu/~tymm), created by Tymm Twillman, consists of a simple command (br) that you can use to operate an X10 Firecracker kit. The br command sends signals to the serial port to which the Firecracker dongle is connected, which are in turn transmitted via RF to the transceiver and then into the electrical power lines.

With your hardware in place, you can use the br command to turn your lights and appliances on and off or to dim your lights. Remember that the Firecracker hardware and BottleRocket software do only one-way communications and can't get feedback or status information from X10 devices.

BottleRocket (actually the br command) assumes that your Firecracker dongle is connected to the first serial port (/dev/ttyS0). If it is connected to a different serial port, you need to identify it to the `br` command line. To do that, add a `-x` option. For example, to use the second serial port (COM2), add `-x /dev/ttyS1` to the `br` command lines shown following.

Here are some examples of the `br` command.

Note

I show the `br` command being run as a regular user (assuming you added that user to the uucp group in the `/etc/group` file, as described earlier). If you prefer, you can simply run the `br` command as root user.

This command simply turns on the X10 device at C1:

```
$ br C1 ON
```

This turns off C1:

```
$ br C1 OFF
```

You can identify a particular house code (`-c`), and then turn several units on (`-n`) or off (`-f`) on the same command line. The following example turns on the device at C1 and turns off the device at C2:

```
$ br -c C -n 1 -f 2
```

You can turn on or off a bunch of devices at once by separating unit numbers by commas. For example, to turn on C1, C2, and C3 and turn off C4 and C5, type the following:

```
$ br -c C -n 1,2,3 -f 4,5
```

You can also turn all lights on for a particular house code. The following commands turn all lights on for house code C, and then turn all lights off.

```
$ br C LAMPS_ON
$ br C LAMPS_OFF
```

There are a few different ways of dimming lights. You can dim and brighten a light by assigning a number to it from -12 to 12. The first command in the following list turns on the light at C1. The next command dims the previous light (`C1`) four notches (`-d -4`). The command after that brightens the light two notches (`-d 2`):

```
$ br C1 ON
$ br -c C -d -4
$ br -c C -d 2
```

You can also use `BRIGHT` and `DIM` options to increase or decrease light on the unit that was most recently turned on or off. The first command that follows turns on the light on unit C1. The next command dims that light:

```
$ br C1 ON
$ br C DIM
```

If the `br` command is working as just described, you can try creating scripts that you can use to set off a sequence of `br` commands immediately or at set times, using the cron facility.

Step 3: Creating BottleRocket Scripts and cron Jobs

You can create your own shell scripts containing BottleRocket commands to control your X10 devices. Gathering together a bunch of `br` commands in one script saves you typing set sequences over and over again. However, it also lets you launch that set of commands at set times using cron.

Here's an example of how to create a script that launches a few `br` commands, and then set it up to be run by cron:

1. From a terminal window (or other shell) create a bin directory in your home directory.

   `$ mkdir $HOME/bin`

2. Using any text editor, open a file in which to create the script. For example, to use the `nedit` command to create a script named `br_script`, you could type the following:

   `$ nedit $HOME/bin/br_script`

   If your Linux system doesn't have `nedit` installed, you can try `gedit` or `kedit` instead.

3. Add the sequence of `br` commands you want to run to the `br_script` file. For example, you could add the following lines to turn on and dim two lights:

   ```
   /usr/local/bin/br A2 on
   sleep 20
   /usr/local/bin/br -c A -d -5
   /usr/local/bin/br A3 on
   sleep 60
   /usr/local/bin/br -c A -d -7
   ```

   This sequence of commands simply turns on A2, waits for 20 seconds (`sleep 20`), and dims it down five notches. It then turns on A3, waits for one minute, and dims that down seven notches. You can use any `br` command lines, along with any shell functions, to set what lights and appliances are turned on, turned off, dimmed, or brightened. When you are done, save the file and close the editor.

4. Make the script executable as follows:

   `$ chmod 755 $HOME/bin/br_script`

5. To run the script, either type the full path to the script or (because it is probably in your path), you can simply type the script name:

   `$ br_script`

Now, to have that script run at a set time, you can set up a cron job. I'll start by giving you a quick review of what the cron facility is and how it works.

The cron facility starts with a daemon program (crond) that runs continuously in the background checking for cron jobs that have been set up. Cron jobs are set up in one of these ways:

- By adding a line to the `/etc/crontab` file that indicates what program to run and when to run it.

- By adding a shell script to a /etc subdirectory cron.hourly, cron.daily, cron.weekly, or cron.monthly, that is then executed hourly, daily, weekly, or monthly, respectively.

- Using the crontab -e command, you can create a crontab file that is personal to the current user. That crontab can be used to launch any command at any time (provided the user has permission to do so).

The vixie-cron package in Fedora (and other Linux systems) provides the crond daemon and crontab command. For our example, I'm using the crontab -e command to set up the br_script to run every day at 7:01 p.m. (presumably to turn on lights each evening at that time).

Before you begin, you should decide which user you want to execute your script. For this example, I have the root user run br_script, which I put in the root user's home directory (/root/bin). If you want to run the script as a different user, you must first make sure that the serial port connected to the Firecracker module is open to that user (run the chmod 666 /dev/ttyS0 command as root to open that port). Also, put the br_script file in the user's own $HOME/bin directory.

Note The crontab command uses vi as the text editor for creating your crontab file. You can use a different editor, however, by setting the EDITOR variable before running crontab. For example, to make it so that crontab uses gedit instead of vi to edit your crontab file, type the following before running the crontab command: # **export EDITOR=/usr/bin/gedit**.

1. From a Terminal window (as root user), type the following:

   # **crontab -e**

2. Because I am setting the br_script to run each night at 7:00 p.m., I added the following information to the crontab file:

   1 19 * * * /root/bin/br_script

   Save and exit the file. Each day at 7:01 p.m. (19:01 on a 24-hour clock), the /root/bin/br_script will run. The first field indicates minutes (1); the second is hours (19). The three asterisks indicate that the script can run on every day of the month, month of the year, and day of the week, respectively.

To check your personal crontab entries, type **crontab -l**. To get rid of your crontab entries, type **crontab -r** or just run crontab -e again and edit the file to remove entries you no longer want. You can indicate when your script is run in a lot of different ways. The crontab entry can be run on particular days of the week, months, hours, or minutes. (To find out more about the format of crontab files, type **man 5 crontab**.)

Step 4: Using a BottleRocket GUI

There are several point-and-click interfaces available that use BottleRocket to control X10 devices. The CD that comes with this book includes the CGI-x10 script (http://bubba.org/cgi-x10) by Brian Wilson, which lets you click radio buttons to select house codes and X10 commands to run from your Web browser.

Caution I don't recommend using this script on a public Web server. Besides the fact that you probably don't want anyone that stumbles onto your Web server to turn your house lights on and off, it also opens other potential vulnerabilities. For example, you need to enable your Web server to run CGI scripts, and you have to open access to your serial port to non-root users.

Setting up the CGI-x10 script is easy. Setting up your Web server on a system such as Fedora, which tries to make your Web server as secure as possible by default, is a bit tricky if you're not used to it. Here are the basic steps to go through.

1. **Run Security Level Configuration.** From the desktop, select Desktop ➔ System Settings ➔ Security Level. In the Security Level Configuration window that appears, your Firewall Options tab tells you whether or not your firewall is enabled and whether or not external Web service is allowed (it can be off and still allow you to run the CGI-x10 script from the local computer).

   The SELinux tab shows you whether or not SELinux is enabled and being enforced. If it is, to be able run the CGI-x10 script, you need to select HTTPD Service and enable `Allow HTTPD cgi support`. You should now be able to run CGI scripts from your Web server.

2. **Open access to serial port.** To use the CGI-x10 interface, the Web server needs to be able to write to the serial port so the `br` command can send X10 signals to it. Because serial ports in Fedora are assigned to root (owner) and uucp (group), with read-write permission open to them (660), you can have that apache user gain access to those ports by simply adding apache to the uucp group. As root user, open the `/etc/group` file with any text editor and change the uucp line to appear as follows:

   `uucp:x:14:uucp,apache`

Note If the serial port for your Firecracker dongle is a port other than `/dev/ttyS0`, you need to indicate that device name in the `x10.pl` script so it is executed on the `br` command line. For example, to use `/dev/ttyS1`, the line in `x10.pl` could read:

```
$exec="/usr/local/bin/br -x /dev/ttyS1"; # location of br
```

3. **Start the Web server.** To start Web service (httpd), run the following commands as root user:

```
# cp /usr/local/bin/x10.pl /var/www/cgi-bin/
# /etc/init.d/httpd start
# chkconfig httpd on
```

4. **Open CGI-x10.** Open any Web browser on the local computer and type the following in the location box:

   `http://127.0.0.1/cgi-bin/x10.pl`

   Figure 7-3 shows an example of the CGI-x10 page.

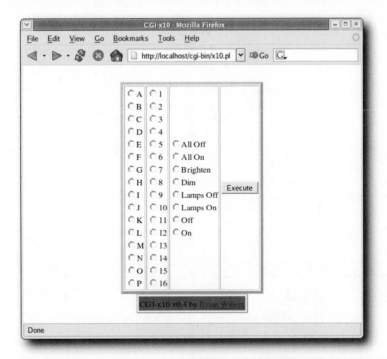

FIGURE 7-3: Turn X10 devices on and off from your Web browser.

5. **Select and execute X10 commands.** Click on a house code, unit number, and command. Then click Execute to run the command. As long as your `br` command was working from the command line, the x10.pl script should be able to turn the selected lights or appliances off or on.

Using Heyu (Two-Way X10)

Typically, for a few dollars more, you can start out with an ActiveHome X10 kit instead of a Firecracker X10 kit. The Heyu project (`www.heyu.org`), created by Daniel Suthers, provides a full-featured interface for managing two-way control over X10 devices from ActiveHome (CM11A) hardware connected to your computer. The project is currently being developed/maintained by Charles W. Sullivan under the name Heyu version 2. (`www.heyu.org/heyu2`).

Figure 7-4 shows the CM11A device that comes with the ActiveHome kit.

The main piece of hardware in an ActiveHome kit is the CM11A unit. A cable comes with that unit that you can plug into a serial port on your computer, and then into the CM11A unit (which in turn plugs into the AC power line). You can add two AAA batteries to the CM11A unit, which allows it to store and execute timed events even if the computer isn't running.

FIGURE 7-4: ActiveHome X10 hardware
(CM11A) allows two-way X10 control.

Step 1: Configuring Heyu

The Heyu software can read from a configuration file to define many features used by the heyu command. That configuration file is typically set up in one of two ways:

- /etc/heyu — By default, the main configuration file for Heyu is /etc/heyu/x10 .conf. If that configuration file is used, related configuration files (such as x10record, x10macroxref, x10image, and report.txt, described later) should be in that directory as well. Only the root user will be able to change configuration files.

- $HOME/.heyu — You can configure a particular user to be the Heyu administrator for your system. In that case, choose the user account and copy the system x10.conf file to $HOME/.heyu/x10config. Other Heyu configuration files will need to go into that directory as well. Because it is preferred to have a user other than root operate Heyu, the rest of this procedure describes how to set up an individual user to administer Heyu for your computer.

Note If you run `heyu` as a regular user, as recommended, the command may fail because of denied access to the `/var/lock` directory. You can remedy this situation by typing `chmod 1777 /var/lock` as root user.

Choose a user to be your system's Heyu X10 administrator. In this example, I create a user account named chris and set it up as the Heyu administrator. From a Terminal window (or other shell) as root user, do the following:

1. Add the user (you can use a name other than chris) and a password for that user by typing the following:

```
# useradd chris
# passwd chris
New UNIX password: *********
Retype new UNIX password: *********
```

2. Next, you need to make your X10 device accessible to the user that will administer X10. With your X10 CM11A unit connected to any serial port (`/dev/ttyS?`), you can simply add the new user to the uucp line in the `/etc/group` file (effectively giving that user access to read and write to all serial ports). As root user, open the `/etc/group` file with any text editor and change the uucp line to appear as follows:

```
uucp:x:14:uucp,chris
```

Note To switch between different X10 software, my uucp line is `uucp:x:14:uucp,chris,apache`. In that way, the CGI-x10 software can access the serial port as well when I switch between my Firecracker and ActiveHome hardware.

3. Log in as the new user. Then copy the `x10.conf` file to `x10config` in that user's home directory (again, you may have a different user name):

```
$ mkdir /home/chris/.heyu
$ cp /etc/heyu/x10.conf /home/chris/.heyu/x10config
```

4. Edit the `x10config` file using any text editor (such as `gedit $HOME/.heyu/x10config`).

With the personal `x10config` file in place, any `heyu` commands run by that user will get configuration information from that file. You can edit the file to set which serial port your CM11A is connected to, the letter identifying your base house code, aliases identifying particular units or groups of units, scenes (for grouping sets of commands), and the location of a log file (none is used by default). One of the more powerful features is the SCRIPT directive, which lets your Heyu software respond to X10 signals by running any Linux command you choose.

Another feature you can use in the Heyu configuration file is the capability to identify schedule files. A schedule file can be created to contain a set of X10 signals to be sent at specific times. That file can be uploaded to the CM11A device, so X10 events can occur when you computer is not on.

Setting the port

Here's an example of a setting you can use in your `x10config` file. This line sets the serial port to which your CM11A device is connected to /dev/ttyS0 (COM1). You could change it to another serial port where it may be connected (`/dev/ttyS1`, `/dev/ttyS2`, and so on).

```
TTY    /dev/ttyS0
```

Setting the default house code

The default house code used by Heyu is A. You can change it to any letter from A to P.

```
HOUSECODE    A    # A B C D E F G H I J K L M N O P
```

Creating an ALIAS

Using an `ALIAS`, you can associate text strings with X10 devices (house code/unit number). This lets you use terms that might be easier to remember, like `back_porch`, `garage`, or `basement_stairs`, instead of something like A3 or J5. `ALIAS`es are case sensitive (Porch is different from porch), limited to 32 characters, and can refer to one or more unit codes.

In an `ALIAS`, you can optionally indicate the type of module you are turning off and on as well. For example, StdLM is a standard X10 one-way lamp module and StdAM is a standard X10 one-way appliance module. (Type **man x10config** to see other supported modules.) The format of an `ALIAS` string is as follows:

```
ALIAS   Label   Housecode/Unitcode_string   [Module_Type]
```

You can identify multiple unit codes with a house code. For example, A1, A2, and A3 can be identified as `A1,2,3` or `A1-3`. Here are several examples that are included in the `x10config` file.

```
ALIAS   front_porch      A1    StdLM
ALIAS   back_porch       A2    StdLM
ALIAS   porch_lights     A1,2

ALIAS   tv_set           A3    StdAM
ALIAS   living_room      A4    LM14A

ALIAS   patio_landscape  A8    StdAM
ALIAS   patio_lamppost   A9    StdLM
ALIAS   all_patio_lights A8,9
```

As you can see, intuitive names such as `tv_set` and `patio_landscape` are each identified with one or more house code/unit number. Some of the `ALIAS`es also indicate which `ALIAS`es represent appliance modules or lamp modules.

Creating a SCENE

The `SCENE` and `USERSYN` (which stands for USER-defined SYNonym) directives are ways of setting up a sequence of X10 signals to be sent. Currently, `SCENE` and `USERSYN` are the same, except that the values you set with them will appear in different Heyu show menus. (Type **man x10config** to find out more about `SCENE` and `USERSYN` directives.)

```
SCENE   blinker   on A1; off A1; on A1; off A1
USERSYN normal_lights   on front_porch; on back_porch
SCENE    tv_on   on tv_set; dimb living_room 10
USERSYN night_lights dimb front_porch $1; dimb back_porch $1
```

The first SCENE, assigned to the name blinker, turns house code/unit A1 on and off two times each. The normal_lights USERSYN uses the aliases set earlier (front_porch and back_porch) to have them turned on. The tv_on SCENE turns on the television and dims lights assigned to the living room so they go down ten notches. Positional parameters can also be added to SCENE and USERSYN directives. So, for example, when the night_lights USERSYN is run later, the $1 parameters will each be replaced by the first option you give on the command line.

Identifying a log file

No log files are used by default with Heyu (LOG_Dir   NONE). However, you can replace NONE with a full path to a directory (for example, /home/chris/.heyu/). You can then use that log file to monitor Heyu activities, such as indications when Heyu scripts are launched and output from those scripts. The following line shows how the modified LOG_DIR option should appear to log to the /home/chris/.heyu/ directory:

```
LOG_DIR   /home/chris/.heyu/
```

Note If you have configured Heyu to be run as the root user (in /etc/heyu/x10.conf), you can put the log file in the standard system log directory, /var/log.

Adding a SCRIPT

The SCRIPT directive is perhaps the most powerful directive you can use with Heyu. By defining a SCRIPT, you can tell Heyu to look for some event to occur (such as an X10 signal to turn on light B1), and react to that event by running any command you like in Linux. Here is an example from the x10config file:

```
ALIAS   doorbell   B1
SCRIPT   doorbell on :: play $HOME/sounds/barking_dog.wav
```

In the previous example, the word doorbell is assigned to house code/unit B1. Then the SCRIPT directive says that if the doorbell is turned on, run the play command on the file $HOME/sounds/barking_dog.wav. The SCRIPT directive and launch condition (doorbell on) are followed by two colons. After the two colons you can enter any command you like.

Using a schedule file (x10.sched)

You can upload a schedule file from your computer to your CM11A device to have X10 signals sent at scheduled times directly from that device. This allows your X10 signals to continue, even when your computer is off. Based on the following entry, the file x10.sched in your $HOME/.heyu directory is used:

```
SCHEDULE_FILE    x10.sched
# SCHEDULE_FILE    normal.sched
# SCHEDULE_FILE    vacation.sched
```

You can see that additional schedule files are commented out, indicating that you can create and use extra schedule files if you like. Heyu comes with a sample schedule file in the /etc/heyu directory (x10.sched.sample) that you can modify to use as you like. (Creating schedule files is covered in more detail later in the chapter.)

Setting MODE

With MODE set to COMPATIBLE, the schedule file sent to the interface is set up to start on January 1 (current year) and will remain in effect for 366 days. So the schedule is active until December 31 on a leap year or January 1 on other years. That's the default, as shown here:

```
MODE      COMPATIBLE      # COMPATIBLE  HEYU
```

With MODE set to HEYU, the CM11A is run with an offset clock, causing the schedule to begin on the date the schedule is uploaded. You can then use the PROGRAM_DAYS directive to set the number of days that the configuration file is valid. (Using the X10 ActiveHome software for Windows can cause trouble if you are running in HEYU mode, if ActiveHome is allowed to reset the CM11A clock to begin on January 1.)

The advantage of HEYU mode is that the schedule file can be re-uploaded at any time before it expires and will be valid for the next 366 days (or shorter period as described following), whereas with COMPATIBLE mode the schedule must be re-uploaded exactly on January 1 if it is to be accurate after that date.

As indicated by the following line, if you are in HEYU mode, PROGRAM_DAYS is set to 366 days (which is the default). Setting this to a shorter period will provide better accuracy when Dawn- or Dusk-relative timed events are included in an uploaded schedule.

```
PROGRAM_DAYS      366              # [number of days 1 to 366]
```

Setting LATITUDE and LONGITUDE

Heyu needs to know the latitude and longitude of your locality in order to calculate the times of dawn and dusk when referenced in a schedule file. They can be omitted until such time as you want to create a schedule file that requires them. The format for these directives is illustrated in the following example for Muleshoe, Texas:

```
LATITUDE   N34:14
LONGITUDE  W102:44
```

In the example, the direction (N/S/E/W) is prefixed to the value of these variables expressed in degrees and minutes. (You can look up your longitude and latitude from the Astrodienst site at www.astro.com/atlas.)

There are other directives you can set in the $HOME/.heyu/x10config file as well. For a description of other available directives, refer to comments in that file itself, or type the command **man x10config** to read the configuration file's man page for a complete list.

Step 2: Running Heyu Commands

The heyu command is the primary tool for using Heyu. There are more than 70 heyu commands, to do everything from administration (such as monitoring activity and resetting house codes), to changing the state of the Heyu engine, to directly sending X10 signals (unit on, off, dim, and the like).

It is possible to use Heyu in the same way that I describe BottleRocket; just add a bunch of heyu commands to a shell script or launch them from a cron job. However, Heyu version 2 has a feature that lets you upload a schedule file directly to the CM11A device, so your X10 scheduled commands can continue to run even if your computer is off.

The following sections describe some ways of using the heyu command to manage your X10 activities.

Sending individual X10 signals

The heyu command is capable of requesting any X10 command that the CM11A is capable of sending to X10 devices. These commands can incorporate any aliases you set, to act on the associated house code(s) or can simply use the house code directly. Here are some examples:

```
$ heyu on F5
$ heyu off F3
$ heyu lightson F
$ heyu lightsoff F
$ heyu allon F
$ heyu alloff F
```

The previous set of commands illustrates a few ways to turn X10 devices on and off. The first command turns on the unit at F5. The second command turns off the unit at F3. The next two commands turn on and off all light modules on house code F, respectively. The next two commands turn on and off all units (lights and appliances) on house code F.

There are several ways to dim and brighten lights as well. Here are some examples:

```
# heyu dim F5 7
# heyu dimb F3 9
# heyu bright F9 4
```

The first command in the preceding code dims the light at unit F5 by 7 from whatever its current brightness is. The next command dims the light at unit F3 by 9 from full brightness. The next command brightens the light at F9 by 4 levels from its current state. The CM11A provides for brightness levels 1–22 between fully dimmed and fully bright.

There are a few dozen direct commands you can try with Heyu. For a complete list, type **man heyu**.

Note

A design goal of Heyu, according to Charles Sullivan, is to, as much as possible, have a command corresponding to every CM11A native command that can go into an uploaded macro. As a result, Heyu has implemented some commands that aren't useful. An example of a useless command is brightb (brighten after first bringing to full brightness).

Administering Heyu

Using administrative options to the heyu command, you can change or just check out the current state of your X10 activities. Here are some examples of commands you can type as the Heyu administrator:

```
$ heyu reset
$ heyu setclock
$ heyu status F7
$ heyu info
```

The `heyu reset` command resets all counters on the CM11A and sets it to the default house code defined in the configuration file. The `setclock` option sets the clock to the time on your computer (using local standard time), or as offset when in MODE HEYU. The `status` option gets and displays the status of the selected device (in this case, unit F7) if that unit is a two-way module. The `info` option displays the time from the CM11A clock, its base house code, and status of units on that house code as maintained in the CM11A's internal registers.

Step 3: Working with the Heyu State Engine

The `heyu` command can launch a heyu state engine daemon (background process), to maintain a record of the state of all your X10 modules (based on signals that are sent to and from each module). If you configured a log file to be used (in the `x10config` file), messages from the state engine are sent to that file.

Along with the state engine, you can open a Heyu monitor screen to monitor all events sent to and from the CM11A device. If you start the monitor from the command line, you can watch the output from your screen (standard output) or direct it to a file. However, the same output is sent to your log file as well, provided one is identified.

To start (or restart) the Heyu state engine, type the following as the user that's set up to administer Heyu:

```
$ heyu engine
```

To see that the heyu state engine is running, type the following:

```
$ ps aux | grep heyu
chris 2216  0.0  0.2  1932 728 ttyS0 Ss+ 15:30 0:00 heyu_relay
chris 2245 50.0  0.2  1924 704 tty1  S   15:32 0:00 heyu engine
```

You can see here that `heyu_relay` and `heyu engine` are running in the background. For this next step, I recommend you have two Terminal windows open. In the first window type the following command to monitor X10 activity live:

```
$ heyu monitor
```

Now, from the second Terminal window (or other shell command line), type a few Heyu commands to turn a light on or off. For example:

```
$ heyu on A3
```

In the Terminal window where you ran `heyu monitor`, you should see that a command was sent to unit A3. The display looks something like this:

```
2005/09/01 07:52:39 sndc address unit 3 : housecode A
(tv_set)2005/09/01 07:52:39 sndc function    On : housecode A
```

This illustrates the basic composition of X10 commands: First a module (or modules) is addressed; then a function code is sent that operates on all addressed modules in that house code. In this example, an address code was sent to house code A, unit 3 (A3). Because there is an alias for A3 set in the `x10config` file (in this case, `tv_set`), you can see that too. (Some commands, such as `alloff` and `lightson`, don't require you to address individual units.)

The `sndc` token indicates the origin of the signal is from the Heyu command line. Signals received by the CM11A interface from the AC power line are identified in the monitor with the token `rcvi`. To quit monitoring your X10 activities live, simply press Ctrl+C. To turn off the state engine, type the following:

```
$ heyu stop
```

Step 4: Creating and Uploading Schedule Files

A Heyu schedule file provides a way to preset your X10 activities in a file that can then be uploaded to the EEPROM memory in the CM11A device. With the schedule file uploaded to the device, you don't need to keep your computer on all the time to continue your X10 activities.

You can start by making a copy of the sample schedule file that comes with the Heyu package (`x10.sched.sample`) and editing it. For example:

```
# cd $HOME/.heyu
# cp /etc/heyu/x10.sched.sample x10.sched
# vi x10.sched
```

The statements in a Heyu schedule file are of three kinds: `macros`, `triggers`, and `timers`:

- **macro** — These statements define sequences of X10 signals to be transmitted over the power line.

- **trigger** — These statements specify a particular macro to be executed upon receipt of a specific X10 On or Off signal over the power line.

- **timer** — These statements specify particular macros to be executed and the times and dates when they are to be executed.

The following are examples of these statements:

```
macro patio_on 0 on A1; on A2; dimb A3 6
macro 0 patio_off off A1; off A2; off A3
timer smwtfs 05/01-11/30 dusk+30 22:00 patio_on patio_off
trigger B1 on patio_on
trigger B1 off patio_off
```

The two `macro` statements define macros named `patio_on` and `patio_off` with the signals to be transmitted to turn on/off/dim the lamps connected to modules with address A1, A2, and A3 after a delay of 0 minutes. (Note that `ALIAS` labels could be used instead of A1, A2, and A3 if aliases for those devices are defined in the configuration file.)

The `timer` statement tells the CM11A unit to execute the `patio_on` macro every day of the week (`smtwtfs`) except Tuesday from May 1 through Nov 30 at 30 minutes after dusk (30 minutes after sunset). That statement also says to execute the `patio_off` macro at 10:00 p.m. (22:00 hours) on those same dates. (Clock times are always programmed as local civil time. Heyu automatically adjusts for periods of Standard and Daylight Savings Time as required.)

The `trigger` statements provide for manual execution of the macros by using a remote controller to send an On or Off signal to address B1. You can have `timer` statements without `trigger` statements and vice-versa.

It may seem that the times in the example `timer` statement correspond to On and Off events similar to a mechanical timer. However, the two time and macro references are entirely independent except for the day-of-week and date range. They can be any two times and any two macros to be executed. For a single timed event, use the reserved name `null` for the unneeded macro and give it any clock time at all.

 Note If you name the `x10.sched` file something different, you need to indicate that by adding a new `SCHEDULE_FILE` entry to your `$HOME/.heyu/x10config` file.

When you are done with the `x10.sched` file, you can check the file for errors before uploading it to the CM11A device by typing the following command.

```
# heyu upload check
```

The results of the check are placed in the `report.txt` file in that same directory. If the check worked without reporting errors, you can compile the schedule file and upload the memory image to the CM11A's EEPROM by typing the following command:

```
# heyu upload
```

If there are no errors in the schedule file, `x10record`, `x10macroxref`, `x10image`, and `report.txt` files are written to the `$HOME/.heyu` directory. The `x10record` file stores the mode and time of the schedule file you uploaded most recently, so that Heyu knows the correct offset to use whenever the CM11A's clock needs to be reset.

The `x10macroxref` file lists EEPROM addresses of the macros that were uploaded, so they can be used by the Heyu monitor and state engine. The `x10image` is a 1024-byte binary image of the EEPROM and is used by some `heyu` commands. Finally, the `report.txt` file contains details about the processing of data that was just uploaded to the EEPROM.

To check when the current uploaded schedule file expires, type the following command:

```
# heyu upload status
Schedule: /home/chris/.heyu/x10.sched
Expanded timers = 89
Max dawn/dusk error over the 366 day period = 3 minutes.
Interface memory free = 185 bytes ( = 18.1% )
See file /home/chris/.heyu/report.txt for details.
Uploading 64 block memory image to interface.
#########################################################
Setting interface clock to current Standard Time.
```

Getting More Information on Heyu

The Heyu home page (`www.heyu.org`) is a good place to start looking for information on Heyu. If software updates or news are available, you should be able find that information there.

For details on Heyu configuration, the following man pages contain excellent coverage of Heyu features: `heyu`, `x10config`, `x10sched`, and `x10scripts`. (Simply type **man** followed by one of those man page names to view its contents.)

If you have questions about Heyu that aren't answered in any of the man pages, you can refer to the Heyu Users Forum (`http://groups.yahoo.com/group/heyu_users/`).

Troubleshooting X10

If you are having trouble getting X10 working properly, here are some troubleshooting tips that might help you out.

- **Noise on power lines** — Power supplies on some electronic devices include conditioning circuits that are designed to clean up noise on power lines. These devices (including some computers, stereo components, surge protectors, and other devices) will actually absorb X10 transmissions. Other electronic devices can block X10 transmissions by putting noise on the power lines (such as electric motors, fluorescent lights, and electric chargers).

  Smarthome.com has noted many customer questions about X10 setups that worked fine for a long time, but suddenly stopped working. They noted that the usual problem is that some new piece of electronic equipment was added to the home. In particular, they noted that certain televisions (Sony, Philips, Magnavox, Hitachi, Emerson), computers (usually off-brand clones), phone and notebook computer rechargers, satellite receivers, fax machines, surge protector power strips, and UPS systems for computers, can suck X10 signals.

  If you think your X10 signals are suffering from noise on your power lines, there are devices you can purchase to clean up the noise. An example of this kind of device is the FilterLinc Plug-in Noise Filter (`www.smarthome.com/1626.html`).

- **Not working on all phases** — Most homes today use a dual-phase electrical system. A transceiver connected to one 110-volt phase of a house may fail to communicate with devices on the other phase. Because 220-volt devices (such as stoves or dryers) are connected to both 110-volt phases in a house, the trick is to get X10 signals to pass through those interfaces. Sometimes, turning on the stove or dryer will allow the X10 signal to get through. A more permanent solution can be to get a device that can pass through X10 signals from a 220-volt outlet. An example of such a device is the SignaLinc Plug-in Coupler-Repeater (`www.smarthome.com/4826B.html`).

- **Transceiver not working** — The firecracker serial dongle may not have a lot of reach. Try moving the transceiver unit closer to your computer and see if that helps.

- **Device stops responding** — If a particular device stops responding to requests, it's possible that it may have just blown a fuse. The fuse is often just a thin wire (as described here at `www.pigselectronics.com/tektips/tip15.htm`). If you are handy with electronics, you might be able to replace this simple fuse yourself (probably voiding the warranty, of course, as the Web site notes).

■ **X10 devices turn on by themselves** — X10 is inherently not secure. There are only 256 total codes and no password or encryption protection. In other words, anyone passing by with an X10 transmitter might be able to turn on your sprinklers, open your garage door, or dim your lights. Other apartments in your building or homes connected to the same transformers at the power company might be able to turn on your devices. And it's not unheard of for modules to be turned on or off by noise or spikes on the AC power line. That's just something to consider when you are deciding what appliances you feel comfortable connecting to your X10 devices.

In most cases, you can simply change the house code on your X10 devices. While A is the most common house code used, if you are in an area where a lot of people may be using X10, you should consider using a later code (such as L, M, or N). In most cases, that should solve the problem (if someone isn't actively trying to get at your X10 devices).

Summary

Although X10 is a fairly simple protocol, it can be a fun and effective way to turn on and off lights and appliances, as well as respond to conditions detected by X10 devices (such as motion detectors). Using open source software, such as BottleRocket and Heyu, not only can you control your X10 devices from Linux, you can also automate when those devices are turned on, turned off, or dimmed.

Setting Up a Game Server with BZFlag

While the number of popular commercial computer games for Microsoft Windows still far outstrips those available for Linux, as a gaming server, Linux is an extremely popular platform. Linux server software is available for hundreds of commercial games, allowing your Linux server to bring together dozens or hundreds of online gamers at a time.

From the pure, open source standpoint, there are some fun games that have completely free client and server software that you can set up and play against others on your LAN or over the Internet. These include board games (such as Go and Atlantik), strategy games (such as freeciv), and battle games (such as BZFlag).

To try your hand at setting up and playing from your own gaming server, I describe how to configure Battle Zone capture the Flag (BZFlag). BZFlag is a fun 3D tank battle game, designed to be played against others over a network. After you set up a BZFlag server, you can have players battle each other over the network using clients on other Linux, BSD, Mac OS X, or Windows systems.

Figure 8-1 illustrates the BZFlag Start Server screen and tanks that might appear on BZFlag clients that run on Linux, Mac OS X, Windows, and BSD systems.

FIGURE 8-1: Play BZFlag tank battles from your Linux server on different clients.

Understanding Battle Zone Capture the Flag

Like many open source projects, BZFlag was begun by a single person as a small idea that just took off. Chris Schoeneman started what became BZFlag as part of his graduate studies in computer graphics at Cornell University in 1993. The project started as a demo program to spin a 3D model with a mouse.

When a friend suggested that Schoeneman make the demo into a game, he created tank models, added the ability to shoot the tanks, and made it so the game could be played against other players on a LAN. The game grew in popularity at Cornell and, over time, features were added such as flags, team bases, and Capture-the-flag–style game play. With the addition of capture-the-flag, the game's name changed from bz to BZFlag.

More than a dozen years later, BZFlag (http://BZFlag.org/) has a thriving community, with more than 3,000 registered users and 34,000 articles at the BZFlag forums (http://my.BZFlag.org/bb). At any given time, there are dozens of public BZFlag servers running and waiting for you to join in. New worlds and new features are constantly being created and made available for BZFlag.

The current BZFlag maintainer is Tim Riker. Many other contributors to the project are listed as well. These include Daniel Léonard, Jeremiah "CobraA1" Moss, Frank Siegert, Frank "Chestal" Thilo, Colin Bayer, David Trowbridge, Daryll Strauss, Dave Brosius, Sean Morrison, Alfredo Tupone, and Daniel Remenak.

Playing BZFlag

Battle Zone capture the Flag (BZFlag) is a tank battle game you can play against others over a LAN or the Internet. Using a tank in first-person shooter mode, you play as an individual or on a team, blowing up opponents along the way while trying not to let others blow you up. There are three major game styles:

- **Free-for-all** — In Free-for-all, you simply try to destroy other tanks more often than they destroy you. The final objective is to score more points than your opponents.

- **Capture-the-flag** — In Capture-the-flag, each team tries to protect its own flag (or flags) from being grabbed by an opponent and taken to the opponent's team base. If you can get hold of an opponent's flag and take it to your base, you destroy all opponents on that team, subtract a point from them, and add a point to your team.

- **Rabbit Hunt** — In Rabbit Hunt, you try to hunt down and destroy the tank designated as the rabbit (typically a white tank). Once that happens, the next leading scorer becomes the rabbit (by default). If you are the rabbit, you try to stay alive as long as you can.

When you join a game, you join as a member of one of the following:

- **A team** — You can join a game as a member of one of four teams, designated by color: red, green, blue, or purple. When you play on a team, you try to work together with teammates to capture opponent flags, protect your own flags, and destroy opponents as much as possible.

- **A rogue** — As a rogue, there is nobody on your team. Other rogues also play alone.

- **An observer** — As an observer, you travel around during battles without playing. Press F8 to change from roaming freely to tracking from the view of one of the players or tracking the team flag. The default mode it to track the winning player. If that player is destroyed, you switch views to the player with the next highest score.

Flags are an important part of BZFlag. Obviously, protecting the flags of your team (which appear in your team's color) is an important part of the Capture-the-flag game. However, in any game type, you can give your tank special skills by picking up flags as you travel around the world. These flags are referred to as *super flags*.

A super flag is white, but has no markings to distinguish it from other super flags. When you pick up a flag (by driving over it), you find out what it is and immediately get its special attributes. (You can also use an identity flag, if you have one, to determine the identity of a flag without picking it up.) Some flags are good, while others are bad. See Table 8-3 later in this chapter for a listing of flags and their attributes.

Figure 8-2 shows an example of a BZFlag world. Two tanks are moving through the foreground, with the one to the left carrying the team's flag. Another tank is blowing up in the background. A white flag on the left side of the screen is a super flag that carries with it some special ability. On the bottom of the screen, you can see a radar view of the world, while messages related to game play and chatting appear on the bottom right.

FIGURE 8-2: Destroy enemy tanks, grab flags, and don't get blown up in BZFlag.

The worlds you battle in with BZFlag are either generated randomly or loaded from specially created world files. The worlds are not that complex by today's gaming standards, but run very efficiently over networks. There are other maps available that you, as an administrator, can load on your BZFlag server. In fact, you can visit another server and save the current world to run on your own server.

Note Some items in a world, such as weapons, are not included when you save a world. However, textures, colors, positions and shapes of buildings, teleporters, and other items (along with many game playing options) will all be copied over when you save a world.

The procedure for setting up a BZFlag server in this chapter focuses on setting up the server for a self-contained LAN or other protected environment. A protected environment lets you get the full feel for the gaming environment, without having the security issues that come with making your server public (and allowing strangers to play who may cheat!).

Setting Up a BZFlag Server

The BZFlag project includes both client (the ones firing the tanks) and server (that connect together lots of players shooting tanks) software that runs on a variety of platforms. Those platforms include many UNIX derivatives (Irix, Linux, FreeBSD, and Mac OS X) and Microsoft Windows.

The example in this chapter illustrates how to configure a BZFlag server to run in Fedora Core Linux. The *Linux Toys II* CD contains an RPM of the BZFlag software that you can install and configure. To begin with, I'll assume you are configuring BZFlag to be played on a LAN, among people in the same home, office, or school. Extending the BZFlag server to share the service on the Internet is fairly simple from a technical standpoint but has security implications I'll go into later.

Step 1: Choosing Server Hardware

Almost any computer that is capable of running Linux can be configured as a BZFlag server. In fact, BZFlag maintainer Tim Riker says they have run a BZFlag server on a Sharp Zaurus and a Linksys WRT54G router! Because we are using Fedora Core Linux in our example, check the hardware requirements for Fedora and install it as described in Appendix C. Aside from basic Linux requirements, here are a few issues you should consider about your hardware.

Networking Hardware

The computer must have networking hardware. Contributors to the BZFlag project suggest that the amount of network bandwidth you need to serve BZFlag should start at about 5Kbps for each player. However, as more players are added, the increase is not linear. So you need more than twice the bandwidth if you have twice the number of players. Therefore, the BZFlag team recommends against using a dial-up 56Kbps modem, which would be limited to a 3 or 4 Kbps transfer rate, to connect your server to the network.

The server will send much more data than it receives, as data received from each client must be sent separately from the server to each of the other clients. So the key to choosing a good networking setup is lots of good bandwith (particularly upstream). Here are some tips from the BZFlag project that relate to the type of network connection you may have:

- **Digital Subscriber Line**(Check if your DSL connection offers different upstream and downstream speeds. Often, the DSL provider will allow much higher downstream speeds, so if they quote you the downstream speed (which they usually do) that number won't reflect how many players you can serve. With a 256 Kbps upstream connection, you should be able to serve up to eight players. You computer typically needs an Ethernet card to use this type of connection.

- **Cable modem**(Your cable modem connection will almost always have lower upstream bandwidth than downstream because these types of connections are generally intended for home use. A cable modem connection limited to a 128 Kbps upstream connection will support up to five players. As with DSL, your computer needs an Ethernet card to connect to a cable modem.

Note Some ISPs specifically don't allow non-business Internet accounts to use their connections. If you get way into the whole gaming server idea, you will probably want to consider co-locating your computer at an Internet service provider or renting access to a server at a company that specializes in gaming servers.

The BZFlag server procedure in this chapter focuses on configuring a BZFlag server in a home, school or other organization (on a LAN and behind a firewall). So, I'll start with the assumption that your server and client computers will all be connected to the same LAN, using wired or wireless Ethernet cards. Unless you are hosting a massive BZFlag LAN party on your server, a normal 100 Mbps Ethernet interface should be able to handle the load quite easily.

Video card

No graphical interface is required if you are just running the BZFlag server. However, if you want to run the BZFlag client on the same computer, you should have a video card that supports OpenGL 3D acceleration. Also, you can use an NVidia graphics acceleration card with proprietary drivers from NVidia, which will work great.

Sound card

As with the video card, no sound card is required on the server. You will probably want sound cards for your client computers, however.

Note BZFlag does not have direct support for aRts (artsd daemon) or other sound servers. So, sound might not work on your BZFlag client if you have a sound server running. To adjust sound levels, you can run alsamixer. I used the Master and PCM sliders to adjust the sound on my Fedora system.

Step 2: Installing Linux and BZFlag Software

Before you begin configuring BZFlag, you need a running Linux system with the BZFlag software installed. Here's how:

1. Install Fedora Core 4 (or other Linux system) on the computer that you want to use as your BZFlag server. You can use a text-only, minimal install (see Appendix C) to run the server. However, you need a graphical interface (GNOME, KDE, or simple X window manager) if you want to play BZFlag from that machine as well.

2. From the installed Fedora Core 4 system, you can install the following RPM packages from the *Linux Toys II* CD:

   ▪ **bzflag** (Contains both the bzflag client and server software

   ▪ **adns** (Contains the adns domain name system client library (used for resolving DNS names and addresses)

Note If you get a later version of BZFlag, it may not require the adns package. The BZFlag project plans to switch to c-ares (http://daniel/haxx.se/projects/c-ares) instead.

You can install the exact packages used to write this chapter from the *Linux Toys II* CD. From an installed Fedora Core system, insert the *Linux Toys II* CD. The CD should mount automatically. If it doesn't, open a Terminal window, become root user (type **su -**) and type the following:

```
# mount /media/cd*
```

With the CD mounted, type the following:

```
# /media/cd*/RPMS/ch08-game/installme
```

Note

If you would like to look for a later copy of BZFlag, the package is part of the Fedora Extras repository. In fact, you can install the bzflag package over the Internet (as root user) by simply typing **yum install bzflag** from a shell. Or you can update the existing package by typing **yum update bzflag**.

If you are installing the BZFlag server on another Linux system, you can use the tarball for BZFlag that is included in the SOURCE directory of the *Linux Toys II* CD. Precompiled packages for other Linux systems are also available. See the BZFlag download page (http://sourceforge.net/project/showfiles.php?group_id=3248) or the unofficial BZFlag Wiki download page for further information (http://BZFlag.org/wiki/Download).

Step 3: Configuring the Server Computer

Before you set up the BZFlag server process (which actually handles the interactions between the BZFlag players), you need to configure the server computer to make it available and secure on the network. To start with, I'll describe how to set up your server on a private LAN, to play among your family or others on your LAN.

Let's assume that besides the server computer, there are computers on your LAN that you want to allow to play BZFlag. If possible, assign a static IP address (one that doesn't potentially change at each reboot) to the server. Then identify a port number from which the service is offered and make the service available to the computers on your LAN.

1. **Get an IP address.** If you are on a private LAN, you can choose your own IP addresses from a set of private IP addresses. If you already have a set of addresses you are using, choose one for the server and assign it to be used each time the network interface is brought up. (For an Internet server, you can get a static IP address assigned from your ISP or your organization's local system administrator.)

2. **Assign the static IP address.** From a desktop on Fedora Core, select the Desktop button in the panel, and then choose System Settings → Network. Double-click the network interface (probably eth0) to see the Ethernet Device window. From that window, select Statically Set IP Address. For the example on my private LAN, I used the IP address 10.0.0.101 and subnetwork mask 255.255.255.0. Other computers on the LAN could be assigned static IP addresses of 10.0.0.102 through 10.0.0.106.

3. **Assign a name.** The client really just needs a way to get to the IP address. If the server is a public, Internet server, you can purchase and register your own DNS name. If you don't know how to do this, you can speak to your ISP or any of a gazillion domain-name registrars on the Internet today. Because I am talking about a LAN, however, in this example, you can simply add the server's host name and address to the `/etc/hosts` file of each Linux client that wants to play the game. For example, if you wanted to call the server `flag`, you could add this entry to each computer's `/etc/hosts` file:

```
10.0.0.101          flag
```

After that, the Linux client could address the server by the name `flag`.

4. **Open a firewall port.** The BZFlag server process (`bzfs`) listens for BZFlag game service requests on a particular port. The registered IANA port number, and default port number used by the server, for BZFlag is 5154 (clients will look for that port number by default). So you need to allow access to that port from your server if your server has an active firewall (which it should).

Linux uses iptables for its firewall by default. The way that iptables is configured in Fedora, you can open access to selected ports from the Security Level Configuration Window (select Desktop ➔ System Settings ➔ Security Level and Firewalls). Add `5154:tcp,5154:udp`. Or you could simply set your entire LAN as a trusted device (if you do trust it).

Note   You can change the default port to any port you like (avoiding popular port numbers such as those listed in the `/etc/services` file). However, the client will have to specify that port number specifically when it connects to you. The default port should be 5154, but you can type the command `bzfs -help | grep p:` to make sure it hasn't been changed on your server.

With your server running on your LAN, you can proceed to configuring the BZFlag server process on that computer.

Step 4: Configuring the BZFlag Server

While you can start the BZFlag server by simply running the `bzfs` server process with lots of options tailing after it, it's more convenient to add options to a configuration file that is then fed to the server process: bzfs. The BZFlag project leaves open the choice of which file to use to put your configuration information in (although `bzfs.conf` is sometimes used in examples). For my example, I'll put the options in the `/etc/bzfs.conf` file.

Note   The same download sites noted earlier for getting software to install the BZFlag server also offer BZFlag client software for various platforms. Software from the SourceForge BZFlag project site (`http://sourceforge.net/projects/bzflag`) includes versions for Windows, Mac OS X, Irix, PowerPC, and several different Linux systems (including Fedora/Red Hat, Mandrake, and Slackware).

1. **Create the configuration file.** Open the /etc/bzfs.conf file using any text editor (such as gedit or vi) and add any options you want to use with your server. There are dozens of options available for the bzfs server utility. To read about them, type **man bzfs**. Here's a sample configuration file you could begin with:

```
# If default port (5154) is busy, use fallback port
-pf

# Give the buildings random height
-h

# Set maximum number of players to 30
-mp 30

# Set maximum simultaneous shots per player to 1.
-ms 1

# Disallow all bad flags
-f bad

# Sets number of super flags existing at a time to 10.
+s 10

# Increase debugging level (twice)
-d
-d

# Quit after serving a single game.
-g
```

I highlighted (in bold) the actual options (lines beginning with # are comments). Save the file when you have entered the information. Because the configuration file could contain information such as the server password that you don't want everyone to see, you should restrict access to the file. For example, you could make it so that the user running the server utility is the only one who can read it, as follows (replacing *username* with the user's name that will run the server):

```
# chown username /etc/bzfs.conf
# chmod 700 /etc/bzfs.conf
```

As I mentioned, there are tons more options you can add to this file to tune how the game is run. But this should be enough to get you started.

2. **Start the bzfs server utility.** You can (and should) run the bzfs server utility as a regular (non-root) user. So, as a regular user from any shell, type the following:

```
$ bzfs -conf /etc/bzfs.conf
style: 2
  super flags allowed
```

```
style: 2
  super flags allowed
There is a voting arbiter with the following settings:
        vote time is 60 seconds
        veto time is 2 seconds
        votes required are 2
        vote percentage necessary is 50.099998
        vote repeat time is 300 seconds
        available voters is initially set to 200
Running a private server with the following settings:
        listening on 0.0.0.0:5154
        with title of ""
        .
        .
        .
```

Because I turned on debugging (-d), you can see some information about the server. The style: 2 setting indicates the default free-for-all style of game is being used. You can ask questions from the server and have players vote on them (timeouts and other settings are shown in the preceding code). You can see that bzfs is running as a private server on all interfaces on the computer (loopback, eth0, and so on) and listening on port 5154 (0.0.0.0:5154).

You can just leave the server running in the Terminal window. Messages that appear indicate players joining and leaving the game, some settings changing, and messages sent to the administrator.

Step 5: Playing BZFlag

To test that everything is working, you can fire up a BZFlag client (bzflag command) and start playing. With the BZFlag server (bzfs) running on the server on your LAN, you can install and start playing BZFlag (bzflag). Here's how:

1. **Start the game.** The BZFlag package contained on the *Linux Toys II* CD contains both client and server software. So, you can install BZFlag for any Linux system you have connected to your network. (As described in Step 1, there is also BZFlag client software available for Irix, Mac OS X, Windows, and other Linux systems.) To start the game from Linux (either from another computer on the network or on the one running the server), type the following:

   $ bzflag

   The initial BZFlag start screen appears.

2. **Join a game.** Select Join Game (using arrow keys) and press Enter. The Join Game screen appears.

3. **Identify server.** Add the information you need to connect to the server you just created (using arrow keys and keyboard), and then highlight Connect and press Enter. Information should include:

- **Callsign**—This is the name you use for signing in to the BZFlag server. This name appears to other players, identifying the activity of your tank and any chatting you do.

- **Password**—You can skip a password for now. If you are signing on to a public server, however, adding a password and identifying yourself with it each time you connect to that server will give you access to some extra features on that server (such as the ability to vote to kick someone off). I'll describe how to identify yourself using a password later on.

- **Team**—You can choose to be a member of a team (Red, Green, Blue, or Purple) or play as a Rogue (no team affiliation). You could also just be an Observer or have the server assign you to a team (automatic).

- **Server**—Here is where you identify the server you just configured. If you are on the same computer as the bzfs server, you can simply type **localhost** or the IP address of the local network interface. Otherwise, you can type the server's name (if you are somehow configured to resolve the name to IP address) or just the server's IP address.

- **Port**—The port number the server is listening on. Unless you specifically changed it when you configured the server, you should enter 5154 (the default port number).

- **Email**—If you want others in the game to email you, you have the option of entering your email address here. You can enter any text here that you would like to display next to your callsign.

Figure 8-3 shows an example of the Join Game information to connect to the server on my LAN that I configured earlier in this procedure.

If you were able to connect to the server, you should see the blinking message `Press Right Mouse or "i" to start.`

4. **Start playing.** As noted, click the right mouse button or press the i key to start. Your tank is now active and ready to start playing.

Of course, it's not very interesting to play yet because nobody else is connected to your server. If you want to have someone to practice on, you can start another BZFlag client (perhaps on the server) and put it into autopilot by pressing the 9 key after that client connects.

Note If you just want to practice game play without using the server you configured, you can type `bzflag -solo 1` and then start a local server. This lets you start a game locally, with one other tank on the field. After you join a game, simply identify the server as localhost and select Start Server. You can play against more tanks by giving a number other than 1 to the `solo` option. To try out BZFlag, you can also select Find Server and connect with games on the Internet that are in progress. You can select Observer as your team if you want to just watch for a while.

FIGURE **8-3: Join the game on the BZFlag server.**

Most of what you do in BZFlag can be done with the mouse. Right-click to start the game and left-click to shoot. Move the mouse to go forward, back, and to spin around. To help you get started with game play, Tables 8-1 through 8-3 contain helpful information on controls and flags. Table 8-1 shows mouse and keyboard actions for controlling your game play.

Table 8-1: BZFlag Mouse and Keyboard Actions

Mouse Action/Keystroke	Description
Moving, shooting, and grabbing	
Mouse position or arrow keys	Control tank position, movement, and aiming.
Left mouse or Enter	Fire shot.
Drive over flag	Pick up flag.
Space bar or middle mouse button	Drop a flag.
Tab	Jump (if allowed).
Delete	Self-destruct or cancel.
Screen information	
B	Toggle binoculars (to get a close-up view of a target).
Right mouse button or I	Identify player (locks on GM).

Mouse Action/Keystroke	Description
Screen information	
W	Toggle console view.
S	Toggle score sheet.
L	Toggle tank labels.
Y	Toggle frame time.
T	Toggle frames per second.
Radar	
1	Short radar range.
2	Medium radar range.
3	Long radar range.
4	Zoom in radar range.
5	Zoom out radar range.
Q	Toggle radar view.
Viewing flags	
H	Toggle radar flags.
J	Toggle main flags.
F	Toggle heads-up flag help.
Messages	
N	Send message to everybody.
M	Send message to teammates.
'	Send message to nemesis.
.	Send message to recipient.
Z	Send message to admin.
Page Up or mouse wheel up	Scroll message log backward.
Page Down or mouse wheel down	Scroll message log forward.
Shift+F1	Main message tab.
Shift+F2	Chat message tab.
Shift+F3	Server message tab.
Shift+F3	Misc message tab.

Continued

Table 8-1 (continued)

Mouse Action/Keystroke	Description
Game controls	
Esc	Show/dismiss main menu.
Pause or P	Pause or resume the game.
F1	Toggle full screen.
F4	Minimize.
F5	Capture current screen image (save to ~/.bzf/screenshots directory).
F8	While in Observer mode, you can change to different roaming modes: free, tracking, following, first person (with a driver), and team flag tracking.
F12	Quit (see /quit in Table 8-2 for information on sending a message as you quit).
A	Slow keyboard motion.
K	Toggle Silence/UnSilence.
O	Server admin.
U	Identify nemesis (Hunt). Scroll player list and press Enter to choose.
9	Auto pilot.
Settings	
-	Set time of day backward.
=	Set time of day forward.

While you are in a message-sending mode (N M , . or Z), there are commands you can enter to make requests. While some commands are available to all users, others are available only to registered users (identified with passwords), operators, or administrators of the game. Table 8-2 shows commands that are available to all users.

Table 8-2: Commands to Send While in a Message Mode

Command	Description
/clientquery	Lists the version of the bzflag client being run by all users.
/date or /time	Displays current date and time (from date command).

Command	Description
/flaghistory	Lists history of flags a player has carried.
/grouplist	Lists groups associated with server.
/groupperms	Lists permissions associated with each group.
/help page	Displays the help text for a selected page.
/idlestats	Displays idle and pause times for each player.
/lagstats	Displays lag statistics for each player.
/msg player message	Replace *player* with the name of a player and *message* with a message you want sent to that player.
/me message	Inserts your user name into a message. For example, /me likes bzflag from the user named chris translates into chris likes bzflag.
/uptime	Tells how long the bzfs server has been up and running.

For other commands available only to registered users, operators, and administrators, refer to the Keys and Commands page (http://BZFlag.org/wiki/KeysAndCommands). With those users' permissions, you can modify the play of a game as it is running (resetting flags, banning hosts or players, or starting and voting in polls). See the Server Commands page for longer descriptions of these commands (http://BZFlag.org/wiki/ServerCommands).

As you travel around the BZFlag world, you encounter different super flags, each of which gives you a special ability (or disability). Some flags are good, while others are bad. To find out what a flag is, you need to pick it up by running over it. Table 8-3 contains a list of available flags and features of each (the flag code appears in parentheses for each flag).

Table 8-3: Good and Bad Super Flags

Flag	Description
Team *color* flags	
Red Team (R)	Flag the Red Team defends and others try to take.
Green Team (G)	Flag the Green Team defends and others try to take.
Blue Team (B)	Flag the Blue Team defends and others try to take.
Purple Team (P)	Flag the Purple Team defends and others try to take.

Continued

Table 8-3 (continued)

Flag	Description
Good Flags	
Agility (A)	Makes a tank better able to avoid getting hit.
Burrow (BU)	Allows your tank to travel mostly underground, so shots sail over your head. You will move slowly, however, and can be destroyed by someone driving over you.
Cloaking (CL)	Makes your tank invisible from other tanks' windows, but still visible on radar.
Genocide (G)	Destroys all players on a team by destroying one.
Guided Missile (GM)	Lets you shoot guided missiles at target you locked on when you fired. Click right mouse to retarget in flight.
Identify (ID)	Shows the identity of the closest flag.
Invisible Bullet (IB)	Makes your shots invisible from other tanks' radar, but still visible from their windows.
Jumping (JP)	Lets the tank jump into the air (but not steer).
Laser (L)	Lets you shoot lasers with, in effect, infinite speed and range, although it doubles your reload time.
Machine Gun (MG)	Increases your shot speed and improves reload speed, but range is dramatically decreased.
Masquerade (MQ)	Causes your tank to look like its teammate to an opponent from that opponent's window. Other viewing methods show the tank team you really belong to.
Narrow (N)	Makes your tank very thin and almost impossible to hit from the front or back, although it doesn't change length.
Oscillation Overthruster (OO)	Lets you drive inside of buildings, although you cannot back up or shoot while you are in one.
Phantom Zone (PZ)	Allows your tank to drive through buildings, making it impossible to destroy, except by a Super Bullet, a Shock Wave or a captured team flag. (Toggle Phantom Zone on and off by driving through teleporters.)
Quick Turn (Q)	Improves turning speed up to 50 percent.
Rapid Fire (F)	Increases the speed of your shots and lets you reload faster, although it decreases your range.
Ricochet (R)	Causes your shots to bounce off of walls.
Seer (SE)	Lets your tank see Stealthed, Cloaked, and Masqueraded tanks as they really are.

Flag	Description
Good Flags	
Shield (SH)	Protects you from being destroyed if you get shot. If you are shot, however, the flag drops and cannot be picked up again in the normal load time.
Shock Wave (SW)	Destroys nearby tanks with shockwaves (including tanks in buildings).
Stealth (ST)	Makes your tank invisible on opponents' radar, but still visible from each tank's window.
Steamroller (SR)	Lets you drive over other tanks to destroy them (but you must be quite close).
Super Bullet (SB)	Uses super bullets that can shoot through buildings. (One way to destroy tanks with an oscillation overthruster flag and phantom zoned tanks.)
Tiny (T)	Changes your tank to a smaller size that's harder to hit.
Thief (TH)	Causes your tank to be small and fast. Shooting an opponent takes its flag instead of killing it.
Useless (US)	Does nothing.
Velocity (V)	Increases top speed up to 50 percent.
Wings (WG)	Lets you drive tank in the air and jump multiple times.
Bad Flags	
Blindness (B)	Darkens your window, making it so you can see only with radar. (Stealth tanks effectively disappear from all view.)
Bouncy (BY)	Bounces the tank at random heights.
Colorblindness (CB)	Prevents you from seeing team information for other tanks. (Can cause you to shoot teammates by mistake.)
Forward Only (FO)	Prevents you from driving backward.
Jamming (JM)	Turns off your radar, but still lets you see from window.
Left Turn Only (LT)	Allows tank to make only left turns.
Momentum (M)	Slows tanks speed and actions.
No Jumping (NJ)	Prevents tank from jumping.
Obesity (O)	Increases your tank's size, making it an easy target and unable to fit through teleporters.
Reverse Only (RO)	Prevents you from driving forward.
Reverse Controls (RC)	Reverses your tank's driving controls.
Right Turn Only (RT)	Allows tank to make only right turns.
Trigger Happy (TR)	Causes the tank to fire continuously.
Wide Angle (WA)	Gives your tank a disorienting, fish-eye lens.

Because the point of this chapter is to focus on setting up a gaming server, the following sections describe BZFlag game play from the perspective of the server. You can learn a lot about playing by reading those sections on the types of games, flags, teams, and other issues related to setting up the server. For more information specifically on game play, however, I recommend the following links:

- **BZFlag First Contact** (`http://shellshock.bzflag.bz/guides-firstcontact.html`) — Contains a good overview of the project and tips for starting out driving your tank.

- **BZFlag.org Official Forums** (`http://my.BZFlag.org/bb/`) — If you have questions about setting up or playing BZFlag, the official forums are a great place to start.

If you decide to try out some public BZFlag servers, consider registering your callsign (user name) and password first. As of BZFlag, version 2, the BZFlag project has been offering a global registration service so each player can keep a consistent user identify across multiple BZFlag servers. Refer to the "Using Central Registration for BZFlag" section later in this chapter for further information on this feature.

Customizing Your BZFlag Server

With dozens of options available to the BZFlag server (bzfs), there are many ways you can configure bzfs to control what players can do and how well you can manage game play. Read through the parts in this section to help make decisions when you create your configuration file. Many administrators will create multiple configuration files to support different types of game play, sometimes even rotating those files to provide different game experiences.

Setting Game Play Features

As administrator of the BZFlag server, you can choose the style of game being played and features that the players in your games can and can't use.

Changing Game Style

If you don't choose a game, BZFlag will run in Free-for-all mode when you start the server. To do a Capture-the-flag game instead, you can add the `-c` option to your configuration file:

`-c`

For Capture-the-flag using a random map, you can use the `-cr` option instead:

`-cr`

After `-cr`, you can add a number indicating building density (the default is 5). Each Capture-the-flag game uses one flag per team by default. You can add more flags using the `+f` option described later.

For a rabbit game (where everyone tries to chase and destroy the tank assigned as the rabbit and the rabbit tries to stay alive), the rabbit can be assigned in different ways. You can have the person with the top score assigned to be the rabbit when the rabbit is destroyed as follows:

-rabbit score

You can have the person who kills the rabbit take over as the rabbit, as follows:

-rabbit killer

Or you could have a random tank assigned to be the rabbit when the rabbit is destroyed:

-rabbit random

Free-for-all is recommended for those learning the game, with super flags (-s) and teleporters (-t) enabled if you want to try out those features. To learn teamwork skills, try a basic Capture-the-flag game.

Enabling Game Features

There are some special game features you can add to make BZFlag more interesting (especially as you become more skilled). For example, you can allow tanks to jump by adding the -j option to your configuration file:

-j

To make regular shots ricochet (guided missiles, super bullets, and shock waves don't ricochet), add the +r option:

+r

Teleporters typically look like mesh screens with black and yellow stripes around them. When a tank drives through a teleporter, it is immediately transported to another teleporter. To enable teleporters, use the -t option:

-t

After each shot (by default), a player needs to reload before shooting again. To increase the maximum number of shots before a reload, use the -ms option. For example, here's how you allow two shots before a reload:

-ms 2

When a player kills a teammate, that player dies too (by default). You can have the player not be killed using the -tk option:

-tk

After a tank is destroyed, it reappears (after the player presses i or right-clicks the mouse) somewhere else on the field. This is referred to as *spawning*. Normally, tanks will spawn on the ground. Adding the following option, however, allows them to spawn on top of box-shaped buildings as well:

-sb

Many other game play options have to do with managing flags, as described in the next section.

Configuring Flags

As a BZFlag server administrator, you can control what flags are in your BZFlag world, what flags are excluded, and how many of a selected flag you want to have. Flags can be in the BZFlag world all the time, or they can be generated at random.

You identify flags by the one- or two-character codes listed in Table 8-3. Use the +f option with a code to guarantee that a particular flag is in the world. Use the -f option to guarantee a particular flag isn't in the world. Here are some examples:

```
+f JP
+f BU
+f CL
+f CL
+f CL
-f T
-f N
```

In the previous example, at least one jumping flag (JP) and one burrowing flag (BU) are assured to be in the world. At least three cloaking flags (CL) are assured of being there. There will be no tiny flags (T) or narrow flags (N).

You can turn off all bad flags by adding a -f bad option. You can add multiple team color flags (there's only one by default in Capture-the-flag) by adding more +f options (for example, +f R to add a red flag).

Flags normally appear on the ground. To allow them to appear on top of box buildings as well, you could add the following option:

```
-fb
```

Use the +s and -s options to indicate an extra number of super flags are available at all times and that up to a certain number of super flags are available at any time, respectively. For example:

```
+s 10
-s 15
```

The preceding lines indicate that there will be at least 10 super flags available at all times and could have up to 15 more available at any time.

When the last player on a team leaves the game, its team flag is reset after 30 seconds. You can change the reset time using the -tftimeout option. For example, for a 45-second timeout, add:

```
-tftimeout 45
```

Options for good flags

You can limit how many shots someone can take with a good flag before dropping it. For example, the following options allow a tank with an invisible bullet (IB) flag to fire 15 times or a rapid fire (F) flag to fire 30 times before losing the flag:

```
-sl IB 15
-sl F 30
```

Options for bad flags

Players don't have to hang on to bad flags forever. Here are some options that allow players to get rid of bad flags:

```
-sa
-st 20
-sw 2
```

The -sa option allows antidote flags in the world to get rid of bad flags. The -st option sets the number of seconds after which a bad flag is dropped (20 seconds here). The -sw option sets the number of wins after which a bad flag is dropped (2 wins in this example).

Setting Game Boundaries

As a BZFlag server administrator, you can set what ends a game. Game ending can be based on time or score. Here are some examples:

```
-time 7200
-timemanual
```

In the example just shown, the game will end 7,200 seconds (two hours) after the first client connects. By adding the -timemanual option, the time will start after the /countdown command is issued, instead of after the first client connection. Instead of time, you can have the game based on score. Here are some examples:

```
-mps 50
-mts 300
```

The first option (-mps 50) ends the game after a player scores 50 points. As an alternative, you could have the game end after a team reaches a certain number of points (-mts 300 ends the game after a team reaches 300 points).

If you want to have a rotating server or if you are doing a timed game, you can indicate that the server should quit after one game. You can do this with the -g option:

```
-g
```

Modifying Worlds and Maps

BZFlag allows you to create your own worlds or include worlds you copy from other servers running BZFlag. There are several options you can use to select and customize the worlds you use with your BZFlag server. With the -b option, you can randomly rotate buildings (only during random Capture-the-flag games):

```
-b
```

Using the -density option, you can control how dense the buildings are. For random worlds, you can set the density to a number between 1 and 10 (with 5 as the default):

```
-density 7
```

If you are using a random map, you can also set buildings to random heights, using the -h option and the size of the world using -worldsize, as follows:

```
-h
-worldsize 800
```

During game play, you can save a world you encounter on another server by selecting Options → Save World. Enter a file name and the world will be stored under that name in the .bzf/worlds directory in your home directory. You can incorporate that saved world into your server using the -world option. For example:

```
-world /home/chris/.bzf/worlds/myworld.bzf
```

Managing Players

If you are running a public BZFlag server, managing the players who use that server is an important task. BZFlag gives you the ability to determine how players are assigned and authenticated. It also gives you the tools for banning players, if necessary.

Managing Player Sign-On

Using the -autoteam option, players are added to your server based on the teams with the lowest number of players and the lowest scores or kill ratios.

```
-autoteam
```

You can also limit the total number of players and the total number of players for each team. Likewise, you can limit how many players can be on each team. Here are examples:

```
-mp 50
-mp 5,5,5,5,5,7
```

In the first example (-mp 50), the server is limited to a total of 50 players. The second example sets limits on each team and observers, in the following order: rogue, red, green, blue, purple, and observer. So, five players are allowed on each team and seven observers are allowed.

Communicating with Players

Players and the server administrator can type messages to each other during a BZFlag game. Table 8-1 includes some keys you can type to start a message, and Table 8-2 includes commands you can use while you are in a message mode. Here are some special ways of communicating with users beyond those already described.

You can have a broadcast message sent to users every 15 minutes, using the -admsg option. Here's an example:

```
-admsg "You are on the XYZ BZFlag Server. Be nice, play fair"
```

You can specify a file where users can report problems, using the -reportfile option as follows:

```
-reportfile myreport.txt
```

Using the -reportpipe option, you can have a report set off a command. In this example, each time a report is filed, a warning message in the warn.txt file is emailed to me.

```
-reportpipe mail chris@example.net < $HOME/warn.txt
```

Adding Passwords

To administer the BZFlag server, you need to add a password, and then enter that password when you connect to the server. Add a password to the server using the -password option in the server configuration file as follows:

```
-password myg00dpwD
```

After you connect to the server (for example, by starting a game with bzflag and identifying the server), you can enter a message mode (for example, type **N**) to send the password. Here's what you would type:

```
/password myg00dpwD
```

The server will say You are now an administrator! if the password was correct. You can then do server administration to your BZFlag process. Managing passwords for the users on your server is a different issue. As the administrator, you identify the password, users, and group file. Then, each user adds a password to his callsign when he connects to the server. Here are examples of options you can add to your server configuration file:

```
-passdb server.pass
-userdb server.users
-groupdb server.groups
```

Just giving file names, as shown above, creates these password files in your current directory. (If you like, you can give a full or relative path instead.) The first time players sign on to a server, they can associate passwords with their callsigns. They can do this from a message mode using the /register command as follows:

```
/register YurGNUpwd
```

Following the /register command is the password associated with the current player (choose your own password). After the player is logged in, the next step is to enter the password again, using the /identify command:

```
/identify YurGNUpwd
```

The player is now registered and logged in. A plus (+) will appear next to the user's name on the score sheet. The player will also have access to extra commands that were not available to unregistered users.

Kicking Off and Banning Players

If you are setting up a BZFlag server for your home or small office, presumably you will not be dealing with cheating and other abusive behavior. However, on public servers, dealing with players who cheat, are abusive, or otherwise disrupt the fun of the game is a major issue with gaming servers (including BZFlag).

As an administrator of a public BZFlag server, there are some tools that you can use to kick out and/or ban users that don't behave properly. The first trick is to detect the bad behavior and the second is to deal with it.

Sometimes a player's client takes too long to respond, causing the player's movements to not be followed by opposing players. This is called *lag*. In most cases, lag is just the result of a long-distance player or someone with a slow Internet connection. If lag occurs repeatedly for long periods of time (600 milliseconds or more), it can disrupt the game experience for all players. It might also be an indication that the person is using lag time to cheat. An administrator who suspects cheating can warn the player and then kick the player off after a certain number of warnings.

The first issue is to set how high a lag is too high. Here, the -lagwarn option is used to set the lag threshold to 600ms. A number above this number results in a warning:

```
-lagwarn 600
```

Using the -lagdrop option, you can set how many times a player is warned about lag before being dropped. Here, players are dropped after four warnings:

```
-lagdrop 4
```

If you notice players who repeatedly cheat or disrupt the game coming from a particular IP address (or set of addresses), you can add those players to a ban list. The following options identify the location of a banlist (-banfile) and indicate which IP addresses to ban (-ban). The ban list takes effect at server startup time and is updated during game play (as users are banned or removed from the ban list). Notice that wild cards (*) can be used to indicate a range of IP addresses:

```
-banfile $HOME/banfile
-ban "10.0.2.*,192.168.1.5,10.2.*.*"
```

Sending the same message repeatedly during a game is considered spamming. You can set the threshold for the time between someone sending out an identical message, and then decide how many warnings about this behavior are given before the person is kicked off. Here are some options that relate to spamming messages during BZFlag play:

```
-spamtime 9
-spamwarn 4
```

In the preceding examples, if an identical message is sent within nine seconds of the first, it is considered a spam message (-spamtime 9). After four warnings of such behavior, the person is kicked off the server.

Killing teammates more often than you kill opponents is considered antisocial behavior as well. The following option kicks a person off a server if more than 25 percent of that person's kills are their own teammates.

```
-tkkr 25
```

BZFlag also includes the ability for servers to offer a voting system to vote a player off the server. An administrator sets the percentage of people needed for a successful vote, number of votes needed to make a vote valid, and other attributes related to voting. (See the poll option on the bzfs man page for details.)

Managing Bad Words

To keep your server family-oriented, you can set up mechanisms to control the use of bad words. To indicate that callsigns (user names) and chat content (ongoing conversations) are free from bad words, you can add the following two options, respectively:

```
-filterCallsigns
-filterChat
```

The BZFlag source code contains two swear lists you can use (`simpleSwearList.txt` and `multilingualSwearList.txt`). You can modify either of these lists to suit your needs. Then incorporate the one you want into your server as follows:

```
-badwords /conf/multilingualSwearList.txt
```

If you decide that the filtering is too aggressive, you can have only exact matches of words on your bad words list cause a hit as follows:

```
-filterSimple
```

Setting Server Name, Address, and Port

When you start your BZFlag server, it listens on all your TCP/IP interfaces for requests to port number 5154 (by default). You can change this behavior by specifying a particular interface and/or port number. You might want to identify a particular interface, for example, if your computer has interfaces to the Internet and to a LAN and you want to offer only the server on your LAN:

```
-i 10.0.0.101
-p 5554
```

In the previous example, the BZFlag server will listen only on the interface associated with the IP address 10.0.0.101 (presumably the interface to your local LAN). To connect as a client from the local host, you would have to indicate this number as well (localhost won't work as the address). The port number the server will listen to is 5554, so any clients using your server would have to know that number as well.

When a client first connects to your server, you can have a message displayed that you choose. You can also add several messages, as shown in the following example:

```
-srvmsg "Welcome to the Linux Toys BZFlag server!"
-srvmsg "Be nice and play fair."
```

Monitoring the Server

There are lots of ways you can keep an eye on the activity of your BZFlag server. For a private server (with no exposure to the Internet), you might get by just doing simple things, such as increasing the debug level as follows:

```
-d
-dddd
```

The first option sets a simple debugging level (-d). By either adding more -d lines or putting a bunch of d's on one line (-dddd) you can increase the amount of debugging information that is output to the server.

If you want to watch the scoring from your server, you can add the -printscore option:

```
-printscore
```

This results in individual scores and team scores being displayed from the server debugging information.

Making Your BZFlag Server Public

This is a *Toys* book, remember. So, what I've described so far is a way of setting up a BZFlag server in a fairly safe environment, such as your home or small office LAN that is either behind a firewall or not connected to the Internet. Because it is so easy to make the BZFlag server public, however, I thought I should throw in a few warnings:

- **Come and get me!** — Listing an unprotected Linux server in a public directory (such as those used with BZFlag) is like holding up a sign to bad guys that you want to get hacked. Don't advertise this, or any other Linux service, until you have properly secured your Linux machine. If you don't know how to do that, start with a book that covers the basics, such as *Red Hat Fedora and Enterprise Linux 4 Bible* (Wiley, 2005). Follow up with a more in-depth book about how not to get hacked, such as *Linux Troubleshooting Bible* (Wiley, 2004).

- **Keep up with patches** — Vulnerabilities in Linux are continually being exposed and fixed. Keep up with available patches to your operating system and server software to limit your exposure.

- **Set up a chroot jail** — Again, to limit your exposure, you can set up your BZFlag server to run in a chroot jail. This can prevent someone attacking your system from getting at your entire file system. Running the server as a non-root user limits an attacker's ability to take over ownership of the machine. The http://BZFlag.org/ site tells how to set up BZFS in a chroot jail: (http://BZFlag.org/wiki/BZFS_20in_20a_20chroot_20Jail).

Actually adding your server to a BZFlag directory for public access is fairly easy. You can do it by adding -public and -publicaddr options to your bzfs configuration file. Here are some examples:

```
-public "Linux Toys Server - Capture-the Flag Tank Battle"
-publicaddr example.com:5154
```

The -public option advertises your server to the Internet and identifies the one-line message that will be displayed from the BZFlag list server that is queried by BZFlag clients. The -publicaddr option is used to indicate the public address of the server (which may be different than the host name your computer might give by default). The name must be a valid, public Internet domain name system name.

Using Central Registration for BZFlag

BZFlag now offers (as of bzflag-2.0) a mechanism for centrally registering users. This service lets a user have a consistent identity on multiple BZFlag servers by keeping the same callsign and password. This same callsign can be used to identify you on BZFlag forums.

The following procedure steps you through the process of registering a user for BZFlag:

1. Open the BZFlag forum page (`http://my.BZFlag.org/bb`).

2. Click the Register button in the upper-left corner of the page. The Registration Agreement Terms page appears.

3. Click to agree to the registration terms. The Registration Information page appears.

4. Add at least your Username (this is your callsign), email address (to receive confirmation of your registration), and password (twice). You also can add other publicly viewable information (ICQ number, AIM address, Yahoo Messenger, and so on) and set preferences (allow HTML, notify of new private messages, and the like). Then click Submit.

5. In a few minutes, check your email. A message welcoming you to BZFlag forums should arrive. Visit the link in that message to activate your account.

The next time you join a BZFlag game (as described earlier in this chapter), enter your user name (callsign) and password. You will see the message `Global Login Approved!` when you connect to the game. You may be asked again to identify yourself to the server. If so, type `/identify password` (using your password of course).

Besides using your callsign to play BZFlag, you can also use it to identify yourself to BZFlag forums. Without a valid callsign, you can read posted forum messages, but you can't post any messages yourself.

Summary

Setting up a private gaming server can be a fun way to play games with your friends or family in your home, school, or other organization. The BZFlag game described in this chapter is easy to set up, but offers fun and challenging game play, as well as many features for a server administrator (that's you) to tailor the game in different ways. While this *Linux Toy* description is meant to be used on a private LAN, BZFlag can be configured as a public network gaming server, as well as a private one.

Building a Dedicated SOHO Firewall

O ne of the rites of ascension for the modern Linux geek is the task of setting up his or her own home network with dedicated firewall/router. Building your own SOHO (Small Office/Home Office) firewall system is simple and cheap, and also a great way to significantly enhance the usability and security of your home or office broadband experience.

At one point, I almost broke down and bought an off-the-shelf firewall/router/gateway combo unit, until a friend convinced me to do it myself. That path opened up a whole world of local and small business consulting opportunities, not to mention the great learning experience that came with it.

Building your own firewall/gateway, router, or any security system for that matter, does more than give you a cheap DIY way around buying something. You gain intimate knowledge about the real security of your own systems. If you take the time to spec, design, and build a system around your specific set of service and security requirements, you'll be way ahead of the guy who just went out and bought some shrink-wrapped solution off the shelf. The commercial solution promises security, without the understanding of what that so-called solution is really doing on the inside, or what its weak points are.

In the original *Linux Toys*, you learned how to set up a home file/print server, firewall, router box that is convenient for running everything under one hood. However, for this chapter in *Linux Toys II* I'm going to drill down and focus on just the SOHO firewall/router functions by showing you what you need to design and build your own Linux-based, hard drive–less, high-availability firewall/router with no moving parts.

This is the type of router/firewall you need if you're going to be using (or installing) a network connection that simply can't go down because of a hard drive crash or a failed CPU fan. This is the type of firewall "device" that you can put on an Uninterruptible Power Supply, stick in a closet, and forget about. After you get one of these dedicated firewalls set up and running, you can often achieve an uptime (time without a reboot) on the order of years instead of just months as with a "do everything" home network server. Also, because there's no hard drive to worry about, backups are a thing of the past.

in this chapter

☑ Choosing a firewall

☑ Picking and modifying the hardware

☑ Designing your network

☑ Booting and configuring your firewall

☑ Securing your firewall and poking holes for access

☑ Other uses for Devil-Linux

Choosing Your Firewall

There are quite a few ways to set up a dedicated firewall. More traditional methods consist of installing a full or partial Linux distribution (or *distro*) to a hard drive, adding a firewall scripting tool or GUI (such as FWBuilder or Firestarter), and then configuring iptables and packet forwarding on that system. An easier commercial way is to buy a specialized firewall distro subscription that installs to a hard drive and gives you a nice point-and-click Web interface, and whose updates and intrusion signatures are centralized (such as Astaro Linux).

These solutions all work, but if you're looking for a cheap, rock solid, "install and walk away"–type system (no hard drive to crash, or subscriptions to maintain), you need to look at one of the CD- or floppy-based dedicated firewall distros covered in this chapter. Their big stability feature is that they boot off the CD or floppy media, and then just run out of the system's RAM. As a result, they require no hard drive, and require very little in the way of hardware resources.

The really great thing about running these CD-based or "Live" distros as a firewall is that most of them simply boot off their CD but store all of your custom configurations on floppy or other media (USB flash drive, or even hard drive). So upgrading to the latest version is usually as simple as downloading the latest version of the ISO (a pre-made CD-ROM image), burning it to CD, and rebooting your dedicated firewall off the new CD. Your system's configuration settings are read off the configuration floppy or USB thumb drive. That makes for the easiest upgrade ever!

And as an added security bonus, with this type of configuration, your CD-ROM is read-only. So after you get your configuration set up and saved out to a floppy, you set the write-protect tab of the floppy (open), and now if your system ever *is* compromised, it's totally non-writeable! That is, you just reboot and any traces of an intruder are gone. (Although after you get such a system locked down and your firewall rules set up, intrusion into the firewall itself is very unlikely.)

Here are some of the more popular and feature-rich live firewall CD/floppy distros to consider:

- **Devil-Linux** (www.devil-linux.org) — Good all-around CD boot firewall distro. Weighing in at around 200MB on CD, and using a configuration floppy, USB thumb drive, CD-ROM, hard drive or CompactFlash card, this seems to be one of the easier and more secure distros. Plus, it can handle both two and three network interface card (NIC) firewall setups just fine.

  Devil-Linux includes all the regular types of expected gateway/router services — everything from internal LAN DHCP and BIND/DNS caching service, to VPN Squid proxy, Apache Web Server with PHP, NTP (network time), and Anti-Spam and Antivirus mail gateway filtering. It features a very nice security model, as all binaries are compiled with the buffer overflow protecting GCC Stack Smashing Protector and GRSecurity. Devil-Linux requires a 486/66 processor, 32MB RAM, a bootable ATA/SCSI CD-ROM/USB drive, and a 1.44MB floppy or a USB flash drive.

- **Sentry Firewall CD** (www.sentryfirewall.com) — Another popular CD booting firewall. This live CD firewall distro takes around 328MB on CD and also uses a configuration floppy. Sentry Firewall includes all kinds of add-on packages that router firewall owners might want, such as OpenVPN, IPSec/PPTP support Snort IDS, Scanlogd, all your common daemons (apache, sendmail, squid, BIND, and so on), plus a Webmin-based Web control panel. Its full-service offering requires a bit more hardware: an i486 processor, 3296MB RAM, CD-ROM, and 1.44MB floppy drives.

- **redWall Firewall** (www.redwall-firewall.com) — This is quickly becoming a popular CD firewall distro. It can store its configurations on floppy or USB flash drive, or even email them! This big boy is based on Red Hat Linux 9 and features much of what Sentry Firewall does plus SMP kernel support, kudzu auto-hardware detection, Anti-Spam and Antivirus mail gateway filtering, centralized multi-firewall config, and more.

  The redWall distro is better suited to meet enterprise firewall/gateway requirements than those of a SOHO router/firewall. redWall also weighs in at a beefy 487MB on CD and, depending on use, has higher hardware requirements: Pentium 133–300 MHz processor (depending on use), 64–128MB RAM (or more), CD-ROM, 1.44MB floppy or USB flash drive, and hard drive for squid caching and logs.

- **Freesco Linux** (www.freesco.org) — This very impressive router/firewall distro boots totally off a single floppy! That's it! It has a full-featured and well-developed set of integrated configuration tools that can support a dedicated Linux router with up to 10 NICs; can serve DHCP, http, ftp, DNS, and ssh; and even includes print services. Plus it has a very cool Web-based administrative GUI. I am very impressed with this little 1.44MB contender, but its functionality as a Linux firewall is not well suited to running only a Linux 2.039/ipchains kernel.

Note Don't discount the small Linux floppy-based firewall distros. They tend to be small and simple, but powerful. Floppy Linux distros are extremely stable and often see years of uptime without reboots. Because there's so little running, so little exists to ever go wrong. They can run on embedded hardware or as little as a 386 processor with 8MB of RAM. And for even higher reliability, these floppy boot images can even be copied out to a USB flash drive or compact flash card for truly embedded-type performance. If you're an IT consultant or this stuff just interests you, other floppy/router distro projects to check out include fli4l, FDLinux, floppyfw, Linux Router Project (LRP), and the Wireless Router Project (WRP).

Figure 9-1 shows what an average SOHO firewall might look. Notice how it is positioned between the broadband provider's hardware and your internal or Trusted LAN switch.

Most firewall setups look similar to the one in the figure. The key with the example firewall in this chapter is that it is designed to be built inexpensively and to be extremely low maintenance. Often the only maintenance to be performed on it is just blowing the dust out of it and maybe upgrading the distro version every two or three years.

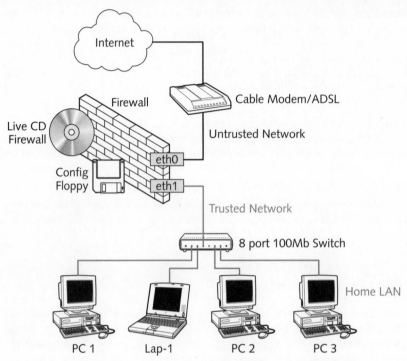

FIGURE 9-1: The average layout of a broadband-connected SOHO firewall

To this end, this chapter steps you through the process of creating the boot CD, building the hardware, and configuring a Devil-Linux–based firewall system. This type of system will be able to run without a hard drive or any moving parts, and can probably be built using nothing more than scrap PC parts that you may have laying around in your computer room or parts closet.

Using the Devil-Linux Live CD Distro

Because you're shooting for a small, stable firewall and not setting up a multifunction, home network, do-it-all server, this chapter focuses mainly on working with Devil-Linux, as it seems to be the easiest to set up, configure, and run.

Devil-Linux is a relatively lean, mean, and secure live firewall CD distro, and its setup automation scripts make it a good introduction firewall distro. But please, if you get the time, check out the other Live CD (and floppy) distros!

Making Your Boot CD

To use Devil-Linux, or any of the Live CD distros, you first need to obtain and burn the ISO. The instructions in his section cover burning ISO images on both Linux and Windows.

Step 1: Get the ISO

You can either use the version of Devil-Linux that is on the *Linux Toys* II CD or download a later copy of Devil-Linux yourself. The following sections describe those two approaches.

Using Devil-Linux from the Linux Toys II CD

The *Linux Toys II* CD contains the Devil-Linux 1.2.5 ISO image. It is contained in the isos/ch09-firewall directory under the following name:

```
devil-linux-1.2.5-i486.tar.bz2
```

Because this chapter was tested against that version, using it gives you the best chance of matching the descriptions in the chapter. So, if you like, you can simply copy this file to your hard disk. For example, from a running Linux system (such as Fedora Core), you could insert the *Linux Toys II* CD and type the following:

```
$ mkdir $HOME/devil-linux
$ cp /media/cd*/isos/ch09-firewall/devil-linux* $HOME/devil-linux/
```

With devil-linux copied to a directory on your hard disk, you can proceed to Step 2.

Getting Devil-Linux from the Internet

You can get a more recent version of Devil-Linux by downloading the Devil-Linux ISO on the Internet (such as from Sourceforge.net). Getting a later version of Devil-Linux gives you a better chance of having the latest features and fixes, but will probably mean some differences from descriptions in this chapter.

To download the ISO, go to www.devil-linux.org or to the SourceForge project site at http://sourceforge.net/project/showfiles.php?group_id=34096. There are several package versions (the latest is usually the best), and also several processor architecture types available: 486, 586-SMP, and 686-SMP.

SMP means Symmetric Multi Processor, and is for multi-processor systems, but the kernel and code work fine on single-processor systems, too. There is also a Server version, which has the GRSecurity feature disabled. This version is not intended for you to use as a firewall, as it is missing a base security feature. The Devil-Linux project provides this version because GRSecurity can interfere with some server applications.

Note

If you don't have a Pentium or better processor, you'll have to use the 486-based ISO, which of course minimally requires a 486. The 486 version will work on higher processors as well. However, if you have at least a Pentium1 or AMD K6, you can use the 586 version. The Intel P-Pro–, PII-, III/Celeron-, and AMD Athlon/Duron–based systems are all 686-class processors, making them appropriate for a 686 version of Devil-Linux.

I recommend downloading the latest architecture that your system can run, and downloading it from one of SourceForge's well-maintained network of mirror sites. Place the Devil-Linux download file into a directory on your hard disk that has at least 400MB of disk space available (for example, you could place it in a $HOME/devil-linux/ directory).

Step 2: Prepare and Check the ISO Image

After you download the image or copy it from the *Linux Toys II* CD to a directory on your hard disk (for example, the $HOME/devil-linux directory), you'll notice that it's not a normal ISO file, but is a compressed tarball of 170–200MB in size:

```
$ cd $HOME/devil-linux
$ ls -lah devil-linux-1.2.5-i486.tar.bz2
-rw-rw-r--  1 tweeks tweeks 179M Mar 29 22:48 devil-linux-1.2.5-i486.tar.bz2
```

Before decompressing the tarball, you should first verify that it's a good download by checking the tar/bz2 file's md5sum, or fingerprint, against what the Web site says it should be:

```
$ md5sum devil-linux-1.2.5-i486.tar.bz2
f902aedea728c72be061d06be02ec3e6 devil-linux-1.2.5-i486.tar.bz2
```

Check that against the MD5 checksums on the page www.devil-linux.org/downloads/. If the checksums match, decompress the tarball with the following command:

```
$ tar xjvf devil-linux-1.2.5-i486.tar.bz2
```

Note Windows users cannot decompress bz2-compressed files with regular WinZip. So to decompress the devil-linux*tar.bz2 file, Windows users will need a zip utility such as ZipZag from http://zipzag.com/ or IZArc from http://izarc.org/. Just realize that this large tar-gzip file will take a while to decompress, as it's several hundred megabytes. As for doing md5sums on Windows, there is no native way to do this. You will have to download a md5sum tool, such as the md5sum.exe command line tool available from www.pc-tools.net/win32/md5sums/. Or you can simply boot the *Linux Toys II* CD and use the md5sum command from a shell once DSL boots.

After you have decompressed the download bz2 file, change into the directory it creates and have a look:

```
$ cd devil-linux-1.2.5-i486/
$ ls -lah
total 201M
drwxr-xr-x  3 tweeks tweeks 4.0K May 15 12:42 .
drwxrwxrwx  3 root   root   4.0K Aug 20 23:22 ..
-rw-r--r--  1 tweeks tweeks 208M May 15 12:42 bootcd.iso
-r-xr-xr-x  1 tweeks tweeks 3.6K May 15 12:42 custom-cd
-rw-r--r--  1 tweeks tweeks 3.4K May 15 12:42 DL-build-config
-rw-r--r--  1 tweeks tweeks  38K May 15 12:42 DL-kernel-config
drwxr-xr-x  3 tweeks tweeks 4.0K May 15 12:42 docs
-rw-r--r--  1 tweeks tweeks 788K May 15 12:42 etc.tar.bz2
-r-xr-xr-x  1 tweeks tweeks  14K May 15 12:42 install-on-usb
```

You want that single 200MB bootcd.iso file, shown in bold. That's what you're going to burn.

Step 3: Burn the ISO to CD

Descriptions of how to burn ISO images to CD in Linux using K3b or cdrecord are contained in Chapter 5. However, for most cases in Linux, assuming that you have a CD-R or CD-RW drive, you can usually burn an ISO to a CD with this command:

```
$ cdrecord -eject bootcd.iso
. . .
```

After a few minutes, the CD will pop out and your firewall boot CD is ready to use.

If that doesn't work, you might have either the wrong default CD-R device or some other application may have control over it. You may need to run a `cdrecord --scanbus` or `killall kscd` command, and then try `cdrecord` with difference settings (for example, `cdrecord dev=0,0,1 boot.iso`).

 Tip — Windows users: Many Windows users seem to be confused about what an ISO file is and how to properly burn one. As most Windows users choose Nero to burn their ISOs, here's the easiest way to do so. Simply run Nero, exit from any easy start wizards, select File → Burn Image, select your `bootcd.iso` image, and let it rip!

Step 4: Set Your Config File Media Aside for Now

Devil-Linux doesn't initially need a configuration medium. At first, you can simply boot with the CD and have the Live distro create a starter config file disk for you. For now, however, just set your floppy configuration media aside until your hardware is ready.

You can take a sneak peek at your new bootable firewall distro, but be careful not to run any of the related services while on a corporate or school network. Even though no dangerous services are run by default with Devil-Linux, consider unplugging your computer from the network when you first try it out.

 Caution — In particular, take care not to inadvertently add services such as DHCP. If your laptop starts broadcasting 192.168.1.x DHCP adverts, then you'll end up unknowingly hijacking half the Windows machines on the LAN. This means that if you're a student, you'll probably get kicked out of school for hacking—or worse, if you're an IT manager, be fired for interrupting your boss's last-second eBay bidding!

Choosing Your Hardware

The great thing about running a dedicated firewall is that it takes almost no horsepower to route and secure a 2 Mbps stream of data between two network interface cards. In fact, on a moderate-speed broadband connection, you can really do quite well with a 386SX25 machine on the low end.

However, as soon as you start wanting to run an internal DHCP service, internal caching DNS, SNAT (masquerading), DNAT (port mapping), and stateful packet inspection, well, then you're going to need a bit more horsepower—but don't worry. You will still be able to build such a system on scrap parts, most of which you can probably find just lying around.

For a very basic SOHO router/firewall configuration with simple DHCP, caching DNS, and basic SNAT IP masquerading, a P100 to P133 with between 32 and 64MB should do just fine.

Note Keep in mind that this firewall/router project is designed for a network that you expect to be small and stable, but for which you still want fast performance. If you decide to start running big apps such as a squid proxy server or a SNORT intrusion detection system (IDS), you're going to need a bit more horsepower and storage. Running applications like those will usually require a hard drive for the large files that will be generated and stored, and more RAM is always a good thing. In fact doubling the amount of RAM that you think you need is usually a good forward-thinking rule of thumb. So where you think you need only 64MB, use 128MB.

How Underclocking Gets You More

The purpose of this section is to help you take a normal, older desktop-quality system and make it run like a high-availability, rock-solid workhorse that can run for years on end without so much as a reboot. To do this, you have to take an already slow older system, turn the speed down a bit (called *underclocking*) to makes it run cooler so that you can then pull the fan off the CPU. Running a system without the need for moving parts such as fans and hard drives will greatly increase its long-term stability and reliability.

The whole idea of high-dollar, high-availability enclosures with redundant power supplies, RAID drive arrays, temperature monitoring, and forced air cooling is fine for big enterprise–level outfits — but remember the engineer's mantra: KISS (Keep It Simple Stupid). Another way to design a system for stability is to simply decrease its operational parameters far, far below normal operating ranges.

For example, my base system is composed of an old AMD K6-2 400 MHz system that I've "tuned down" to 250 MHz and a large heat sink from which I've removed the fan. When underclocking and pulling off the fan, the only thing you have to worry about is the size of your heat sink and watching the temperature of the processor (see the related sidebar on heat sinks). You can't just pull the fan off and put the system on line or the CPU will quickly cook itself. You first want to decrease the CPU speed (usually by around one-half) and then pull the fan off the CPU heat sink (it's usually screwed on).

If you have a motherboard/BIOS configuration that gives you real-time temperature feedback, check the temperature before and after you turn down the CPU MHz and pull off the fan. The actual CPU speed is usually controlled either via the BIOS/software settings, or via a DIP switch or jumper settings on the motherboard. The CPU speed is achieved by multiplying the bus-clock speed by the CPU multiplier. Don't bother messing with the front side bus (FSB) clock speed (rated in MHz). Instead, just turn down the clock multiplier. Usually AMD and some Pentium systems have multiplier settings of something like 2, 2.5, 3, 3.5, 4, 4.5, 5, and 5.5. With a 100 MHz FSB clock, that will result in anything from 200 to 550 MHz.

Caution You might want to have a hair dryer handy to blow room-temperature air on your CPU/sink just in case, after removing the fan, the CPU/sink gets too toasty.

Because I started out with a CPU clock speed multiplier of 4x and a 100 MHz FSB/clock, for example, I just powered down the system, removed the fan, and changed the multiplier down to around 50 to 65 percent of the rated CPU speed (2–2.5x multiplier). After you try that yourself, power the system back up and watch the CPU temperature in the real-time BIOS readings if you have that option. Hold down an arrow key for 5 minutes while watching the BIOS temperature to give it *some* type of CPU load (which makes heat). Most BIOS utilities are extremely inefficient and do place some demands on the CPU. While testing, you don't want your older P2/P3/586/686 system to get much hotter than 125°F (or ~52°C).

If you don't have built-in BIOS temperature indicators, you can do intensive system RAM tests using Devil-Linux's included `memtest` utility (from the Memtest-86 package) and placing your hand on the side of the heat sink. To do this, boot your Devil-Linux CD to the main CD `boot` menu (making sure your BIOS boot order has CD-ROM listed first), and at the Devil-Linux boot menu, type **m** to run `/boot/memtest`. It will hammer your system's RAM and load the system enough to get some type of "busy temperature reading." Use the hand temperature test as your benchmark: If it's too hot to hold your hand on for more than 2 seconds, then you need to step down by half a multiplier notch and try it again.

Importance of Heat Sink Size and Thermal Interfacing

If you're running a system without a fan, you need to be sure that your heat sink can dissipate the heat from the CPU quickly enough, even when under-clocked. This boils down to two main things: Is your heat sink large enough to dissipate the CPU's thermal output and is your CPU–to–heat sink interface good enough to allow that heat to migrate out of your CPU and into the sink, and be radiated into the air.

The size of your heat sink matters. If you have one of those little 1-inch-high heat sinks with a fan, that probably won't do without the fan. I recommend one of the larger 2- to 2.5-inch heat sinks (see Figure 9-2) before attempting this fan-less underclocking trick. Otherwise you could damage your CPU and/or your system. As for the CPU-to-heat sink interface, for this project I recommend thermal conductive compound (silicone grease) to thermally connect and conduct heat from your CPU to your heat sink.

Some say that heat sink silicon compound is no good because on/off power cycling causes what's called *thermal migration* or *"edge pooling,"* so most modern PC manufacturers now use Thermal Pads or Phase Changing materials. While thermal compound migration is a problem on most desktop PC systems that are constantly turned on and off day after day, because your firewall will stay on months or years at a time, this is not a problem. Just be sure that both your heat sink and CPU surface are clean of any other materials, smooth to the touch, and that you apply the compound no thicker than you would if you were lightly painting the surface. Globs are bad and messy.

Last, if you want to really increase the efficiency of your heat sink, check out the information in Chapter 4, in the section "Assembly Tips." There is a useful link on how to lap (hone or polish) your heat sink's CPU-side interface to easily knock 10–20 degrees off your CPU temperature.

The "under load" temperature target range of around 120°F is a figure with safety in mind. If you can get the loaded CPU temperature under 125°F without a fan by adjusting the CPU speed multiplier (while running memtest), then operationally you'll be okay once you start up and run a GUI-less Linux firewall.

Yes, different operating systems and applications have different average operating temperatures (depending on what they're doing, of course). As compared with other operating systems, Linux actually runs very cool indeed. So if you can get the BIOS temperature down to between warm-warm to warm-hot while doing your memtest load testing, it should run pretty cool in Linux (under 100°F) even under full network load.

As a point of reference, my AMD 400 underclocked down to 250 MHz was running memtest at around 120° (warm-hot to touch) under load, but running the firewall under full throttle it's actually cool to the touch (under 98°!).

Don't forget to have a good heat sink–to–CPU thermal interface (with silicon compound), or the sink may actually feel cool to the touch while your CPU is actually burning up, as the heat never gets conducted away from the CPU into the heat sink!

Networking Hardware

Assuming that you're hooking up to some form of SOHO broadband (2–6 Mbps ADSL or cable modem), you want at least a 10 Mbps card on the outside, and a 100 Mbps card on the inside. Common and supported 10 Mbps cards are any ne2000 (or ne driver in the Linux kernel) or 3COM 3c509 (3c509 module in the kernel). Either of these older card types may require a non-PNP memory I/O option setting of io=0x300 (or whatever the IO memory address is set to on your card).

For a common and inexpensive 100 Mbps card, the RealTek 8139–based chipset is very common (look on the little black chip itself). The kernel module for the 8139 is usually 8139too. On the higher-end 100 Mbps cards you also commonly see the nicer Intel Pro 100 series chipset (which uses the eepro100 kernel module). In general you should try to use PCI network cards if possible, as they're easier to set up and usually faster. I address all these NIC1 driver configuration issues later in the chapter in the section on configuring Devil-Linux.

While you can't see it in the black-and-white figure, note that the external Internet facing, or untrusted, interface cable is red (for danger) and the internal cabling, or at least the cabling going from the firewall to the switch, is green to indicate the trusted side of the firewall. Some security buffs prefer this use of firewall cable color-coding so that the interfaces, and relative risk levels of the two connections, are never confused. As for the hardware itself, it can be mounted in any old PC case, or in a custom 19-inch rack mount. It is essential, however, that you not use a cheap power supply with a cheap fan that will burn out within a year of continuous use.

FIGURE 9-2: This is the precarious hardware test environment that I did my initial testing in.

Switch Recommendation

When building one of these SOHO firewalls, I also recommend getting a very small, very cheap 100 Mbps auto-crossover detecting switch for interconnecting your other internal clients to your firewall/gateway. The auto-crossover detecting feature will save you much eye strain as you squint at CAT5 cables, trying to discern between a crossover color arrangement of those eight little CAT5 wires, and a straight-through CAT5 cable wire arrangement.

Get a switch with at least eight ports so that you can provide connections for several home/office machines, and have a couple extra ports for guests or stringing line out to another switch or even a WiFi (wireless) Access Point.

Tip

A very cheap, very small, fairly robust little switch that I've fallen in love with for this purpose is the GigaFast EZ800-S 8-Port 10/100Mbps Network Switch (see Figure 9-3), available from most online computer parts and networking e-tailers such as www.newegg.com or www.tigerdirect.com. This powerful and cheap switch is built reliably, has eight auto-sensing, auto-negotiating, auto-crossover detection ports, and can be had for around $16! You really can't go wrong.

If you need a larger switch, GigaFast also offers 16- and 24-port models, and their pro line has a built-in mini AC power supply so you can bypass the wall wart DC power supply. These eight-port models are perfect for this purpose because they just slide into a 5.25-inch drive bay and can be screw mounted if desired. Very nice indeed for a single enclosure design!

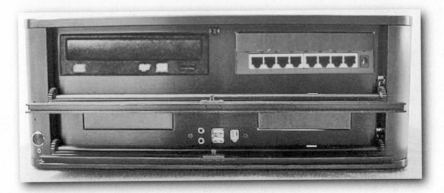

FIGURE 9-3: See how versatile these little EZ800S switches are!

CD-ROM, Floppy, and USB Thumb Drives

As for the last two major components, all you need are a general purpose ATA CD-ROM drive that's less than five years old (no CD-R media reading issues) and a 1.44MB floppy drive. If you're like me, you can probably assemble all of this from parts lying around in your geek closet. If you're using a newer motherboard that supports USB, you can use a small USB thumb drive instead of the floppy drive. The smallest thumb drives available, 8 or 16MB, are more than you'll ever need.

Designing Your Network

This section addresses some additional variables to consider in planning and laying out a small office or home network. These variables include items such as your internal network's IP space, IP pre-allocation or static mappings, file servers, print servers, as well as alternate DNS servers, network devices, alternate network gateways, and the like.

DHCP Configuration

The network that comes by default on most firewall distros is a single block of usable IP addresses, ranging from 1 to 254. You need to decide how you want to slice up the IP space to allocate static IPs for known internal machines, known network devices, as well as dynamic IPs for guests or unknown visitors to your network (such as a friend's laptop).

Because you may have always-on PCs or servers as part of your network, and you want the IPs on those machines to remain static and never change, the IPs of 2 through 9 should be reserved (1 is the internal address of the firewall/gateway/router itself). Usually, at the upper end of the network you also have a few IPs (perhaps 251–254, with 255 being the reserve broadcast IP for your LAN) that you want to reserve for various network devices (such as a wireless gateway-router or Access Point).

About DHCP and Network Address Translation on Router/Gateways

Dynamic Host Configuration Protocol (DHCP) is the protocol by which a machine can ask for an IP address, and a DHCP server (running dhcpd) answers the client and leases (or allows it to borrow) an IP address for the duration of its time on that given network. In the configuration in this example, the Internet firewall/gateway/router gets its external IP address (on eth0) from the broadband provider. This is done by the cable modem (for cable broadband) when it serves DHCP to give your firewall its IP address.

The firewall in turn is running DHCP internally to serve out multiple IP addresses to all the internal clients. The firewall also serves as a gateway/router that does Network Address Translation (NAT) to masquerade all of your IP addresses internally behind the single external IP address on the firewall.

Some uninitiated think because you are creating many IPs for free that this is in some way illegal. This is simply not the case. Running a NAT gateway with private IPs internally is not illegal; it is simply the standard way of allowing many machines in your home or office to share and use a single externally routable Internet IP address, without taking more Internet IPs from your broadband provider (or the Internet). This is very similar to the way that a company's phone PBX system abstracts or masquerades many private phone extensions behind a single main telephone phone number.

So with this logic, your average SOHO network IP space layout might look something like Table 9-1.

Table 9-1: Network IP Assignments

IP Address	Assigned to
192.168.1.1	Static firewall/gateway/router to Internet
192.168.1.2	File, media, fax, and print server
192.168.1.3	Backup server
192.168.1.4	Admin PC #1
192.168.1.5	Admin PC #2
192.168.1.6	Admin remote access machine
192.168.1.7	Staging/development workstation
192.168.1.8	Reserved
192.168.1.9	Reserved

Continued

Table 9-1 *(continued)*

IP Address	Assigned to
192.168.1.10 through 192.168.1.250	Miscellaneous employee or guest machine IP leases
192.168.1.251	Reserved
192.168.1.252	Reserved
192.168.1.253	Reserved
192.168.1.254	WiFi Access Point reverse gateway/router (trusted side)

This type of arrangement offers a well laid out IP space arrangement with a little room for growth. What other IP ranges do you think you could use in a small office environment? Might you need additional static IPs? If you're not sure, then double the ones that you currently have allocated. What about if this were a home configuration? Just remember that if you are going to have servers, workstations, or other devices that people need to access on a regular basis, consider giving them a static IP address.

Other Network Services and Configuration Options

In most SOHO gateway/router configurations, the machine that gives out IP addresses also runs caching name services (or DNS) for the internal group. This saves on company bandwidth and increases the overall speed of using Internet name-based services because shared recursive DNS services like this also do what's called DNS caching.

After the first user on your network browses out to google.com or ebay.com, that DNS record is cached and stored locally on your DNS server for all internal network users to access more quickly in the future. To enable this service on your Devil-Linux gateway, you need to turn on DNS, and set up DHCP to point the internal clients to your internal Devil-Linux gateway's IP address for DNS resolution. You'll find more on this in the section "Configuring the Network and Startup Services" later in this chapter.

Other internal services that small gateway servers sometimes provide include ssh (Secure Shell) access, so that administrators can log in and check things out and make small changes to the server from their desktop. You may also want to offer Network Time Protocol services or NTP from your small gateway server. With NTP properly set up, your gateway will go out and sync itself against Internet-connected atomic clocks, and in turn allow your client and server machines to sync against it. This is an often overlooked but strongly recommended configuration.

Some other services that you might want to kick the tires on and check out internally are NTOP and THTTPD. NTOP is a very powerful little network monitoring tool that shows you the traffic type flowing across your gateway as well as the source and destination IPs by country. You get to it by internally pointing a Web browser to http://192.168.1.1:8080.

Caution You want to be very careful about running too many services on your firewall/gateway. The more programs that you run, the more you expose your network to attack, even from the inside. Remember, 80 percent of all successful hacker/cracker attempts come from within an organization!

Booting up and Configuring Your Firewall

Now that you have all your hardware together and your network plan laid out, you should run through a quick hardware setup checklist. Verify the following before you proceed:

- Your CPU is running cool enough.
- Your CD-ROM is hooked up correctly and configured as the master ATA device.
- Your floppy drive cable isn't on backward (if it is, the light will stay on).
- Your config floppy is formatted ext2 (done via the command `mke2fs /dev/fd0` from Linux).
- Your motherboard BIOS is set to boot off the CD-ROM first.

The rest of this section shows you how to boot the system from a CD and use a default configuration, start applying your network layout settings and required services, configure your specific network card drivers, and configure your DHCP and firewall settings.

Note Before booting Devil-Linux, consider booting the *Linux Toys II* CD first to determine the modules representing your network interface cards. Open a Terminal window and type `lsmod | less`. Page through the list of loaded modules to find ones representing your two NICs. If you're not sure which they are, type **modprobe module**, replacing *module* with the name of the one you suspect of being for a NIC. That displays a description of the module. Discovering the modules for your NICs can save you some trouble when you go to configure your network interfaces during Devil-Linux setup.

Starting the Boot

At the boot menu (where you previously pressed m for memtest), press Enter. The boot screen should look something like Figure 9-4.

Let the machine boot normally, verifying again that your blank ext2 configuration floppy is in the drive with the write-protect tab closed. The boot process will see the blank floppy and will prompt you as follows:

```
*** Found empty configuration media ***
Should I copy default configuration to it? (y/n) y
```

FIGURE **9-4:** Devil-Linux boot screen

Press **y** to use a default configuration to boot from, as just shown. When you are prompted for a SCSI controller, press **n** because you're not even running a hard drive (unless you've installed a SCSI card/drive for some reason).

The first-time boot process will then load, using a minimal default configuration, and start a generic boot.

> **Note**   While this firewall project doesn't include (in fact, it doesn't even recommend) having a hard disk attached to the firewall, if your computer does have one, you should be aware of one thing. If Devil-Linux spots a hard disk when it first boots, it places the configuration file (etc.tar.bz2) on a hard disk partition. After that, it will continue to use the config file from that location and bypass your floppy disk. To get around that problem you can either remove the hard disk or move (not copy) the config file from the hard disk to the floppy disk. Devil-Linux will then happily use the config file from the floppy going forward.

Configuring the Network and Startup Services

Now the system is booted, and you need to use the default login before you can start configuring the system. At the `devil login:` prompt, log in as the user `root` with no password and at the # root prompt, type the following:

```
# setup
```

At the Devil-Linux System Configurator screen that is displayed, you see the menu options shown in Figure 9-5.

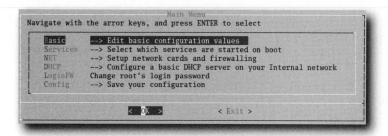

FIGURE 9-5: The Devil-Linux setup text menu

The following sections help you use this menu to configure your firewall system per your requirements. Refer back to Figure 9-1 and note that this firewall/gateway is meant to:

- Get a DHCP IP address on eth0 from your broadband provider
- Serve DHCP on your internal eth1 interface
- Run DNS (BIND) for your internal network
- Run SSH internally so that your administrator(s) can internally administer the firewall
- Possibly run other internal services to assist in monitoring the firewall traffic (ntop, thttpd)

During any point of the following setup procedure you can select Config from the Main Menu to save your current settings. In that way, you can exit from Devil-Linux setup before completing the procedure (if you need to) without losing the work you have done.

Basic

From the Basic screen of the Main Menu, you set the host name and domain name (if you're using a fully registered domain name), and select your time zone.

```
Hostname     firewall
Domain       example.com <--Replace if using a real domain name
TIMEZONE     CST6CDT
. . .
```

Note If you do not have a registered domain name that you want your machines to be associated with, you should list the host and domain name to match the reverse FQDN (full host name) of the IP address that your broadband provider gave your firewall's eth0. You can look this up by logging into the firewall (later), running `ifconfig` to determine the IP of eth0, and then running `host <IP>` to see what the full name of your firewall is on the Internet. You can then use that in the preceding settings.

Check if there are other setting you need to change (such as your default keyboard or mouse) and select Back to continue to the next menu.

Services

The Services section of the configuration menu controls what services start when the firewall boots. These services include the initialization scripts that actually turn on the router/gateway and firewall features of Devil-Linux, as well as common SOHO gateway required services such as DNS (named), network time (ntpd), and ssh.

```
[X]    CRON           Periodic command scheduler
[X]    FIREWALL       Execute firewall script on boot
[X]    IPV6_ROUTING   New Internet Protocol
[X]    NAMED          The BIND name (DNS) daemon
[X]    NTOP           Network traffic probe reporting tool
[X]    NTPD           Network time protocol daemon
[X]    ROUTING        Enable routing (between interfaces)
[ ]    SHOREWALL      Alternate firewall creation/startup
                      (recommend against now)
[X]    SSHD           Secure shell for secure logins & file xfer
[X]    THTTPD         Small, fast & secure web server
                      (be careful!)
```

The DHCP service will be configured a bit later when you configure the network layout for your internal LAN. For now, select OK when you have selected the services indicated above, so you can save your selections and continue to the next menu.

 Note I recommend not setting the shorewall firewall startup script at the beginning. Shorewall is a great firewall config script automation tool, but you need to get the system up and running with the default 2 NIC firewall script first, and then look at customizing or writing your own firewall script from scratch, or using a script writer such as shorewall or fwbuilder. Trust me — you do not want to be troubleshooting DHCP, DNS, and IPtables rules all at the same time! For information on shorewall or fwbuilder, check out www.shorewall.net/two-interface.htm, and for fwbuilder see www.linuxjournal.com/article/6625 and www.linuxjournal.com/article/6715.

NET

From the NET option of the Main Menu, you must configure the first NIC (external/Internet) for your specific kernel module (for example, ne, rtl8139, eepro100, and so on). You will need to supply your io address (in hex) if you're using an older NIC that requires this (such as ne-based NIC on an ISA bus), although modern PCI cards don't require this information. Finally, you will need to tell the system to get its external IP address via DHCP request to your ISP's system.

```
1NIC
    MODULE      [ne]
    OPTMOD      [io=0x320]
    UseDHCP     [yes]
        <Load Module>
```

Selecting <Load Module> will perform a modprobe, and then display a module listing. After this, you should see the module name on the left, but you may see (unused) on the right. You may also see additional PCI-based NICs drivers are already loaded. After you have this section set up, press Esc or select <BACK>.

Note If you're running all PCI or motherboard-integrated NICs, you probably will not have to issue any io= or irq= options settings for the NIC kernel modules. However, on older ISA hardware (as seen in this example), you will often have to fight this config battle. This requires that you change BIOS settings of the motherboard (reserving the proper IRQ for the card), set up the card (with either jumpers on the card, or a DOS boot config disk), and then match that in the NIC module config area under the NET section of the main menu. PCI is nice, eh?

This is what the second, internal NIC configuration would look like for a Real Tek 8139 PCI network card:

```
2NIC
    MODULE       [8139too]
    OPTMOD       [ ]
    UseDHCP      [no]
    DHCPSERVER   [yes]
    IP           [192.168.1.1]
    NETMASK      [255.255.255.0]
        <Load Module>
```

Do you see your driver after the Load Module tries to determine the module to use for your NIC using modprobe? If not, then you will need to enter the driver for your second NIC card manually. If everything looks okay, you can continue.

Next you want to indicate that you will use a standard two-network firewall configuration. To do that, you need to back out of the current menu, select FW2, and select <yes> to configure this type of firewall, as follows:

```
            <Back>
FW2         <enter>, <yes>
            <Back>
```

DHCP

Next you need to configure the internal DHCP service that will provide private IP addresses to all the machines on your internal LAN. Select DHCP from the main menu and configure your DHCP server as follows:

```
Domain       [example.com]
PrimaryDNS   [192.168.1.1] (your firewall internal IP)
...
1st IP       [192.168.1.20]
2nd IP       [192.168.1.250]
Gateway      [192.168.1.1]
             <Save>
```

There you go.

Note

If you do not have the CPU and RAM resources to run a full caching BIND/named name server on your devil-linux gateway, consider running the lightweight dnsmasq service. It is a simple way of using the NAT feature of Devil-Linux along with the dnsmasq service for doing DNS forwarding and caching for a small network of internal machines. Dnsmasq is not configurable from the Devil-Linux text GUI, so you will have to configure it manually. More information on this service can be found at `http://thekelleys.org.uk/dnsmasq/doc.html`. Also see the example configuration file `/etc/dnsmasq.conf.example`.

LoginPW

You need to change the default blank login password to something a bit more secure. The LoginPW configuration option on the Main Menu (see Figure 9-5) is the firewall's root password that you will be asked for whenever logging into the system from console or via `ssh` as root. Make it something secure that you will remember, but something that you don't have to write down.

Config

The Config option on the Main Menu allows you to save all your changes out to the configuration floppy disk, a critical step to remember.

The system compares your changes to the files on the floppy and asks you if you still want to save your config to floppy. Press **y**. It will take a minute or so to save the changes.

Now exit out of the configuration screen, and when back at the root prompt, type **reboot**:

```
root@Devil:~ # reboot
```

Now you should be able to let the system reboot unattended.

After Devil-Linux reboots, hook a laptop or any of your internal PCs up to the switch that your SOHO firewall is serving DHCP on now, and boot the internal laptop or PC. Does it get onto the internal network? Type **/sbin/ifconfig** on the internal system to see if your internal machine has an IP address (on Windows, use **ipconfig**).

Next. from the internal laptop or PC, try `ping 192.168.1.1` (the internal firewall interface), and then try `ping 216.239.37.99` (the `google.com` IP). Finally, try `ping google.com`. Did they all work? If so, your internal machines are now online and using your firewall and its DNS and it all works! Congratulations! But don't start hooking up all your machines to the LAN just yet. You should change the stock DHCP configuration to meet the requirements of the network design that you previously planned (refer to Table 9-1).

Customizing Your DHCPD Network Configuration

Now you have basic functionality and Internet access. Before hooking all your other computers up and handing out DHCP IP assignments and leases, consider what settings you need to customize (see Table 9-1) on your firewall/gateway/router. This level of configuration detail can't be done with the regular text-GUI configuration interface of Devil-Linux. To modify these DHCP server settings for the IP addresses on your inside LAN, you must manually edit your `dhcpd.conf` file.

Log in at the console directly or remotely (using ssh) into the firewall (from the inside LAN, use ssh root@192.168.1.1), and edit the DHCP daemon config file located in /etc/dhcpd.conf (using vi /etc/dhcpd.conf).

Tip

If you're new to Linux, or just not keen on vi, you can use either the included pico or joe editors. If you're not familiar with pico, after pulling up your config file with pico /etc/dhcpd.conf, just press F1 for help, and Ctrl+X to save and exit. Appendix B provides a quick tutorial of the vi text editor.

Here's what my /etc/dhcpd.conf file looks like, given the settings mentioned in the DHCP configuration section:

```
# to restart DNS on Devil Linux:
#   /etc/init.d/dhcpd stop
#   /etc/init.d/dhcpd start
#
######## My Network Layout ########
## 1              The LAN firewall/gateway
## 2-10           Reserved for our machines
## 10-250         Guest/DHCP IPs
## 251-254        Special edge devices (wap)
##################################
authoritative;
default-lease-time 14400;
max-lease-time 14400;
get-lease-hostnames false;
use-host-decl-names on;
ddns-update-style none;
option domain-name "example.com";
option subnet-mask 255.255.255.0;
### This is my inside LAN Dynamic/Guest IP range definition ####
subnet 192.168.1.0 netmask 255.255.255.0 {
  option domain-name-servers 192.168.1.2;
  option routers 192.168.1.1;
  option broadcast-address 192.168.1.255;
  range 192.168.1.10 192.168.1.250;
}
### These are my known machines w/MAC addr mapped static IPs
host fileserver {
        hardware ethernet 00:e0:29:3d:a0:93;
        fixed-address 192.168.1.2;
        }
host janice3 {
        hardware ethernet 00:08:54:d1:94:21;
        fixed-address 192.168.1.3;
        }
host fixed4 {
        hardware ethernet 00:00:c0:a8:80:04;
        fixed-address 192.168.1.4;
        }
```

```
host fixed6 {
        hardware ethernet 00:00:c0:a8:80:06;
        fixed-address 192.168.1.6;
        }
host fixed7 {
        hardware ethernet 00:00:c0:a8:80:07;
        fixed-address 192.168.1.7;
        }
host fixed8 {
        hardware ethernet 00:00:c0:a8:80:08;
        fixed-address 192.168.1.8;
        }
host fixed9 {
        hardware ethernet 00:00:c0:a8:80:09;
        fixed-address 192.168.1.9;
        }
#### Net Devices ####
host wap {
        hardware ethernet 00:0c:66:0c:2f:14;
        fixed-address 192.168.1.254;
        }
```

To make each static IP address persist, you need to enter the MAC address from each network card in each internal machine in the respective `hardware ethernet` field, as shown in the code. You can see the unique address of a NIC by typing **/sbin/ifconfig** from the shell prompt, or **ipconfig /all** from any Windows command line. Just be sure that you get the right NIC, especially in Windows. Look for the manufacturer name on your network card. Be sure not to use the fake MAC addresses associated with virtual dial-up and VPN adapters.

Caution

If you set up a machine with a static IP address on your LAN, be sure *not* to have the IP that you assigned it also co-existing in the `range` field of the DHCPd config file that your DHCP server uses to assign dynamic guest IPs. If you do, you will run into some pretty serious network problems as your DHCP/firewall, guest dynamic client who gets that IP, and your statically assigned client all get into a network/DCHP IP address "It's Mine!" brawl on your network, effectively bringing your whole LAN to its knees. This is a classic DHCP newbie problem. Be mindful of your dynamic versus static IP assignments and do not allow them to overlap.

Save that file and restart `dhcpd`:

```
# /etc/init.d/dhcpd restart
Stopping ISC DHCP Server daemon on eth1 ... [  OK  ]
Starting ISC DHCP Server daemon on eth1 ... [  OK  ]
```

Verify that this works by plugging in a guest laptop or PC that you have not taken the MAC address of. If all is well, the resulting IP address should be in the dynamic "guest range" of 192.168.1.10 to 192.168.1.250.

Make any additional changes to your system or config files in `/etc/` that you feel the need to, test them, and run the command `save-config` to save all your changes to the floppy so that they will take after a reboot.

Locking Down Your Firewall

Now that you have a basic, assumed secure firewall in place, you can start looking at ways to customize it.

Note Why do I say "assumed" secure? Because of the fundamental security tenet that if you don't truly understand how the inside of your security system works and what its weaknesses are, that security is just an illusion. In light of this principle, I encourage you to at least know where your firewall script is located (in case anyone ever asks you about it), and even have a peek inside and try to follow the flow of its Access Control List (ACL) style logic.

If you want to look over the default 2NIC firewall startup script (assuming that's the configuration you chose), it is very well documented and easy to modify. The running Devil-Linux firewall rule set is located at `/etc/init.d/firewall.rules`.

Tip If you're not comfortable with iptables and don't want to bother with learning it, check out some of the firewall script-building tools such as FWbuilder or Shorewall (mentioned earlier). If you wouldn't mind getting to know more about iptables however, check out related chapters of *Linux Troubleshooting Bible* or *Linux Bible, 2005 Edition*, both from Wiley. Another great online iptables beginner guide is `www.siliconvalleyccie.com/linux-hn/iptables-intro.htm`, or if you want a bit more, see `http://iptables-tutorial.frozentux.net/`.

Some aspects of your firewall you may want to secure further than what the default config includes, while others you may want to loosen. For example, you may want to loosen firewall rules in order to do DNAT or port forwarding (discussed shortly). Another reason to loosen your firewall settings is to poke holes in your firewall to allow certain protocols to traverse it to all your internal hosts (not recommended unless required).

Tip A good security tip is to disable root ssh logins all together. To do this, simply open the configuration file `/etc/ssh/sshd_config` and change the `#PermitRootLogin yes` line to `PermitRootLogin no`. Restart the sshd service and save your configuration to your config media. This will force you to log in as a non-root user, and then use the `su -` or `sudo` command to perform root-privileged operations. To do this, you would need to add a new user to your Devil-Linux configuration, because no non-administrative users are configured by default.

Before you do anything, however, take a look at the setup that you have, and what it currently looks like to people both on your LAN as well as in the outside world.

Give It a Sniff, Inside and Out

First you will want to see how the network profile of your firewall looks to someone on the inside of your network, so that you can see if anything is unexpectedly exposed. Use the following command:

```
# nmap -sS -Oo 192.168.1.1
Starting nmap 3.70 ( http://www.insecure.org/nmap/ ) at 2005-04-01 23:15 EST
Interesting ports on 192.168.1.1:
```

```
(The 1653 ports scanned but not shown below are in state: closed)
PORT      STATE     SERVICE
22/tcp    open      ssh
53/tcp    open      domain
135/tcp   filtered  msrpc
137/tcp   filtered  netbios-ns
138/tcp   filtered  netbios-dgm
139/tcp   filtered  netbios-ssn
445/tcp   filtered  microsoft-ds
1720/tcp  filtered  H.323/Q.931
Device type: general purpose
Running: Linux 2.4.X|2.5.X
OS details: Linux 2.4.0 - 2.5.20
Uptime 0.871 days (since Fri Apr  1 02:21:01 2005)
```

To the experienced eye, this is actually pretty funny — and a bit confusing. From the ports that appear to be present (135–1720), but filtered, this Linux gateway/firewall actually looks like a Windows XP box, except for that port 22 ssh daemon that's running. If this firewall/gateway is for a small office and you want to really secure the firewall from the inside (yes, you have to worry about deviants on the inside of your network, too), you may want to shut off ssh and use only console to make firewall adjustments.

If this firewall/gateway is just for a home office LAN, it's probably not a big issue. Port 53 is just the DNS service that you're offering on the gateway. The fact that this type of simple scan did reveal the OS and running kernel version is disturbing, though. Take note of that so you can lock it down later.

If you can get a Linux connection on the outside and scan the Internet, or untrusted, side of your firewall, that would be a good way to see what the crackers are going to see:

```
# nmap  -sS -O 172.24.24.61
Starting nmap 3.81 ( http://www.insecure.org/nmap/ ) at 2005-04-03 20:33 CDT
Warning:  OS detection will be MUCH less reliable because
we did not find at least 1 open and1 closed TCP port
Interesting ports on firewall (24.243.0.221):
(The 1662 ports scanned but not shown below are in state: filtered)
PORT    STATE  SERVICE
113/tcp closed auth
Too many fingerprints match this host to give specific OS details
Nmap finished: 1 IP address (1 host up) scanned in 31.835 seconds
```

Not too bad. Only one port visible, and even it's closed, plus no OS detection from the outside. That's a good thing. However, the fact that you can see anything at all is troubling. If someone can ping you (which that last scan used), people are more likely to target you. You fix that in the next step.

Note   The external IP 172.24.24.61 is not a real, public Internet IP address. The actual IP scanned has been changed to protect the innocent.

DROP External Ping Packets (Optional)

One problem that I had with the default 2NIC setup was that it does everything but drop ICMP on the outside of the firewall. While some people say that you should leave ICMP on (ping/echo reply included), it has been my observation that the easier it is for people to see you (or your firewall), the more you get attack attempts and the deeper the scans are.

To cut down on the number of potential intruders who can even find you, disabling ICMP seems to be the quickest, easiest fix. To change this setting on the default firewall script that comes on Devil-Linux, simply `cd` into the running `/etc/init.d/` directory, and back up your `firewall.rules` file like this:

```
# cd /etc/init.d/
# ls -1 firewall.rules*
firewall.rules          <--- This is the live firewall script
firewall.rules.2nic     <--- Only used as a template
firewall.rules.3nic     <--- Only used if running a DMZ
#
# cp -a firewall.rules firewall.rules-BAK <---"archive" the file
```

Tip   You should always back up important configuration files like this before editing them. If something goes terribly wrong, having a fallback position can be a real lifesaver.

Now open your `firewall.rules` file, and add the following line to your iptables rule:

```
...
# Allow Ping and friends.
## TWW: but drop all ext. pings Bv>
${IPTABLES} -A INPUT  -p icmp -i ${OUT_DEV} -j DROP
${IPTABLES} -A INPUT  -p icmp -j ACCEPT
${IPTABLES} -A OUTPUT -p icmp -j ACCEPT
...
```

To make these changes to the `firewall.rules` file live, rerun the firewall `init` script:

```
# etc/init.d/firewall start
```

Now, with the following command, rescan your firewall from the outside:

```
# nmap -sS -O 172.24.24.61
Starting nmap 3.81 ( http://www.insecure.org/nmap/ ) at 2005-04-03 20:36 CDT
Note: Host seems down. If it is really up, but blocking our ping probes, try -P0
Nmap finished: 1 IP address (0 hosts up) scanned in 2.565 seconds
```

Great! Not only can no ports be seen, but with the ICMP packet DROP rule, now nothing can be seen from a regular ping sweep (the fastest way that crackers scan for machines).

Don't forget to save your work, and reboot just to make sure all your changes are persistent:

```
# save-config
```

DNAT or Port Forwarding (Optional)

The last common change people like to set up, especially in a small office environment, is a Destination NAT or DNAT configuration, also referred to as *port forwarding*. This is an optional configuration by which you can direct all incoming traffic on a specific destination port to a specific internal destination IP and port.

Port forwarding is commonly done with HTTP, for example. In this process, an incoming request on port 80 gets redirected to an internal IP address. For example, in the example network design you had a staging/development server on 192.168.1.7. With DNAT/forwarding set up, you could redirect all traffic coming in on port 80 or 8080 to this staging Web server. You can set this up very easily using the well-documented example included in the `firewall.rules` file:

```
# Uncomment/modify the next 4 lines to forward a service to an internal IP.
# SERVER_IP=192.168.1.1               # Internal IP of server.
# PORT=22              # 22 = SSH.  Change to 80 for web server, etc.
# ${IPTABLES} -A PREROUTING -i ${OUT_DEV} -t nat -p TCP -dport
 $PORT -j DNAT --to ${SERVER_IP}:${PORT}
# ${IPTABLES} -A FORWARD -p TCP -d ${SERVER_IP} --dport $PORT
 -i ${OUT_DEV} -o ${INT_DEV} -j ACCEPT
```

Just uncomment the four last lines (being mindful of the line wrapping) and modify them to redirect incoming port 80 (Web) requests to the 192.168.1.7 on port 80, like this:

```
# Uncomment/modify the next 4 lines to forward a service to an internal IP.
SERVER_IP=192.168.1.7            # IP of internal web server.
PORT=80                          # Web traffic directed to staging web server.
${IPTABLES} -A PREROUTING -i ${OUT_DEV} -t nat -p TCP -dport
 $PORT -j DNAT --to ${SERVER_IP}:${PORT}
${IPTABLES} -A FORWARD -p TCP -d ${SERVER_IP} --dport $PORT -i
 ${OUT_DEV} -o ${INT_DEV} -j ACCEPT
```

Again, test this change by rerunning the firewall `init` script:

 # etc/init.d/firewall start

Do some testing, and if all looks good, save your new config to floppy using the `save-config` command.

 By setting up your firewall to forward requests for a port to another computer on your network, you are adding great risk to your internal network. In the preceding example, any attack on port 80 (used for Web service) of your firewall will be forwarded to your internal server. If that internal server is not kept patched, and someone on the outside launches a Web server attack on it, there is the very real possibility that someone could compromise (or crack into) your internal server. In other words, port forwarding effectively bypasses your firewall security for those ports you allow forwarding on. Firewalls do not preclude you from having to take other foundational security steps such as good OS/service patching and secure password policies.

If you are going to allow DNAT or port forwarding, you definitely want to look into running your firewall with a third network card in what's called a Demilitarized Zone, or DMZ, as described in the following section.

Other Uses for Devil-Linux

Various open source firewall/router/gateway distros have been popping up all over the place. I've seen them installed everywhere from small offices and libraries to lawyers' offices and car dealerships, and they really do empower small-to-medium IT consultants. For example, by simply turning on and configuring the built-in squid proxy, AntiVirus/AntiSpam mail relay software, and Snort IDS systems, just about any moderately tech-savvy person is empowered to offer quality IT consulting services to the community or small business sector.

This type of free open source empowerment has revolutionized the IT industry as nothing before. Even big companies such as Linksys are using these types of solutions in the little blue boxes that you see at WalMart and CompUSA. The application, scope, and use are up to you, and because it's all GPL open source, the software is free, and you can modify it to meet your specific needs and services, as it should be.

Running WiFi Access Points

Another SOHO/consulting use of open source firewalls that's quickly gaining popularity is the placement of the hardware into a rugged, weatherproof, Pelican case (www.pelican.com) with a WiFi card and cable ports. These weatherproof systems are then set up as wireless access points with packages like NoCatSplash configured for free (or for fee) WiFi hot spots. (In this type of a configuration you would want to ditch the floppy and go with a USB flash or CF storage device for higher reliability.)

You can see the obvious advantage of a ruggedized DIY WiFi system for under $200, as compared to the $800–$4,000 similar commercial setups. Often, the commercial solutions use some of the same software that I've covered here!

Running a 3NIC DMZ Firewall Configuration

If you're doing any DNAT or port redirection, as a small company might do if it had a Web server inside its network, you might want to look into running a Demilitarized Zone (DMZ) configuration to protect your inside network by putting your Web server in a protective bubble.

A DMZ can be configured in Devil-Linux by simply adding a third network card, selecting the 3NIC firewall configuration from the setup system, and then just entering the hardware and service setup variables for it. This allows you to run a Web server, mail server, or any externally accessible system securely from within a "DMZ bubble," if you will.

The DMZ area is not fully exposed to the Internet, but does not have access to your internal LAN either. Just as you select and customize the 2NIC firewall.rules file, you can also select and customize the 3NIC `firewall.rules` config file. See the Devil-Linux documentation for more information on this very popular and secure configuration.

Rolling Your Own Devil-Linux System

These small distros don't lock you in; they are designed to be open ended. Instead of just burning the preconfigured `boot.iso` CD and starting with that software set, the Devil-Linux system, for example, comes with all the tools and documentation that you need to customize, build, and burn your very own customized distro ISO image.

For a more physically hardened solution that you could potentially sell to a client, you can even build a custom Devil-Linux distro that boots and runs totally from a 128MB CompactFlash card. This level of customization is not only possible; it's encouraged! With these types of flexibility in place, the list of customized uses is literally endless.

Summary

You can build your own SOHO firewall system with nothing more than spare parts, some planning, and a little patience. You can take a single PC broadband connection, and put several hundred machines on that one connection behind a firewall/gateway/router.

The hardware can be specially tuned to be extremely reliable with uptime on the order of years. Combine this with all of the additional software services that you can simply enable or modify on your dedicated firewall, and you suddenly have a plethora of options for what you can do with such a system.

Remember, before you dive in, be sure to sit down and figure out what you actually want to do first, iron out the types of services that you need, and then plan your resulting network layout. After doing those tasks, you can intelligently choose the firewall distro that best suits your needs, detail the hardware requirements of the project, as well as conceptualize and design your specific security needs into the solution.

After you put together a system in this manner, you will really understand the security that the system does and does not provide you and your internal LAN. Security is no longer an illusion for you. It's real, you know where its boundaries are, and as a result, you will be ahead of the guy who just went out and bought his firewall off the shelf.

Small Business Projects

part

IV

Running an Internet Radio Station with Icecast

D
o you aspire to be the next Al Franken, Rush Limbaugh, or other political ideologist with a mass market radio audience? Or, do you believe that you can create a better mix of music than any local DJ? If so, you don't have to wait for a major radio network to discover your talent. You can set up your own Internet radio station with Icecast and start streaming your choice of music and talk today.

With your own Internet radio station you can:

➤ Broadcast live lectures or commentary on sporting events

➤ Promote a rock band, high school musical, or other performing arts event

➤ Play whatever you like 365 days a year, 24 hours a day to anyone who will listen

At the heart of this Internet radio station chapter is the Icecast project. Icecast is a powerful and versatile tool for streaming audio across computer networks. It can be configured to stream audio in Ogg Vorbis or MP3 format (with other audio formats, and now even some video formats, available as well).

To feed content to your streaming Icecast server, you can grab audio from a playlist (of songs or speech files), your sound card, microphone, or a mixture of those input types. Several different source client applications are available to feed that content, including IceS2, MuSE, and Oddcast.

Note There are two distinctly different IceS source clients that are maintained by two active, but different, development efforts. I focus on the IceS2 source client that is used for broadcasting audio in Ogg Vorbis format. The IceS0.x source client is also available, and can be used to broadcast audio in MP3 format to an Icecast server. (By the way, IceS is short for Icecast Source.)

Linux applications that can play audio streams from Icecast over the network include XMMS, Rhythmbox, and MPlayer. Often, the URL to an Icecast audio stream is embedded in a Web page, from which your browser can launch a helper app to play the content or use an inline plug-in (such as the mplayer plug-in) to play the content. You can also publish the URL to your radio station on public Icecast Stream Directories (sometimes referred to as YP directories).

Figure 10-1 shows how you can put together different open source software components to create your own radio station.

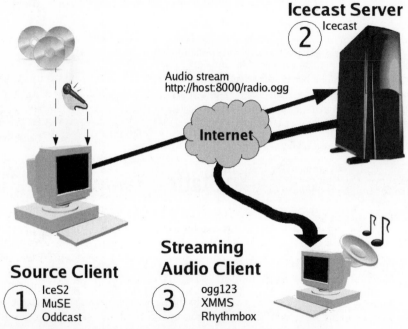

FIGURE 10-1: Stream audio from a microphone, sound card, or playlist on a client machine through an Icecast server to the public.

The path for starting your Internet radio station begins with starting up the Icecast server. Next, you configure the type of audio input you want by creating a playlist or configuring your sound card. Then you start a source client (such as IceS2) to direct that audio input in a stream to the Icecast server.

It's important to understand the difference between the *Icecast server* and the *source clients* that produce the audio content that the server broadcasts. The Icecast server never decides what content to play. The source client, such as IceS2 or MuSE, is responsible for directing stream-ing content to the Icecast server, which simply broadcasts that audio stream to *audio players* on your LAN or on the Internet. It's possible (in fact, it's quite normal) for the source client, Icecast server, and audio players to all be running on different machines.

If you are using your Internet radio station to support a cause or promote a band, you can simply add a URL to your Icecast stream on your own Web page. You can provide your own images and text, and then offer links that play a live stream or select from static files or playlists. You can also list your radio station with public Icecast directory sites called Icecast Stream Directories.

At that point, it's up to clients of your Internet radio station to use an audio player that supports Icecast to connect to the URL (something like `http://hostname:8000/newradio.ogg`) to play the audio stream. Most Linux systems come with several different clients that are capable of playing Icecast audio streams, including Rhythmbox, XMMS, and ogg123. WinAmp is a popular Windows audio player that can play Icecast audio streams.

This project takes you through the process of configuring an Internet radio station based on Icecast. I then recommend (and describe) several different tools for delivering the audio source to the Icecast server and playing it back from a client.

Note   I was fortunate to have Michael Smith, one of the key developers of Icecast, IceS2, vorbis-tools and other Xiph.Org projects, review this chapter for technical accuracy. His perspective on how the different components fit together and which need special descriptions has greatly improved the chapter.

Overview of Internet Radio Station Setup

To help you create and play your Internet radio station, I've divided the Internet radio station into five major components. The text in this chapter follows the audio content from its source to the final playback by someone listening to the station (although this is generally how the sound travels from one end to the other, you'll need to configure the stream in a somewhat different order):

- **Audio source** — With the tools described in this project, you can take your audio source from a playlist of files (containing Ogg Vorbis or MP3 audio files) or audio stream from your sound card (line in, microphone, and so on), or another audio stream that is streamed from somewhere else. In Linux, that source can come through ALSA or OSS sound systems.

- **Source client** — The audio stream is taken by the source client, which then forwards it to the Icecast server. There are several good choices for source clients. The `ices` command (which is associated with the Icecast project) relies on a simple configuration file for setting up where it gets and directs the audio stream. MuSE (Multiple Streaming Engine) provides an intuitive graphical interface for configuring Ogg Vorbis or MP3 (Lame) streams that can connect specifically to Icecast servers. There are also Windows clients you can use to direct an audio stream to Icecast, including the Oddcast plug-in for Winamp.

Note Although the streaming server (Icecast) and the source client (IceS2 or other) can be running on the same computer, they don't have to. I describe the Oddcast Winamp plug-in with this project because it is not uncommon to stream your music collection or microphone hook up from your desktop computer (often Windows) to a server computer (Linux, of course).

- **Icecast server** — Although there are other projects for streaming audio over the Internet, Icecast is the most often used open source project for the job. Creating a configuration file (typically `icecast.xml`) and launching the Icecast server are about all you need to get going. Within the `icecast.xml` file, you define where and how the Icecast service listens, set passwords that let users gain access to stream audio to the Icecast server, and choose the directories that contain Icecast configuration files.

  While Icecast is running, you can keep an eye on it by monitoring the log files (`access.log` and `error.log`). There is also a Web interface for checking the status of your Icecast server.

- **Stream Directories and Web sites** — Because your Internet radio station (that is, the Icecast stream) can be identified by a simple URL, you probably want to add some way of making that URL available to your target audience. Icecast itself is set up to help you list your radio station in a Stream Directory of other Icecast stations, to show its availability. If you are promoting a cause or an organization along with the Internet radio station, you probably want to create a Web page where you offer the link to your radio station, along with related information. Related information might include links to pre-recorded shows or music.

- **Audio players** — To play streams of audio in Ogg Vorbis or MP3 format from an Icecast server, your listening public can choose from a bunch of different players. In Linux, you can play Icecast audio streams from Rhythmbox, xmms, ogg123, kaffeine, and other players. Winamp is a popular audio player for Windows that is capable of playing Ogg Vorbis and MP3 streams.

Note For a list of audio players that can handle Ogg Vorbis content, refer to the Xiph.Org Vorbis Software Players page (`http://wiki.xiph.org/VorbisSoftwarePlayers`).

About Xiph.Org Foundation

Icecast and IceS2 are projects of the Xiph.Org Foundation (`www.xiph.org`): the Mecca of open source multimedia efforts. While all the commercial computer industry big guns have tried to control the formats of streaming audio and video, Xiph.Org has championed high-quality open source audio and video format, including:

- **Ogg Vorbis** — The best open source audio encoding software available today. It is an open source functional equivalent of MP3 (used for encoding and compressing music and speech).

- **Ogg Theora**—A developing open source video codec. Theora is intended to improve on the VP3 video codec, using the Ogg multimedia container format. For the associated audio, Theora is usually combined with the Vorbis audio codec. The VP3 format was developed as a proprietary format by On2 Technologies (www.on2.com), but was released as open source with a full patent grant in September 2001, so it can be used freely.

- **FLAC**—This is a Free Lossless Audio Codec (FLAC) that can be used to preserve audio content without harming audio quality.

- **Speex**—An audio compression format that is particularly suited for handling speech data.

I mention Theora in the preceding list because, if you want to expand your Internet radio station to broadcast video as well as audio, Icecast recently began supporting streaming video in Theora format (you need at least Icecast 2.2.0 and Theora alpha 4). For the project described in this chapter, I use Ogg Vorbis (because it provides high-quality compressed audio and is free). In the near future, you can expect Icecast to support Speex as well, so you could consider substituting Speex for Ogg Vorbis, particularly if you are streaming speech instead of music.

Xiph.Org has mailing lists devoted to Icecast development and general use (see http://lists.xiph.org/icecast/list.html). There is also an Icecast IRC channel where you can chat about Icecast and IceS2 (irc.freenode.net: #icecast). Sometimes, simply downloading the latest version of the software can take care of a problem you are having (visit www.icecast.org/download.php). There is also a fairly new Icecast Streaming Media Server forum (http://forum.icecast.org) where you can ask questions about Icecast use and development issues.

About Other Open Source Audio Projects

Other software projects I go into for the Internet radio station include Oddcast (www.oddsock.org) and MuSE (http://muse.dyne.org), which I describe as alternative source clients you can use instead of IceS2. Also consider the XMMS (www.xmms.org) and Rhythmbox (http://rhythmbox.org) projects, which you can use instead of Xiph.Org's own ogg123 player to ultimately play the audio stream.

Note If you enjoy the software from these projects, consider making contributions of code, documentation, or money, to help keep the projects going.

Installing Internet Radio Software

I tested Icecast and the other components in this project using Fedora Core 4, installed as described in Appendix C. When you do your Fedora Core install, be sure that the following packages are installed:

- libxml2 and libxml2-devel
- libxslt and libxslt-devel

- curl and curl-devel

- vorbis-tools, libvorbis and libvorbis-devel

A graphical desktop (such as KDE or GNOME) is not required to run the Icecast or IceS software. However, if you choose to run some of the graphical software for playing audio (such as Rhythmbox or XMMS), you will need to have desktop software installed.

To install the RPM software packages described in this chapter from the *Linux Toys II* CD to a Fedora or RHEL system, do the following:

1. Insert the *Linux Toys II* CD in your CD drive. If your CD mounts automatically, you can skip the first command. If it doesn't, run the following (possibly replacing */media/ cdrecorder* with the location where your CD was mounted) as root user from a Terminal window:

   ```
   # mount /media/cdrecorder
   ```

2. Next, change to the RPMS directory for Icecast and run the installme script as follows:

   ```
   # cd /media/cdrecorder/RPMS/ch10-icecast
   # ./installme
   ```

   This will install all RPMs needed for this project. One piece of software this does not install, however, is the oddcast Windows client in the Sources/ch10-icecast directory. To use that software, copy it to a Windows system and execute the oddcast executable file.

Configuring Your Internet Radio Station

Installing the Internet radio station software, as described in the previous section, should give you all the software you need to begin creating and broadcasting your own streaming audio. Because the intent of this project is to offer your radio station as a public Internet service, you should consider preparing your Linux system as you would for any service you enter on the Internet. Here are some things you should consider:

 As I noted in other server projects (including Gallery in Chapter 3 and BZFlag in Chapter 8), setting up a public Internet server should not be done without careful consideration. Any unprotected server will almost certainly eventually get attacked and possibly taken over. Use the following items as a partial list of things you should consider when setting up an Icecast server. Be sure to keep up with the latest security bulletins and patches for your Linux system.

- **Domain name and IP address** — It is possible to simply broadcast your Internet radio station from the IP address of your home broadband connection. However, to have the service be more permanent, consider getting a static IP address and permanent domain name for the service. If you have access to a public Linux server computer, you can simply add the Icecast service to the public server. The source client (IceS2 or other) and your audio input, playlist, and music can all be streamed to the Icecast server from any desktop system with an Internet connection that is fast enough to keep up with the streaming.

- **Firewall** — If the Icecast server system includes a firewall, you need to configure it to allow connections to the port offering the Icecast service (TCP port number 8000 is the default). Otherwise, you want to lock down the server, closing off any inactive ports from access.

- **Bandwidth** — Most ISPs will charge for the amount of bandwidth that is consumed by your streaming audio server. You can save on bandwidth costs by reducing the quality of the audio streams.

- **Broadcast fees** — Just because the broadcasting software I describe in this chapter is free doesn't mean that you can broadcast any content you want for free. If you want to broadcast material covered by copyright or play-by-play of a professional sporting event, someone will expect you to pay for those things. To see what your potential costs and liabilities are for broadcasting recorded music, visit the ASCAP (`www.ascap.com/weblicense`) and BMI (`www.bmi.com/licensing/broadcaster/radio/webanswers.asp`) Web sites.

- **Licensing fees** — To legally use MP3 to do streaming audio to your Icecast server, you need to pay licensing fees. Ogg Vorbis, which is the audio format described in this chapter, requires no licensing fees. Ogg Vorbis can also be less expensive to use than MP3 because it allows lower bitrates, which can save you bandwidth costs. Because there are no quality advantages to using MP3, you really can't lose by using Ogg Vorbis.

The following procedure describes how to set up your Internet radio station. Step 1 describes how to configure Icecast to stream audio to the Internet. Step 2 tells how to set up a source client (either on the same computer or a different one) to feed content to that server. In Step 3, I describe different ways of presenting your radio station to the public (directories and Web pages). The last step describes applications that you can use to play back your radio station.

Step 1: Setting up and Starting the Icecast Server

Before you can start your Internet radio station with Icecast, you need to edit the Icecast server's configuration file (`icecast.xml`).

Note Extensible Markup Language (XML) is a simplified subset of the SGML standard for describing data types. It helps to have some familiarity with XML to work with the `icecast.xml` file. In particular, you need to know that lines between this marker `<!--` and this marker `-->` are comments and ignored. Most of an XML file consists of nested elements. For example, in the `icecast.xml` file, the `<authentication>...</authentication>` nested element holds password information. If you have not worked with XML files before, you should always be aware of which nested element(s) you are working in.

1. **Edit the** `icecast.xml` **file.** As a root user, open the `/etc/icecast.conf` file using any text editor. The following text takes you through parameters you should consider changing.

   - **Authentication** — You need to set the passwords for the users named `source`, `relay`, and `admin`. In the following examples, passwords are set to `kuul4wrd`, `leet5wrd`, and `nkon2B9`, respectively.

```
<authentication>
  <!-- Sources log in with username 'source' -->
  <source-password>kuul4wrd</source-password>
  <!-- Relays log in with the username 'relay' -->
  <relay-password>he8getgo</relay-password>
  <!-- Admin logs in with the username given below -->
  <admin-user>admin</admin-user>
  <admin-password>nkon2B9</admin-password>
</authentication>
```

   The IceS2 application (described later) will use the `source` password to be allowed to pass an audio stream to the Icecast server. The relay password is not used in this case, but you should add a password anyway, to keep others from accessing that feature. You will use the `admin` password to gain access to Icecast administration through your Web browser.

   - **Server name, IP address, and port** — You need to identify the name of your host computer (used mostly for generating URLs in playlists and Stream Directory listings) and the particular port number the Icecast service will listen on for on the server's network interfaces. (By default, it will listen on all network interfaces.) In this example, I used the name `LinuxToys.net` as the server name and `8000` as the listening ports (which is the default).

```
<!-- This is the hostname other people will use to connect to
your server.
It affects mainly the urls generated by Icecast for playlists
and yp listings. -->
<hostname>LinuxToys.net</hostname>
<listen-socket>
    <port>8000</port>
</listen-socket>
```

   - **Directory locations** — Set the directory where the Icecast log files (`access.log` and `error.log`), static Web content (such as audio files), and administrative files are stored. (Note that I changed the location of the log directory from `/usr/var/log/icecast` to `/var/log/icecast`).

```
<logdir>/var/log/icecast</logdir>
<webroot>/usr/share/icecast/web</webroot>
<adminroot>/usr/share/icecast/admin</adminroot>
```

These should be enough changes to get the Icecast server started. There are other settings I haven't covered because they are not required in most simple Icecast setups. To read about other available settings for your `icecast.xml` file, open this file in your Web browser: `/usr/share/doc/icecast2.2.0/icecast2_config_file.html`.

2. **Save changes.** Save the changes you made to the `icecast.xml` file and close it.

3. **Create `icecast` log directory.** Type the following to create the `icecast` log directory:

```
# mkdir /var/log/icecast
# chown icecast /var/log/icecast
```

Notice that, in this example, I changed the ownership of the `icecast` directory to nobody. If you are running Icecast as another user, you should change ownership of the `icecast` log to belong to that user.

4. **Start the Icecast server.** Instead of just running the Icecast server as the root user, in this example I run it as the `icecast` user. This happens automatically, whether you launch `icecast` as root or the icecast user. The reason n for running Icecast as some user other than root is so that, if the Icecast service is exploited, the person doing the exploit will not gain full access to the computer.

As root user, start the `icecast` server, which will cause it to run as the user named `icecast`.

```
/usr/bin/icecast -c /etc/icecast.xml
```

This command opens a bash shell as the user nobody, then executes the `icecast` command, using the `icecast.xml` configuration file. (If you created a different user account earlier to run `icecast`, you can substitute that user name for nobody in the procedure just shown.)

5. **Check that `icecast` is running.** If `icecast` is not able to start, you will get an error message and the `icecast` process will exit. Go back to your `icecast.xml` file and try to debug the problem. If `icecast` appears to be running, check it by opening the following location from Firefox or another Web browser:

```
http://localhost:8000/admin/stats.xsl
```

When prompted, enter the user name **admin** and the associated password you added to your `icecast.xml` file earlier. (As an alternative, you could simply enter `http://localhost:8000` to see a basic status page that shows less information, but requires no authentication.) If the Icecast Status Page (shown in Figure 10-2) appears, the server is running properly.

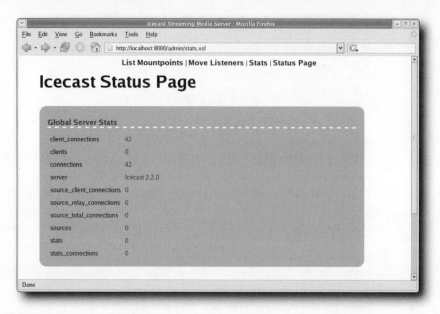

FIGURE 10-2: If you see the Icecast Status Page, the Icecast server is running.

6. **Check Icecast remotely.** Next you want to check that your Icecast server is accessible from the network. If your computer is connected to a LAN, you can try to open the Icecast Status Page from another computer on your LAN. Otherwise, if your Icecast server is connected to the Internet, you can try it from any computer on the Internet.

Using the IP address or host name of your Icecast server, enter the address of the Icecast Status Page into the location box of any Web browser on a computer that can access your server. For example:

```
http://10.0.0.3:8000/admin/stats.xsl
```

This shows an example of a private IP address (10.0.0.3) for the Icecast server on your LAN. Instead of 10.0.0.3, if your computer has a fully qualified domain name, the 10.0.0.3 might be replaced with something like icecast.linuxtoys.net. As you did before, type the admin user name and password to access the page.

If you can't access the Icecast Status Page, go through the standard things you would do to check accessibility of any machine. From the other computer, check that you can ping the machine (ping 10.0.0.3). If you can, then make sure that your firewall has been configured to allow access to port 8000.

7. **Add audio content to test.** To test that the client can play content from your Icecast server, you can simply copy a file of a supported format (I suggest an Ogg Vorbis file) into the server's Web directory. For example, to copy the file test.ogg from the current directory on the server so it can be accessed on an Icecast client, type this:

```
# cp test.ogg /usr/share/icecast/web
```

To play the content you just added to your Icecast server, you could enter the following URL from any of the audio players described in "Step 5: Listening to Your Internet Radio Station":

```
http://10.0.0.3:8000/test.ogg
```

If all has gone well, your Icecast server should be ready to start accepting audio to stream out to the Internet or other network. The next step is to set up the source client with the content that you will be streaming to the Icecast server.

Step 2: Setting Up Audio Input or Playlists

With Icecast set up and ready to stream audio to the Internet, you are ready to begin configuring the computer that will provide source content to the Icecast server. The computer you use to do this can be either:

- An **Icecast server** — You can install the IceS2 or MuSE source client on the Icecast server and provide both the audio source and Internet stream from the same computer.

- A **Desktop system** — If your sound card, microphone, or music files are on your home computer and Icecast is on a server somewhere in Texas, you can configure your Desktop system to stream your audio content to the Icecast server before broadcast.

Icecast doesn't care if the content you direct to it is on the same computer, a remote Linux system, or a remote Windows system. Regardless of which system you use, however, here are some steps to prepare your streaming audio content.

Configuring the Sound Card

The source clients I describe later can stream audio input from your sound card through either OSS or ALSA sound systems in Linux. A PCI audio card should be detected and configured when you boot your computer. To check what sound card has been detected for your computer, type:

```
# lspci -vvv |grep -i audio
```

If your sound card doesn't work, use the information from this output to check a forum or do an Internet search to find out if there is a problem with that audio card in Linux. The ALSA project supports a sound card page (www.alsa-project.org/alsa-doc) where you can search sound cards by manufacturer.

If your audio card is working properly, you need to select which device you want to use to capture input (mic, line, and so on) and turn down the others. To change audio levels and select the capture device for your sound card, use a mixer application such as aumix or alsamixer. In aumix, click the "R" on the line for the device you want to record from so that it turns red. In alsamixer, use the arrow to move the cursor to the device you want to capture from and press the space bar (so a red CAPTURE appears over the device).

See Chapter 5 for information on aumix and using it to select a recording device.

Setting up Playlists

The IceS2 source client can stream Ogg Vorbis audio to an Icecast server from a playlist or from live audio input. For this example, I'm using IceS2 to stream audio from a playlist of pre-recorded music.

If metadata was included with a song when it was encoded in Ogg Vorbis, that information will be transmitted with the audio file as well. That way, the audio player that connects to your Icecast server can display the artist and song as it is playing.

From an IceS2 source client, the playlist can be a simple list of files that represents your songs or speech files. Those songs can be copied using a variety of tools, including oggenc (which is part of the vorbis-tools package that includes ogg123, ogginfo, and other Ogg Vorbis tools) and cdparanoia.

The original *Linux Toys* book includes a music jukebox project that rips, compresses, and stores songs from music CDs in Ogg Vorbis format. Besides sorting songs into directories by artist and album, the stored songs include metadata identifying the song title, artist, and album. Using that project, you could create files for streaming with IceS.

If you are interested in viewing the metadata included in an Ogg Vorbis audio file, you can use the vorbiscomment utility that comes with the vorbis-tools package. Here's an example:

```
# vorbiscomment -l "01-My_Music_Song.ogg"
TITLE=My Music Song
ARTIST=Chris Negus
TRACKNUMBER=1
TRACKTOTAL=18
ALBUM=Greatest Open Source Hits
GENRE=Classical
```

Using the vorbiscomment utility, you can also append or modify comments in an Ogg Vorbis audio file. To find out other information about an Ogg Vorbis file, such as its bitrate and playback time, you can use the ogginfo command.

Step 3: Streaming Audio to Icecast

With the Icecast server running, you can now direct streaming audio content to it using several different tools (referred to as source clients). The Icecast project itself offers the ices streaming audio command with Ices2 (for streaming live audio or audio from a playlist). However, you can also use other tools. To give you a nice cross-section of source client tools that are available, this step describes how to deliver audio source from:

- A playlist, using IceS2 on a Linux system

- A sound card, using MuSE (http://muse.dyne.org) on a Linux system

- A microphone, using the Oddcast Winamp plug-in (www.oddsock.org/tools/oddcastv3) on a Windows system.

Feeding Audio from a Playlist (IceS2)

To feed audio using the ices command and a playlist, you need to edit an ices-playlist.xml file. Create a directory to hold your playlist files, and then copy the ices-playlist.xml file there as follows:

```
# mkdir $HOME/myices
# cd $HOME/myices
# cp /usr/share/doc/ices-*/ices /ices-playlist.xml $HOME/myices/
```

In the ices-playlist.xml file, you can identify log files and information (metadata) about the audio stream, the input type (in this case, a playlist), and each instance of the stream. You can have multiple instances to send the audio stream to multiple servers or to the same server that will forward the stream under different names (mount points) or bitrates.

A mount point in IceS2 is the part of the URL of a stream that identifies that particular stream uniquely on an Icecast server. The mount point name always begins with a slash (/).

Step 1 contains examples of changes I made to a stream section of the ices-playlist.xml file. The steps that follow describe how to create a playlist, start the ices command, and check the log files.

1. **Edit** ices-playlist.xml **file.** Open your $HOME/myices/ices-playlist.xml file using any text editor. The following text takes you through parameters you should consider changing.

   - **Logging** — Information about ices activity is, by default, sent to the file /var/log/ices.log. You can change that location (as I changed mine to /home/chris/myices), the maximum size of the log (2,048KB), or level of log messages (3). You can also set consolelog to 1 (instead of 0) to have log messages go to the console instead of the log file.

   ```
   <logpath>/home/chris/myices/</logpath>
   <logfile>ices.log</logfile>
   <!-- 1=error,2=warn,3=info,4=debug -->
   <loglevel>4</loglevel>
   <consolelog>0</consolelog>
   ```

   - **Metadata** — Information in the following metadata example sets the name, genre, and description of the audio stream to anything you like.

   ```
   <metadata>
       <name>MusicBlitz Radio</name>
       <genre>Alternative, rock and hip-hop</genre>
       <description>Eclectic mix of music, 24x7</description>
   </metadata>
   ```

■ **Input**—For the input modules (because I'm describing playlists as input at the moment), the following input settings cause `ices` to take input from a playlist.

```
<input>
    <module>playlist</module>
    <param name="type">basic</param>
    <param name="file">/home/chris/myices/playlist.txt</param>
    <!-- random play -->
    <param name="random">0</param>
    <!-- if the playlist get updated, start at beginning -->
    <param name="restart-after-reread">0</param>
    <!-- if set to 1 , plays once through, then exits. -->
    <param name="once">0</param>
</input>
```

I didn't change any of the input values in this code, except for the location of the `playlist.txt` file. Using the default, IceS2 takes its input from a playlist (`playlist.txt` shown here in the `/home/chris/myices` directory). Files (songs or speech files) are played in order by turning off the random option (`random 0`) and are repeated after the whole list has been played (`once 0`). The playlist begins playing again, from the beginning, if the playlist is updated.

■ **Instance**—You can have one instance, or many instances, of this audio stream. You can direct an instance of an audio stream to a different mount point or a different server. Each instance can be encoded at a different bitrate. Having multiple instances of a stream going to different servers allows transmission to continue, even if a particular Icecast server goes down. Having multiple instances on the same server enables you to offer different levels of audio quality, to work better on different download speeds.

```
<instance>
        <hostname>LinuxToys.net</hostname>
        <port>8000</port>
        <password>kuul4wrd</password>
        <mount>/myplaylist.ogg</mount>
</instance>
```

As Icecast was configured in a previous step (to listen on all interfaces at LinuxToys.net), you could run `ices` from another computer. In that case, the host name would look something like this (depending on the name or IP address of your Icecast server):

```
<hostname>LinuxToys.net</hostname>
```

There are a bunch of other parameters associated with an instance that are probably not necessary for you to change. For example, if `ices` fails to connect to the machine containing the Icecast server, it will attempt to reconnect five times (with two seconds between each attempt) before failing. (Change `reconnectattempts` to -1 to continue trying forever.)

The final set of instance parameters determines the nominal bitrate (64,000), sample rate (44,100) and channels (2) assigned to the stream. (These settings must match the input data for channels and sample rate.)

The section labeled <encode> can be used to turn on the re-encoding feature. You want to use re-encoding only if you want a stream sent at a lower bitrate than the bitrate at which the files were recorded. Having this feature on can consume lots of CPU time. By disabling the feature, the audio is streamed as it is.

2. **Create playlist.** The playlist can be a simple text file that contains a list of audio files in formats that are supported by Icecast. Because I keep my music files in the /usr/local/share/music directory, I created a file containing all my songs by typing:

```
$ cd /home/chris/myices
$ find /usr/local/share/music -name *.ogg > playlist.txt
```

I can then edit the playlist.txt file to put songs in the order I want and remove songs I don't want. Notice that I added /home/chris/myices/playlist.txt to my ices-playlist.xml file earlier in this procedure. That file has to be accessible to the ices command you run in the next step.

3. **Start ices command.** To begin playing the audio files from your playlist and stream them to your Icecast server (as you configured in your /etc/ices-playlist file), simply run the following command:

```
$ /usr/bin/ices $HOME/myices/ices-playlist.xml
```

If ices plays successfully, you won't see any feedback from the command. However, you can look in my $HOME/myices/ices.log file to see what's happening.

4. **Check ices.log file.** Open the $HOME/myices/ices.log file. The following shows examples of messages that appear at a successful ices startup:

```
[2005-08-01 14:44:51] INFO ices-core/main IceS 2.0.0 started...
 [2005-08-01  14:44:51] INFO playlist-basic/playlist_basic_get_next_filename
        Loading playlist from file "/home/chris/myices/playlist.txt"
[2005-08-01  14:44:51] INFO playlist-builtin/playlist_read Currently playing
        "/usr/local/share/music/Chris-Album1/10-Lots_of_Rain.ogg"
[2005-08-01  14:44:51] INFO stream/ices_instance_stream Connected to server:
        10.0.0.3:8000/myplaylist.ogg
[2005-08-01  14:44:51] DBUG reencode/reencode_page Reinitialising reencoder
        for new logical stream
[2005-08-01  14:44:51] INFO encode/encode_initialise Encoder initialising
        in VBR mode: 2 channels, 44100 Hz, nominal 64000
```

After showing that ices starts, the playlist (/home/chris/myices/playlist.txt) is read and the first song from that list should start playing (10-Lots_of_Rain.ogg, from the /usr/local/share/music/Chris-Album1 directory). The audio stream is directed to the network interface of the computer where the Icecast server is running (10.0.0.3:8000) under the name /myplaylist.ogg. You can also see the chosen encoding data (2 channels, 44100 Hz, nominal 64000).

If you don't see messages like those in this example, you will probably need to either check your settings in your ices-playlist.xml file or find out if the Icecast server is running properly and able to accept connections from you.

If you are happy with your configuration to stream audio from a playlist, you can jump to "Step 4: Making Your Internet Radio Station Public" or "Step 5: Listening to Your Internet Radio Station." To try creating live audio feeds, continue on to the next section.

Feeding Audio Live

The Multiple Streaming Engine (MuSE) application offers both a command line and graphical interface for configuring audio streaming to your Icecast server. Using MuSE, you can take input from your sound card, as well as from up to six encoded audio streams. The output can be directed to an Icecast server. From there it can be streamed over the Internet.

The following procedure provides an example of using MuSE (in graphical mode) to stream audio from a sound card to your Icecast server. Using MuSE, you can also mix additional audio streams into a single output stream to your Icecast server.

1. **Start MuSE.** To start MuSE in graphical (gtk) mode, type the following:

```
# muse -g gtk2
```

The MuSE window appears. From there, you can select the microphone icon to have MuSE take input from the device on your sound card that is set up to capture audio.

2. **Prepare to stream.** Select the plug icon (Let's Stream) from the MuSE window and select the Ogg/Vorbis Streaming tab. The MuSE Add Server window appears alongside the main MuSE window, as shown in Figure 10-3.

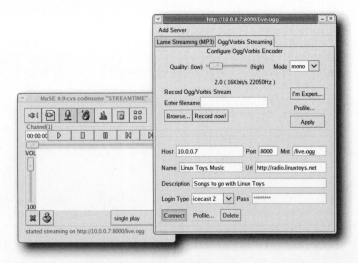

FIGURE 10-3: Configure Icecast information from the MuSE window.

3. **Create Icecast configuration.** Fill in much of the same information that you entered when you configured IceS2. The key information you need in this example includes the following:

   ■ **Host/port.** Enter the IP address of the computer on which the Icecast server is running and the port number (probably 8000).

   ■ **Identify a mount point.** This is the name given to the stream that the audio player will need to enter later to play the stream.

   ■ **Name/URL/Descriptions.** Add a name and description for the streams, along with any URL you want to be associated with the stream. In this case, the URL is the URL of the Web site that was set up and not the URL of the stream itself.

   ■ **Login type/password.** Here we're using an Icecast 2 server. You need to enter the source-password associated with the Icecast server to be able to connect this audio stream to it.

4. **Connect.** Click the Connect button on the Icecast configuration window. On the main MuSE window you should see a message like `started streaming` on `http://10.0.0.7:8000/live.ogg`.

5. **Test the connection.** From another computer, you can test that the stream is working using any player that supports Icecast. From a Linux system, you can type the following to connect to the stream you just created:

```
$ ogg123 http://10.0.0.7:8000/live.ogg
```

Feeding Audio from Windows

Your Icecast server may be running at a hosting service in Texas and you're sitting at somebody's Windows system in Wisconsin. Don't worry. If you have a network connection to the server, you can stream your audio content from the Windows system to the Icecast server using the Oddcast streaming media tool.

Here's a procedure for using the Oddcast plug-in for Winamp to broadcast from a Windows system using a microphone:

1. **Download Winamp.** Download and install Winamp to your Window system. You can get it from www.winamp.com.

2. **Download Oddcast.** Download and install the Oddcast Winamp plug-in (at least version 3) from the Oddsock Web site (www.oddsock.org/tools/oddcastv3).

3. **Start Winamp.** From the Start menu on your Windows system, start Winamp.

4. **Configure Oddcast.** To configure Oddcast, select Options ➜ Preferences from the Winamp window. From the Oddcast configuration window that appears, right-click the Vorbis entry in the Encoder Settings box and choose Configure. A configuration window appears, as shown in Figure 10-4.

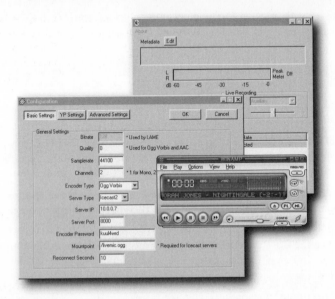

FIGURE 10-4: Configure Icecast settings in the Oddcast configuration window.

5. **Select Icecast settings.** Enter the settings needed to connect to your Icecast server. You should recognize these settings from when you configured Icecast. Click OK when you have the settings the way you would like.

6. **Start recording.** To begin recording, click the microphone icon in the Live Recording, and then click the Connect button. Audio immediately should begin streaming to your Icecast server.

Step 4: Making Your Internet Radio Station Public

So far, you have only a URL, such as `http://example.com:8000/live.ogg`, representing your Internet radio station. There are a lot of ways you can go about making that URL more accessible to your adoring radio fans. For example, you can advertise your server on an Icecast Stream Directory or you can create your own radio station Web site.

Note   While the term "YP Directory" is often used in the Icecast configuration files to identify an Icecast Stream Directory, the term "Stream Directory" is always used when identifying one of these directories to someone using the Stream Directory. Over time, the term YP is expected to be phased out from the configuration files.

Stream Directories

Icecast servers can register their audio streams with Icecast Stream Directories. These directories allow people to choose from among hundreds of Internet audio broadcasters. By default, your Icecast audio streams are not registered with any Stream Directory servers. But you can fix that.

First, you can edit the `icecast.xml` file and uncomment the directory listing entries by removing the `<!--` and `-->` characters that surround them so that they appear as in the following code. The directory entries that are enabled will allow any source clients that allow Stream Directory listings on your Icecast server to be listed at Xiph.Org and oddsock.org Stream Directories:

```
<directory>
    <yp-url-timeout>15</yp-url-timeout>
    <yp-url>http://dir.xiph.org/cgi-bin/yp-cgi</yp-url>
</directory>
<directory>
    <yp-url-timeout>15</yp-url-timeout>
    <yp-url>http://www.oddsock.org/cgi-bin/yp-cgi</yp-url>
</directory>
```

Next, for each source client audio stream, you must configure the source client to allow Stream Directory registration. To do that for IceS2, you can simply turn on the yp value in the IceS2 configuration file (`ices-playlist.xml`) within an `<instance>` block. For example:

```
<yp>1</yp>
```

After selecting Stream Directory from the Xiph icecast.org site, I searched on the term "Toys" and an entry for my *Linux Toys* Music radio station appeared in the directory listing. The listing shows that it is an Ogg Vorbis stream, available on the mount point `/live.ogg`. By selecting that link, the Web browser can open a plug-in or external player to play the Internet radio station. Figure 10-5 shows the listing that appeared in the Icecast Stream Directory.

FIGURE 10-5: Have your Internet radio station appear in a Stream Directory.

Adding Your Radio Station to a Web Site

How you add your radio station to your Web site, once it is up and running, is entirely up to you. To make it accessible to visitors to your personal or business Web site, simply add a link to the radio station's URL (such as `http://example.com:8000/mymusic.ogg`). Once your visitors select the link, the player that is configured for their browser to play Ogg Vorbis content will open and begin playing your streaming audio.

Step 5: Listening to Your Internet Radio Station

To play your streaming radio station, you need an application that can play Icecast audio streams from a Web address (URL). Don't worry. There are a lot of them available. Given the IceS2 and MuSE source client examples shown earlier, the URLs you would enter to listen to Icecast streams started from those clients could look like the following:

```
http://linuxtoys.net:8000/myplaylist.ogg
http://10.0.0.3:8000/live.ogg
```

Here are a few examples of audio players that are available to play Icecast broadcasts:

- **Rhythmbox** (`http://rhythmbox.org`) — Launch Rhythmbox from a menu or by typing `rhythmbox`. From the toolbar, select Music → New Internet Radio Station. Type in the URL to the radio station for it to start playing.

- **XMMS** (`www.xmms.org`) — Launch from a menu or by typing `xmms`. Right-click on the player and select Play Location. Type in the URL to the radio station for it to start playing.

- **ogg123** (`www.xiph.org/ogg/vorbis`) — For this command line Ogg Vorbis player, simply type the command name with the URL to the radio station (`ogg123 http://host:8000/live.ogg`) to begin playing.

- **Winamp** (`www.winamp.com`) — From this popular Windows audio player, select File → Play URL. Then type in the URL to the radio station for it to start playing.

Administering Your Radio Station

Once your Internet radio station is up and running, there is a lot you can do to check on it and make sure it is running smoothly. Here are a few ideas:

- **Check status** — The Icecast Status Page can be displayed from any Web browser by simply typing the IP address and port number (for example, `http://localhost:8000`). The status page shows the name of the current stream, the stream title, and stream description. You can also see information about how many listeners are accessing the stream at the moment, the quality of the recording, and the song that is currently playing. Click the Click to Listen link to hear the stream. Click the Reload button on your browser to update the current song and number of listeners.

■ **Check admin information** — In the admin directory (`/usr/share/icecast/admin`), there are several administrative XSL files you can call up to see information about your Icecast server from a Web page. To access this information, you need to use the admin login and associated password (you added it to the `icecast.xml` file) when you are prompted.

For example, type `http://localhost:8000/admin/listmounts.xsl` to see the current mount points that are active. Or, you can enter `http://localhost:8000/admin/stats.xsl` to see global server statistics.

■ **Watch log files** — As we configured logging in the sample Icecast server, information about Icecast activities is stored in the `/var/log/icecast` directory in `access.log` and `error.log` files. To keep an eye on your Icecast server, type something like the following to watch as songs change, directory listings are made, and other activities occur:

```
# tail -f /var/log/icecast/error.log
```

Because `ices` was run as a regular user, and logged to the user's home directory (`$HOME/myices/`), you can watch the log for a particular IceS2 stream by monitoring the log file from there as follows:

```
# tail -f $HOME/myices/ices.log
```

Troubleshooting Your Internet Radio Station

I've found the Icecast server and IceS2 source client to be very reliable and fairly simple to use, once you get the hang of how they work. For problems with those projects, I recommend that you try the Icecast mailing list (`http://lists.xiph.org/icecast/list.html`). And, as I mentioned earlier, there is also an Icecast Streaming Media Server forum (`http://forum.icecast.org`) where you can ask questions. Many of your questions will probably be answered from those resources, but if they are not, participants seem to be responsive to questions.

Bigger problems you might have with your Internet radio station might relate to simply getting audio working the way you would like in Linux. For general information on Linux audio and specific information on developing audio applications, I'd recommend the following references:

■ **Linux Audio Users Guide** (`www.djcj.org/LAU/guide/index.php`) — Great reference site for information about Linux audio. Lots of information for new Linux audio users.

■ **Linux Audio Developers Mailing List** (`www.linuxdj.com/audio/lad`) — Topics related to development of audio applications in Linux are discussed here.

There are many tools that come with most Linux distributions that you can use to work with audio. For example, in Fedora and RHEL distributions, you can check out commands in the alsa-utils and vorbis-tools packages to work with general sound recording and mixing and Ogg Vorbis audio content, respectively.

Summary

With high-quality open source tools for streaming audio available today, it's possible for anyone with a PC (running Linux) and an Internet connection to have his own Internet radio station. The *Linux Toys II* Internet radio station project is based primarily on tools created by the Xiph.Org Foundation. The Icecast project provides an extraordinarily flexible and reliable audio streaming mechanism. Source content can be directed to the Icecast server using software from the IceS2, MuSE, Oddcast, or other software projects.

To make your radio station available to the public, Icecast has built-in features that allow you to register your radio station with a public Stream Directory. People can search for, find, and launch links to your radio station from a Stream Directory. You can also create your own radio station front page, to include such things as audio archives and other supporting information about your cause, organization, or music broadcasts.

The Icecast project also comes with several ways for watching over your Internet radio station. Log files in /var/log/icecast and or a personal ices directory track activities of those two software components. You can also display basic statistics about your streaming audio server from your Web browser.

Building a Thin Client Server with LTSP

U sing a nicely loaded Linux server and a bunch of throwaway PCs, you can fill your small office, home, or classroom with usable workstations while saving thousands of dollars. With a little bit of setup (described in this chapter) you can reuse equipment destined for the scrap heap, often with no discernable loss of performance compared to running more expensive PCs.

The Linux Terminal Server Project (http://ltsp.org) was designed to use minimal hardware for workstations referred to as thin clients that are driven by a central server. Because the clients need little more than a LAN card and the ability to drive a display, mouse, and keyboard, almost any standard PC made in the past ten years can be used as a client.

While setting up this project can be a stretch for new Linux users, it provides an opportunity to become familiar with a wide range of Linux features. In the process of setting up your LTSP server and clients, you will learn about configuring services (DHCP, TFTP, NFS, and XDMCP), working with boot images, and tuning and troubleshooting thin client workstations.

Note Although LTSP will run on a variety of UNIX and Linux systems, it entails using a set of features that can vary from one system to the next. Using a Fedora or Red Hat Enterprise Linux system will make the procedures a bit easier because Red Hat systems are used as examples in this chapter.

Understanding Thin Clients, Servers, and LTSP

Most of the work you do to use the LTSP project involves setting up the server so that all the software the thin client workstations need to run is added to the server, configured, and ready to be grabbed. After the server is configured and networked to the clients (via a wired or wireless LAN), all you have to do is boot each workstation in a way that it can get what it needs from the server (I describe PXE and Etherboot methods for doing this).

The first step is to choose a powerful enough server to handle the load and connect it to your workstations via a LAN. After that, the rest is setting up software. Figure 11-1 illustrates the general process of configuring your LTSP server and clients.

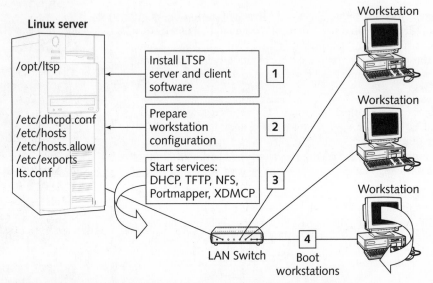

FIGURE 11-1: Set up software on an LTSP server and boot the workstations.

The LTSP server is designed to run on a Linux or UNIX server system. That server should also include software for providing DHCP, TFTP, NFS, and XDMCP services. The LTSP software you add to that system consists of a few administrative commands (for getting the LTSP client software needed) and making sure that the server is configured for supplying that client software to workstations when they boot. (The administrative utilities let you download the client software from the network or get it from a local disk.)

The ltsp-utils package contains the utilities ltspadmin (to download and install the LTSP client software onto the server) and ltspcfg (to check and configure services needed by LTSP). The CD that accompanies this book includes ltsp-utils as both an RPM for Red Hat Linux systems or gzipped tar file for all others. In case you don't have an Internet connection (which is the common method of grabbing LTSP software during the install procedure), the *Linux Toys II* CD also includes the LTSP ISO images to provide all the software for the project.

LTSP stores the directory structure needed by each workstation to operate in the /opt/ ltsp/i386 directory of the server. While most of the same files and directories will be shared by all client workstations, you can edit the /opt/ltsp/i386/etc/lts.conf file to add specific settings relating to each workstation's video card, mouse, run level, and other features.

Services that you configure on your server for LTSP are there so the workstations can request what they need to run. DHCP must be set up to give each workstation its IP address and locations of such things as routers and DNS servers on the network. However, LTSP also uses DHCP to identify the location of the bootstrap or Linux kernel each workstation needs to boot from. The TFTPD service is used to actually download the bootstrap or kernel file to each workstation.

After a workstation boots, it is presented with a login screen (which is configured on the server using the XDMCP service). The user can log in through that login screen using a regular user account on the server. The desktop, files, directories, processes, devices, and other components the user sees after logging in all come from the server. The directory structure is provided from the server using the NFS service to share the /opt/ltsp directory (for the file system) and the /var/opt/ltsp/swapfiles directory (to provide a swap area).

I cover two ways for the workstation to boot: PXE and Etherboot. Although there are other boot methods available, PXE will work for most diskless workstations that have a PXE-enabled card. Etherboot lets you build ROM images that can be put on a floppy disk, copied to a CD, or burned to an eprom to boot the workstation.

Caution

Although there are many features available in Linux for securing its services, some of the features included in this project (such as NFS, TFTP, and X over a network) are not inherently very secure. For that reason, I recommend using this project, as described here, only behind a secure firewall. If your LTSP server has an Internet connection, be sure that you block access to the LTSP services in your firewall so they are accessible from your LAN, but not from the Internet. Look to the LTSP.org project periodically for newer versions to patch potential security problems that might have been discovered after this book was printed.

Advantages of Thin Client Computing

While being able to save money on workstations is a big incentive for doing this project, there are other advantages to administering a group of workstations from a central server using LTSP:

- **Backups** — Because data for the workstations are all stored on one computer, you don't have to manage separate data backups from every computer in the group.

- **Peripherals** — Instead of adding peripherals to every workstation, any peripherals (printers, scanners, removable media, and so on) attached to the server can be immediately made available to every workstation without additional configuration.

- **Central administration** — You can focus your security and administration efforts on the server. You don't need to worry about the firewall on each person's workstation or what is being downloaded to hard disks all over your LAN. You can focus your attention on managing user accounts, checking system load and watching network activity from the server.

If you need to add workstations or there is an increase in system load, you can simply add resources (more RAM, processors, or hard disks) to the server. Total resource usage can be much more efficient because you don't need to add all the resources a person might need to each workstation.

About the LTSP Project

The Linux Terminal Server Project (ltsp.org) is an open source project covered under the GPL. LTSP is actively being developed and includes a very rich set of features that go well beyond the scope of this chapter.

Jim McQuillan is the leader of the LTSP project and kindly agreed to review this chapter for accuracy. The primary contributors to the project include Jim McQuillan, Ron Colcernian, Erick Tyack, Richard June, Andrew Williams, Jim Glutting, Scott Balneaves, Steve Switzer, Mike Collins, Robbie Stanford, Gideon Romm, David Johnston, Chuck Leibow, Ragnar Wisloff, and Bill Cavalieri.

The LTSP project itself offers excellent documentation and support options. If you run into snags during this chapter, here are some other LTSP resources you can turn to:

- **Documentation** — The LTSP documentation page (`www.ltsp.org/documentation`) provides links to a full set of LTSP documentation in English and Dutch, as well as translations in progress for French, Italian, Brazilian Portuguese, German, Norwegian, Spanish, and Zulu. Earlier versions of LTSP also include Greek, Polish, and Finnish documentation.

- **Support** — LTSP offers several mailing lists, an IRC channel, and some support options in different languages (`www.ltsp.org/support.php`). There is also Wiki where you find more ways to learn and contribute (`http://wiki.ltsp.org`).

While this chapter is geared more toward reusing old equipment as clients, LTSP is also an excellent project for building higher-performance thin client configurations in professional settings (which can still save a lot of money). If you want help developing that type of environment, or simply want to purchase certified LTSP workstations, you can visit the LTSP project's DisklessWorkstations.Com company site (`www.disklessworkstations.com`). Purchasing products from this site helps support the people who bring you LTSP.

Getting a Server and Workstations

The hardware you need for this LTSP project depends on the amount of load you expect to have. However, there are some guidelines that will help you choose the hardware you need for your LTSP server and workstations.

Choosing a Server

It is a bit of an art form to choose the server to support your LTSP workstations. Here are some things to consider:

- **Disk space** — Beyond the operating system (which can consume from about 2GB to 7GB of disk space for Fedora Core), you need an additional 400MB of disk space for the LTSP software. You must then consider how much disk space will be required for the users from each workstation. For a user who is just writing some documents and storing a few images, 500MB might be plenty of space. For someone working with video or ISO images, 10GB may not be enough.

- **RAM** — Because all applications being used from each workstation are actually running on the server, RAM is not a place to skimp if you want good performance for your clients. Luckily, one of the biggest memory hogs (the X server) is running on each workstation. Start with the minimum RAM requirements from the Linux you installed and build from there. The LTSP documentation says that the project has successfully run 50 workstations from a machine with 4GB of RAM.

- **Processors** — While RAM is potentially the biggest bottleneck, processor speed is probably next. For the 50-workstation configuration mentioned by LTSP, the processor was a dual–Pentium 4, 2.5 GHz configuration.

- **Ethernet NIC** — You will need an Ethernet NIC supported by Linux to communicate with the workstations.

- **Other hardware** — Because, presumably, this server will be serving multiple users, you need to think about what you need to support all of those users. By consolidating everyone on one server, you might find it cost-effective to invest in good backup hardware, printers, CD/DVD writers, and other hardware your users may need to access.

Choosing Client Workstations

The list for choosing client workstations is more a list of what you don't need than what you do. You don't need to have a hard disk, floppy drive, CD/DVD drive, or any storage medium (provided you have network interface cards that have boot capabilities).

The client workstations really require only enough horsepower to be able to run a minimal Linux system geared mainly to running the X Window server. The processor can be an ancient 486. Because swap space is on the server, RAM can be as little as 32MB on each workstation.

The one tricky part, especially for older PCs, is making sure that you have a supported video card. If LTSP is unable to autodetect your video card, you will have to do some special configuration in your `lts.conf` file to indicate how to handle that card. Although I describe how to set up a graphical workstation in this chapter, you also have the option of using the workstation without a GUI (shell-only login).

While the view from the GUI on your workstation is the server's processor and file system, there are ways of accessing some local hardware using LTSP. For example, the LTSP documentation describes how to connect a local printer to a workstation so that you and others can access it from the server and other workstations.

Networking Hardware

Each workstation and server will need at least one network interface card, appropriate cabling, and a network switch (or a hub). (You can also use wireless NICs as opposed to using a wired Ethernet network.) On the workstations, if you are not booting from floppy disk or CD, you will need to have a network-bootable NIC (I describe how to use PXE to do network boots). NICs are available for under $10, so you might consider buying a new one if yours isn't supported.

A 10/100 Mbps switch can be found for under $20. An older hub will work (and you might be able to find one being thrown away). But keep in mind that nearly every transaction from an LTSP workstation causes network traffic. So even a free 10 Mbps hub, where all workstations will see your network traffic, may not be worth the price.

Setting Up the Server

If you have already chosen the computer you will use as the server for this project, you are ready to set up the software. Here is how your LTSP server must be set up before you begin installing and configuring that server:

- **Operating system** — Most Linux and UNIX systems should work as the server for this project. In my example, I use Fedora Core because it includes all the server packages that LTSP needs and there is an easy-to-install RPM package of ltsp-utils that works well. When I installed Fedora Core, I had to make sure that these packages were installed: nfs-utils, portmap, tftp-server, dhcp, and a set of xorg-x11 packages (selecting to install GNOME or KDE when you install Fedora will get the X packages you need). I also used the default run level for a desktop system, which is run level 5. (That causes the GNOME display manager to be enabled so it can be used by the clients as well.)

  For other Linux systems, you will need to use the ltsp-utils package. That package is in TGZ format, which you have to un-tar and install as described later in this chapter. (There is nothing to compile because the utilities are all written in perl.) As for the Linux services that LTSP requires, packaging, configuration files, start-up scripts, and other features related to the services LTSP needs vary among different Linux distributions.

- **Internet connection** — During the setup process, `ltspadmin` grabs the latest client software from the LTSP repository. So, to complete this procedure, you need an active Internet connection from the server machine you are configuring. That machine should eventually have a LAN connection to your client machines. (You can bypass the Internet connection by using the LTSP ISO image, as described later in the procedure. That ISO image is included on the *Linux Toys II* CD.)

The following sections describe how to install and set up the LTSP software to allow your computer to run as an LTSP server. In general, you will be doing the following on the server:

- Installing LTSP software
- Setting up the software needed by LTSP client workstations
- Configuring services on the server so that clients can get what they need from the server

The way your LTSP server is configured will be based on how your thin clients are configured to boot up and how the server verifies that each client is allowed to access the server. There are many ways to configure thin client access to the server. The example in this chapter manually assigns just a few computers specifically to be thin clients, based on the MAC address of each computer's network card and the type of boot each does (such as Etherboot or PXE boot). This makes sure that only computers with specific network interface cards are allowed to use the LTSP server. Figure 11-2 shows an example of a network configuration consisting of one LTSP server and four thin clients.

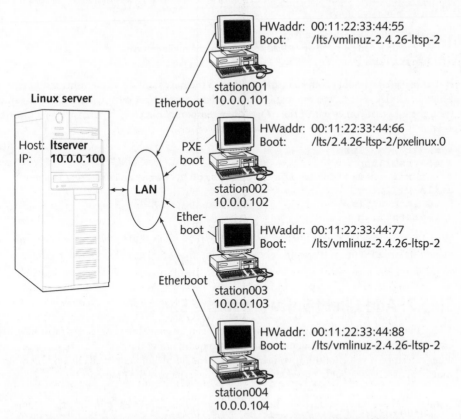

FIGURE 11-2: Specific thin clients can access the server, based on a MAC address.

The configuration shown in Figure 11-2 is used to set up the services on your server in the rest of this procedure. It shows a single LAN with one server and four thin clients (IP addresses 10.0.0.100 through 10.0.0.104). The server acts as a route to the Internet for the thin clients, and also provides the services they need to boot and communicate on the network.

I suggest that you keep your own set of information, either on a diagram like this or in a list, that contains the data you need to set up your own LTSP configuration. Some information will be specific to your situation. For example, you will get your own DNS server addresses from your ISP and assign your own domain name to the computers on your LAN.

Step 1: Install the Server Software

In Fedora Core or Red Hat Enterprise Linux, you can install the ltsp-utils RPM. (On other Linux or UNIX systems, install the ltsp-utils TGZ package, as explained in the text that follows.)

To install from RPMs, insert the *Linux Toys II* CD on your CD drive. If your CD mounts automatically, you can skip the first command. If it doesn't, run the following (possibly replacing /media/cdrecorder with the location of where your CD was mounted) as root user from a Terminal window:

```
# mount /media/cdrecorder
# cd /media/cdrecorder/RPMS/ch11-terminalserver
# ./installme
```

If that installed without error, you can continue to the next step. If you are using a different Linux or UNIX system, you can install from the ltsp-utils tgz package instead. Copy that file from the CD that comes with *Linux Toys II* to a temporary directory. Then, with that directory as your current directory, type the following as root user:

```
# mkdir /tmp/ltsp
# cd /tmp/ltsp
# tar xzf /media/cdrecorder/Sources/ch11-terminalserver/ltsp-
utils-0.11.tgz
# cd ltsp_utils
# ./install.sh
```

Whether you installed from an RPM or TGZ file, the result should be that three new commands are installed on your system. The commands are ltspinfo, ltspadmin, and ltspcfg.

Step 2: Add Client Software to the Server

To begin installing LTSP software that will be needed by your thin clients, you must have at least 400MB of disk space available in the partition containing the /opt/ltsp directory (or other directory, if you choose). If you already have the LTSP software available on CD or on your hard disk, you shouldn't need any additional disk space at the moment.

Note   If you don't have an Internet connection, you can install the LTSP files from the ltsp ISO image contained on the *Linux Toys II* CD. First you need to burn the ltsp-4.1.0-1.iso file from the isos/ch11-terminalserver directory on the *Linux Toys II* CD to a blank CD. (Chapter 5 includes a description of how to burn a CD.) Insert the CD into your computer and continue with the following procedure.

1. As root user, type the following command:

```
# ltspadmin
ltspadmin - v0.14                    LTSP dir: /opt/ltsp

LTSP Administration Utility

   Install/Update LTSP Packages
   Configure the installer options
   Configure LTSP

   Quit the administration program
```

2. Use the arrow keys to move the cursor to the `Install/Update LTSP Packages` line and press Enter. You are asked where you want to retrieve the LTSP packages (as shown in the code that follows). You can use the default (`http://www.ltsp.org/ltsp-4.1`) or choose a different location.

```
LTSP Installer configuration

Where to retrieve packages from?
[http://www.ltsp.org/ltsp-4.1]
```

Note If the LTSP packages are available locally, you can type the directory name. For example, you could type **file:///media/cdrecorder** or **file:///mnt/cdrom**, if they are on a local CD ROM drive, depending on where the CD drive is mounted on your system.

Note The LTSP project offers an LTSP ISO file that contains all the software needed to install LTSP clients and servers. If you download and mount that ISO, you can indicate its location when prompted in the preceding step. This allows you to install the LTSP software without being connected to the Internet. Get the ISO from `http://ltsp.org/download` page. Follow instructions there for downloading and installing from the ISO image.

3. Press Enter to get packages from the default location. You will be prompted to provide the following information for installing the LTSP software:

   ▪ **Location of LTSP client tree** — Your client file tree will be set up in the `/opt/ltsp` directory by default. Press Enter to accept that location, or type your own location and press Enter.

   ▪ **HTTP or FTP proxy** — If you need to use an HTTP or FTP proxy, enter it in this option (for example, **http://example.com:3124**). Otherwise, type **none** and press Enter (twice) to not use a proxy server.

   ▪ **Correct?** — Type **y** and press Enter if you have entered the information correctly (or **n** if you want to go back and enter it again).

A list of available LTSP software packages will appear on your machine.

4. Press **A** to select all packages (or **I** to select each package individually or **U** to unselect a package).

5. Press **Q** to end package selection, and then **y** and Enter to begin installing the packages. (By default, these package will be downloaded to the `/opt/ltsp/pkg_cache` directory.)

6. When package downloading is done, press Enter to continue as instructed. You are returned to the main ltspadmin display.

7. Select Q to exit from ltspadmin.

Next you need to check that the services you need on your LTSP server are available.

Step 3: Configure Services for the Workstations

The LTSP server must be able to provide several services to the LTSP thin clients. Those services include:

- **DHCP** — Using Dynamic Host Configuration Protocol (DHCP), the server can pass information to the client that it needs to begin its boot procedure. This can include its IP address, DNS servers, gateways, and other information.

- **TFTP** — The Trivial File Transfer Protocol (TFTP) server is a simple file transfer server, used primarily for booting diskless workstations (as you are doing here) so that each client can copy the files it needs from the server.

- **NFS** — With Network Files System (NFS) software, a server can make a directory (and its subdirectories) available to computers on the network. A client, given proper permissions, can then mount that directory locally and access the files in that directory as though they existed locally. Because LTSP clients may have no disk at all, any files that are not stored in local RAM are made available using NFS from the server.

- **XDMCP** — The X Display Manager Controller Protocol (XDMCP) is a protocol used to implement graphical login displays. It has been implemented in most popular X Window System display managers (such as XDM, GDM, and KDM) to handle how the clients' graphical displays are launched and how the initial graphical login screen appears and acts.

The following steps check your Linux or UNIX system for the services just listed, as well as the existence of needed configuration files (such as hosts and exports files). If there are services missing, the procedure will help you get them installed and running.

Note   I started with a fairly complete install of Fedora Core 4 on my LTSP server. I had everything LTSP needed to get started. Consider adding the software packages shown in the preceding list from your Linux distribution, as they should already have been tested to work with your distribution. Components needed by XDMCP come in the x11-xorgs packages, which you get with most GNOME and KDE installs.

1. Run the `ltspcfg` command to check that the components needed by your LTSP server are already installed on your Linux system:

```
# ltspcfg

ltspcfg - Version 0.11

Checking Runlevel....: 5
Checking Ethernet Interfaces
Checking Dhcpd.....
Checking Tftpd.......
Checking Portmapper...
Checking nfs....
Checking xdmcp...Found: xdm, gdm, kdm  Using: none!
Checking /etc/hosts.
Checking /etc/hosts.allow.
Checking /etc/exports.
Checking lts.conf.
Press <enter> to continue..
```

2. Press Enter to continue. The following selections appear:

```
lstpcfg Linux Terminal Server Project (http://www.LTSP.org)

S - Show the status of all services
C - Configure the services manually

Q - Quit

Make a selection: S
```

3. Press S to check which of the needed services are installed and properly configured. Figure 11-3 shows an example of the output of `ltspcfg` on a Linux system running Fedora Core.

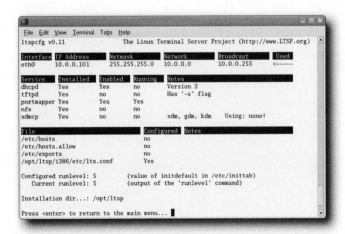

FIGURE 11-3: Check that services needed on your LTSP server are available.

The output shown in Figure 11-3 would be typical for a system that included a Desktop install of Fedora Core, with several server packages added. If you had done just a Desktop type of install, you might have to install more of the server packages.

From this output, you can see that dhcpd, tftpd, portmapper, nfs, and xdmcp are all installed, but only portmapper is actually running at the moment and set to run on an ongoing basis. Likewise, the hosts, hosts.allow, exports, and lts.conf configuration files were all found, but only lts.conf was properly configured.

4. Press Enter to leave the status display, and then press **C** to configure the services. The following list of services that you can configure appears:

```
ltspcfg The Linux Terminal Server Project (http://www.LTSP.org)
   1 - Runlevel
   2 - Interface selection
   3 - DHCP configuration
   4 - TFTP configuration
   5 - Portmapper configuration
   6 - NFS configuration
   7 - XDMCP configuration
   8 - Create /etc/hosts entries
   9 - Create /etc/hosts.allow entries
  10 - Create /etc/exports entries
  11 - Create lts.conf file

   R - Return to previous menu
   Q - Quit

Make a selection:
```

Here is where you get into the nitty-gritty of setting up the services on your LTSP server. Because these features may or may not be already installed on your system, I'm going to go through each selection and describe what needs to be done.

Note For most of the preceding configuration selections, you need to modify a configuration file after the ltspcfg command has done its work. When that is the case, you can exit the ltspcfg command, edit the file as described, and then go back and restart ltspcfg to go to the next configuration choice.

Run-Level Configuration

After starting the ltspcfg command, type **1** to change the run level. For Fedora and other Red Hat Linux systems, the default run level is usually 5 (causing a graphical login screen to appear on the console). Run level 3 can be used if you want a text prompt to appear for login instead. Other Linux systems may use different run-level values for graphical and text-based logins.

Interface Selection

After starting the `ltspcfg` command, type **2** to select which Ethernet network interface from your server connects to the thin clients. Your server might have two (or more) network interface cards (NICs) if, for example, it is connected both to a LAN (that goes to the thin clients) and an Internet connection (such as DSL or ISDN hardware). Select the appropriate interface so that an arrow (`<-----`) appears under the Used column.

DHCP Configuration

After starting the `ltspcfg` command, type **3** to set up your DHCP service (dhcpd). After you have responded to the prompts, you will need to further edit the `/etc/dhcpd.conf` file (as described a bit later). Here are descriptions of those prompts and the results on a Fedora or other Red Hat system:

- **Enable dhcpd daemon** — Type **y** to turn on the DHCP service (to start the dhcpd daemon each time the system starts up).

- **Build a dhcpd.conf file** — Type **y** to create the configuration file used by the dhcpd daemon (`/etc/dhcpd.conf`). If you already have a `dhcpd.conf` file, the LTSP information is created in a different file: `/etc/dhcpd.conf.sample`.

Note   There are lots of ways to set up a DHCP server. I recommend that you refer to the dhcpd.conf man page (type **man dhcpd.conf**), as well as other man pages (dhcrelay, dhcpd, dhcpd.leases, and dhcp-eval) for further information on configuring DHCP.

On a Fedora system, after the preceding steps are done, the dhcpd service should be set to run when the system starts (run level 5) and the `dhcpd.conf` file should be filled with some default settings. At this point, you can open the `/etc/dhcpd.conf` file in another Terminal window and tailor it to suit the needs of your thin client network. The following text steps you through that sample file and how you might want to change it.

In the following three lines, dynamic DNS is off (check the dhcpd.conf man page for Dynamic DNS Updates if you want to learn more about this feature) and default and maximum lease times are set to 21,600 seconds (6 hours). Lease values set the amount of time a client can keep an IP address before it needs to be renewed.

```
ddns-update-style          none;
default-lease-time         21600;
max-lease-time             21600;
```

The next lines are critical to how you lay out your network. You will need to edit these lines to suit your environment. Refer back to Figure 11-2 to see how we configured our sample thin client configuration.

For our example, we chose to set up a LAN using private IP addresses 10.0.0.100 through 10.0.0.104 (you can use up to IP address 10.0.0.254 in this arrangement). The IP address of the server that faces the LAN is 10.0.0.100 (it has an additional IP address facing the Internet on another network interface card).

You must get IP addresses of DNS servers from your ISP to enter on the `domain-name-servers` lines. (The ones shown are not real IP addresses because no IP address can start with a number above 255, so be sure to fix them to match your situation.) Replace the *example.com* domain-name with your own name.

```
option subnet-mask          255.255.255.0;
option broadcast-address    10.0.0.255;
option routers              10.0.0.100;
option domain-name-servers  310.0.0.1;
option domain-name-servers  310.0.0.2;
option domain-name          "example.com";
```

The root-path line indicates the location of the Linux operating system files that will be used by each thin client (referred to as the LTSP client tree). The first part (10.0.0.100) indicates the LTSP server that contains the LTSP client tree and the directory path (/opt/ltsp/i386) indicates the location on the server of that directory structure.

```
option root-path            "10.0.0.100:/opt/ltsp/i386";
```

Next I define the network itself and the thin client workstations within that network. For this example, I have one set of IP addresses operating on a single physical LAN. Then, within the subnetwork, each host computer is defined individually, with a separate host entry.

```
subnet 10.0.0.0 netmask 255.255.255.0 {
    use-host-decl-names    on;
    option log-servers     10.0.0.100;

    host station001 {
        hardware ethernet    00:11:22:33:44:55;
        fixed-address        10.0.0.101;
        filename             "/lts/vmlinuz-2.4.26-ltsp-2";
    }
    host station002 {
        hardware ethernet    00:11:22:33:44:66;
        fixed-address        10.0.0.102;
        filename             "/lts/2.4.26-ltsp-2/pxelinux.0";
    }
    host station003 {
        hardware ethernet    00:11:22:33:44:77;
        fixed-address        10.0.0.103;
        filename             "/lts/vmlinuz-2.4.26-ltsp-2";
    }
    host station004 {
        hardware ethernet    00:11:22:33:44:88;
        fixed-address        10.0.0.104;
        filename             "/lts/vmlinuz-2.4.26-ltsp-2";
    }
}
```

Make sure that each file name matches the name of the Linux boot file in the /tftpboot directory tree on the server. When you indicate the location of the file, remove the /tftpboot part of the path (hence, /lts/vmlinuz-2.4.26-ltsp-2) because the

TFTP services runs in a chroot environment in Red Hat Linux systems. (The location may be different on other Linux systems.)

The workstation `station002` in the preceding code shows an example of a configuration for a workstation that will do a PXE network boot (see the section "Booting Up the Workstations"). The `pxelinux.0` file on the server is a 16KB bootstrap file (rather than the nearly 2MB `vmlinuz` file used to boot the machine). It's necessary for the bootstrap file to start first, and then load the kernel because the PXE feature on the network card cannot handle more than a 32KB file.

You can add as many workstations (host entries) as you want. You can use the IP address scheme and the host-naming scheme, or come up with your own. You will, however, need to determine the MAC address of each network card from each workstation and use them for each hardware Ethernet entry.

Tip If a version of Linux is running on the workstation, you can determine the MAC address by typing **/sbin/ifconfig**. From a DOS window in a Windows system, type **ipconfig /all**. The MAC address will be listed as HWaddr or Physical Address, respectively.

The example I've just presented is a fairly secure way of configuring LTSP, as only computers with specific network cards (based on unique MAC addresses) can connect to the server. In many cases, however, you might simply want to let any machine that connects to your LAN be able to boot up on the LTSP server. Here is how the subnet section might look in a more open LTSP setup:

```
subnet 10.0.0.0 netmask 255.255.255.0 {
    range 10.0.0.102 10.0.0.200;
    if substring (option vendor-class-identifier, 0, 9) = "PXEClient" {
     filename  "/lts/2.4.26-ltsp-2/pxelinux.0"; # PXE NBP Boot Loader
    }
    else {
      filename  "/lts/vmlinuz-2.4.26-ltsp-2";   # Etherboot kernel
    }
  }
```

In this example, the DHCP service will hand out addresses in the range of 10.0.0.102 to 10.0.0.200 to any computer that asks for an address. To tell what kind of boot loader to use, the DHCP server checks if the vendor-class-identifier from each client is PXEClient. If it is, the pxelinux.0 boot kernel (PXE) is used. If it's not, the vmlinuz-2.4.26-ltsp-w boot kernel (Etherboot) is used.

This example was adapted from the LTSP DHCP page, where a longer example (including PPC boots) is shown (`http://wiki.ltsp.org/twiki/bin/view/Ltsp/DHCP`). Refer to that page for more ideas on setting up DHCP for and LTSP server.

TFTP Configuration

After starting the `ltspcfg` command, type **4** to set up your server's TFCP service (tftpd daemon). When prompted, type **y** to enable the service. In Fedora or other Red Hat system, this sets tftpd to start when the system reboots (or when the xinetd service restarts), but it doesn't start the service immediately. (Press Enter to return to the menu.)

Portmapper Configuration

After starting the `ltspcfg` command, type **5** to set the portmapper service (portmap daemon) to start. On many systems this will already be running (`lspcfg` will tell you so if it is already running). If you are prompted to start the service, type **y**. Portmapper is required to use the NFS service. (Press Enter to return to the menu.)

NFS Configuration

After starting the `ltspcfg` command, type **6** to set up NFS (nfsd daemon) to run on your system. Type **y** to enable the service and press Enter to return to the menu.

XDMCP Configuration

On Fedora and Red Hat Enterprise Linux systems, the X display manager does not listen for XDMCP or Chooser requests as a security precaution. You must change this behavior to allow graphical logins for your LTSP workstations. The easiest way to do this is from the Login Screen setup window (before you enable the XDMCP service using the `ltspcfg` command). From the LTSP server, do the following:

1. From the desktop panel, select Desktop ➔ System Settings ➔ Login Screen.
   (If prompted, login as root user.)

2. Click the XDMCP tab. A set of XDMCP settings appears.

3. Select Enable XDMCP. All XDMCP fields are enabled, as shown in Figure 11-4.

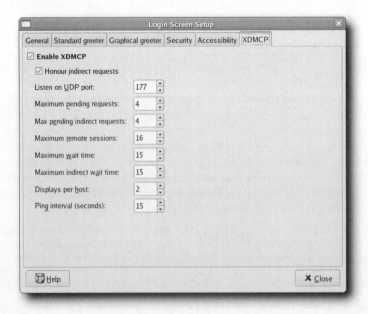

FIGURE 11-4: Enable XDMCP to present login screens to client workstations.

4. Adjust the XDMCP settings, if necessary. For example, you might change the maximum number of remote sessions (if you need more or less than the default 16 remote sessions).

5. You may need to restart your graphical login for the XDMCP changes to take effect. There may be a better way to do this, but in Fedora, I usually close all windows except a Terminal window and type **init 3** as root user. Then, after X is shut down, I type **init 5** to restart the graphical login screen.

Caution

XDMCP service is offered through port 177. Because this service is not secure, you should block access to that port from any network interfaces on your server that face the Internet.

While you have the Login Screen Setup window open, you can do several things to adjust how the login screen will behave on your workstations. Here are some things you should consider changing:

- **Remote greeter** — The Remote greeter is set to "Standard greeter," which means that the login screen will have a plain, single-color background. You can change it to "Graphical greeter," which will cause remote workstations to see the same Fedora Core or Red Hat Enterprise Linux login screen that they would see from the server's console.

- **Remote welcome string** — By default, the Remote welcome string (on the General tab) is set to Welcome to %n where %n is later replaced by the name of your server. You can change that string to anything you want to appear on the login screen each remote workstation sees.

- **Backgrounds and themes** — On both the Standard and Graphical greeter tabs (depending on which you end up using), you can change the look and feel of the login screen. Instead of a plain blue background, you can choose a different color or an image. You can add a different logo (other than those used by Red Hat) or change the whole theme of the graphical greeter.

You can also enable or disable features related to security and accessibility on the Login Screen Setup window.

At this point, you can go back to your ltspcfg command and type **7** (to configure the XDMCP display manager to allow the user at each workstation to login to the server). Type **y** to enable XDMCP. Next, you are given the option to have a text-based login on the server, and not use the graphical login (while retaining its use on the workstations).

Host Name/Address Setup (/etc/hosts)

Because you are creating only one server and a few workstations in this configuration, the /etc/hosts file is an acceptable way to map host names to addresses. For the server and each workstation, I'm going to add its name and associated IP address. (The alternative is to configure the computers in a DNS server or remember and use only IP addresses.)

After starting the ltspcfg command, type **8** to add entries to your /etc/hosts file. By typing **y** when asked to configure /etc/hosts, a bunch of dummy entries are added to the /etc/hosts file. Next, you should use a text editor (as root user) to edit the /etc/hosts file. For this example, the entries added for your LTSP entries would appear as follows:

```
10.0.0.100      ltspserver
10.0.0.101      station001
10.0.0.102      station002
10.0.0.103      station003
10.0.0.104      station004
```

These names and addresses should match the ones you added to the dhcpd.conf file.

Service Permission Setup (/etc/hosts.allow)

You can add entries to the hosts.allow file on the server so that the workstations can access the services they need. After starting the ltspcfg command, type **9** to add the following entries into the /etc/hosts.allow file:

```
bootpd:       0.0.0.0
in.tftpd:     10.0.0.
portmap:      10.0.0.
```

The first entry allows bootpd service to other computers from any address. The next two entries allow anyone from the 10.0.0. network to access the TFTP (in.tftpd) and portmap services. If you are using different IP address pools than those that appear here, be sure to change these entries.

NFS Share Setup (/etc/exports)

The files and directories you need to share from your NFS service need to be added to the /etc/exports file on the server. After starting the ltspcfg command, typing **10** and selecting **y** adds the necessary entries to your /etc/exports file. Here is how those entries appear:

```
/opt/ltsp                10.0.0.0/255.255.255.0(ro,no_root_squash,sync)
/var/opt/ltsp/swapfiles  10.0.0.0/255.255.255.0(rw,no_root_squash,async)
```

These two entries cause the /opt/ltsp and /var/opt/ltsp/swapfiles directories to be shared with any computers on the 10.0.0. network. Both shared directories will allow the root user from client workstations to read and write files as the root user (no_root_squash). The ltsp directory tree, however, is shared only as a read-only file system (ro) and allows new requests to the file system only when previous requests have been committed to storage (sync). Alternatively, the swapfiles directory will allow read and write requests to take place (which it must do to act as swap space for the clients) and allow new requests to take place before previous ones complete (async), which can improve performance.

Note   Type **man exports** to see other options available to be set in the exports file for the NFS system.

Workstation Configuration Setup (lts.conf)

The `lts.conf` file (located in the `/opt/ltsp/i386/etc` directory on the server) contains important information needed by each client workstation. After starting the `ltspcfg` command, typing **10** and selecting **y** creates an `lts.conf` file you can begin with.

The Default entry in the `lts.conf` file looks like the following:

```
[Default]
        SERVER                = 10.0.0.100
        XSERVER               = auto
        X_MOUSE_PROTOCOL      = "PS/2"
        X_MOUSE_DEVICE        = "/dev/psaux"
        X_MOUSE_RESOLUTION    = 400
        X_MOUSE_BUTTONS       = 3
        USE_XFS               = N
        SCREEN_01             = startx
```

Make sure that the SERVER line represents the IP address of your LTSP server. The XSERVER line tells each client to try to auto-detect the type of video card it has, so the client can start up the right video driver for the X display. By default, a PS/2, three-button mouse (`/dev/psaux` device) is configured. By default, each client grabs the fonts it needs from the NFS shared directory (USE_XFS = N), so no additional font server is used. The X Window System is started on the first screen by launching the `startx` command.

Note The `lts.conf` file has a format that is similar to that of old Windows .INI files. The `[Default]` section can be used for all of the workstations, while specific workstation entries, `[station001]` for example, can override settings from the `[Default]` section. Besides using host names, you can also use IP addresses or MAC addresses in the brackets.

In many cases, this default setting will work fine for allowing the workstations to start up. However, if you need additional tuning, you can add a separate entry for any workstation that needs it. For example:

```
[station001]
        XSERVER        = XF86_SVGA
        RUNLEVEL       = 3
```

In this case, X.org cannot detect the video card of the workstation (`station001`) so the XF86_SVGA driver (from the XFree86 project) is used instead. I also choose to start this workstation in run level 3 (instead of 5), so it will boot to a text-based prompt.

Note There are many parameters you can enter into the `lts.conf` file. For details on many of these parameters, I recommend you refer to "Chapter 9 - lts.conf Entries," from the LTSP manual (`www.ltsp.org/documentation`). Also, later in this chapter, I describe how to add an entry to open a local shell on a workstation.

Step 4: Startup Services on the Server

Although you should have configured the services needed by your workstations to boot up, they may not all be started yet. To check that those services are running, run the `ltspcfg` command again and select S to check the status of the services. Figure 11-5 shows an example of the ltspcfg screen.

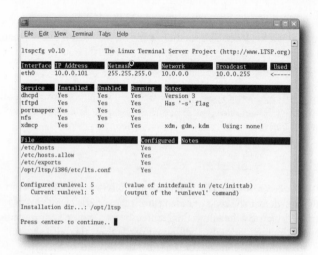

FIGURE 11-5: ltspcfg displays installed, enabled, and running services.

As you can see from Figure 11-5, the Ethernet interface of the server is indicated as being used by the LTSP server. All configuration files have been configured (Yes) and the system is set to start at run level 5 (graphical boot screen). The installation directory (where files needed by the workstations are stored) is /opt/ltsp.

Where you may have to do some work is on the services. Although all services are shown as enabled and running in Figure 11-5, that may not be the case for your setup. Here's what you should check:

- **Installed** — If any one of the services is not installed you need to install it. Software packages containing all required services are available on Fedora and Red Hat Enterprise Linux distributions, as well as most other Linux systems.

- **Enabled** — A Yes under Enabled for any of the services indicates that it is set to start when the system boots. If, for example, the dhcpd service is not yet enabled and you are using a Red Hat system, you can enable that service using the chkconfig command. For example, type the following (as root user) to enable dhcpd in a Red Hat Linux system:

chkconfig dhcpd on

You can repeat that command for tftp, portmap, or nfs to set those services to start automatically at boot time. On other Linux distributions, you may need to enable the service's daemon to start up in an init file (such as an rc.* file in the /etc/rc.d directory).

- **Running**—Just turning on a service won't immediately start that service. On a Red Hat Linux system, to start a service you can use the `service` command. For example, as root user type the following to start the dhcpd service immediately:

  ```
  # service dhcpd start
  ```

  Likewise, you can start portmap or nfs (replace `dhcpd` on that command line). Because tftpd is handled by the xinetd daemon, after enabling tftpd you can be sure that it is running by restarting xinetd (`service xinetd start`).

After you have started all the necessary services, you can type the `ltspcfg` command again, to make sure that all the required services are running. You are now ready to start choosing how to boot your workstations to take advantage of your LTSP server.

Step 5: Add Users

The server that you just configured is ready to provide a network boot service to thin client workstations. When you configured XDMCP, you set a login screen that each workstation will see when it boots. Before anyone can login from those screens, however, they need to have a user account name and password set up.

The quick way to add a new user account to Linux is by running the `useradd` command as root user, followed by the `passwd` command. Here's an example of how to add a user named jim:

```
# useradd jim
# passwd jim
Changing password for user jim.
New UNIX password: ********
Retype new UNIX password: ********
```

By default, the new user (`jim`) will be assigned a home directory (`/home/jim`) that includes a set of start-up files to provide the desktop environment he will see when he logs in from a workstation. The password he will need is represented here by a set of asterisks because it is not visible when you type it.

Give a user name and password to each person you want to allow to log in to your server from an LTSP client. Encourage them to run the `passwd` command the first time they log in and to keep that password secure.

Booting Up the Workstations

With just about everything you need to start your thin client workstations configured on the server, the next thing to do is decide how each workstation will boot up and ask for the stuff it needs from the server. The type of hardware available on the thin client may limit the type of boot method you can use. In this section, I describe two workstation boot methods, one of which at least should work in most cases:

- **PXE booting** — If your computer hardware supports PXE booting, this is probably the easiest method to use. To use this method, your network interface card must be PXE-enabled and your computer's BIOS must be able to select PXE as a boot method.

- **Etherboot booting** — You can create an Etherboot image that you put on a CD or floppy disk. Once that medium boots, your workstation can get the rest of the data it needs over the network from the LTSP server.

The following sections describe how to prepare for and boot your LTSP workstations using either the PXE or Etherboot methods.

Booting Workstations Using PXE

The Pre-boot eXecution Environment (PXE) is a feature available on most Ethernet network interface cards (NICs). It allows a client computer to get a small boot program from another computer on the network to begin the boot process. Using PXE (pronounced "pixie"), a completely diskless client computer can boot from the network — no floppy, CD, or hard drive is required.

When you power up the workstation, the PXE client checks the network for a DHCP server that is configured to supply the bootstrap program, and then uses TFTP to copy the bootstrap program into the computer's RAM. Luckily for us, we have already configured a server to provide these services (see the description of station002 in the "DHCP Configuration" section earlier).

To get a PXE boot to work on your workstation, you probably have to do a few things to your computer BIOS:

- **Check the BIOS** — Power up your computer and quickly press the key required to go into setup mode. It is probably something such as the Del, F1, or F2 function key.

- **Enable PXE** — Some computers will have a separate way of enabling or disabling PXE functionality. While you are checking BIOS settings, look for Network Boot or PXE Boot and make sure that it is enabled. If you have multiple NICs, you may also need to select which one to use as the PXE card.

- **Add PXE first in the boot order** — When a computer powers up, it checks the boot order set in the BIOS to determine how to start the operating system. Typically, it will check removable media (CD or floppy drive), and then the computer's hard disk to find a bootable operating system. To use PXE, you need to set PXE as the first boot device in the BIOS.

With the BIOS properly set, save the changes and continue the boot process. If everything is working properly, you should see a series of messages that show PXE sending out a DHCP request, gathering IP address information, downloading the bootstrap file, and starting up the Linux kernel that will drive your local display.

Note The bootstrap file used with the release of LTSP included with this book is called `pxelinux.0`. In the `/etc/dhcpd.conf` file, it is identified as `/lts/2.4.26-ltsp-2/pxelinux.0` (although, because `tftpd` operates in a chroot environment, it is actually located in the `/tftpboot/lts/2.4.26-ltsp-2` directory). The `pxelinux.0` file is only 16KB. If you tried to load the `vmlinuz` file directly (which is 1.9MB), you would get an error message from TFTPD, telling you that the files are too large.

Given the way that you configured the LTSP server earlier in this chapter, you should boot directly to a login screen. Log in using a user account added earlier. You can then work from the workstation as though it were directly connected to the server. Instead of seeing the files and devices on the workstation as you work, your view will be as though you were working from the server.

Booting Workstations Using Etherboot

Instead of booting from a bootstrap file downloaded from the server (as with PXE), you can create a boot image for starting the boot process. The Etherboot project (`www.etherboot.org`) offers software that you can use to create the boot image you need to start your LTSP workstations from a CD or floppy.

You can create Etherboot ROM images from the `www.ROM-o-matic.net` Web site. The following procedure can be used to create a floppy disk or CD Etherboot image (based on instructions from the `www.ROM-o-matic.net` site):

1. **ROM-o-matic.net.** Open the `www.ROM-o-matic.net` Web site from your browser and select the link to the latest production release (I used Etherboot 5.4.0). You will see a page for dynamically generating an Etherboot ROM image.

2. **Choose NIC.** The ROM image must contain the PCI ID of your network interface card, so the proper driver can be added to the image. You can determine the NIC in your computer using the `lspci` command (assuming that either Linux is running or that you can boot a Linux Live CD such as the *Linux Toys II* CD). Here's how:

   ```
   # lspci -n | grep 200
   02:06.0 Class 0200: 10ec:8139 (rev 10)
   ```

   The `lspci` command lists information about PCI cards on your system. Most supported NICs appear as Class 0200. The identifier after the class number identifies the family (10ec for a RealTek NIC) and the specific identifier (8139 for the RLT8139 Fast Ethernet controller). Use the number that was output for your card and select it in the NIC/ROM box.

3. **ROM format.** You can output the ROM as a bootable ISO image (that can be used on CD, DVD, or floppy medium) or zdsk (that can be used to produce a floppy image). There are other formats available as well. I used "Floppy bootable ROM Image (.zdsk)" to create a boot floppy and "ISO bootable image without legacy floppy emulation (.iso)" to create a CD/DVD image.

4. **Customize ROM (optional).** You have the option to customize a few dozen settings on your ROM. I used the defaults (which worked fine in my case), but it doesn't hurt to look through them before proceeding to the next step.

5. **Generate ROM.** Select the Get ROM button to create and download the ROM image. When asked, indicate where to download the ROM. The name of the image I created when I generated a floppy and CD-ROM reflected that each image is an Etherboot image (eb), the version number (5.2.6), the NIC (rt18139), and the disk format (iso or zdsk). Your image names will differ but still reflect the same type of information.

6. **Copy ROM to medium.** You need to copy the ROM from your disk to the medium you created it for. To create a boot floppy, insert a blank floppy disk into the floppy drive. Then type the following to copy the ROM image to floppy disk (your ROM image name and floppy device might be different):

```
$ cat eb-5.2.6-rt18139.zdsk > /dev/fd0
```

To copy a boot image to CD or DVD, use the `cdrecord` command. Insert the appropriate disk into your CD or DVD writer and type the following (your ROM image name and CD/DVD writer device might be different):

```
$ cdrecord -data /dev/hdb - eb-5.2.6-rt18139.iso
```

As with the PXE boot, you need to be sure that your computer can boot from the medium you just created. It's quite possible that the workstation is already configured to boot from floppy or CD, so you may not have to do anything to the BIOS. Just reboot and wait for the login screen to appear.

Troubleshooting the Workstations

After login, think of it as though you are running from the monitor on the server. You will use the server's processor to run programs and see the server's file system. The small Linux kernel that is running on the workstation is there primarily to make sure the X Window System (in other words, the most basic part of your GUI) is running properly. Everything else comes across the network from the server.

After you have your workstation set up to use PXE or Etherboot booting, most of the preferences relating to how your desktop is arranged, how your files are organized, and how you launch and manage applications can all be done from the workstation by using the desktop. In fact, given proper permission (such as access to the root user account), you could also make changes to the server or to your LTSP client configuration from any client workstation.

The proof of whether your LTSP configuration is working or not comes from booting a workstation, logging in, and running an application from the desktop. If you can't do that, here are some things you can try:

- **Check the hardware** — You need to make sure that all your hardware is properly connected. In its most basic form, you can simply connect all your workstations and server to a single switch. From each workstation, run the `ping` command (available in both Linux and from a DOS window in Windows) to the server's IP address. If you can't reach the server, you need to configure your network interfaces before continuing.

- **Can't boot PXE** — If you are trying a PXE boot and your computer keeps bypassing it and going to the hard disk to boot, try these steps:

  - Recheck the BIOS to see that PXE is enabled and booting first.

  - Consider whether your NIC supports PXE.

  - Check that you are plugged into your LAN. If you see a message that mentions PXE and shows your MAC address, PXE is probably working.

- **Can't boot Etherboot** — With an Etherboot boot from floppy or CD, you should see a `Loading ROM image` message and then `Etherboot 5.4.0 (GPL)....` If you don't see those messages, you may have a bad CD or floppy, or your machine may not be set to boot from that media (check the BIOS). The next issue is that you may have chosen the wrong driver for your NIC, in which case, the boot might stall after the message: `Probing PCI NIC`. Build a new Etherboot image and try to pick the correct NIC driver (or get a new NIC if there is no driver for your card).

- **DHCP failure** — If the boot stalls when your workstation starts searching for a DHCP server, check the server to make sure the DHCP service is running. Because I suggested individual DHCP entries for each workstation, make sure that the MAC address for your NIC exactly matches the entry in the server's `dhcpd.conf` file (in particular, make sure you didn't put the letter "O" when you need the number "0").

- **TFTP failure** — Make sure the TFTP service is enabled on the server. For a PXE boot, LTSP needs to be configured on the server to provide a tiny bootstrap file (`pxelinux.0`). If you try to load the larger kernel directly (`vmlinuz`), it will fail with a `TFTP files too large` message. Change the `/etc/dhcpd.conf` file so that the correct file is indicated for the workstation you are trying to boot.

- **NFS mount failure** — If you see a message that includes `...opt/ltsp/i386 on /mnt failed`, for some reason your workstation is not able to mount the NFS resource. Check that the NFS service is configured (as described earlier) and running on the server. If NFS is running, the server's firewall may be blocking you from doing the mount, or your particular workstation may be blocked in the `/etc/hosts.allow` or `/etc/hosts.deny` file.

- **Graphical interface fails** — If you see a bunch of X11 failure messages, it means that the X Window System process failed to start on the workstation. LTSP was probably unable to detect the video card on the client. (Remember that the video card on the server is not relevant because X is running on the client. In fact, the server doesn't even need to have a video card.)

In the several video cards I tried, only the NVidia card was not autodetected (although I'm sure there are others that will also not work automatically). For the NVidia card, I added a the line `XSERVER = nv` to the station definition in the `lts.conf` file. If you need to further configure your X server, refer to the documentation at the ltsp.com site.

- **No graphical login screen** — If you see a gray screen with an X mouse pointer, your X server is running, but the graphical login screen is not. Make sure that the XDMCP service is enabled on the server.

- **Trouble logging in to server** — At this point, we are into basic Linux stuff. Make sure that you have added a user account to the server and have assigned it a password. After you have successfully logged in, you can use the controls that come with your Linux system's desktop environment to adjust the look and feel of that interface.

 Note Don't change a workstation's video card settings from the workstation. Make those changes to the `lts.conf` file on the server instead on behalf of the workstation. Changing the `/etc/X11/xorg.conf` file from a workstation using a tool such as system-config-display can result in X not being able to start on the server (because the workstation's and not the server's video card will be configured).

Again, I suggest using the ltsp.org site for documentation if you have further problems. In particular, look for settings you can add to the `lts.conf` files that are specific to the workstation you are using.

Expanding on LTSP

After following the instruction so far in this chapter, you should have a fairly efficient set of workstations running off your server. Once you log in, your session from each workstation should look exactly as if you were logging in to the monitor that is directly connected to the server itself.

Because you directly log into the server, after the workstations are up and running, there is no need for special configuration between the clients and server. Standard Linux user permissions will allow users to share files, printers, an Internet connection, and any hardware configured on the server, without special server settings.

To wrap up this chapter, I've added some ways to extend your LTSP project. They include the following:

- **Drawing more from each workstation** — You are actually running a separate, small Linux operating system on each workstation (which, for the most part, should be invisible to you). The section "Playing with Local Workstation Features" suggests some opportunities for drawing further on your workstations' processors and hardware. You can have more applications than just the X server running locally on your workstation and you can take advantage of printers and other hardware connected there.

- **Locking down workstations as kiosks** — A common use of thin clients is to lock them down as controlled, special-use stations for a specific application. One such application is to run each workstation as a Web browser kiosk, allowing only a browser window to run at each workstation, serving up a limited set of content. The section "Using Workstations in Schools and Public Places" describes some efforts to use LTSP workstations as public kiosks.

Playing with Local Workstation Features

If your client workstations are capable of handling more than an X server, why not take advantage of that? Here are a few things you can do to add printers and applications directly to your workstation.

Getting to Your Workstation's Operating System

If you want to open up the inner workings of your workstation, you can add LTSP "screen scripts" to open shell access to that workstation. Using screen scripts, you can open additional virtual terminals on the workstation that give you a view of the local system.

By default, only one screen is open on each workstation, based on this entry in the `lts.conf` file `Default` section:

```
SCREEN_01  = startx
```

You can add an additional `SCREEN_??` entry in a workstation section to allow you to open a shell on that workstation. For example, to have the second virtual terminal on the workstation named station003 that can open to a shell, you could add an entry as follows:

```
[station003]
    SCREEN_02   = shell
```

Because `SCREEN_01` is the GUI, I used the `SCREEN_02` line to be able to open a shell from the second virtual terminal on the workstation (press Ctrl+Alt+F2 on the workstation to see a shell prompt and Ctrl+Alt+F1 to go back to the GUI). In this arrangement, while SCREEN_01 give you a view of the server system (files, directories, processes, devices, and so on), SCREEN_02 lets you view processes and files on the local file system. The second view shows you the limited Linux system running locally in RAM (type **ps ax**), providing just enough features to allow the GUI framework (X Window System) to run.

Besides "shell" there are also ways of having a virtual terminal open to other types of sessions. You can open a telnet session (SCREEN_02 = `telnet hostname`) or log in to a windows server (SCREEN_02 = `rdesktop -f hostname`).

Using a Workstation Printer

LTSP also includes features for connecting a printer to your local workstation and making that available to all the workstations in your LTSP group (if you choose). The workstation operating system includes a utility called lp_server to add print server capability to the workstation. Here's how you set that up:

1. Connect your printer hardware to your workstation.

2. On the server, add entries for `PRINTER_0_DEVICE` and `PRINTER_0_TYPE` to the definition for the workstation in the `lts.conf` file. For example, to add a printer to station002 that is connected to the first parallel port on the workstation, you could enter the following:

```
[station002]
    PRINTER_0_DEVICE = /dev/lp0
    PRINTER_0_TYPE = P
```

The lp_server daemon will listen on port 9100 for printing requests from the server. To the server, it will appear as a JetDirect printer (a type of printer that can be connected directly to a TCP/IP LAN).

3. On the server, configure the printer as a JetDirect printer. From a Fedora or other Red Hat Linux system, open the Printer Configuration window (Desktop ➜ System Settings ➜ Printing). Then, configure a JetDirect printer. During that process, you need to add the workstation's IP address or host name and identify port 9100 as the printer port.

4. To add up to three printers to a workstation (provided you have available ports), you can add more entries to lts.conf. Set the second printer to PRINTER_1_DEVICE and PRINTER_1_TYPE and the second device as /dev/lp1 (and so on).

Running Applications from the Workstation

If your workstation still has some juice after running the local X server, you can add other applications to run locally. This can be particularly useful for applications that might place extraordinary demands on your LAN or that could gain from accessing local hardware (such as a microphone or speakers). These can also be a bit of a pain to set up because the LTSP operating system running on the workstation is not configured to support multiple users and applications.

The steps for adding local applications to your LTSP workstations are detailed in the Local Applications section of the LTSP manual (www.ltsp.org/documentation). Here are the general steps you need to follow:

1. **Share user information.** Because each workstation's operating system has no concept of regular users (only administrative logins), you need to add a user environment to be loaded on the workstation. That requires sharing user information by configuring a service called NIS. That information is then identified in the server's lts.conf file (LOCAL_APPS, NIS_DOMAIN, and NIS_Server entries).

2. **Share home directories.** The LTSP workstation also has no /home directories, so use NFS to mount /home from the server.

3. **Set up applications.** Because the operating system on each workstation is started using the file system from the /opt/ltsp directory structure, applications have to be added to that directory structure before they can run. Again, because this is a reduced operating system, you might also need to add more device drivers and libraries, along with the applications themselves. Because the workstation's architecture can be different from the server's architecture, you might need to compile the applications for the workstation and then add them to a local directory (such as /opt/ltsp/i386/usr/local/, which will show up on the workstation simply as /usr/local).

4. **Run applications.** When you log in from the GUI at an LTSP workstation, your view is of the server's operating system. An application run locally on the workstation, conversely, views the local hardware, file system, and processes. Now, this is a good thing, if

you want to use the workstation's sound system or hardware. To launch a local application from the workstation, however, the LTSP project recommends using a remote execution program such as rsh or ssh to run the application. That requires enabling rshd or sshd on the workstation (which they are not set up to do by default).

Essentially, by setting up LTSP to run applications from the workstation, you are asking it to do something it wasn't really designed to do. If you are configuring the server so that the work of setting up one set of users and applications can be spread across multiple workstations, the effort might be worth it. If you have one workstation you want to set up and it has a hard disk, you might consider just installing its own Linux system.

Note With the LTSP project running on a few old PCs I pulled from the closet, my personal on-going project is to make the workstations into communications centers and plant them around my home. To make the stations, I plan to add microphones, speakers, and Web cams to each one. Then I'll use applications such as GAIM (instant messenger) and GnomeMeeting (video conferencing) to communicate among the different stations. My wife cringes a bit when I tell her about it.

Using Workstations in Schools and Public Places

While the "playing" features I described involve adding features to your thin client workstations, configuring an LTSP workstation as school workstations or in kiosk mode mostly involves taking features away. Also, if kiosks are going to be used in public places, they need to be secured (both physically and in terms of the software they can run).

Libraries and schools, where budgets are often tight, have made excellent use of the LTSP project to create specialized workstations so they can continue to use old or low-cost hardware. Here is some information about LTSP-related projects used in libraries and schools:

- **K12LTSP.org** — This project created a custom version of Fedora Core for configuring LTSP servers and workstations that are appropriate for schools.

- **Linux and Library Web Kiosks** — This presentation by Sam Deeljore at St. Louis University (www.ala.org/ala/lita/litaevents/2004Forum/PS_Linux_ Web_Kiosks.ppt) describes advantages of Linux and LTSP in libraries. (It's a PowerPoint presentation, but it runs fine in OpenOffice.org.)

A Web browser is a natural application to run in kiosk mode. The idea is to configure your workstation clients once on the server, after which you can have lots of workstations that:

- Boot directly to the Web browser or other application in full-screen mode

- Restrict users from running different applications or otherwise accessing the operating system

- Display only a limited set of locations to restrict what the users can see

Here are a couple of projects aimed specifically at locking down Web browsers to operate in kiosk mode:

- **Kiosk Browser** (`http://tln.lib.mi.us/~amutch/pro/phoenix/kiosk.htm`) — Describes work done by Andrew Mutch to modify the Firefox Web browser to operate in Kiosk mode. This effort has been used in library online catalogs (including the Chattanooga-Hamilton County Bicentennial Library).

- **Kiosk Using LTSP** (`www.edu.helsinki.fi/atk/ltsp_kiosk`) — Describes work by Matti Lattu to create a Web Kiosk based on Firefox, Linux, and the LTSP project. The site provides some good information for modifying XUL files to limit or enhance what your Firefox browser can do.

The key here is that, whether you want to add to or lock down your LTSP thin client software, by creating an environment on your LTSP server to support your workstations, that one configuration can be used to support as many workstations as your server can handle. All you have to do is boot up the workstation and go.

Summary

The Linux Terminal Server Project (ltsp.org) is one of the best open source projects for making use of old or inexpensive computer hardware. Configure an LTSP server to provide the software that workstations on your LAN need to boot. Multiple workstations can then all browse the Web, use email, write documents, or do thousands of other things you can do with Linux, through the LTSP server.

LTSP provides a way of centralizing the administration and resource allocations on one server. All the client workstation has to do is connect to the server over a LAN, boot up (using special PXE or Etherboot features), and log in. Using standard Linux user accounts, desktop applications, and configuration tools, users can operate their LTSP workstations as though they were working directly from the server's monitor and keyboard.

Once you understand the basic LTSP technology, you can enhance your LTSP server and workstations in various ways. A workstation can be configured to access a local printer or run local applications. Workstations can be locked down to provide special-use kiosks, for tasks such as Web browsing or library catalog searches. You can adapt and deploy your own specialized Linux distribution, as the K12LTSP.org project did when they created an LTSP-enabled distribution of Fedora Core suitable for schools.

Appendixes

Using the Linux Toys II CD

The software needed to create the *Linux Toys II* projects described in this book come from various open source projects, covered by the GPL or similar licenses. Most of the software you need is included on the CD that comes with *Linux Toys II*. The form that most of the software comes in includes:

> **RPM binary packages** — These are prebuilt binary packages that you can install on a Fedora or Red Hat Enterprise Linux system. In other words, just install the RPMs and start stepping through instructions in the chapter.

> **Source code tarballs** — These are compilations that include the source code for all necessary files for each chapter. In most cases, you must compile these files yourself to run on whatever Linux system you are using. Because of differences among Linux distributions, there is no guarantee that descriptions in this book will work exactly as written when you install from source code on a Linux distribution other than the ones we recommend.

> **Source code RPMs** — These include the source code associated with the binaries included with each RPM. You can use the source RPMs to rebuild RPM binaries yourself.

> **ISO images** — Some of the *Linux Toys II* projects can be booted or installed from ISO images included in the `isos/` directory on the *Linux Toys II* CD. An ISO image is a single file that typically includes a set of software, organized in a file system, that can be burned to a CD, DVD, or other removable medium. Often that image can be booted directly or used as a medium for installing software permanently in Linux.

Many of the projects require that you install a Linux operating system before you begin. I recommend Fedora Core or Red Hat Enterprise Linux because the prebuilt RPMs included with this book should just run on those systems without modification. However, most Linux systems should work fine, provided you can adapt to differences among Linux systems (such as different locations of configuration files and ways of starting services).

The purpose of this appendix is to describe how the software included with *Linux Toys II* is organized on the CD, tell you how to install that software for the projects contained in each chapter, and tell you how to get later versions of that software as it becomes available.

Using the Linux Toys II CD

The *Linux Toys II* CD contains a small, bootable Linux system and the software packages you need to create the projects described in this book. It can be used in one of two ways:

- **Install software from the CD** — With Linux running, you can insert the CD into your CD drive and install the software for each chapter to your Linux system (using the RPMs or tarballs).

- **Boot the CD directly** — You can insert the CD into your computer's CD drive and reboot the computer, to boot directly to a version of Linux called Damn Small Linux. With Damn Small Linux running, you can do the project described in Chapter 6 for configuring a custom pen drive. You can also run client software for some of the other projects described in this book.

To view the contents of the *Linux Toys II* CD, insert the CD into your computer's CD drive while the computer is running. In Fedora or RHEL, you should see an icon representing the CD on your desktop. Double-click the icon to display the contents of the CD in a folder window. Here's what you should see:

- **RPMS/** — The RPMS directory contains separate directories for each chapter in the book that requires software. Each chapter directory has the RPM files that are needed with that chapter and an installme file that can be run to install all the RPMs in that directory. Each RPM package ends in a .rpm suffix.

- **Sources/** — The Sources directory includes a directory for each chapter that contains the tarballs in tar/gzip format that are available. Each tarball ends in .tar.gz or .tgz suffixes. In most cases, you can use the tarballs to compile the software for each project from source code. In other cases, such as the Gallery project (see Chapter 3), the software is in a form where it doesn't need to be compiled. (In the case of Gallery, the software consists of perl scripts and HTML code.) You can also find some ISO images (for example, the eMoviX ISO image for Chapter 5) that can simply be burned to CD or other removable medium.

- **SRPMS/** — The SRPMS directory includes separate directories for each chapter that contain the source code needed to modify and rebuild RPM files. Each source RPM ends in a .src.rpm suffix.

- **isos/** — The isos directory contains ISO images used for several of the projects. For the eMoviX project I include the MoviX bootable media player. ISO images are also included for the LTSP and Devil-Linux projects.

- **KNOPPIX/** — The KNOPPIX directory contains the bootable image of Damn Small Linux. Other files needed to boot Damn Small Linux are contained in the isolinux directory. No installation is required to use the Damn Small Linux files from those directories (although the project in Chapter 6 describes how to install Damn Small Linux to a pen drive).

Decide which form of the software you want to use, and then proceed to the next section for general information on using the *Linux Toys II* software in different forms.

Installing from RPMs

Within each chapter directory is a file called installme. You can run the installme file for a chapter to install all the RPM files available for that chapter. For example, as root user from a Terminal window, you could install all RPM packages for Chapter 8 as follows:

```
# /media/cd*/RPMS/ch08*/installme
```

This action runs the rpm command to install each RPM file in the directory. The name of your CD drive (shown as cd*) may have any of several names (cdrom, cdrecorder, and so on). Instead of installing all RPMs for a chapter at once, you could instead use the rpm command directly:

```
# cd /media/cd*/RPMS/ch08*
# rpm -Uhv *.rpm
```

Using the rpm command directly, you can also pick and choose which RPMs to install. The installme script will simply force all RPMs to be installed.

If you want to see information about any of the RPMs, you can query an RPM using the -q option. For example, to see information about the BZFlag RPM that comes with this book (see Chapter 8), type the following:

```
# rpm -qi bzflag
```

If you decide later you want to remove an RPM package, you can use the -e option. For example, to remove the bzflag RPM, type the following:

```
# rpm -e bzflag
```

Installing from tarballs

The tarballs included on the *Linux Toys II* CD can include several different types of files. If a tarball contains the source code for the project, an INSTALL or README file included in the tarball will describe exactly how to install the contents of the tarball. That procedure typically includes the following:

- Using the tar command to unzip and extract the files from the CD to a directory on your hard disk
- Running a configure command to configure the software
- Running one or more make commands to compile and install the software

Each package can be a little different in how it wants you to create and install its components. Therefore, I recommend that you copy the expanded tar archive file to a directory, then go to that directory and look for the INSTALL or README file for specific instructions on how to proceed. If there are any specific instructions you need for installing the project from a tarball, they will be included in the chapter that describes that project.

The following is a general procedure that you should run as root user from a Terminal window to unzip and extract the files for a particular project. In this example, the tarball is named *whatever.tar.gz* and is located in the sources/ directory on the CD.

1. Insert the *Linux Toys II* CD in your computer's CD drive.

2. If the CD doesn't mount automatically (which it should), mount it by typing something like the following (your drive may have a slightly different name):

   # **mount /media/cdrecorder**

3. Create a directory where you want to put the source code and change it to:

   # **mkdir ~/LinuxToys**
   # **cd ~/LinuxToys**

4. Unzip and extract the source code from the tarball as follows:

   # **tar xvfz /media/cdrecorder/sources/*whatever.tar.gz***

5. Change to the directory created by the tar command and read through the INSTALL or README file for further instructions:

   # **cd ~/LinuxToys/*whatever***
   # **less INSTALL**

Typical instructions for compiling and installing from source code include ./configure, make, and make install. As I said, however, instructions vary from project to project. You will be expected to have a compiler (gcc) and the make command (such as gmake) to build the binary utilities you need from source code.

Installing from SRPMs

The CD includes the source code RPM (SRPM) for each binary RPM package included with *Linux Toys II*. You can install these SRPMs using a standard rpm command (for example, rpm -Uhv *whatever.src.rpm*). However, instead of placing commands, config files, and directories on your system to use, the rpm command places the source code files in subdirectories of the /usr/src directory. You can then modify the source code as you please and rebuild a new RPM and/or SRPM file that includes your changes using the rpmbuild command.

There are a few ways to go about rebuilding SRPMs into binary RPM packages. If you simply want to rebuild a binary package from the SRPM, without changing any of the source code, you can do the following:

$ **rpmbuild --rebuild *whatever-1.1.src.rpm***

To change an SRPM and rebuild an RPM from those changes requires additional setup and is beyond the scope of this book. However, if you are interested in trying it yourself, refer to the RPM-HOWTO (`www.rpm.org/RPM-HOWTO/build.html`) for further information.

Finding Software for Each Chapter

Each chapter contains details on how to install the software from the *Linux Toys II* CD needed to build each project. This section describes how the software packages for each chapter are organized on this CD.

Because open source software is constantly being updated and improved, you should look for updates to that software. The following sections also describe where to look for updated packages from the primary open source projects used in each chapter.

Chapter 3: Gallery

For the Gallery project, I've included the original tarball directly from that project. You can find it in the `Sources/ch03-gallery` directory. Because nothing needs to be compiled for this project, starting the project is as simple an unpacking that project to a directory that's accessible to your Web server.

The Gallery software featured in Chapter 3 is available from the Gallery Web site. From the project's home page (`http://gallery.sourceforge.net`), select the link to Download Now! I strongly recommend keeping up on updates for Gallery, or any other project where the software will be exposed to the Internet or other network.

Chapter 4: MythTV

Prebuilt RPMs for MythTV are available from the ATRPMS.net repository, which you can access via the Fedora Myth(TV)ology page (`http://wilsonet.com/mythtv`). To get source code, try the `www.mythtv.org` site. Look for the Downloads link.

On the CD, Check the directories `RPMS/ch04-mythtv` and `SRPMS/ch04-mythtv` for `README` files that describe the RPM situation for this project.

Chapter 5: eMoviX

Check the `RPMS/ch05-emovix` directory for RPMS you can use with the eMoviX project for creating and playing video content, as well as the emovix RPM itself. An ISO image for creating your own bootable, standalone MoviX2 player is contained in the `isos/ch05/emovix/movix2*` directory.

Check for new versions of eMoviX from the MoviX SourceForge.net site (`http://sourceforge.net/projects/movix/`).

Chapter 6: Damn Small Linux

An actual Damn Small Linux distribution is used as the basis for the bootable portions of the *Linux Toys II* CD. Components of Damn Small Linux are included in the KNOPPIX and boot/ directories on the *Linux Toys II* CD. However, several image files (.iso, .img, and .zip) are included in the isos/ch06-damnsmall directory so that you can configure the project in various ways.

To get a later version of Damn Small Linux, refer to the Damn Small Linux home page (www.damnsmalllinux.org). Go to the download page to find a list of DSL mirror sites (www.damnsmalllinux.org/download.html).

Chapter 7: Heyu and BottleRocket

RPMs for Heyu and BottleRocket software described in Chapter 7 are contained in the RPMS/ch07-x10 directory. Software in other forms for the X10 projects is included in the Sources/ch07-x10 directory.

The latest versions of Heyu version 2 are available from the Heyu home page (www.heyu.org). For updated BottleRocket software, check the BottleRocket home page (http://mlug .missouri.edu/~tymm).

Chapter 8: BZFlag

Get RPMs for the BZFlag project in the RPMS/ch08-bzflag directory on the *Linux Toys II* CD. There is also source code available in the Sources/ch08-bzflag directory.

To find official later versions of BZFlag software, check the SourceForge.net BZFlag project page (http://sourceforge.net/projects/bzflag). For unofficial packages of BGFlag in various formats, see the BZFlag WIKI (http://bzflag.org/wiki/Download).

Chapter 9: Devil-Linux

Devil-Linux comes on a single disk image that is included on the *Linux Toys II* CD. You can find it in the isos/ch09-firewall directory.

You can replace the existing Devil-Linux firewall distribution as it becomes available. From the Devil-Linux home page (www.devil-linux.org), select the Downloads link.

Chapter 10: Icecast

RPMs for the Icecast project, and related software, are included in the RPMS/ch10-icecast directory on the *Linux Toys II* CD.

Follow the links from http://xiph.org to find Icecast software downloads. Refer to Chapter 10 for information on how to get third-party client software that you can use with Icecast.

Chapter 11: Linux Terminal Server Project

Software for the Linux Terminal Server Project is in the RPMS/ch11-terminalserver and Sources/ch11-terminalserver directories. If you don't have an Internet connection, you can use the ISO image included in the isos/ch11-terminalserver directory (which contains all software needed for the project).

Check http://ltsp.org for the latest software available for the Linux Terminal Server Project.

Customer Care

If you are having trouble with the CD-ROM, please call the Wiley Product Technical Support phone number: (800) 762-2974. Outside the United States, call 1(317) 572-3994. You can also contact Wiley Product Technical Support through the internet at http://support.wiley .com. Wiley Publishing will provide technical support only for installation and other general quality control items. For technical support on the applications themselves, consult the program's vendor or author.

To place additional orders or to request information about other Wiley products, please call (877) 762-2974.

Summary

Software for *Linux Toys II* comes in different forms. You can install from RPMs, SRPMs, or tarballs. Some of the projects also include ISO images you can use. Continue to check project Web sites for information on the latest updates available for each project.

ABCs of Using Linux

While I try to make the *Linux Toys II* projects as foolproof as possible, there's going to be a time when file permissions are wrong, a piece of hardware isn't detected properly, or a server just plain doesn't work. For those times, you're going to have break out of our step-by-step procedures and get around in Linux yourself.

Because I recognize that everyone who buys *Linux Toys II* is not a Linux expert, I've devoted this appendix to giving you some basics on using Linux. These basics are not purely introductory-level Linux commands and concepts. Instead they cover features that will help you use, troubleshoot, and enhance your Linux Toys projects.

If you are brand new to Linux, stepping through this whole appendix is a good place to start. Beyond this appendix, I recommend that you consider getting a more complete, general Linux book that will cover commands, administration, services, and other Linux features in more depth. *Red Hat Linux Bible* (the latest edition is titled *Red Hat Fedora and Enterprise Linux 4 Bible*) is a good place to start if you are using any Red Hat Linux system. *Linux Bible, 2005 Edition* covers a broader range of Linux distributions and will help you select a Linux distribution and start working with it.

Note If you don't currently have a Linux system installed on a computer, you can try the shell commands described in this chapter by booting the CD that comes with this book to Damn Small Linux (DSL). Because DSL contains a reduced set of Linux features, you will have to do a permanent install of Fedora Core (or other Linux) to use some of the graphical administrative tools described here.

Using the Shell

The Linux shell is the most basic way of working with a Linux system. While not every Linux system offers a graphical interface, they all offer a shell interface. Once you learn to run commands, get around the file system, and deal with administrative tasks from the shell, you have skills that are useful for any Linux and UNIX system that you encounter.

You may see a shell prompt when you login (if you don't boot to a graphical interface). If not, to get to a shell you can open a Terminal window from a graphical interface by clicking the right mouse button and selecting Terminal Window or Xterm from that menu (or XShells from Damn Small Linux). The following two examples show what your command line prompt might look like:

```
[chris@mycomputer ~]$
```

or

```
[root@mycomputer tmp]#
```

A dollar sign ($) at the end of a command line prompt indicates that you are logged in as a regular user. A pound sign (#) shows you are logged in as the root user (also often referred to as the *super user*). The command line prompt is configurable. However, the information contained in these examples is typical for many Linux systems. Your current user name and computer name are separated by an @ character (chris@mycomputer). That's followed by the name of the current directory. A ~ indicates the user's home directory (which is /home/chris in the first case). Otherwise, you will just see the name of the current directory (in the second example, the current directory is /tmp).

A full install of a typical Linux system can offer more than 3000 user commands and nearly 1000 administrative commands. But don't worry. For the most part, you can get started with a couple dozen commands.

Tips for Using Commands

Before I start showing some commands, here are a few tips to help you understand how to use Linux commands:

- **man pages** — If you ever want to find out more about a command (or for that matter, a configuration file, programming function, system call, device name, or most other Linux components), you should try reading man (short for manual) pages. Man pages were used to document the first UNIX systems and continue to be the way that Linux command line and programming components are documented today.

  The downside of man pages is that you need to know what you are looking for and they don't typically lead you through a whole task. So they are best used as a way of learning or remembering particular options for a command. For example, if you just want to know what option to use with the df command to view how much disk space you have available, you can type:

  ```
  # man df
  ```

Note   Man pages aren't included with Damn Small Linux. However, if you have a connection to the Internet, running man in Damn Small Linux will get the man page you request from the Internet.

■ **Finding commands** — Sometimes you will type a command and get an error message such as:

```
bash: whatever: command not found
```

Two common reasons why this may happen are that the software was not installed, or the command is not in your path. To solve the first problem, you have to install the software package containing the command. (Appendix A explains how to install Linux software.) The second problem requires a bit more explanation.

When you type a command, the shell looks for that command in a set of predefined directories called your *path*. You can see what directories are in your path by typing:

```
$ echo $PATH
/usr/local/bin:/bin:/usr/bin:/usr/X11R6/bin:/home/chris/bin
```

This is an example of a PATH for a regular user (in this case, chris). If you were to simply type the date command, the shell would first look in the /usr/local/bin directory then the /bin directory (where it would find the date command and run it). In other words, the shell will go from left to right, checking each directory in your path until the command is found.

On occasion, a software package will put a command in a non-standard location. If a command is not in your path (or if it appears in more than one directory), you can type the full path to run the command, for example, /bin/date. Or, you can add a directory to your path. For example, to add the directory /opt/bin to your path, add this line to the .bashrc file in your home directory:

```
export PATH=/opt/bin:$PATH
```

Many administrative commands are not in the path of a regular user, since they are intended for the root user. If you run echo $PATH as the root user, you will see /sbin and /usr/sbin directories in the root user's path, in addition to those in the regular user's path. (Unlike in other Linux systems, in Damn Small Linux, you will see all major directories in your PATH, but only be able to use administrative commands as root user or by running sudo, as described later.)

Besides commands that sit in directories on your computer, there are also shell built-in commands (such as cd, pwd, and echo), aliases, and functions. Those items will override any commands in your path directories. For example, the rm command is often aliased as rm -i, to cause you to be prompted to confirm each file before removing it.

Here are a few ways to find out the commands that are available:

```
$ alias
$ man builtins
$ type mount
```

The alias command shows any aliases that are set. The man builtins shows a list and descriptions of shell built-in commands. The type command shows the location of any command you give it as an argument (in this case, it will shown that the mount command is in /bin/mount).

- **Use command completion** — Using command completion can save you a bunch of typing. By typing part of a command and pressing the Tab key, bash will try to complete the rest of the command from the commands it finds in your path, aliases and shell builtins. If there is potentially more than one command that could be used to complete what you have typed, press Tab again and the shell displays all possible values. For example:

```
$ us<Tab><Tab>
usbview      usermount    users     ustar
userinfo     userpasswd   usleep
$ us
```

The output here shows that there are seven commands in the user's path that begin with the letters us. At this point, you could type a few more letters and hit Tab again, or simply type the command name you want. Completion is also available for directories (type /var/sp<Tab> to complete the /var/spool directory), user names (type ~ro<Tab> to complete the root user's home directory), and environment variables (type $PA<Tab> to complete the $PATH variable).

- **Recalling commands** — The bash shell keeps a history of the commands you have run with it. You can recall those commands in several different ways. This can be very handy, especially if you want to repeat a long command line. After you recall a command, you can edit it and run it again. Here's an example of the history command for displaying some of your command history:

```
$ history 5
968  cd /usr/sbin
969  ls | wc
970  man mount
971  pwd
972  tail -f /var/log/messages
```

The number following the history command determines how many of the most recent commands you want to see (here, you see the five most recent). Simply typing history displays your entire history list.

There are a few different ways you can run a previous command. Use an exclamation mark (!), to refer to command lines from your history by number or by position in the list. Here are a few examples:

```
$ !968
$ !-5
$ !!
```

The first example (!968) runs the 968th command line in your history list. The next example (!-5) runs the command line you ran five commands ago. The last example (!!) repeats the previous command you ran.

Step through your command history using the up and down arrows. With the command you want to run displayed, use the right and left arrows to move to any part of the command line you want to change. After making your edits to the command, press Enter to run the modified command.

Moving among Files and Directories

The Linux file system is represented by a hierarchy of directories and files, each level of which is separated by a slash (/). The root of the file system (not to be mistaken for the root user) is simply a / mark.

Major directories below the root are /etc (which contains configuration files), /home (which contains user directories), /bin and /sbin (which contain commands), /dev (which contains device files for accessing hardware), and /var (which hold changeable system data). The home directory for the root user is /root. Temporary files can be put in the /tmp directory. There are other directories at the root level as well, but we'll start with these.

As you begin using Linux, you will use your home directory (for example, if your user name were chris, your home directory would be /home/chris) to store most of your personal data. Most configuration files you need to change are in the /etc directory. To set up a public server, you would put data in /var/www (Web server), /var/ftp/pub (FTP server), /var/mail (mail server), or /var/named (Domain name system server), to name a few.

To familiarize yourself with the Linux files system, you should try running some file system commands. Here are some common commands for moving around the Linux file system and working with files and directories:

```
$ echo $HOME
/home/chris
```

The echo command can be used to display an environment variable or just a string of characters. In this case, by echoing the value of $HOME, you can see that the current user's home directory is /home/chris. The home directory of a regular user is typically in the /home directory under the user's name. The /root directory is typically the root user's home. To change to a directory, you can use the cd command. Here are examples:

```
$ cd
$ cd /tmp
$ cd /usr/share/doc
$ cd /var/log
$ cd public_html
$ cd -
$ cd ..
```

The cd command with no options takes you to your home directory. An option beginning with a slash (/) indicates that it is the full path to the directory you want (/tmp, /usr/share/doc, and /var/log). With no beginning slash, the option is assumed to be a relative path (so if you were in /home/chris, the command cd public_html would move you to /home/chris/public_html). A dash (-) option take you to the previous directory and two dots (..) takes you to the directory above the current directory.

Type this to see your current directory:

```
$ pwd
```

To refer to your home directory, or a subdirectory of your home directory, you can refer to either $HOME or a tilde character (~). For example, either of the two commands could be used to go to the public_html directory in your home directory (for example, /home/chris/ public_html):

```
$ cd $HOME/public_html
$ cd ~/public_html
```

Listing Files and Directories

The ls command lists the contents of a directory. For example, to show a short list the contents of your home directory, a long list, and a list that also includes hidden files (that begin with a dot), change to your home directory and type the following:

```
$ cd ~
$ ls
$ ls -l
$ ls -a
```

You can display your file listing in many different ways using options available for ls. For example, -t sorts files by the time they were last modified, -C lists files in columns, and -S lists files by size. Often, you will use options together (for example, ls -lS lets you sort files by size and show the actual size, along with other information about each file).

Creating and Removing Files and Directories

You can create a new directory using the mkdir command. For example:

```
$ mkdir ~/mydocs/
```

The result is a directory named mydocs in your home directory. You could remove that directory (provided it were empty) by typing:

```
$ rmdir ~/mydocs/
```

If the directory were not empty, you could use a command such as the following to remove it and its contents:

```
$ rm -rf ~/mydocs/
```

To remove a file, you can simply use the rm command. For example:

```
$ rm ~/myfile
```

To rename a file or directory (or actually, move it to a different name), use the mv command as follows:

```
$ mv ~/README.txt ~/README_SHELL.txt
```

To make a copy of a file, use the cp command as follows:

```
$ cp ~/README_SHELL.txt /tmp
```

Understanding File and Directory Permissions

Every file and directory in a Linux system is assigned a set of permissions. Those permissions define what the user who owns the file, the group assigned to the file, and anyone else who has access to the file can do with it. There are three type of permissions assigned to the user/group/other for a file:

- **read** — Read permission defines whether or not the person has permission to view the contents of the file or directory.

- **write** — Write permission determines if the person is allowed to change or delete the contents of the file or directory.

- **execute** — Execute permission means different things to files and directories. A file with execute permission can be run as a program. A directory with execute permission can be accessed (for example, without execute permission, you could not make a directory your current directory).

You can see the permissions on a file or directory using the ls command with the -l (long list) option. For example:

```
$ ls -l $HOME
drwxr-xr-x   1 chris      sales      4096 Jun 10 21:17 Desktop
-rw-rw-r--   1 chris      sales      4096 Jun 15 02:05 phone.txt
```

This output shows that there is a directory called Desktop and a file called phone.txt. Besides showing whether the item is a directory (d), file (-), character device such as a terminal (c), block device such as a hard disk (b), or some other type of component, the first set of letters and dashes indicates the permissions associate with the item.

The last nine bits of the permission section are split into three parts: owner, group and other. For the Desktop directory shown above, you can see that the owner (chris) has full read/write/execute permission on the directory (rwx). The group (sales) has only read and execute permission (r-x), allowing anyone in the sales group to change to that directory and view its contents (the dash indicates that write permission is not turned on). All other users who have access to the computer also have read/execute permissions to the directory.

As for the file phone.txt, the owner can read (view the contents) or write (change or delete) the file (rw-). Those who belong to the sales group also have read/write permission to the file. All others, however, can only view the contents of the file, but not change it.

While this type of permissions make your system more secure by doing such things as preventing a normal user from destroying critical system files, it also can sometimes make things fail that you don't want to fail. Here are permission issues you should look out for:

- **Can't run a program** — You try to run a program and it fails with a permission error, such as unable to lock password file or can't create transaction lock. Chances are you are trying to run a program as a regular user that requires root access. To run the command, you probably need to gain root access (as described in the "Administering Linux" section later in this chapter).

- **Can't find a program** — You might create a program, put it in a directory in your path (such as `/usr/local/bin`), and try to run it, only to get a message that the command was not found. This could be caused by the program not having its execute bit turned on. The shell will only find programs, even if they are in your path, that have the execute bit set. You'll have to add execute permission.

- **Others can't access content** — In order for someone to be able to change to a directory you own and access your files, you need to have execute permission set on that directory in a way that it can be used by those you want to access it. For example, if you create a `/home/chris/public_html` directory for a user to upload content to your Web server, if execute permission is not on so that the apache user can access the directory, you may find that your Web server can't display the content.

  Likewise, if you are setting up a user account and find that the user can't access a file or directory, make sure that any files you put in that user's directory are not owned by root. For example, if you want to create a `/home/chris/public_html` directory for a user while logged in as root, you can change the ownership and permissions to it as follows (changing `chris` to the user name you are using and `sales` to an appropriate group):

  ```
  # chown chris:sales /home/chris/public_html
  # chmod 755 /home/chris/public_html
  ```

As I've just shown, the `chown` command can be used to change ownership and `chmod` can be used to change the permissions of a file or directory. With `chown` you can simply change ownership (`chris`) or follow the owner name with a group name to set that as well (`chris:sales`). In Red Hat Linux systems, each user has a default group name that is the same as the user name (for example, `chris:chris`). You can create more groups by adding them to the `/etc/groups` file.

The owner/group/other permission on files and directories can be assigned by numbers or by using letters. The number 777 represents full permission on a file; no permissions on a file would be 000. You can figure out the number to set by adding up the numbers for each read/write/execute set. Here's a visual representation:

```
Owner  Group  Other
r w x  r w x  r w x
4 2 1  4 2 1  4 2 1
```

So, for example, to make a directory fully accessible to a user, but only executable to group and other, you would set permissions to 711. A file that was read/write enabled for owner and group, but only readable everyone could be set to 664. Common permission settings are 755 for directories and 644 for files. This essentially makes everything accessible to everyone to access, but only accessible for the owner to change. Here are some examples of `chmod` commands using numbers to set permissions:

```
$ touch test1 test2 test3
$ mkdir dir1 dir2
$ chmod 711 test1
$ chmod 000 test2
$ chmod 644 test3
```

```
$ chmod 777 dir1
$ chmod 700 dir2
$ ls -ld test* dir*
drwxrwxrwx  2 chris chris 4096 Jun 26 13:57 dir1
drwx------  2 chris chris 4096 Jun 26 13:57 dir2
-rwx--x--x  1 chris chris    0 Jun 26 13:57 test1
----------  1 chris chris    0 Jun 26 13:57 test2
-rw-r--r--  1 chris chris    0 Jun 26 13:57 test3
```

The chmod command can also be used with the letters u (user, meaning you), g (group), and o (others) to assign permission to r (read), w (write), or x (execute) on a file or directory. Here are a few examples:

```
$ chmod og+r test1
$ chmod u=rw test2
$ chmod uog=rwx test3
$ chmod go-w dir1
$ chmod go+x dir2
$ ls -ld test* dir*
drwxr-xr-x  2 chris chris 4096 Jun 26 13:57 dir1
drwx--x--x  2 chris chris 4096 Jun 26 13:57 dir2
-rwxr-xr-x  1 chris chris    0 Jun 26 13:57 test1
-rw-------  1 chris chris    0 Jun 26 13:57 test2
-rwxrwxrwx  1 chris chris    0 Jun 26 13:57 test3
```

Notice that you can use plus (+) and minus (-) signs to add or subtract a permission type (rwx) to a user, group, or other. Or, you can use the equal sign to reset the permissions for user, owner, or group to a specific set of rwx permissions.

Editing Text Files

Most configuration files in Linux are stored as plain text files. While there are graphical tools for managing many of these files, you will almost surely find yourself needing to change a configuration file manually at some point. To do that, you will need to learn to use a text editor.

There is no shortage of text editors available with Linux. If you are using a graphical desktop with your Linux system, there are some very easy-to-use text editors that let you move around a file using your mouse and menus (such as gedit). Nice forms-based editors that provide menus right from a shell (no GUI required) include the joe editor. Damn Small Linux includes a graphical text editor named beaver (right-click the desktop and select Apps → Editors → Beaver or type **beaver**). Old-school Linux and UNIX users tend to use either vi or emacs editors.

Using the gedit Editor

To try out gedit from a Fedora or Red Hat Enterprise Linux desktop, you can select Applications → Accessories → Text Editor (or just type **gedit** from a Terminal window). An example of the gedit window is shown in Figure B-1.

There isn't much explanation required to use gedit. You can highlight text with your mouse, right-click for a menu to cut, copy, paste or delete text, and just type to add text where you want it. Menus and toolbars let you save, open, print, and do other basic text editing functions.

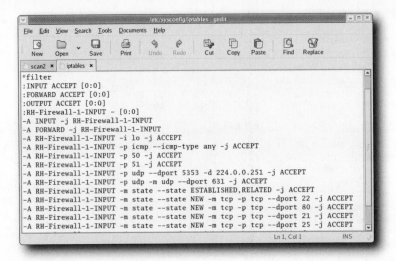

/etc/sysconfig/iptables - gedit

FIGURE B-1: The gedit text editor provides a simple, graphical text editor in Linux.

Using the joe Editor

For editing directly from the shell, the joe editor is fairly easy to use. To open a file with the joe editor, simply type

```
$ joe filename
```

where *filename* is the name of the file you want to edit. To get some help with getting around in joe, press Ctrl+K, then H. To edit, you can use arrow keys to move around and just start typing to make changes. Using Ctrl keys, you can move the cursor, go to specific places in the document, and work with blocks of text. When you are done editing, type:

- **Ctrl+C** — To exit without saving changes.
- **Ctrl+K D** — To save current changes and continue editing.
- **Ctrl+K X** — To save changes and quit.

Using the vi Editor

The vi editor is the least intuitive of the text editors described in this section. It was one of the first, if not the first, screen-based text editors available with UNIX-like systems. To start vi from any shell (virtual terminal or Terminal window), simply type

```
# vi filename
```

where *filename* is the name of the file you want to edit. The resulting screen that appears is second only to the shell itself as the world's most non-intuitive interface. If you were to edit /etc/hosts file using vi, the screen would look something like this:

```
# Do not remove the following line, or various programs
# that require network functionality will fail.
127.0.0.1       localhost.localdomain     localhost
10.0.0.1        toys.linuxtoys.net
~
~
~
~
~
"/etc/hosts" 4L, 178C                        1,1       All
```

Information at the bottom of the screen shows that the file name is /etc/hosts, that there are four lines and 178 characters in the file, that you are currently on line 1 and character 1, and that the entire text in the file is currently being displayed (All). There are two modes that vi operates in:

- **Command mode** — This is the mode that vi begins in. In this mode, you can move around the file, search for text, or enter a command that lets you begin input.

- **Input mode** — After you type a command that lets you input text, you are in input mode. Text that you type will appear where the cursor is after you enter input mode. To leave input mode, press the Esc key.

Here is a quick tutorial on using vi:

1. Type **vi /tmp/testfile.txt**.

2. Press the **i** key (for insert). The editor just switched from command mode to input mode and you can begin adding text immediately before the cursor.

3. Type **Here are a few words that we can begin testing with.**

4. Press the Esc key. You are back in command mode.

5. Press the **H** key to go to the first character of the first line.

6. Press the **w** key a few times to move ahead a word at a time.

7. Press the **b** key a few times to move back a word at a time.

8. Type **o** to open a line below the current line and type another line of text, then Esc to return to command mode.

9. If you don't like the line you just typed, type **u** to undo what you just did. (The u command to undo what you just did can be a good friend!) Then repeat the previous to type a line you like.

10. Use the **j**, **k**, **l**, and **h** keys to move up and down and across the file one character (or one line) at a time.

11. Put your cursor on the first character of a word and type **dw** to delete the word (no need to Esc after a deletion since you are still in command mode after a deletion).

12. Type **A** and begin typing to add text to the end of the current line. Type **I** to add text to the beginning. (These are opposed to lowercase **a** and **i**, which would add text after or before the current character, respectively.) Press Esc to return to command mode.

13. Type **/*word*** (where *word* is replaced by a word in the file) and press Enter. Type **n** to continue to search for other occurrences of the word in this file.

14. Type **:w** to save changes you made to the file. Type **:wq** to save and exit the file. To quit without saving changes, type **:q!** (which causes all unsaved changes to be lost).

There is a lot more to vi than I've just explained. In most cases, typing the vi command actually runs an expanded version of vi called vim. One advantage of vim is that it has available help text. If you get stuck while using vim, type **:help** to get further information.

Note   In order to edit most administrative files, you need to have root privilege. To do that, you can either login as the root user before opening the editor or use a command such as su to temporarily become the root user. In Damn Small Linux, you can become root user for a single command using sudo (for example, sudo beaver /etc/resolv.conf would let you edit the resolve.conf file using the beaver text editor as root user). Without root privilege you won't be able to save changes to most administrative files. These issues are discussed in the "Administering Linux" section of this appendix.

Using the Desktop

In recent years, extraordinary improvements have been made to the graphical interfaces that are available with Linux systems. Along with those changes have come improved graphical tools for administering the system.

Whether or not you have a graphical interface on your Linux system depends on whether or not X and related software has been installed and whether or not it has been set to start automatically. If you see a graphical login screen, you already have a GUI running. If you see a text-based login prompt, you will need to start the GUI yourself (using something like the startx command).

If you have a powerful enough computer and a full install of KDE or GNOME desktop environments, using one of those desktop environments gives you the advantage of integrated applications (with such things as shared clipboards and drag-and-drop features). However, if you are using a low-end computer, you might want to use a more streamlined GUI (X and a simple window manager), as we recommend in several of our projects. Damn Small Linux uses the efficient fluxbox window manager.

Most Linux distributions use either XFree86 or X.org projects for X Window System software. Because many of the most popular Linux systems have moved to X.org in the past few years, I'm going to describe what you need to know to get a desktop working in Linux using X.org as your X server.

Configuring Your Video Card and Monitor

When you first install most Linux systems, you are asked to configure your video card at some point during the install process. If you are not able to find the exact video card and monitor in the list you are presented, you can often just choose a generic setting to get going. Then you can tune it further after the system is installed.

Red Hat Fedora and RHEL systems offer a Display Settings window that lets you choose a monitor type and video card, and then set the screen resolution and color depth. To start the Display Settings window, select Desktop → System Settings → Display.

If your display is so broken, however, that you can't even get to a Display Setting window, you can try to configure your basic X setup from the command line. The trick is to run the Xorg command to probe your hardware and create a basic xorg.conf file. First, exit from the broken X display and return to a shell by pressing Ctrl+Alt+Backspace. Then create, tune, and insert an X configuration file where it can be used by your system when X starts. Here's an example:

```
# Xorg -configure
# X -xf86config /root/xorg.conf.new
```

The Xorg command probes your video hardware and creates an xorg.conf.new file in your home directory (presumably /root). Next, run the X server, identifying the xorg.conf.new file you just created as your X configuration file using the -xf86config option, as shown.

If this doesn't get you a working X screen (plain gray with an X for your mouse cursor), you may have broken or unsupported video hardware. Check the Xorg.0.log in the /var/log directory for information about the graphics chipset that is detected. Use a search engine, with the chipset and the word Linux as keywords to find information on other people's experiences with your video hardware.

If the graphics seem to be working, but the mouse is not (you see the cursor and a gray screen, but the cursor doesn't move), exit from X (Ctrl+Backspace) and run the mouseconfig command to configure your mouse. Once the configuration file is working, copy it to its permanent location as follows:

```
# cp /root/xorg.conf.new /etc/X11/xorg.conf
```

For more information about how to configure your xorg.conf file, type **man xorg.conf**.

Video cards from NVidia have Linux drivers available that will work, but will not take advantage of all features of the video card. Many people download drivers directly from nvidia.com to use in Linux, or download a prepackaged RPM for the driver from a Fedora Core software repository. These drivers are proprietary, non-open source drivers, so they are not officially supported by any Linux distributions.

Starting the Desktop

Assuming desktop software is installed and configured, the desktop usually starts up in one of two ways. Either you boot directly to a graphical login and start the GUI automatically or you boot to a text-based login and start the GUI manually (usually with the startx command).

In Chapter 11, which describes how to set up thin clients and a thin client server, I describe different ways of configuring X that suit different hardware and software configurations. For bootable Linux systems, such as Damn Small Linux, you usually bypass a graphical login and boot directly to a graphical desktop.

Desktop Administration Tools

Desktop tools for administering the Linux system are generally more intuitive, but less powerful than command line tools. For many of the *Linux Toys II* projects, you need to set up network connections, configure firewalls, add users and do other administrative tasks. Graphical administration tools that might be available with your distribution include:

- **YaST** — SUSE Linux includes the YaST interface for graphically administering a Linux system.

- **Webmin** — Webmin is a Web-based graphical administration tool that is not specific to any Linux distribution. You can learn about it at www.webmin.com.

- **system-config tools** — Red Hat Enterprise Linux (RHEL) and Fedora Core come with a set of graphical administration tools. The names of the commands to launch these tools typically begin with *system-config*, such as system-config-network and system-config-users. However, the more common way to launch these tools is from the Desktop or Applications buttons on a Fedora or RHEL desktop.

Because I'm recommending that you use Fedora Core or Red Hat Enterprise Linux as your installed operating system for *Linux Toys II*, I want to describe a few of the graphical tools you can use in those systems. The following is a list of tasks that can be done with administrative tools that you can run from the Desktop menu:

- **Add users** — Click Desktop → System Settings → Users and Groups. From the User Manager window that appears, you can add a user, add a group or change properties associated with Linux users and groups.

- **Configure networking** — Click Desktop → System Settings → Network to open the network configuration window. From that window, you can configure connections to your network using Ethernet, ISDN, modem, token ring, wireless, or xDSL networking equipment. Through this window, you can even configure virtual private network connections, using IPsec, for secure point-to-point communications over the Internet. Figure B-2 shows the Network Configuration window.

- **Set up firewalls** — Click Desktop → System Settings → Security Level and Firewall to open the Security Level Configuration window. From that window, you can configure a basic firewall that will let you secure your system from unwanted network access, while opening access to services you select (such as your web server, ftp server, ssh login server, or mail server). You can also configure some advanced security features referred to as Security Enhanced Linux.

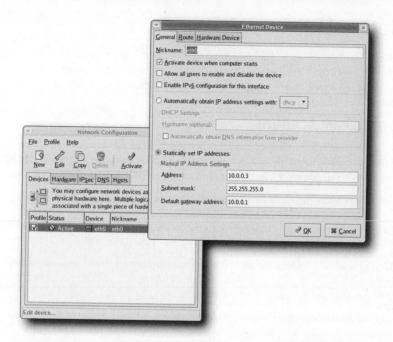

FIGURE B-2: Use Network Configuration to configure your Ethernet card.

- **File sharing**—To share files among computers that you have on your LAN (safely behind a firewall), there are several services you can configure through the GUI in Fedora and Red Hat Enterprise Linux systems. From the Desktop menu, select System Settings → Server Settings, then choose NFS (to share files among Linux and UNIX systems) or Samba (to share files among Linux and Windows systems).

- **Software packages**—If a Fedora software package that you didn't add when you first installed the system is needed for a *Linux Toys II* project, you can add it later from the Package Management window. To access that window, click Desktop → System Settings → Add/Remove Applications.

The graphical administrative tools just mentioned are some that you are likely to find useful as you set up, or expand on, your *Linux Toys II* projects. You should check out other tools, available from the System Settings and Applications → System Tools menus, to see how else you might enhance your Linux system. There are graphical tools for managing printers, languages, keyboards, sound cards, system services, domain name system, Bluetooth wireless devices, and a variety of other Linux features.

Administering Linux

Whole books are written on the subject of administering Linux systems. In a few paragraphs in this appendix, however, I want to point you toward a few important things you should know to get you on the right path to administering your Linux system.

The root User Account

Every Linux system has a root user account. The root user is the owner of most system configuration files and administrative applications. So, to do such things as add users, configure the network, start and stop services, and install software, you need access to the root user account.

There are several ways to access your system as the root user:

- **Login** — You can login with the root user name and password. Then, all commands you run from the shell or start from the desktop will run as the root user.

- **Run graphical administration** — When you run any graphical administration tool, you can launch it as a regular user. Before the window opens, you are prompted to enter the root password to have access to the window.

- **Use the su command** — Using the su command from the shell, while you are logged in as a regular user, gives you root privilege from the shell. To use su to become the root user, type the following:

```
$ su -
Password: *******
#
```

Enter the password, as requested, and your shell prompt changes from a dollar sign to a pound sign (#). Note the dash following the su command. This causes the entire root environment to start up when you get root privilege. Without the dash, you won't have such things as /sbin and /usr/sbin added to your path or any special shell environment variables (from the /root/.bashrc file) added to your shell environment.

You should run any administrative commands you choose at this point. When you are done, exit the root shell environment by typing **exit**. You will become the original user again.

- **Use the sudo command** — If you want certain users to have limited access to root privileges, without giving away the root password, you can configure the sudo facility. Add a user to the wheel group (in /etc/group) and uncomment one of the %wheel lines in the /etc/sudoers file to allow that user full access to administrative command, while that user is logged in as himself. Or, you can configure certain users to only have access permission to run particular administrative commands.

Some bootable Linux systems, including Damn Small Linux, come with the /etc/sudoers file already configured to allow the default user name (such as knoppix or dsl) to run sudo on all commands without entering a password. The presumption is that the system owner is running the bootable Linux system. So there is no restriction on what you can run, but to protect you from changing a system file by mistake, you explicitly have to ask for root permission using sudo.

Caution It's generally considered good security practice to not stay logged in as root user for long periods of time. For general desktop use, you should log in as a regular user, then only become root user to do the administrative tasks you need. When you are done running administrative commands, exit the root shell or close the administrative window.

Administrative Tasks

The responsibility you have for completing administrative tasks on your Linux system varies based on such things as the number of users you support on the system and the amount of exposure the computer has to the Internet. In the case of *Linux Toys II*, aside from a few server-related projects, most administrative tasks you do will be to get your Linux system to work, and keep working, the way you want it to.

I've added a few common tasks below and divided them up into the categories "Common Linux tasks," "Multi-user tasks," and "Network server tasks." This is by no means an exhaustive set of system administrative duties. They are just meant to give you the feel for some of the most common administrative procedures and to help give you the confidence to set out on your own when you find you need to do some tasks that are not covered here.

Common Linux Tasks

The following are some common administrative tasks you might do with any Linux system, from a personal desktop to an enterprise-level server.

Checking System Resources

There is no shortage of tools for checking on the status of your Linux system. You want to make sure that you are not running out of disk space, that your processor is not being overloaded and that you have enough RAM to run the applications you need to run. Here are a few tools you can run to do those things.

Note Try checking the man pages for any of the commands listed in the following sections for more options you can use with them.

- **Check file system space usage**. You can use the df command to check how much space has been used and how much is available on each file system. Here is an example:

```
$ df -h
File system     Size  Used  Avail Use% Mounted on
/dev/hda6       9.7G  8.0G  1.3G  87%  /
/dev/hda1        99M   11M   83M  12%  /boot
/dev/hda2        49G   16G   31G  34%  /home
```

The df command lists how much space is available on your mounted file systems. This will mostly cover your hard disk partitions, but it will also show space on mounted CDs, flash drives, floppies, or other removable media as well. The -h option displays the output in human-readable form (megabytes and gigabytes, instead of 1K blocks).

- **Check directory space usage**. You can check the space used in a directory and all its sub-directories using the du command as follows:

  ```
  $ du -h /home/chris | less
  ```

  With the du command (again with the -h to make it human-readable), you can see how much disk space is being consumed in a particular directory structure (in this case, all files and subdirectories under the /home/chris directory). By piping the output to the less command, you can page through the output. To just see the total disk space used in a directory and its subdirectory, you can type the du -sh command instead.

- **Check what processes are running**. The ps command lists information from the system process table about running processes. Here is an example:

  ```
  $ ps -ef | less
  ```

  The ps command lists the processes that are currently running on your system. The -ef options give you a good set of information relating to all processes currently running. You can see which user is running the process, the process ID, the date the process was started, and how much CPU time it has consumed. At the end of each line, you can see the full command line that is running.

- **Check running processes live**. Using the top command, you can see the list of currently running processes, sorted in different ways. To start the top command, simply type the following:

  ```
  $ top
  ```

  The top command shows all running processes in a live, changing format. By default, processes are displayed by how much CPU time they are currently consuming (most to least from the top down). You can sort output by how much memory each is using (type m), CPU usage (type c) or other attributes. Information at the top of the screen shows how much memory and swap space are available and being used.

Monitoring Logs and Mail

Errors and many activities associated with hardware detection and system services are logged in files in the /var/log directory. You can check logs in this directory manually (using any text editor, paging through with the less command, or watching them live as in tail -f /var/log/messages). Red Hat Enterprise Linux systems come with a handy graphical tool for checking out log files. From a RHEL desktop, select Applications → System Tools → System Logs to see the System Logs window (shown in Figure B-3).

If you have difficulty detecting problems during boot-up, you can check the Boot Log, Kernel Startup Log, or System Log. Check the X.Org X11 Log for troubles with your video card. Check the Mail Log regularly to make sure no one has taken over your box as a spam relay. The System Log (/var/log/messages file) is probably the best place to check for the on-going, general health of your computer.

The System Logs window flags any message that look like a potential problem by adding a red X in the left column. In the example shown in Figure B-3, there were problems reading a DVD I had inserted that were flagged in the System Log file.

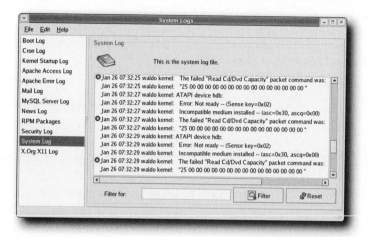

FIGURE B-3: View and search system logs to keep tabs on your system.

Another way to keep up on your system health is to check the root account's mailbox on the system. Often, email to the root user is forwarded to another user account, especially in the case where the system administrator is managing a lot of systems. There are several background processes (called daemons) and cron jobs (commands set up to run at particular times) that monitor various system activities and send email to the root user with any potential problems. Here are some examples:

- **diskcheck** — This script runs hourly to check if any of your partitions has low disk space. It sends an email to the root user if a partition is low on space.

- **logwatch** — The logwatch package is configured to scan through your log files and create reports of interesting and suspicious activities (which it mails to the root user).

- **sudoers** — If some user who is not configured to use sudo to gain root access tries to do so, an email is sent to the root user to note that fact.

There are other software packages that run programs using the cron facility (from /etc/cron.d, /etc/cron.daily, /etc/cron.hourly, /etc/cron.monthly, and /etc/cron.weekly) that send messages containing information or problems related to their processing to the root user. It's a good idea to check out the cron directories to get a sense of the kind of applications your system is running on an on-going basis.

Working with Storage Media

File systems that are contained on CDs, DVDs, hard disks, and other media are connected to the Linux file system by *mounting* the device on a directory in the file system. When you first install Linux, you typically determine where the parts of your hard disk (referred to as *partitions*) are connected to your Linux file system.

Linux stores information about hard disk partitions and removable media that it expects to consistently mount in a particular location in the /etc/fstab file. Typically, the hard disk partitions will be mounted automatically when you boot Linux. Removable media will be mounted when the media is inserted or connected.

Different Linux systems have different ways of dealing with automounting of removable media. However, the Linux Standards Base, which seeks to standardize many aspects of Linux systems, is moving away from mounting removable media in the /mnt directory and toward mounting that media in the /media directory. (Damn Small Linux still uses /mnt to mount removable media.)

Beginning with Fedora Core 3, Red Hat has done a lot to improve the handling of removable storage media (CD, DVD, and floppy drives, as well a USB storage media such as pen drives). There are also many good tools for managing fixed storage media (such as hard disks).

The Hardware Abstraction Layer daemon (hald) is configured in many Linux systems (including Fedora Core) to detect when removable media are inserted or attached. It then tries to mount those media in subdirectories of the /media directory. If you are running the GNOME desktop, those items should show up automatically as desktop icons. Just double-click on the icon to open the CD, DVD, USB disk, or other medium.

You should know the naming conventions used to identify your storage media devices. IDE hard drives are identified by the letters hd, so the first IDE hard disk on your system would be accessible through the /dev/hda device; the second would be /dev/hdb, and so on. Primary partitions on each device are numbered from 1 to 4 (hda1, hda2, and so on), with the first logical partition starting at hda5. SCSI disk drives are named similarly, starting with /dev/sda, /dev/sdb, and so on. So the first partition on the first SCSI drive is /dev/sda1, then /dev/sda2, and so on.

Both IDE and SCSI devices can represent removable media as well as fixed hard disks. For example, on the computer I am using right now, the CD/DVD burner is located at /dev/hdb and my digital camera (when I connect it to a USB port) shows up as /dev/sda1.

Why do you care about all this? Because there may come a time when you want to manually mount and unmount file systems. At some point, you will probably want to add a hard disk, define partitions, and create file systems on partitions. (For more depth on these topics, I recommend *Red Hat Fedora and Enterprise Linux 4 Bible*.) For now, here are a few examples of commands for working with your storage media:

mount /dev/hdb /media/cdrecorder

Assuming your CD/DVD burner is the second IDE drive (/dev/hdb), the mount command just shown will make the contents of the CD or DVD in that drive available from the /media/cdrecorder directory. To unmount the drive, you can run the following command:

umount /media/cdrecorder

At this point, you can eject the medium (type eject /media/cdrecorder or just press the button on the drive). If the unmount fails, there is probably something still accessing the drive. Quit any applications that have files open on the drive and change directories (cd $HOME) from any shell for which the current directory is on the removable medium.

There are many options associated with the mount command that are specific to the file system types you are using. Type man mount to read more about the mount command.

Other commands you can look into for managing your storage media include the following: fdisk (for listing, adding, deleting and modifying disk partitions); mkfs (to create a file system on a fixed medium); mkisofs (to create a file system that you can later burn to a CD or DVD); and fsck (for checking file systems for bad blocks). Each of the commands just mentioned is used at some point in this book.

Managing Hardware Devices

While hardware detection has much improved in recent years with Linux, there are times when Linux will either not detect a hardware device or improperly identify it. At those times, it helps to know something about tools for listing, modifying, and loading drivers in Linux.

Device drivers and modules define the interface between your computer's hardware and the applications you run. Because there are so many potential device drivers that you might need, only the most basic drivers are built into the Linux kernel that you are running. The code needed to handle other devices is added to the kernel, typically when you boot the computer or plug in a removable device, using what are called *loadable modules*.

If your hardware device is properly detected, it will either run from a driver that is built into the kernel or have an appropriate module loaded to handle it (if that module is known and available). If some piece of hardware isn't working when you install Linux (maybe a sound card or Ethernet card, for example), here are some things you can do to figure out what is wrong:

1. **Check the boot log.** Run the following command to print the kernel ring buffer, which contains information about your bootup process:

   ```
   # dmesg > bootinfo.txt
   ```

   Look at the bootinfo.txt file you just created. It should contain information about what happened when the hardware was detected and what might have gone wrong. If you can't solve the problem yourself, someone in a Linux mailing list or online forum will need this information to help you debug the problem.

2. **Search the Web for a solution.** Use your favorite search engine to search for the name of the hardware that is not being detected and the word Linux or kernel. Chances are that someone else has run into a problem with the same hardware and might offer insights.

3. **Try Damn Small Linux or KNOPPIX.** Live bootable Linux CDs, such as KNOPPIX and Damn Small Linux, are known for doing a good job detecting hardware and loading the correct driver. If you suspect there might be a problem with some piece of hardware on your computer in regards to Linux, it can even be a good idea to try KNOPPIX or DSL before you install Linux permanently on your hard drive. DSL is included on the *Linux Toys II* CD, so you can boot straight to DSL and check how well Linux can run on your computer.

In some cases, you will need to get a module that is not included with your Linux distribution. Once it is installed, the next reboot might properly load the module. Or you might have to manually load the module yourself. The following are examples of commands that can be used to work with loadable modules.

- To list the modules that are currently loaded into your kernel, type the following:

    ```
    # /sbin/lsmod
    ```

- To list information about a particular module (such as the snd sound module), use the `modinfo` command. Here's an example:

    ```
    # /sbin/modinfo snd
    filename:        /lib/modules/2.6.10-1.737_
                     FC3/kernel/sound/core/snd.ko
    author:          Jaroslav Kysela <perex@suse.cz>
    description:     Advanced Linux Sound Architecture
                     driver for soundcards.
    license:         GPL
    parm:            major:Major # for sound driver.
    parm:            cards_limit:Count of auto-loadable
                     soundcards.
    alias:           char-major-116-*
    alias:           char-major-116-*
    vermagic:        2.6.10-1.737_FC3 686 REGPARM
                     4KSTACKS gcc-3.4
    depends:         soundcore
    srcversion:      31957A6940EB9CDD5702831
    ```

Note The amount of information included with loadable modules varies a great deal. Look for parm lines that indicate parameters you can add to the driver to tune how it behaves.

- If you know of a driver that you want to load, you can load it with the modprobe command. Here's an example of loading the pwc driver for a Logitech Webcam:

    ```
    # modprobe pwc
    ```

    When you run `modprobe`, any other modules that the one you are loading depends on are loaded into the kernel as well. Module dependencies are stored in the `/lib/modules/kernel/modules.dep` file (where *kernel* is replaced by the associated kernel version number).

- If you want to remove a module from the kernel, because you don't need the device anymore or you want to access the hardware with a different module, you can use the modprobe command with the `-r` option as follows:

    ```
    # modprobe -r pwc
    ```

    Here, the `modprobe` command removes the pwc modules, as well as any other dependent modules that were loaded when the pwc module was first added.

Multi-user Tasks

If you are managing a multi-user machine (one where many people have login accounts), there are some additional tasks you will need to do. If you are doing a project such as the Web Photo Gallery in Chapter 3, you might want to allow different family members to each have their own user accounts, so they can upload their own images to the family gallery. Here are a couple of tasks related to managing users in Linux.

Adding and Removing Users

From the command line, the useradd command is a convenient way to add user accounts your Linux system. Here's an example:

```
# useradd -m jjones
```

The useradd command just shown adds a user named jjones to the system (actually, into the /etc/passwd file). By default, it also creates a home directory for that user (in this case, /home/jjones). The standard place for adding Web content for the user would be in that user's public_html directory (for example, /home/jjones/public_html).

Check the useradd man page to see many other options you can put on the command line. You can modify user attributes later, using the usermod command. You can delete the user account using the userdel command (userdel jjones).

Note A user's home directory and mailbox are still intact, by default, when you delete a user account. An ls -l of those items will show them being owned by the user ID number that was once assigned to the user. To remove the home directory and mail spool file, add the -r option to the userdel command line when you delete the user.

Limiting Disk Space

A greedy or careless user can consume all of your hard disk space. Using the quota software package, you can limit the amount of disk space a user can consume. Quota software comes with Red Hat Linux systems, as well as with other Linux distributions.

A full description of setting up quotas is outside the scope of this book. However, you can find out how to set up quotas in *Red Hat Fedora and Enterprise Linux 4 Bible* or in the Quota mini-HOWTO (www.tldp.org/HOWTO/Quota.html).

Network Service Tasks

You don't really tap into the full power of Linux until you connect it to a network. By adding an Ethernet connection to almost any of the Toys projects, you can expand them in ways that are only limited by your imagination. Especially if your *Linux Toys II* computer is set up on an entertainment system or in a remote building, a network connection lets you:

- Copy content to or from the *Linux Toys II* computer across the network. For a media player, such as MythTV or MoviX, this can greatly expand the audio, video, and other multimedia content you can play and where you can play it.

- Do remote administration and maintenance. With a network connection, you don't even need a monitor or keyboard on the computer. Just login from the network when you need to enhance or fix something.

- Broadcast or publish your data on the Internet or private network.

The following sections describe some network services you might want to enable on your *Linux Toys II* machines.

Enabling Secure Shell (ssh) Service

When many Linux users set up a machine, one of the first network services they turn on is the secure shell service (sshd daemon). The sshd daemon listens for network requests that allow you to log in, copy files, or remotely execute commands securely from across the network.

After installing Red Hat or many other Linux systems, the ssh service is often on by default. Type **ps -ef | grep sshd** to see if the sshd daemon is running. If not, you can start the service in Red Hat Linux systems by typing the following (as root user):

```
# /etc/init.d/sshd start
# chkconfig sshd on
```

With the sshd daemon running, you can log in to the computer from your LAN or other network using the ssh command. You can identify your computer either by name (provided you are using DNS or have mapped your host names to IP addresses in your /etc/hosts file) or by IP address. Here is an example:

```
$ ssh john@example.com
The authenticity of host 'example.net (10.0.0.1)' can't be established.
RSA key fingerprint is 8b:21:08:e7:41:c0:9d:b2:93:w1:ad:fa:af:e5:7d:a2.
Are you sure you want to continue connecting (yes/no)? yes
john@example.com's password: ******
[john@example ~]$
```

In this example, you are logged in as the user named john to the host named example.com. Once you are logged in, you can use the same commands you would if you were logged into the console. Because ssh is a secure shell, all transmissions are encrypted, so someone snooping the line can't watch what you are doing. You can even log in directly as root, although good practice is to log in as a different user and become root as needed.

The scp command is another command you can use to communicate with a computer that is running the sshd daemon. With scp, you can securely transfer files across your network connection. Here's an example of an scp command:

```
$ scp -r /home/chris/mygallery/ chris@server:/home/chris/
chris@server's password: *******
```

The command line just shown, recursively (-r) copies the entire contents of the mygallery directory (and all its subdirectories and files) to the /home/chris directory on the machine called server as the user named chris. This is a handy and safe way to pass files from one machine to another.

Note If you are using a firewall on your sshd server and you are not able to log in (using ssh) to the computer, make sure that port 22 is accessible. Otherwise the machine will not let another computer request the ssh service.

Enabling Other Network Services

Other networking protocols can be useful for exchanging information between your Linux Toys projects and the other machines on your LAN. In particular, you should look into enabling the Samba service (to share files and printers with Windows systems on a LAN), FTP service (to transfer files to and from your Linux Toys machine), NFS (to share files among Linux and UNIX systems), and Web service (to be able to share Web content with others on your network).

Summary

Becoming proficient in Linux takes a lot of time and hard work. This appendix was intended to give you some of the basics needed to run and use a Linux system effectively. Although this appendix should be a good starting point for learning Linux, you might consider a more complete reference (such as *Red Hat Fedora and Enterprise Linux 4 Bible*) to be able to dig deeper into the topics discussed here.

Installing Linux

Before you start any of the projects in this book, you should have an installed Linux system to work on. Even those projects that run without installing Linux on your hard disk (such as eMoviX and Linux Terminal Server Project) require that you have a running Linux system to set them up.

The projects were tested on Fedora Core 4, which is the free Linux operating system sponsored by Red Hat, Inc. (One exception is the MythTV project in Chapter 4, for which Fedora Core 3 is recommended.) You can also use Red Hat Enterprise Linux 4 to install and build these projects. In both of those systems, you can install the RPMs that come with this book for each project.

This appendix describes several different Linux distributions you might want to install as the basis for *Linux Toys II* projects. Because I recommend using Fedora Core to build most of the *Linux Toys II* projects, I have included a complete description of the Fedora Core installation procedure in this appendix as well.

Note	Once you have a Linux system installed, refer to Appendix A for information on how to install the *Linux Toys II* projects from the software contained on the CD that comes with this book. That includes installation of packages in both RPM (`*.rpm`) and compressed TAR (`*.tar.gz`) formats.

Choosing a Different Linux Distribution

If you want to use a Linux distribution other than Fedora Core or RHEL to install your projects, you are free to do so. It's possible that you already have a Linux system installed, in which case you can just dive right into the project you want to try. However, if you are interested in installing a different Linux distribution for *Linux Toys II*, here are a few places you can go to choose one:

- *Linux Bible, 2005 Edition* — The book (written by this author) contains ten different Linux distributions on CD and DVD. It also contains descriptions for choosing one and installing it.

- **Debian GNU/Linux** — To obtain Debian, refer to the Getting Debian page (www.debian.org/distrib). To install Debian, check out the Installation Manual (www.debian.org/releases/stable/installmanual).

- **Slackware** — Refer to the Get Slack page (www.slackware.com/getslack) for information on getting Slackware. To install Slack, refer to the Slackware Installation Help page (www.slackware.com/install).

- **Gentoo** — To find Gentoo Linux download sites, refer to the Gentoo Linux Mirrors page (www.gentoo.org/main/en/mirrors.xml). For information on installing Gentoo, go to the Gentoo Documentation Resources page (www.gentoolorg/doc/en/?catid=install).

- **SUSE** — To get SUSE Linux, go to the SUSE LINUX Professional downloads page (www.novell.com/products/linuxprofessionals/downloads). For help installing, refer to the SUSE Forums (Select Install/Boot from www.suseforums.net).

While we haven't tested all of these Linux distributions with *Linux Toys II*, many of the projects will probably just work by installing the tarballs included on the *Linux Toys II* CD. Most of these tarballs were created directly by the project developers themselves. So, often they will run on other Linux systems without modification. You should check whether the project's Web site has its software specifically packaged for your version of Linux (such as a .deb package for Debian or a package in the portage tree for Gentoo that you can install using emerge).

If you made the choice to use Fedora or Red Hat Enterprise Linux (RHEL), you can follow the installation procedure contained in this appendix. Most of the descriptions in this appendix were taken from *Red Hat Fedora and Enterprise Linux 4 Bible*. By obtaining that book, you will have media (both DVD and CDs) that you can use to install Fedora Core 4.

Installing Fedora Core 4

This chapter details how to install Fedora 4 from a DVD or CD set. Other methods for installing Fedora Core 4 from a hard disk or over a network are also noted in this section.

Choosing an Installation Method

Fedora offers several flexible ways of installing the operating system. As noted earlier, you can get the installation media from *Red Hat Fedora and Enterprise Linux 4 Bible*. Or, you can obtain the Fedora Core 4 DVD or four-CD installation set by downloading disk images of those CDs from the Internet and burning them to CD yourself. Go to http://fedora.redhat.com/download for information on downloading images of the DVD or CDs.

Installing Other Red Hat Linux Systems

Much of the installation procedure described here is the same as you will find when you install a Red Hat Enterprise Linux system. However, here are a few issues you should be aware of if you are using the installation procedure in this chapter to install Red Hat Enterprise Linux.

- Instead of having a DVD or four-CD installation set, Red Hat Enterprise Linux consists of a different boot CD for AS and WS installs. After starting installation with the appropriate boot CD, both install types use the same set of additional CDs (marked disc2, disc3, and disc4).

- Installation classes for Fedora and Enterprise are different.

- The names and logos used for Fedora and Enterprise are different.

- Unlike the Fedora installation, which installs all CDs in order, Red Hat Enterprise Linux requires that you insert the boot CD again near the end of the install process.

Aside from those differences, an installation of Red Hat Enterprise Linux 4 should closely match the instructions in this chapter. There are differences in which packages are included with the Fedora and Enterprise distributions, however.

In addition to installing Fedora from the DVD or CDs, you have the option to use several different types of installation (hard disk, PXE, HTTP, or FTP, to name a few). Most of those methods involve copying the Fedora Core software to an accessible hard disk or network location and launching a special install type (such as `linux askmethod`) at the installation boot prompt.

Install or Upgrade?

First you should determine if you are doing a new install or an upgrade. If you are upgrading an existing Red Hat Linux or Fedora system to the latest version, the installation process will try to leave your data files and configuration files intact as much as possible. This type of installation takes longer than a new install. A new install will simply erase all data on the Linux partitions (or whole hard disk) that you choose.

Note While you can upgrade to Fedora Core 4 from previous Fedora or Red Hat Linux systems (such as Red Hat Linux 8 or 9), you cannot upgrade to Fedora Core 4 from a Red Hat Enterprise Linux system.

If you choose to upgrade, you can save yourself some time (and disk space) by removing software packages you don't need. An upgrade will just skip packages that are not installed and will not try to upgrade them.

From DVD/CD, Network, or Hard Disk?

When you install Fedora, the distribution doesn't have to come from the installation DVD or CD. After booting the installation DVD or CD and typing **linux askmethod** at the boot prompt, you are offered the choice of installing Fedora from the following locations:

- **Local DVD or CDROM** — This is the most common method of installing Fedora and the one you get by simply pressing Enter from the installation boot prompt. All packages needed to complete the installation are on the DVD that comes with this book or the set of four install CDs available from the Fedora project that contain the same software.

- **HTTP** — Lets you install from a Web page address (`http://`).

- **FTP** — Lets you install from an FTP site (`ftp://`).

- **NFS image** — Allows you to install from any shared directory on another computer on your network using the Network File System (NFS) facility.

- **Hard drive** — If you can place a copy of the Fedora Core distribution on your hard drive, you can install it from there. (Presumably, the distribution is on a hard drive partition to which you are *not* installing.)

If you don't have a bootable DVD or CD drive, there are other ways to start the Fedora installation. Unlike earlier Fedora and Red Hat Linux versions, Fedora Core 4 doesn't support floppy disk boot images (the Linux 2.6 kernel is too large to fit on a floppy disk). Therefore, if you don't have a bootable DVD or CD drive, you need to start the install process from some other medium (such as a USB device, PXE server, or hard drive).

The following specialty installation types also may be of interest to you:

- **Boot CD** — You can create a boot CD from the boot images contained on the Fedora installation DVD or CD. Copy and burn the file `boot.iso` from the `images` directory on the DVD. You can use the CD you create from that image to begin the install process if you have a DVD drive that is not bootable or if you have the Fedora Core 4 software available on any of the media described earlier (HTTP, FTP, NFS, and so on).

- **USB or other bootable media** — If your computer can be configured to boot from alternate bootable media, such as a USB pen drive, that are larger than a floppy disk, you can copy the `diskboot.img` file to that medium and install from there. That image is contained in the `images` directory on the DVD or first CD.

- **Kickstart installation** — Lets you create and save a set of answers to the questions Fedora asks you during installation. This can be a time-saving method if you are installing Fedora on many computers with similar configurations.

Supported Computer Hardware

This may not really be a choice. You may just have an old PC lying around that you want to use for the *Linux Toys* projects. Or you may have a killer workstation with some extra disk space and want to try out the toys in Fedora on a separate partition or whole disk. To install the 32-bit PC version of Fedora, the computer must have the following:

- **x86 processor** — Your computer needs an Intel-compatible CPU. With the latest version, Fedora recommends that you at least have a Pentium-class processor to run Fedora. For a text-only installation, a 200 MHz Pentium is the minimum, while a 400 MHz Pentium II is the minimum for a GUI installation. Although some 486 machines will work, they cannot be counted on.

- **DVD or CD-ROM drive** — You need to be able to boot the installation process from a DVD, CD-ROM, or other bootable drive. (Other drives can include a USB pen drive that you can use with a `diskboot.img` image included on the DVD.) Once you have booted from one of the media just described, you can use a LAN connection to install Fedora Core software packages from a server on the network or figure out a way to copy the contents of the DVD to a local hard disk to install from there.

- **Hard disk** — The minimum amount of space you need varies depending on the installation type and packages you select. If you are an inexperienced user, you want at least 2.3GB of space so you can get the GUI with a Personal Desktop or 3GB for a Workstation install:

  - **Personal Desktop** — Requires 2.3GB of disk space.

  - **Workstation** — Requires 3.0GB of disk space.

  - **Server** — Requires 1.1MB of disk space.

  - **Everything** (Custom) — Requires about 6.9GB of disk space.

  - **Minimal** (Custom) — Requires at least 620MB of disk space.

  - **RAM** — You should have at least 64MB of RAM to install Fedora Core (text mode only). If you are running in graphical mode, you will want at least 192MB. The recommended RAM for GUI mode is 256MB.

Note With demanding applications such as the Openoffice.org office suite and automatic features for monitoring your desktop being added, Fedora demands more RAM to use effectively than it used to. A developer at Red Hat recommends at least 512MB of RAM to get good performance from a Desktop system in Fedora.

- **Keyboard and monitor** — Although this seems obvious, the truth is that you need only a keyboard and monitor during installation. You can operate Fedora Core quite well over a LAN using either a shell interface from a network login or an X terminal.

Fedora Core versions are available for the AMD64 architecture. For other hardware, such as Intel Itanium, IBM PowerPC, and IBM mainframe, versions of Red Hat Enterprise Linux are available (which you have to purchase from Red Hat, Inc.). The installation procedures presented here, however, are specific to 32-bit PCs. (Check `fedora.redhat.com/download/mirrors.html` for sites that offer Fedora for different computer hardware architectures.)

Note The list of hardware supported by Red Hat Enterprise Linux is available on the Internet at `http://bugzilla.redhat.com/hwcert`.

Installing Fedora on a Laptop

Because laptops can contain non-standard equipment, before you begin installing on a laptop you should find out about other people's experiences installing Linux on your model. Do that by visiting the Linux on Laptops site (www.linux-on-laptops.com).

Most modern laptops contain bootable CD-ROM and/or DVD drives, If yours doesn't, you probably need to install from a device connected to a USB or PCMCIA slot on your laptop. PCMCIA slots let you connect a variety of devices to your laptop using credit card–sized cards (sometimes called PC Cards). Linux supports hundreds of PCMCIA devices. You can use your laptop's PCMCIA slot to install Fedora from several different types of PCMCIA devices, including:

- A DVD drive

- A CD-ROM drive

- A LAN adapter

If you would like to know which PCMCIA devices are supported in Linux, see the SUPPORTED. CARDS file (located in the /usr/share/doc/pcmcia-cs* directory).

Beginning the Installation

If you have properly prepared to install Fedora, you can begin the installation procedure. Through-out most of the procedure, you can click Back to make changes to earlier screens. However, once you go forward after being warned that packages are about to be written to hard disk, there's no turning back. Most items that you configure can be changed after Fedora Core is installed.

Caution

If your computer contains any data that you want to keep, be sure to back it up now. Even if you have multiple disk partitions, and don't expect to write over the partitions you want, a backup is a good precaution in case something should go wrong.

1. **Insert the DVD or first CD-ROM.** This procedure assumes you are booting installation and installing from either the DVD or CD set that is available from the Fedora project mirror sites or from books, such as *Red Hat Fedora and Enterprise Linux 4 Bible*.

2. **Start your computer.** If you see the Fedora Core installation screen, continue to the next step.

Tip

If you don't see the installation screen, your DVD or CD-ROM drive may not be bootable. Creating a bootable floppy is no longer an option because the 2.6 kernel doesn't fit on a floppy. However, you may have the choice of making your DVD or CD-ROM drive bootable or copying a boot image to a bootable USB device (such as a pen drive). Here's how: Restart the computer. Immediately, you should see a message telling you how to go into Setup, such as by pressing the F1, F2, or Del key. Enter setup and look for an option such as Boot Options or Boot from. If the value is A: First, Then C: change it to CD-ROM First, Then C: or something similar. Save the changes and try to install again.

If installation succeeds, you may want to restore the boot settings. If your DVD or CD drive still won't boot, you may need to use an alternate method to boot Fedora installation.

Choosing Different Install Modes

Although most computers will enable you to install Fedora in the default mode (graphical), there may be times when your video card does not support that mode. Also, though the install process will detect most computer hardware, there may be times when your hard disk, Ethernet card, or other critical piece of hardware cannot be detected and will require you to enter special information at boot time.

The following is a list of different installation modes you can use to start the Fedora install process. You would typically try these modes only if the default mode failed (that is, if the screen was garbled or installation failed at some point). For a list of other supported modes, refer to the /usr/share/doc/anaconda*/command-line.txt file (if the anaconda package is installed) or press F2 to see short descriptions of some of these types.

- linux text — Type **linux text** to run installation in a text-based mode. Do this if installation doesn't seem to recognize your graphics card. The installation screens aren't as pretty, but they work just as well.

- linux lowres — Type **linux lowres** to run installation in 640 × 480 screen resolution for graphics cards that can't support the higher resolution.

- linux nofb — Type **linux nofb** to turn off frame buffer.

- linux noprobe — Normally, the installation process will try to determine what hardware you have on your computer. In noprobe mode, installation will not probe to determine your hardware; you will be asked to load any special drivers that might be needed to install it.

- linux mediacheck — Type **linux mediacheck** to check your DVD or CDs before installing. Because media checking is done next in the normal installation process, you should do this only to test the media on a computer you are not installing on.

- linux rescue — The linux rescue mode is not really an installation mode. This mode boots from DVD or CD, mounts your hard disk, and lets you access useful utilities to correct problems preventing your Linux system from operating properly.

- linux vnc vncconnect=hostname vncpassword=****** — Run the install in VNC mode to step through the installation process from another system (a VNC client represented by *hostname*). The optional password must be entered by the client to connect to the installation session.

Continued

Continued

- `linux dd` — Type **linux dd** if you have a driver disk you want to use to install.

- `linux expert` — Type **linux expert** if you believe that the installation process is not properly auto-probing your hardware. This mode bypasses probing so you can choose your mouse, video memory, and other values that would otherwise be chosen for you.

- `linux askmethod` — Type **linux askmethod** to have the installation process ask where to install from (local DVD/CD, NFS image, FTP, HTTP, or hard disk).

- `linux nocddma` — Type **linux nocddma** to turn off DMA. Errors with some CD drives can be overcome by turning off the DMA feature. This is a good option to try if an install CD or DVD you know to be good fails media check.

- `linux updates` — Type **linux updates** to install from an update disk.

You can add other options to the `linux` boot command to identify particular hardware that is not being detected properly. For example, to specify the number of cylinders, heads, and sectors for your hard disk (if you believe the boot process is not detecting these values properly), you could pass the information to the kernel as follows: `linux hd=720,32,64`. In this example, the kernel is told that the hard disk has 720 cylinders, 32 heads, and 64 sectors. You can find this information in the documentation that comes with your hard disk (or stamped on the hard disk itself on a sticker near the serial number).

3. **Start the boot procedure.** At the boot prompt, press Enter to start the boot procedure in graphical mode. If your computer will not let you install in graphical mode (16-bit color, 800 × 600 resolution, framebuffer), refer to the sidebar "Choosing Different Install Modes." Different modes let you start network installs and non-graphical installs (in case, for example, your video card can't be detected). There are also options for turning off certain features that may be causing installation to fail.

4. **Media check.** At this point, you may be asked to check your installation media. If so, press Enter to check that the DVD or CD is in working order. If the DVD or one of the CDs is damaged, this step saves you the trouble of getting deep into the install before failing. After the media are checked, select Skip to continue.

5. **Continue.** When the welcome screen appears, click Release Notes to see information about this version of Fedora Core. Click Next when you're ready to continue.

6. **Choose a language.** When prompted, indicate the language that you would like to use during the installation procedure by moving the arrow keys and selecting Next. (Later, you will be able to add additional languages.) You are asked to choose a keyboard.

7. **Choose a keyboard.** Select the correct keyboard layout (U.S. English, with Generic 101-key PC keyboard by default). Some layouts enable dead keys (on by default). Dead keys let you use characters with special markings (such as circumflexes and umlauts).

8. **Choose install type.** Select either "Install Fedora Core" for a new install or "Upgrade an existing installation" to upgrade an existing version of Fedora.

Note To upgrade, you must have at least a Linux 2.0 kernel installed. With an upgrade, all of your configuration files are saved as `filename.rpmsave` (for example, the hosts file is saved as `hosts.rpmsave`). The locations of those files, as well as other upgrade information, is written to `/root/upgrade.log`. The upgrade installs the new kernel, any changed software packages, and any packages that the installed packages depend on being there. Your data files and configuration information should remain intact. By clicking the Customize box, you can choose which packages to upgrade.

Caution The personal desktop and workstation installation types do not install server packages or many system administration tools. To use administration and server features, you must either select to add additional packages to those install types, or add extra packages as you need them with the system-config-packages tool or `yum` command.

For a new install, you must choose one of the following types (also referred to as *classes*) of installation. For any of these installation types, you will have the opportunity to install a set of preset packages or customize that set.

- **Personal Desktop** — Installs software appropriate for a home or office personal computer or laptop computer. This includes the GNOME desktop (no KDE packages) and various desktop-related tools (word processors, Internet tools, and so on). Server tools, software development tools, and many system administration tools are not installed.

- **Workstation** — Similar to a Personal Desktop installation but adds tools for system administration and software development. (Server software is not installed.)

Caution Any Linux partitions or free space on your hard disk(s) will be assigned to the new installation with the Personal Desktop or Workstation types of installation. Any Windows partitions (VFAT or FAT32 file system types) will not be touched by this install. After installation, you will be able to boot Linux or Windows. If there is no free space outside of your Windows partition, you have to resize your hard disk to free some space or add an extra hard drive.

- **Server** — Server installs the software packages that you would typically need for a Linux server (in particular, Web server, file server, and print server). It does not include many other server types (DHCP, mail, DNS, FTP, SQL, or news servers). The default server install does not include a GUI (so you'd better know how to use the shell). This install type also erases all hard disks and assigns them to Linux by default.

Caution This is a big one. In case you didn't catch the previous paragraph, Server installs erase the whole hard disk by default! If you have an existing Windows partition that you want to keep, change the Automatic Partitioning option that appears in the next step either to remove only the Linux Partitions or to use only existing free space.

- **Custom** — You are given the choice of configuring your own partitions and selecting your own software packages. Minimal and Everything installs can be selected during a Custom install.

Note If you are just trying out Linux, an Everything custom install gives you all of the desktop, server, and development tools that come with Fedora Core. If you have the disk space, an Everything install saves you the trouble of installing packages you need later. However, it can also leave you vulnerable to attacks on software that might not otherwise be installed and can slow software updates and upgrades. If you plan to use the computer as an Internet server, you should be more selective in the packages you install.

At this point, the procedure will continue through a Custom System installation. Even though different install classes choose different partitioning methods by default, in all cases you have the choice to see and change the partitioning that was chosen for you.

9. **Choose your partitioning strategy.** You have two choices related to how your disk is partitioned for a Fedora installation:

- **Automatically partition** — With this selection, all Linux partitions on all hard disks are erased and used for the installation. The installation process automatically handles the partitioning. (It does give you a chance to review your partitioning, however.)

- **Manually partition with Disk Druid** — With this selection, the Disk Druid utility is run to let you partition your hard disk. If the installer has chosen default partitioning for you, move your cursor to each partition and press Enter. The box that appears lets you see how each partition is set and change it if you want to. Choose to reformat any partition that should be completely erased. Choose not to reformat partitions with data you want to keep.

Click Next to continue.

10. **Choose partitioning.** If you selected to have the installer automatically partition for you, you can choose from the following options:

- **Remove all Linux partitions on this system** — Windows and other non-Linux partitions remain intact with this selection.

- **Remove all partitions on this system** — This erases the entire hard disk.

- **Keep all partitions and use existing free space** — This works only if you have enough free space on your hard disk that is not currently assigned to any partition. (Choose this option if you resized your Windows partition to make space for Linux. You can use tools such as the parted utility or qtparted GUI to resize a disk partition. Those tools come on bootable Linux CDs, such as KNOPPIX and System Rescue CD. You can also use the Fedora installation CD or DVD as a rescue disk by typing `linux rescue` at the prompt when you boot those media. You can use the `parted` command in rescue mode to partition most Linux and Windows VFAT file systems.)

If you have multiple hard disks, you can select which of those disks should be used for your Fedora Core installation. Turn the Review check box on to see how Linux is choosing to partition your hard disk. Click Next to continue.

After reviewing the Partitions screen, you can change any of the partitions you choose, providing you have at least one root (/) partition that can hold the entire installation and one swap partition. A small /boot partition (about 100MB) is also recommended.

The swap partition is often set to twice the size of the amount of RAM on your computer (for example, for 256MB RAM you could use 512MB of swap). Linux uses swap space when active processes have filled up your system's RAM. At that point, an inactive process is moved to swap space. You get a performance hit when the inactive process is moved to swap and another hit when that process restarts (moves back to RAM). For example, you might notice a delay on a busy system when you reopen a Window that has been minimized for a long time.

The reason you need to have enough swap space is that when RAM and swap fill up, no other processes can start until something closes. Bottom line: Add RAM to get better performance; add swap space if processes are failing to start. Red Hat suggests a minimum of 32MB (text mode only) and a maximum of 2GB of swap space.

Note Fedora uses Logical Volume Manager (LVM) software to set up your disk partitions by default. While this feature is useful if you think you want to expand a partition by just adding more space from another disk or partition, there are some cases where you may not want to use LVM partitions. For example, you will not be able to access your LVM partitions from Damn Small Linux (as described in Chapter 6) because DSL can't read LVM partitions. For that reason, it might be better to assign your Linux file system partitions to ext3 type.

Click the Next button (and select OK to accept any changes) to continue.

11. **Configure boot loader.** All bootable partitions and default boot loader options are displayed. By default, the install process will use the GRUB boot loader, install the boot loader in the master boot record of the computer, and choose Fedora Core as your default operating system to boot.

Note With the GRUB boot loader, you have the option to add a GRUB password. The password protects your system from having potentially dangerous kernel options sent to the kernel by someone without that password. This password can be different from the root password you are asked to enter later.

The names shown for each bootable partition will appear on the boot loader screen when the system starts. Change a bootable partition name by clicking it and selecting Edit. To change the location of the boot loader, click "Configure advanced boot loader options" and continue to the next step. If you do not want to install a boot loader (because you don't want to change the current boot loader), click "Change boot loader" and select "Do not install a boot loader." (If the defaults are okay, skip the next step.)

12. **Configure advanced boot loader.** To choose where to store the boot loader, select one of the following:

    ■ **Master Boot Record (MBR)** — This is the preferred place for GRUB. It causes GRUB to control the boot process for all operating systems installed on the hard disk.

    ■ **First Sector of Boot Partition** — If another boot loader is being used on your computer, you can have GRUB installed on your Linux partition (first sector). This lets you have the other boot loader refer to your GRUB boot loader to boot Fedora Core.

You can choose to add kernel parameters (which may be needed if your computer can't detect certain hardware). If some piece of hardware is improperly detected and preventing your computer from booting, you can add a kernel parameter to disable that hardware (for example, add `nousb`, `noscsi`, `nopcmcia`, or `noagp`). You can select to use linear mode (which was once required to boot from a partition on the disk that is above cylinder 1,024 but is now rarely needed).

13. **Configure networking.** At this point, you are asked to configure your networking. This applies only to configuring a local area network. If you will use only dial-up networking, skip this section by clicking Next. If your computer is not yet connected to a LAN, you should skip this section.

Network address information is assigned to your computer in two basic ways: *statically* (you type it) or *dynamically* (a DHCP server provides that information from the network at boot time). One Network Device appears for each network card you have installed on your computer. The first Ethernet interface is `eth0`, the second is `eth1`, and so on. Repeat the setup for each card by selecting each card and clicking Edit.

With the Edit Interface eth0 dialog box displayed, add the following:

- **Configure using DHCP** — If your IP address is assigned automatically from a DHCP server, a checkmark should appear here. Most computers simply use DHCP to connect to the network. With DHCP checked, you don't have to set other values on this page. Remove the checkmark to set your own IP address.

- **IP address** — If you set your own IP address, this is the four-part, dot-separated number that represents your computer to the network. (How IP addresses are formed and how you choose them is more than can be said in a few sentences.) An example of a private IP address is 192.168.0.1.

- **Netmask** — The netmask is used to determine what part of an IP address represents the network and what part represents a particular host computer. An example of a netmask for a Class C network is 255.255.255.0.

- **Activate on boot** — You should indicate also whether you want the network to start at boot time (you probably do if you have a LAN).

Click OK. Then add the following information on the main screen:

- **Set the host name** — This is the name identifying your computer within your domain. For example, if your computer is named `baskets` in the `handsonhistory.com` domain, your full host name is `baskets.handsonhistory.com`. You can either set the domain name yourself (manually) or have it assigned automatically, if that information is being assigned by a DHCP server (automatically via DHCP). You can also leave the default name, which is `localhost.localdomain`.

- **Gateway** — This is the IP number of the computer that acts as a gateway to networks outside your LAN. This typically represents a host computer or router that routes packets between your LAN and the Internet.

- **Primary DNS** — This is the IP address of the host that translates computer names you request into IP addresses. It is referred to as a domain name system (DNS) server. You may also have Secondary and Tertiary name servers in case the first one can't be reached. (Most ISPs will give you two DNS server addresses.)

14. **Choose a firewall configuration.** The use of a firewall has significant impact on the security of your computer. If you are connected to the Internet or to another public network, a firewall can limit the ways an intruder can break into your Linux system. Here are your choices for configuring a firewall during installation:

    - **No firewall** — Select this security level if you are not connected to a public network and do not want to deny requests for services from any computer on your local network. Of course, you can still restrict access to services by starting up only the services you want to offer and by using configuration files to restrict access to individual services.

    - **Enable firewall** — Select this security level if you are connecting your Linux system to the Internet for Web browsing and file downloading (FTP). By default, only services needed to allow Web browsing and basic network setup, DNS replies, and DHCP (to serve addresses) are allowed at this level.

    If you enable the firewall, and you know you want to allow access to particular services, you can click the appropriate check boxes and allow incoming requests for those services. These services include: SSH (secure shell to allow remote login), HTTP/HTTPS (act as a Web server), SMTP (act as a mail server), and/or FTP (act as an FTP server).

    On the Firewall Configuration screen you can also select to Enable SELinux (Active), have it disabled but warn you when requests would be denied (Warn), or have it turned off (Disabled). SELinux has improved enough to leave it enabled in most cases. Most of the restrictions it puts on your system, by default, apply if you are turning on network services such as NFS or HTTP.

Tip

Adding firewall rules results in rules' being added to the `/etc/sysconfig/iptables` file. The rules are run from the `/etc/init.d/iptables` startup script when you boot your system. To make permanent changes to your firewall rules and to SELinux features, you can use the Security Level Configuration window (run `system-config-securitylevel`).

15. **Choose a time zone.** Select the time zone from the list of time zones shown. Either click a spot on the map or choose from the scrolling list. To see a more specific view of your location, click World and choose your continent. From the UTC Offset tab, you can choose a time zone according to the number of hours away from Greenwich Mean Time (GMT), known as the UTC offset.

16. **Set root password.** You must choose a password for your root user at this point. The root password provides complete control of your Fedora Core system. Without it, and before you add other users, you will have no access to your own system. Enter the Root Password, and then type it again in the Confirm box. (Remember the root user's password and keep it confidential! Don't lose it!) Click Next to continue.

17. **Select packages.** You are presented with groups of packages at this point. Which packages are selected by default depends on the type of installation you chose earlier. In general, either more workstation-oriented or server-oriented packages are selected.

    You can override your package selections by choosing Minimal or Everything install groups. Disk space requirements for those install types are described earlier in this appendix. The disk space required for the package selections you make will appear at the bottom of the Package Selection screen.

    Because each group represents several packages, you can click the Details button next to each group to select more specifically the packages within that group. Because Workstation and Personal Desktop installations don't add any server packages, this is a good opportunity to add server packages for the services you expect to use. When you are done selecting groups and packages, click Next.

Note Each project description contains information about the packages it needs from an installed Fedora Core system. If you are doing a fresh install to create a particular project, you might save yourself some time if you check the procedure for that project and add any necessary packages now.

18. **About to install.** A screen tells you that you are about to begin writing to hard disk. You can still back out now, and the disk will not have changed. Click Next to proceed. (To quit without changes, eject the DVD or CD and restart the computer.) Now the file systems are created and the packages are installed. This typically takes from 20 to 60 minutes to complete, although it can take much longer on older computers.

    For CD installs, you are prompted to insert additional installation CDs as they are needed.

19. **Monitor configuration.** You may be asked to configure your monitor at this point. If it was probed properly, you should be able to just continue.

20. **Finish installing.** When you see the Congratulations screen, you are done. Note the links to Fedora information, eject the DVD or CD, and click Exit.

Your computer will restart. If you installed GRUB, you will see a graphical boot screen that displays the bootable partitions. Press the up or down arrow keys to choose the partition you want to boot, and press Enter. If Linux is the default partition, you can simply wait a few moments and it will boot automatically.

The first time your system boots after installation, the Fedora Setup Agent runs to do some initial configuration of your system. The next section explains how Fedora Setup Agent works.

Running Fedora Setup Agent

The first time you boot Fedora Core after it is installed, the Fedora Setup Agent runs to configure some initial settings for your computer.

Note The Fedora Setup Agent runs automatically only if you have configured Fedora to boot to a graphical login prompt. To start it from a text login, log in as root and type the following from a Terminal window:

```
# rm /etc/sysconfig/firstboot
# /usr/sbin/firstboot
```

The first screen you see is the Welcome screen. Click the Next button to step through each procedure as follows:

- **License agreement** — Read and agree to the Fedora License Agreement to be able to continue.

- **Date and time configuration** — You can manually enter the date (click the calendar) and time (select hour, minutes, and seconds) or use the Network Time Protocol tab to have your date and time set automatically from a known time server. Click Enable Network Time Protocol (NTP), and then select a time server by clicking the down arrow and selecting a site. Then click Add to add it to the list. Network Time Protocol (NTP) is a service that allows computers to synchronize their date and time clocks with reliable time servers.

Tip Fedora offers two time servers you can use (click the down arrow in the server box to see them). Or you can type in your own time server. It is better to type an IP address than a name for your time server.

Setting NTP in this way adds your chosen NTP server to the /etc/ntp.conf file (see the server option). To check that time has been synchronized, type the ntptrace command. You should not have to change your firewall for NTP to work because NTP attempts to punch a hole through your firewall to synchronize your time.

- **Monitor configuration** — You may be asked to configure your monitor. Linux should already know your monitor model and allow you to select your screen resolution and color depth. If your video card is improperly detected, select Configure to fix it.

- **User account** — For your daily use of Fedora Core, you should have your own user account. You should typically log in with this user name (of your choosing) and use the root user to perform administrative tasks only. In the first of the four text boxes on the screen, type a user name (something like jparker or alanb). Next, type your full name (like John W. Parker or Alan Bourne). Then type your password in the Password text box and again in the Confirm Password text box. Click Next.

  If some form of network authentication is used, such as LDAP, Kerberos, or SMB authentication, you can click the Use Network Login button. See the "Enabling Authentication" sidebar for information on choosing different authentication types.

- **Sound card** — Select to play a test sound. If you can hear the sound at all, click Yes when prompted. You may need to turn up the volume to hear it.

- **Install additional software** — If you have a Fedora CD other than the Fedora four installation CDs or DVD, you can install it now. Insert the CD you want to install and click the appropriate button.

Enabling Authentication

In most situations, you will enable shadow passwords and MD5 passwords (as selected by default) to authenticate users who log in to your computer from local `passwd` and `shadow` password files. To change that behavior, you can select the Use Network Login button during the User Account setup in Fedora Setup Agent (`firstboot`).

The `shadow` password file prevents access to encrypted passwords. MD5 is an algorithm used to encrypt passwords in Linux and other UNIX systems. It replaces an algorithm called crypt, which was used with early UNIX systems. When you enable MD5 passwords, your users can have longer passwords that are harder to break than those encrypted with crypt.

If you are on a network that supports one of several different forms of network-wide authentication, you may choose one of the following features:

- **Configure NIS**—Select this button and type the NIS Domain name and NIS server location if your network is configured to use the Network Information System (NIS). Instead of selecting an NIS server, you can click the check box to broadcast to find the server on your network.

- **Configure LDAP**—If your organization gathers information about users, you can click this button to search for authentication information in an LDAP server. You can enter the LDAP server name and optionally an LDAP distinguished name to look up the user information your system needs.

- **Configure Hesiod**—If your organization uses Hesiod for holding user and group information in DNS, you can add the LHS (domain prefix) and RHS (Hesiod default domain) to use for doing Hesiod queries.

- **Configure Kerberos Support**—Click this button to enable network authentication services available through Kerberos. After enabling Kerberos, you can add information about a Kerberos Realm (a group of Kerberos servers and clients), KDC (a computer that issues Kerberos tickets), and Admin server (a server running the Kerberos kadmind daemon).

- **Configure SMB**—Click this tab to configure your computer to use Samba for file and print sharing with Windows systems. If you enable SMB authentication, you can enter the name of the SMB server for your LAN and indicate the Workgroup you want your computer to belong to.

The Fedora Setup Agent is complete. Click Next to continue.

When Fedora starts up the next time, it will boot up normally to a login prompt. A graphical boot screen is displayed (instead of a scrolling list of services starting up). If you miss the old scrolling list, you can view it by clicking the Details button or by pressing Ctrl+Alt+F1. Then go back again by pressing Ctrl+Alt+F8.

Caution   If you have multiple operating systems on your computer (such as Windows and Fedora), and after a Fedora install you find that the other operating system is no longer available on your boot screen, don't panic and don't immediately reinstall. You can usually recover from the problem by booting the Fedora install disk in rescue mode (type `linux rescue`) and using the `grub-install` command to reinsert the proper MBR. If you are uncomfortable working in emergency mode, seek out an expert to help you.

Going Forward After Installation

If your Fedora Core system installed successfully, you are ready to start using it. Before you head off to start installing *Linux Toys II* software, however, there are a few things that I strongly recommend you do:

- **Get updates** — As bugs and security vulnerabilities are discovered in Fedora or RHEL, updates to your software packages are made available. The Red Hat Network icon in the panel will alert you if updates are available (with a blinking red exclamation point). If you have an Internet connection, either select that icon to run up2date, or (as root user) run `yum update` to get available updates downloaded and installed on your computer.

- **Check your security** — Any computer connected to a public network, such as the Internet, needs to be secured. In particular, if you are offering services to the Internet, as you can with the Gallery (see Chapter 3) or Icecast (see Chapter 10) projects in this book, you need to make sure that your computer is properly secured and monitored. Security features that you should learn more about include user accounts, file/directory permissions, iptables firewalls, and SELinux. You can learn about these features in books such as *Red Hat Fedora and Enterprise Linux 4 Bible* or by reading HOWTOs available from the Linux Documentation project (`http://tldp.org`).

- **Learn the desktop and the shell** — Refer to Appendix B for some basics on using the desktop and the shell to work with Fedora. Many of the topics covered there apply to other Linux systems as well.

Index

Continued

Continued

Continued

Continued

GNU General Public License

Version 2, June 1991

Copyright © 1989, 1991 Free Software Foundation, Inc.

675 Mass Ave, Cambridge, MA 02139, USA

Preamble

The licenses for most software are designed to take away your freedom to share and change it. By contrast, the GNU General Public License is intended to guarantee your freedom to share and change free software—to make sure the software is free for all its users. This General Public License applies to most of the Free Software Foundation's software and to any other program whose authors commit to using it. (Some other Free Software Foundation software is covered by the GNU Library General Public License instead.) You can apply it to your programs, too.

When we speak of free software, we are referring to freedom, not price. Our General Public Licenses are designed to make sure that you have the freedom to distribute copies of free software (and charge for this service if you wish), that you receive source code or can get it if you want it, that you can change the software or use pieces of it in new free programs; and that you know you can do these things.

To protect your rights, we need to make restrictions that forbid anyone to deny you these rights or to ask you to surrender the rights. These restrictions translate to certain responsibilities for you if you distribute copies of the software, or if you modify it.

For example, if you distribute copies of such a program, whether gratis or for a fee, you must give the recipients all the rights that you have. You must make sure that they, too, receive or can get the source code. And you must show them these terms so they know their rights.

We protect your rights with two steps: (1) copyright the software, and (2) offer you this license which gives you legal permission to copy, distribute and/or modify the software.

Also, for each author's protection and ours, we want to make certain that everyone understands that there is no warranty for this free software. If the software is modified by someone else and passed on, we want its recipients to know that what they have is not the original, so that any problems introduced by others will not reflect on the original authors' reputations.

Finally, any free program is threatened constantly by software patents. We wish to avoid the danger that redistributors of a free program will individually obtain patent licenses, in effect making the program proprietary. To prevent this, we have made it clear that any patent must be licensed for everyone's free use or not licensed at all.

The precise terms and conditions for copying, distribution and modification follow.

TERMS AND CONDITIONS FOR COPYING, DISTRIBUTION AND MODIFICATION

    0. This License applies to any program or other work which contains a notice placed by the copyright holder saying it may be distributed under the terms of this General Public License. The "Program", below, refers to any such program or work, and a "work based on the Program" means either the Program or any derivative work under copyright law: that is to say, a work containing the Program or a portion of it, either verbatim or with modifications and/or translated into another language. (Hereinafter, translation is included without limitation in the term "modification".) Each licensee is addressed as "you".

Activities other than copying, distribution and modification are not covered by this License; they are outside its scope. The act of running the Program is not restricted, and the output from the Program is covered only if its contents constitute a work based on the Program (independent of having been made by running the Program). Whether that is true depends on what the Program does.

1. You may copy and distribute verbatim copies of the Program's source code as you receive it, in any medium, provided that you conspicuously and appropriately publish on each copy an appropriate copyright notice and disclaimer of warranty; keep intact all the notices that refer to this License and to the absence of any warranty; and give any other recipients of the Program a copy of this License along with the Program.

   You may charge a fee for the physical act of transferring a copy, and you may at your option offer warranty protection in exchange for a fee.

2. You may modify your copy or copies of the Program or any portion of it, thus forming a work based on the Program, and copy and distribute such modifications or work under the terms of Section 1 above, provided that you also meet all of these conditions:

   a) You must cause the modified files to carry prominent notice stating that you changed the files and the date of any change.

   b) You must cause any work that you distribute or publish, that in whole or in part contains or is derived from the Program or any part thereof, to be licensed as a whole at no charge to all third parties under the terms of this License.

   c) If the modified program normally reads commands interactively when run, you must cause it, when started running for such interactive use in the most ordinary way, to print or display an announcement including an appropriate copyright notice and a notice that there is no warranty (or else, saying that you provide a warranty) and that users may redistribute the program under these conditions, and telling the user how to view a copy of this License. (Exception: if the Program itself is interactive but does not normally print such an announcement, your work based on the Program is not required to print an announcement.)

   These requirements apply to the modified work as a whole. If identifiable sections of that work are not derived from the Program, and can be reasonably considered independent and separate works in themselves, then this License, and its terms, do not apply to those sections when you distribute them as separate works. But when you distribute the same sections as part of a whole which is a work based on the Program, the distribution of the whole must be on the terms of this License, whose permissions for other licensees extend to the entire whole, and thus to each and every part regardless of who wrote it.

   Thus, it is not the intent of this section to claim rights or contest your rights to work written entirely by you; rather, the intent is to exercise the right to control the distribution of derivative or collective works based on the Program.

   In addition, mere aggregation of another work not based on the Program with the Program (or with a work based on the Program) on a volume of a storage or distribution medium does not bring the other work under the scope of this License.

3. You may copy and distribute the Program (or a work based on it, under Section 2) in object code or executable form under the terms of Sections 1 and 2 above provided that you also do one of the following:

a) Accompany it with the complete corresponding machine-readable source code, which must be distributed under the terms of Sections 1 and 2 above on a medium customarily used for software interchange; or,

b) Accompany it with a written offer, valid for at least three years, to give any third party, for a charge no more than your cost of physically performing source distribution, a complete machine-readable copy of the corresponding source code, to be distributed under the terms of Sections 1 and 2 above on a medium customarily used for software interchange; or,

c) Accompany it with the information you received as to the offer to distribute corresponding source code. (This alternative is allowed only for noncommercial distribution and only if you received the program in object code or executable form with such an offer, in accord with Subsection b above.)

The source code for a work means the preferred form of the work for making modifications to it. For an executable work, complete source code means all the source code for all modules it contains, plus any associated interface definition files, plus the scripts used to control compilation and installation of the executable. However, as a special exception, the source code distributed need not include anything that is normally distributed (in either source or binary form) with the major components (compiler, kernel, and so on) of the operating system on which the executable runs, unless that component itself accompanies the executable.

If distribution of executable or object code is made by offering access to copy from a designated place, then offering equivalent access to copy the source code from the same place counts as distribution of the source code, even though third parties are not compelled to copy the source along with the object code.

4. You may not copy, modify, sublicense, or distribute the Program except as expressly provided under this License. Any attempt otherwise to copy, modify, sublicense or distribute the Program is void, and will automatically terminate your rights under this License. However, parties who have received copies, or rights, from you under this License will not have their licenses terminated so long as such parties remain in full compliance.

5. You are not required to accept this License, since you have not signed it. However, nothing else grants you permission to modify or distribute the Program or its derivative works. These actions are prohibited by law if you do not accept this License. Therefore, by modifying or distributing the Program (or any work based on the Program), you indicate your acceptance of this License to do so, and all its terms and conditions for copying, distributing or modifying the Program or works based on it.

6. Each time you redistribute the Program (or any work based on the Program), the recipient automatically receives a license from the original licensor to copy, distribute or modify the Program subject to these terms and conditions. You may not impose any further restrictions on the recipients' exercise of the rights granted herein. You are not responsible for enforcing compliance by third parties to this License.

7. If, as a consequence of a court judgment or allegation of patent infringement or for any other reason (not limited to patent issues), conditions are imposed on you (whether by court order, agreement or otherwise) that contradict the conditions of this License, they do not excuse you from the conditions of this License. If you cannot distribute so as to satisfy simultaneously your obligations under this License and any other pertinent obligations, then as a consequence you may not distribute the Program at all. For example, if a patent license would not permit royalty-free redistribution of the Program by all those who receive copies directly or indirectly through you, then the only way you could satisfy both it and this License would be to refrain entirely from distribution of the Program.

If any portion of this section is held invalid or unenforceable under any particular circumstance, the balance of the section is intended to apply and the section as a whole is intended to apply in other circumstances.

It is not the purpose of this section to induce you to infringe any patents or other property right claims or to contest validity of any such claims; this section has the sole purpose of protecting the integrity of the free software distribution system, which is implemented by public license practices. Many people have made generous contributions to the wide range of software distributed through that system in reliance on consistent application of that system; it is up to the author/donor to decide if he or she is willing to distribute software through any other system and a licensee cannot impose that choice.

This section is intended to make thoroughly clear what is believed to be a consequence of the rest of this License.

8. If the distribution and/or use of the Program is restricted in certain countries either by patents or by copyrighted interfaces, the original copyright holder who places the Program under this License may add an explicit geographical distribution limitation excluding those countries, so that distribution is permitted only in or among countries not thus excluded. In such case, this License incorporates the limitation as if written in the body of this License.

9. The Free Software Foundation may publish revised and/or new versions of the General Public License from time to time. Such new versions will be similar in spirit to the present version, but may differ in detail to address new problems or concerns.

Each version is given a distinguishing version number. If the Program specifies a version number of this License which applies to it and "any later version", you have the option of following the terms and conditions either of that version or of any later version published by the Free Software Foundation. If the Program does not specify a version number of this License, you may choose any version ever published by the Free Software Foundation.

10. If you wish to incorporate parts of the Program into other free programs whose distribution conditions are different, write to the author to ask for permission. For software which is copyrighted by the Free Software Foundation, write to the Free Software Foundation; we sometimes make exceptions for this. Our decision will be guided by the two goals of preserving the free status of all derivatives of our free software and of promoting the sharing and reuse of software generally.

NO WARRANTY

11. BECAUSE THE PROGRAM IS LICENSED FREE OF CHARGE, THERE IS NO WARRANTY FOR THE PROGRAM, TO THE EXTENT PERMITTED BY APPLICABLE LAW. EXCEPT WHEN OTHERWISE STATED IN WRITING THE COPYRIGHT HOLDERS AND/OR OTHER PARTIES PROVIDE THE PROGRAM "AS IS" WITHOUT WARRANTY OF ANY KIND, EITHER EXPRESSED OR IMPLIED, INCLUDING, BUT NOT LIMITED TO, THE IMPLIED WARRANTIES OF MERCHANTABILITY AND FITNESS FOR A PARTICULAR PURPOSE. THE ENTIRE RISK AS TO THE QUALITY AND PERFORMANCE OF THE PROGRAM IS WITH YOU. SHOULD THE PROGRAM PROVE DEFECTIVE, YOU ASSUME THE COST OF ALL NECESSARY SERVICING, REPAIR OR CORRECTION.

12. IN NO EVENT UNLESS REQUIRED BY APPLICABLE LAW OR AGREED TO IN WRITING WILL ANY COPYRIGHT HOLDER, OR ANY OTHER PARTY WHO MAY MODIFY AND/OR REDISTRIBUTE THE PROGRAM AS PERMITTED ABOVE, BE LIABLE TO YOU FOR DAMAGES, INCLUDING ANY GENERAL, SPECIAL, INCIDENTAL OR CONSEQUENTIAL DAMAGES ARISING OUT OF THE USE OR INABILITY TO USE THE PROGRAM (INCLUDING BUT NOT LIMITED TO LOSS OF DATA OR DATA BEING RENDERED INACCURATE OR LOSSES SUSTAINED BY YOU OR THIRD PARTIES OR A FAILURE OF THE PROGRAM TO OPERATE WITH ANY OTHER PROGRAMS), EVEN IF SUCH HOLDER OR OTHER PARTY HAS BEEN ADVISED OF THE POSSIBILITY OF SUCH DAMAGES.

END OF TERMS AND CONDITIONS

How to take it to the Extreme.

If you enjoyed this book, there are many others like it for you. From *Podcasting* to *Hacking Firefox*, ExtremeTech books can fulfill your urge to hack, tweak and modify, providing the tech tips and tricks readers need to get the most out of their hi-tech lives.